AMERICAN
INDEPENDENT CINEMA

A Sight and Sound Reader

AMERICAN
INDEPENDENT CINEMA

A Sight and Sound Reader

Edited by Jim Hillier

 Publishing

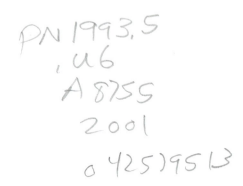
First published in 2001 by the
British Film Institute
21 Stephen Street, London W1T 1LN

Reprinted 2002, 2006

The British Film Institute promotes greater understanding
and appreciation of, and access to, film and moving image
culture in the UK.

Cover image: Heather Graham as Rollergirl in *Boogie Nights* (Paul Thomas Anderson, 1998)
Set by Design Consultants (Siobhán O'Connor)
Printed in Great Britain by St Edmundsbury Press Limited,
Bury St Edmunds, Suffolk

British Library Cataloguing-in-Publication Data
A catalogue record for this book is available from the British Library

ISBN 0-85170-759-9 (paperback)
ISBN 0-85170-758-0 (hardback)

Contents

Introduction

Looking back from 2000, the landscape of US cinema since the 1980s would be significantly poorer without what has become known – loosely but meaningfully – as American independent cinema. Many people, myself included, would go further and argue that it is to this American independent cinema that we owe most of what is enduringly valuable in US cinema as a whole during this period. It is largely to this 'indie' sector that we owe transformed representations of ethnic minorities – particularly African Americans (but also Hispanics and Chinese Americans; the latter, for instance, in the work of Wayne Wang) – and of gays and lesbians, as well as experimentation with narrative forms and generic expectations – and sometimes all these combined. Also, it is to this sector that we would look for most of the distinctive voices in recent US cinema.

Although American independent cinema has a relatively specific meaning – as much to do with economics as with aesthetics – within this relatively short period, it is a loose, slippery label. Historically, 'independent' has always implied work different from the dominant or mainstream, whether this relationship is defined primarily in economic terms (production and distribution) or in aesthetic or stylistic terms. In the period covered by this book, these differences are sufficiently widely understood for us to be able to ask how and why these developments and transformations came about. In doing so, we should not underestimate the achievements of the independent film-makers themselves in the 1980s and 1990s, but nor should we overestimate them, or see them out of context. The influences which feed into the apparent emergence of an independent cinema in the 1980s are complex, reaching back into recent and older developments in both mainstream and experimental cinema.

As an obvious example, the sense of renewal and experimentation in Hollywood-related film-making in the late 1960s and early 1970s – with such films as Arthur Penn's *Bonnie and Clyde* (1967) and *Little Big Man* (1970), Dennis Hopper's *Easy Rider* (1969) and *The Last Movie* (1971), Bob Rafelson's *Head* (1968), *Five Easy Pieces* (1970) and *The King of Marvin Gardens* (1972), Monte Hellman's *Two-Lane Blacktop* (1970), Sam Peckinpah's *The Wild Bunch* (1969), *Junior Bonner* (1972) and *Bring Me the Head of Alfredo Garcia* (1974), Robert Altman's *M*A*S*H* (1970), *McCabe and Mrs Miller* (1971), *The Long Goodbye* (1972) and *Nashville* (1975) – has much in common with the sense of renewal in later independent film-making. The looser, less consequential narratives of many of these films are frequently led more by character than plot. Their often more introvert than extrovert characters and their play with generic expectations make them close to much later independent work. Like the later period, the late 1960s and early 1970s generated much optimism about the possible renewal of narrative forms. This was also, of course, the time when audience attendances reached a nadir brought

to an end by the huge success of blockbusters such as *Jaws* (1975) with the advent of
'New Hollywood' and such practices as saturation release.

From that point, innovative work within the mainstream became more difficult.
There is some justification, however, in arguing that this innovative strand of
American film-making resurfaced in the independent film-makers in the 1980s and
1990s. All the same, the career of a consistently independent film-maker such as Alan
Rudolph (*Welcome to L.A.*, 1977; *Remember My Name*, 1979; *Choose Me*, 1984; *Trouble in
Mind*, 1985), sustained by the growth of independent production as the video boom
began in the late 1980s, suggests continuity rather than a break. Robert Altman
himself, of course, continued to make films throughout this period, though their
nature certainly reflects an adjustment to changes in economic opportunities, as
Justin Wyatt has suggested. Altman's 1970s features were generally financed by the
major studios, but his survival through the 1980s depended on minor independents
(such as Cinecom, Cannon and New World) and television, with curious low-budget
projects such as *Come Back to the Five and Dime, Jimmy Dean, Jimmy Dean* (1982),
Streamers (1983) and *Tanner '88*, before he returned to larger scale, though still
'independent', projects such as *The Player* (1992) and *Short Cuts* (1993) (for Fine Line
and Miramax) in the 1990s. Similarly, at the outer edges of independent feature
production, in the more politicised, narratively challenging, no-budget work of a film-
maker such as Jon Jost there is a continuity of production from *Speaking Directly* (1974)
and *Last Chants for a Slow Dance* (1977) through to *Slow Moves* (1983) and *Sure Fire* (1990).

But this is to see the apparent emergence of independent film-making in the 1980s
only in its most immediate context. Historically, there have been other kinds of
independent cinema operating at the far end of the American film-making spectrum
from Hollywood. Leftist film-makers such as those grouped in Frontier Films (*Native
Land*, 1942) grew up in the socialist climate of the 1930s. Although the strand was
eclipsed in the virulently anti-communist postwar period, *Salt of the Earth* (1953) –
made independently by necessity by blacklisted former Hollywood film-makers –
remains a major achievement and an exemplary work, rediscovered, significantly,
during the 1980s and 1990s. This politically committed tradition in US film-making
has been carried on by documentary film-makers such as Emile de Antonio, Fred
Wiseman and Errol Morris, and the work of John Sayles makes sense only within this
long tradition.

The 1940s also saw the rise of an American avant-garde cinema – in the same period
as the rise of Abstract Expressionist painting – with Maya Deren, Kenneth Anger and
later Stan Brakhage as major figures. Their short films, mostly shot on 16mm and
funded by the film-makers themselves or by public subsidy, placed the emphasis on
new ways of seeing, new forms which broke free from mainstream conventions and
new subjects, including issues centring on gender. From Anger's *Fireworks* (1947)
through to Jack Smith's *Flaming Creatures* (1962) – and on into Andy Warhol's work –
the focus was often on groups marginalised by the mainstream – particularly gay
figures, but also lesbians and blacks – a focus that helped lay the groundwork for the
'new queer cinema' of the 1990s. Their vocal public championing of the avant-garde
and efforts to establish a network of venues for screening such work enabled underground cinema of the 1950s and 1960s to enjoy a relatively high critical profile. This

was to exert an important influence on independent American film-making from the 1970s onwards. Given David Lynch's background in avant-garde film and other visual arts, it becomes perfectly possible to speculate about what Lynch's 1996 *Lost Highway* might owe to Maya Deren's seminal *Meshes of the Afternoon* (1943).

The role of John Cassavetes, who features in this volume as a pioneer, was also crucial to the development of today's US independent cinema. In awarding Cassavetes' 16mm-shot *Shadows* the 1959 Independent Film Award, film-maker and critic Jonas Mekas referred to it as 'a film that doesn't betray life or cinema, whereas Hollywood films (and we mean Hollywoods all over the world) reach us beautiful and dead'. This was also the moment of the New American Cinema Group, established in 1960, whose founders included Shirley Clarke, Lionel Rogosin, Robert Frank, Jonas and Adolfas Mekas, Emile de Antonio, Peter Bogdanovich and others, which set itself against 'official cinema' in terms of both production and distribution. The group's diversity reflected earlier independent traditions from the aesthetic avant-garde to more leftist documentary-oriented work.

Cassavetes' relationship to Hollywood was always ambivalent. His struggles to secure finance and distribution for his movies – many of which he funded himself, shooting and editing over periods of years – and his occasional flirtations with the system (whether the majors or independents such as Cannon) made clear the conditions in which an American independent cinema that retained a strong narrative element was bound to exist. To some extent, Cassavetes benefited from the relative decline in Hollywood cinema in the 1960s and the vitality and popularity of European art cinema – predominantly the French New Wave. These led to the establishment of an art-house circuit, a vital condition for the flourishing of the homegrown equivalent of the European films. By the 1960s, there was a growing number of film schools which took over the function of training future film-makers from the studios, and their students were increasingly exposed to work that represented alternatives to mainstream Hollywood fare. Certainly, the French New Wave gave the New American Cinema Group a sense of the possibilities for a new US cinema and, twenty years later, a film such as Spike Lee's *She's Gotta Have It* is still borrowing its stylistic cues not from the New American Cinema Group, but from the New Wave. The politicisation of film-making in France, particularly in the work of Jean-Luc Godard, had a direct effect on the work of film-makers such as Jon Jost, whose later movies combine this influence with a stripped-down visual style and moments of lyricism reminiscent of Brakhage.

Andy Warhol, another pioneering underground film-maker who more or less went 'overground', exerted an influence far beyond the small audiences that saw his films. The work of the American independents characterised as 'minimalists' in this volume owes much to the visual and narrative spareness of Warhol's style. Jonas Mekas's characterisation of Warhol – 'the world seen through a consciousness that is not running after big dramatic events, but is focused on more subtle changes and nuances' – applies also to 'structural' film-makers such as Michael Snow, whose *Wavelength* (1967) Fred Camper contrasts with 'the attention-getting density of narrative events in a Hollywood film'. Such characterisations are very suggestive of major strategies in the work of Jim Jarmusch or Richard Linklater. Where Cassavetes is intense – 'hot' – with much camera movement and editing, Warhol is 'cool', often with minimal editing, so that where the films of Martin Scorsese (or certainly his earlier work) might be seen in a line coming from Cassavetes, those of Jim Jarmusch or Richard Linklater might be seen as owing a debt to Warhol.

In their very different ways, Cassavetes and Warhol combined extreme realism with modes of stylisation that diverged from the norms of mainstream illusionist cinema, with the result that both raised, indirectly, questions about form. Cassavetes' dramas resembled Hollywood's, but approached their material from a very different perspective: the narrative organisation was expanded beyond what would be considered necessary in a mainstream film, but was also fractured and wayward – qualities that find echoes in American independent films of the 1980s and 1990s. Meanwhile, David Thomson's striking account of Warhol provides a suggestive perspective on other recent US independent work:

> Very little attempt was made in the films to achieve a professionally polished image, let alone one that was 'radiant' or 'artistic', or to eliminate boring passages. Nor was there any sense of a meaning being contained in the films that a sensitive viewer could digest. Instead, there was an obsession with the phenomenal nature of human spectacle and performance. The experience was enough to make the viewer... ask himself the abiding questions – 'What happens in the cinema? What is cinematic narrative? What is acting? How do we tell fiction from documentary? What is an audience?' What has always seemed... important and exciting in Warhol is the instant touching on those questions with a directness that makes Godard look like a prevaricator.

These qualities, inducing reflection upon the very nature of the medium of film and the dominant conventions it has accumulated, are among the most important elements of the excitement generated by the independent film-makers of the 1980s and 1990s, their sense of, if not 'reinventing' cinema, at least rethinking it.

These perspectives might be seen to be placing too much emphasis on new forms, new styles, and not enough on new contents. However important formal innovation may have been, a renewal of subject matter was equally important, and nowhere less so than in African-American, or 'black', film-making and in gay and lesbian film-making. In both cases, form and content cannot be easily separated and the reaching for new representations was seen to demand a new black or queer aesthetic: the experimental aspects of, say, Spike Lee's *Do the Right Thing* (1989), Julie Dash's *Daughters of the Dust* (1991) and Marlon Riggs's *Tongues Untied* (1989) or Todd Haynes's *Poison* (1990) and Gus Van Sant's *My Own Private Idaho* (1991) can only be understood in this light. Even here, the new queer film-making owes much to earlier experimental work and, as Ed Guerrero reminds us, independent black film-making draws upon the debates and practices initiated by the LA School in the 1970s (with film-makers such as Julie Dash and Charles Burnett constituting a very clear link).

Spike Lee's work was returned to again and again in *Sight and Sound* in the 1990s – reflected in this volume – and quite rightly so. No one did more, or did it more consistently and in higher profile, than Lee to foreground issues of race in both social and film industrial terms, in his films and other pronouncements. But Lee's prominence here immediately raises the question: was – and is – he an 'independent film-maker'? *She's Gotta Have It* was certainly independent (distributed by Island) and an important early (1986) example of a cheaply made film which could earn significant revenue (and it is as interesting as a film of ideas about cinema as about representations of black male and female sexuality). Thereafter, Lee's next big films were less obviously energetically innovative in visual style and narrative organisation; the larger the budgets of his films, the less 'independent' they became (even if one argues that *Do the Right Thing* might be the best fusion). Although produced by his own company, Forty Acres and a Mule, they were financed and distributed through major studios (Universal for *Do the Right Thing*, 1989, and *Jungle Fever*, 1991; Warner's for *Malcolm X*, 1992).

As Ed Guerrero argues, the quandary, felt particularly sharply by African-American film-makers and others for whom so much is at stake, was: be stylistically and thematically more independent and adventurous and reach a limited audience, or work via a major distributor and appear more conventional – but have the potential to reach a much larger audience. We might think of this quandary as the Julie Dash strategy – to innovate boldly with *Daughters of the Dust* (1991), using alternative routes to its (significant) audience, but finding little other work during the 1990s – against the Spike Lee strategy. But Lee himself has recognised the dilemma by coming back to less conventional and more independent projects in a variety of forms, with *Girl 6* (1996), *Get on the Bus* (1996), *Four Little Girls* (1997) and *Kings of Comedy* (2000). Tommy Lott's description of Lee as 'a crossover black independent' sums up his position admirably: Lee seeks the widest possible audience for his films – for which he needs the major studios – but this does not mean he has to abandon the radical formal and thematic choices open to him as an independent. Although many have argued that *Jungle Fever* and *Malcolm X*, say, are less formally innovative than the earlier films, others maintain that independent and mainstream qualities can mix.

No doubt some of these same dilemmas have come into play among gay film-makers such as Gus Van Sant and even an arch iconoclast such as Gregg Araki. The career trajectory of Van Sant – from the experimentation of *Mala Noche* (1986) to the relative 'realism' of *Drugstore Cowboy* (1989) and the richly convoluted *My Own Private Idaho* (1991) to the mainstream conventionality of *Good Will Hunting* (1997) and the simply puzzling remake of *Psycho* (1998) – seems to tell a story of incorporation into the mainstream, although this is not yet quite clear. In any case, such issues are not only relevant to black or gay film-makers. Steven Soderbergh, the high priest of 'indie' film-making after the Sundance and subsequent commercial success of *sex, lies and videotape* in 1989, has maintained a career veering wildly between the extreme experimentation of *Kafka* (1991) and *Schizopolis* (1996), the mainstream-with-some-indie-qualities *Out of Sight* (1998) and *The Limey* (1999), and the frankly commercial *Erin Brockovich* (2000). Through such changes, Soderbergh maintains – so far – a recognisably 'indie' stance, as his interview with Sheila Johnston makes quite clear.

Although the primary focus of our discussion here has been on the style and the content of recent American independent cinema, economics have never been far behind. Speaking historically, economics has often been the primary factor in different forms of 'independent production'. We may today identify American independent cinema against the dominant of Hollywood – both as a mode of production and as a set of stylistic norms – but Hollywood itself was originally associated with a break from the dominant. The first attempt at monopoly in US cinema – the Motion Picture Patents Company, formed in 1909 by the leading East Coast motion-picture manufacturers and distributors – was challenged by independent distributors who migrated west in the period 1908–13. Among those who fled to Hollywood (which, as well as offering good conditions for filming, was physically distant from the New York-based MPPC and close to the Mexican border in case of the need for further flight) were figures soon to become key players in the studio system: Carl Laemmle, later chief executive of Universal Pictures, and William Fox, later boss of the Fox Film Corporation.

Matthew Bernstein reminds us that 'there have always been many types of independence', including the long tradition of 'commercial independent production' by companies with no corporate relationship with a distributor, but whose product was destined for distribution by one of the major studios (although one of the majors, United Artists, was set up in 1919 by Charlie Chaplin, Mary Pickford, Douglas Fairbanks and D. W. Griffith precisely to provide a distribution alternative to the increasingly powerful majors). But such 'independents' were neither truly independent – since they relied on the major studios for distribution – nor trying to make films that were significantly different from those of the major studios. In essence, they both depended on and fed the system. As David Thomson argues in his biography of one of Hollywood's greatest 'independents', David O. Selznick:

> There has never been a viable independence in Hollywood – ask D. W. Griffith or Francis Coppola. The geniuses have to deal with the dirt and, sometimes, late in the day, they may realise how far their genius has been darkened. Sam Goldwyn had the best working estimate of independence: make the pictures you want to make and produce them in the spirit of someone saving silver foil to build bombers; then make the best deal you can with someone who will take the risk and responsibility of selling your picture – so that you may move on and make more.

The divorce between the major studios' production and distribution functions and their monopoly on exhibition after central government moved in 1947 to free up theatre ownership is often seen as a milestone in the encouragement of independent production. But this did not necessarily change the kinds of films the new wave of independent companies set out to make. As Kevin Hagopian remarks of Cagney Productions: 'During the years 1936–1949, James Cagney sought a formula that would maximise his freedom as an artist and his economic remuneration as a businessman.' The same could be said for the many other stars, including Kirk Douglas and John Wayne, who went into independent production in the 1950s, but made films similar to those of the majors to whom they went for distribution. Even before 1947, the major studios used independent production companies to fill vacant studio space and facilitate more flexible release patterns, so much so that Leo McCarey in 1949 referred to the majors as having become 'just indie combines'. However, as Bernstein's work on

Fritz Lang's Diana Productions (formed in 1945 with Joan Bennett and Walter Wanger) has shown, in such situations the major distributors exercised firm control on the films produced.

This pattern of semi-independent production continues in Hollywood today. In the 1980s and 1990s, such blockbusters as *Terminator 2: Judgment Day* (produced by Carolco, 1991) were not financed directly by a major studio. Rather, they used studio deals assuring them national and/or international distribution to secure funding from other sources, allowing the majors to profit from distribution without risking too much up front. This type of deal led truly independent producers such as Lloyd Kaufman of Troma and Roger Corman to claim that 'the word [independent] has been corrupted. Independent no longer means "independent". It now means "appendage"' (Kaufman). Or Corman: 'a true independent is a company that can finance, produce and distribute its own films. Most are partial independents, connected in some way to a major studio. They are independent producers but not truly independent companies.' During the 1990s, the majors have reeled in even this level of independent production: Carolco has gone out of business and Castle Rock was taken over by Turner (since taken over by Time Warner, now Time Warner AOL).

The contents of this volume imply the emergence of a recognisably different and new American independent cinema during the second half of the 1980s and into the 1990s. I have argued here that there was more continuity with earlier work than the selection implies, and that this apparently new phenomenon can only be understood in a complex historical context. Perhaps this is why various commentators have had trouble in locating and dating this American independent cinema in time. The acclaim that greeted Steven Soderbergh's *sex, lies and videotape* at Sundance in 1989 has been taken by many to mark the advent of American independent cinema as a major force in the landscape of US movie-making. In retrospect, it may represent the assimilation of that cinema. During the 1980s and early 1990s, independent cinema was driven by independent distributors such as Cinecom, Island/Alive, Goldwyn, New Line and Miramax. Seeing the potentially profitable market niche independent films might occupy, the major studios took steps to control what benefits might accrue. It was the familiar commercial pattern of smaller companies taking initial advantage of new market opportunities, only to be later ousted by major players – as happened with video, and as we now see happening with dot.com businesses. Disney took over one of the largest independent producer–distributors, Miramax, and Turner took over the other, New Line (since acquired by Time Warner). Other majors set up production–distribution units, such as Fox Searchlight (staffed largely by former Goldwyn staff), to exploit independent-type material (although Fox, Orion and Sony had all dabbled in 'classics' divisions earlier).

Other commentators such as John Pierson see American independent cinema as an earlier phenomenon, locating Jarmusch's 1984 *Stranger than Paradise* as the starting point. In this perspective, 1989 – Pierson's the 'Year It All Changed' – becomes a midpoint and 1994–95 and *Pulp Fiction* an end point. Pierson argues that 'you have to bend over backward and jump through hoops to define *Pulp Fiction* as independent' since it starred John Travolta and Bruce Willis, cost $8 million, was originally set up at TriStar and was released in 1200 prints by Miramax, by then a division of Disney.

'One thing is clear,' Pierson concluded in 1995, 'the definition "independent" is much more elusive now than a decade ago.'

Certainly, the roll call of film-makers discovered or boosted by Sundance between 1989 and 1992 – Reggie Hudlin, Maggie Greenwald, Whit Stillman, Hal Hartley, Julie Dash, Todd Haynes, Richard Linklater, Matty Rich, Jennie Livingston, Allison Anders, Alexandre Rockwell, Tom DiCillo, Gregg Araki, Tom Kalin and others – supports the importance of these years. But Pierson's sense that American independent cinema was a largely spent force by the mid-1990s has surely been called into question by the consistency and renewal of Jarmusch – with *Dead Man* (1996) and now *Ghost Dog* (1999) – and the appearance of such inventive independent works as Paul Thomas Anderson's *Magnolia* (1999), Errol Morris's *Fast, Cheap & Out of Control* (1997) and *Mr Death* (1999), Kimberly Peirce's *Boys Don't Cry* (1999), Spike Jonze's *Being John Malkovich* (1999) and Mike Figgis's digital four-screen experiment, *Timecode* (2000).

But are *Boys Don't Cry*, *Timecode* and *Being John Malkovich* 'independent'? By all rights, they should be and are – in spirit. But *Boys Don't Cry* was produced by Fox Searchlight and distributed by Fox, *Timecode* was produced by Figgis's own Red Mullet for Screen Gems, a subsidiary of Columbia/Sony and distributed by Columbia-TriStar, and *Being John Malkovich* was backed by Polygram, subsequently taken over by Universal. Should we take this as a sign that 'American independent cinema' is alive and well, but living in sin, a sign that the spirit of independence has permeated some levels of the mainstream? Or that the meanings of 'independence' remain as elusive as ever? In part, of course, this arises because independent film-making today is doing what it always did – offering films made on modest budgets with potential for considerable success, reinvigorating narrative and generic conventions and providing a source of new film-makers, some of whom are only too ready to graduate to dependency.

* * *

The contents of this volume have been collected from the 'new' *Sight and Sound* from 1991 to 2000, and we have tried to achieve a balance of material – articles, interviews, reviews – which reflects the balance of typical issues of the journal. However, the vagaries of film distribution and exhibition, and the desire of a monthly journal to be up to date when possible have inevitably meant both a certain unevenness in coverage and a general impulse to cover what is 'hot' at any particular time. The coverage of American independent cinema in *Sight and Sound* during the 1990s has generally been good, especially during the first part of the decade when the phenomenon was at its hottest and most debated – partly because it also seemed, during this period, most clear-cut as a distinct category. As a result, the contents of this volume are skewed slightly towards the earlier part of the decade, rather than the later. This is especially so in the case of areas such as African-American and queer cinema, where developments were especially vital in the earlier 1990s and less marked by the end of the decade.

Inevitably, too, *Sight and Sound*'s coverage of particular films and film-makers was not consistent and this is obviously a constraint on the choices available for an anthology such as this; choices could only be made from what actually appeared in the journal. As an example, although Jim Jarmusch's films – and what he has to say about them and his work in general – are never less than interesting, it is doubtful whether *Night on Earth* (covered in a featured article) will be considered over time as important a Jarmusch work as *Dead Man* (covered only by a review). However, in this case as in others, the end of the decade coinciding with the end of the century and the millennium – and with the appearance of new and challenging films – has prompted retrospective looks at some film-makers and trends. We have played a part in this ourselves by commissioning new essays with retrospective views. Two of these – B. Ruby Rich's 'Queer and Present Danger' and Ed Guerrero's 'Be Black and Buy' – have also appeared in *Sight and Sound.* Murray Smith's 'Parallel Lines', tracing some of the experimentation with narrative forms, and Kim Newman's 'Independents Daze', looking at, among other things, the continuing importance of generic forms in independent work, are new to this book.

In terms of the structure of the book, I hope the categories and sections into which the material is grouped help to make sense of some of the major different strands in American independent cinema. Even so, there are entries which could well fit elsewhere in the structure. Kobena Mercer's piece on Marlon Riggs's *Tongues Untied* – in the African-American section – for example, would also have been appropriately placed under 'Queers', while Nick James' review of Carl Franklin's *One False Move* would certainly fit under 'African Americans'. Elsewhere, it may be too soon, clearly, to assume that film-makers such as Paul Thomas Anderson, Spike Jonze or Harmony Korine are really 'mavericks', despite the distinctive individuality of their work so far.

References

Andrew, Geoff, *Stranger than Paradise: Maverick Film-makers in Recent American Cinema* (London: Prion, 1998).

Balio, Tino, 'When Is an Independent Producer Independent?: The Case of United Artists after 1948', *The Velvet Light Trap*, no. 22, 1986.

Bernstein, Matthew, 'Fritz Lang Incorporated', *The Velvet Light Trap*, no. 22, 1986.

Bernstein, Matthew, 'Hollywood's Semi-Independent Production', *Cinema Journal*, vol. 32, no. 3, Spring 1993.

Camper, Fred, '1966–1967', in Singer, Marilyn (ed.), *A History of the American Avant-Garde Cinema* (New York: American Federation of Arts, 1976).

Guerrero, Ed, 'A Circus of Dreams and Lies: The Black Film Wave at Middle Age', in Lewis, Jon (ed.), *The New American Cinema* (Durham, NC & London: Duke University Press, 1998).

Hagopian, Kevin, 'Declarations of Independence: A History of Cagney Productions', *The Velvet Light Trap*, no. 22, 1986.

Hillier, Jim, *The New Hollywood* (London: Studio Vista; New York: Continuum, 1993).

James, David, *Allegories of Cinema: American Film in the 60s* (Princeton, NJ: Princeton University Press, 1989).

Kleinhans, Chuck, 'Independent Features: Hopes and Dreams', in Lewis, *op cit*.

Lott, Tommy L., 'Hollywood and Independent Black Cinema', in Neale, Steve & Smith, Murray (eds), *Contemporary Hollywood Cinema* (London & New York: Routledge, 1998).

Pierson, John, *Spike, Mike, Slackers and Dykes: A Guided Tour across a Decade of Independent American Cinema* (New York: Hyperion/Miramax, 1995; London: Faber & Faber, 1996).

Schamus, James, 'To the Rear of the Back End: The Economics of Independent Cinema', in Lewis, *op cit*.

Thomson, David, *Showman: The Life of David O. Selznick* (New York: Alfred A. Knopf; London: André Deutsch, 1993).

Thomson, David, *A Biographical Dictionary of Film* (London: André Deutsch, 1994).

Wyatt, Justin, 'Economic Constraints/Economic Opportunities: Robert Altman as Auteur', *The Velvet Light Trap*, no. 38, 1996.

Wyatt, Justin, 'From Roadshowing to Saturation Release: Majors, Independents, and Marketing/ Distribution Innovations', in Lewis, *op cit*.

Wyatt, Justin, 'The formation of the "major independent": Miramax, New Line and the New Hollywood', in Neale & Smith, *op cit*.

Shadows (John Cassavetes, 1959)

Section I: Pioneers

STATE OF GRACE

Michael Ventura

'This picture, *this* picture – I don't give a fuck what anybody says. If you don't have time to see it, don't. If you don't like it, don't. If it doesn't give you an answer, fuck you. I didn't make it for you anyway.'

John Cassavetes, after shooting *his* Las Vegas, eight summers ago. It is 110 in the shade and he is filming a couple of scenes of his last film, *Love Streams*. He has begun to suspect, and will soon know, that he is dying. One day at dailies he says to no one in particular, 'This is a sweet film. If I die, this is a sweet last film.' For the moment, he chooses to take the possibility of death as just another part of the atmosphere, significant but not central, in the creation of his new work. 'I don't direct a film,' he is fond of saying, 'I set up an atmosphere and the *atmosphere* directs the film.'

Night and day

John's 'atmosphere' takes place night and day, without let-up, whether the cameras are rolling or not, and now it's taking place at a joint called The Tower of Pizza on the south end of the Vegas Strip. Several of us are drinking wine and being loud, especially Cassavetes and his cousin, the film's art director and John's staunch ally, Phedon Papamichael.

They are driving the waitress crazy. Phedon wants absolutely no garlic. Cassavetes wants to have a discussion with the cook. Phedon is insisting that even a place called The Tower of Pizza shouldn't mind preparing special, slightly exotic dishes that are not on the menu. The waitress is barely restraining herself from throwing something not very exotic all over us.

Cassavetes eggs her on because he likes her toughness. I've become used to this way of his, how he'll see a quality he likes in a stranger, and he'll goad and push until he gets a good taste of it. If the food starts to fly tonight, he won't care. He likes flying food. A young actor in our party is explaining to John why she can't stand his character in the film: 'He's a creep with his kid.' John comes back at her with something he loves to say and says often, that he understands everybody in the movie but his own character. Then John's eyes get brighter: he doesn't want to understand his own character; he doesn't want to understand himself either; on or off the screen, what people call 'understanding' is over-rated. 'I love motion, change, and I hate answers – because they stop change.'

'You're a phoney sonofabitch,' Phedon says, matter-of-factly.

'I'm phoney?' John explodes. Phedon has done his part, given John a hook for another riff, and now he sits back and watches the show, just like the rest of us. 'I feel sorry for *you*,' John says with glee, 'because *you're* phoney, because you think you know what's right, what's good. I don't know and I don't wanna know.'

'You put your life into the movie,' Phedon tells him, 'and then you say that you don't.'
'What?'
'You know. Don't tell me like you don't know.'

A beat of silence – something rare in their exchanges. Then John says, 'I put *everything* into the movie. What I know *and* what I don't know. And that's as far from phoney as Kelsey's you-know-what.' (Nobody ever knew what 'Kelsey's you-know-what' was.)

Which makes me think of another John-and-Phedon exchange a couple of months earlier during pre-production, when an argument about the colour of upholstery digressed into a discussion of love (talks with John often did). 'That was the biggest discovery I ever made,' John said at the time, 'that love stops. Just like a clock. Or anything. Then you wind it and it goes again. Because if it stops forever, then you die.'

'Love,' Phedon started to say, but John interrupted with: 'I know what love is.'
'You don't.' Phedon said quietly.
'You know I know,' John said just as quietly.
'And, if you know?'
'Love – is the ability of not knowing.'

I was in the institution at the time. The institution of marriage, I mean. Testing for myself some quaint and/or self-destructive ideas about love. I heard 'Love is the ability of not knowing' as Cassavetes' way of saying, 'Love is having faith.' John had a dismissive shrug he reserved for ideas and people not worthy of his attack, and I can see now how he would have shrugged off the word 'faith'. His films begin at the moment when a person has been forced beyond such words – the moment, as he put it, 'when you can't find your way home'. ('That's when I consider it's worth it to make a film,' he added.)

What if, as he always insisted, there are no answers? What if there's just the unknown within you, between you, behind you and in front of you? And what if that unknown is impenetrable by love? What, then, can your bond with another human being consist of? When that bond is tested (for it will be), *what* will be tested?

In Cassavetes' film, what is tested is what he called, in his peculiar grammar, 'the ability of not knowing'. How much can you allow yourself to feel, or share, or be, when you'll never know? When there can be no security, since anything that can serve as security, any promise of insurance, can be taken from you in an instant? When there is nothing but what you feel, what you sense the other person feels, and the unknown? What if this is the way it is, beyond all philosophies, arts, therapies – all those palliative constructs? Welcome to the laughter of John Cassavetes.

That high, wheezy, witchy laugh that he let loose on film only three times: in short bursts during *Husbands*; in a graveyard with Peter Falk during *Mikey and Nicky*; and at full blast in the last moments of his last performance, *Love Streams*. I think about that sometimes, about the last things John Cassavetes did on film. He laughed that laugh, then he said goodbye to Gena, and then he waved goodbye to the camera.

The last drink

Las Vegas, the summer of 1983, later that night, in John's room. The walls are coloured puke green. 'A perfect room,' he says, 'a room where lots of people have lost. Lost things important to them, not just money.'

There are a few of us, we're quiet, it's the end of the night, the last drink. I'm thinking that it's incredible that his films, while so merciless, so furious, aren't depressing. Fury and laughter were John's ways, not depression. Did he owe that to his ability of not knowing? As the summer goes on it'll be clearer that he's dying, but we won't speak of it. Much later, a few months before his death, he'll say to me, 'Is life about horror – or is it about those few moments we have?'

As always, he won't pretend that the question has an answer. But now, in this terrible room which he really does relish, he's thinking about his art and he says, more to himself than to any of us: 'What people *like* is different from what they want, not what they like. They see insincerity and they hate it – but they don't say what they really feel. Why do people throw away all their mentality, all of what they really feel, in lieu of a promise – fake, made by the society – of how everybody's supposed to live?'

Goodnight, John.

AS TIME GOES BY

Richard Combs

Since his death three years ago, John Cassavetes seems to be everywhere, references to him setting off a chain reaction of other names, film-makers who might have been influenced by him, have benefited from his example, their films made possible by his pioneering work. It would be interesting to describe Cassavetes through the Cassavetes effect, to construe his own work from that of film-makers who have been likened to him.

So Robert Altman would exemplify a certain narrative messiness, characters who talk over each other or at cross-purposes; Martin Scorsese represents the ethnic side, the documentary of street life, the passion for music, and how all the above can turn a genre movie into something personal (Scorsese and Cassavetes dreamed up the basic plot of *Chinese Bookie* together); Mike Leigh shows the pain of minutely scrutinised reality. Leigh is also as impatient as Cassavetes used to be with the assumption that 'improvisation' means making it up as you go along (Cassavetes usually took a script credit on the films he directed).

In his day, Cassavetes cut a lonely figure in the film world. He apparently had no cinematic antecedents; his experimentation, his attitudes and objectives, appeared self-contained and even formulated in anti-film terms. He became a film director by accident, or, as he himself saw it, as a by-product of something else. In the late 1950s, he had helped to set up an actors' workshop in New York, for developing theatrical skills through improvisations. One of these produced the idea for *Shadows*, which became a film after private sponsors responded to an appeal on a radio show.

But even when the film was completed, Cassavetes still thought of it as a means to an end. 'When we made *Shadows* we had no intention of offering it for commercial distribution. It was an experiment all the way, and our main objective in making it was just to learn. It was an attempt for people to know their craft' (*Films & Filming*, February 1961). Cassavetes also had a private grudge against the cinema: 'I had worked in a lot of films and I couldn't adjust to the medium. I found I wasn't as free as I could be on stage or in a live television show. So for me, it was primarily to find out why I was not free – because I didn't particularly like to work in films…' At one point in *Shadows*, Lelia (Lelia Goldoni) replies grumpily to an invitation to go to the cinema. 'I don't like the movies,' and, although she has other reasons for being put out, to do with life, sex and race, it's tempting to think that she is speaking for her creator.

Shadows was shot in 16mm on the streets of New York, without a script, but with detailed character descriptions out of which the actors spun the different narrative threads. The freshness of the performances and the looseness of the shooting style made an immediate impact; harder to categorise as 'improvisation' or 'documentary', however, is the way the idiosyncratic dialogue establishes a density of character, mood and social scene without explaining anything. Three main storylines jostle along in a happy serendipity which turns into a complex reflection on race and identity. They involve the black Lelia, her brother Ben (Ben Carruthers), who with two white friends drifts aimlessly through parties and coffee bars, chatting up girls and putting down intellectual pretension, and their elder brother Hugh (Hugh Hurd), a struggling night-club singer.

To the American critic Parker Tyler, *Shadows* couldn't even be pigeonholed with the Beat counterculture, with the 'alternative' cinema of Robert Frank and Alfred Leslie's *Pull My Daisy*, with its free-form commentary by Jack Kerouac and participation by poets Allen Ginsberg and Gregory Corso. To Tyler, Cassavetes' method was different from other attempts to bring a documentary realism to feature film-making.

'*Shadows* has been surprisingly well appreciated while mostly for the wrong reasons… No one, I believe, except the author of an article on Cassavetes in a small West Coast film magazine, has noticed the relation between the method of *Shadows* to that of Chekhov in his plays and especially his short stories. *Shadows* approaches its subject with the same casual directness as Chekhov his subjects… It takes a few characters and reveals their true life situation; the situation moves behind the veil of full consciousness and yet it communicates' (*Film Culture*, no. 24, 1962).

It's an intriguing connection – and more than that, the 'Chekhovian' element of *Shadows* becomes a continuity through Cassavetes' career, which otherwise does seem to break down into discrete, self-enclosed actors' experiments happening at irregular intervals. Time is the essence of this element, and the core of the drama: time as something to be enjoyed in a moment-to-moment way, in the camaraderie of Ben and his two friends, but time also as a pressure, as something that can never quite be seized and forever provokes feelings of loss, failure and disappointment. *Carpe diem* is one thing, but Ben and his friends occasionally worry – or others worry for them – about their lack of purpose. 'No more of this jazz for me, baby.' Even more wistfully, his younger sister Lelia confesses, 'I feel I should be further ahead than I am. Everything is passing me by.'

And within this flux, this pressure, there's an intractability to problems of love and family that is beyond the power of time to heal or resolve. Ben and Lelia are black, but so light-skinned that they can 'pass' in the white world – which is evidently responsible for the feelings of indefiniteness, of waste and guilty drifting, that they express in different ways. But their brother Hugh is unequivocally black, a quality which leaves them feeling both grateful and resentful. Lelia learns something unpleasant about her white lover Tony when he first meets Hugh, and Ben reacts aggressively when a black woman, a friend of Hugh's, makes advances to him at a party. Hugh, meanwhile, has his own problems with passing time, with his musical career stalled, at the beginning and end of the film, in bus and train terminals to third-rate out-of-town bookings.

It was nearly ten years before Cassavetes was again able to make a film completely on his own terms, and by the time of *Faces* much of what had been praised as radical in techniques or original in setting about *Shadows* had disappeared or been transformed. Cassavetes, whose films after all begin with his own reality – and who now lived in California, where he began using his home as a location – had discovered that his reality was different.

'It is a picture about the middle-aged, high middle income bracket people that are made fun of in our society … One day I woke up and realised that I'm part of that society and almost everyone I know is … And I knew there was something to be said about these people and about their insular existence and about their place in a society that is frowned upon today' (*Cinema*, Spring 1968). In between these two films, Cassavetes directed two Hollywood pictures, *Too Late Blues* (1961) and *A Child Is Waiting* (1962). On both, he felt he had less than a free hand, and both have therefore been largely ignored in the Cassavetes 'canon'.

Social milieu aside, there are obvious similarities between *Shadows* and *Faces*. There's the helter-skelter camerawork that gives all possible leeway to the actors' freedom of movement and expression, the rambling conversational sallies and challenges, the tenderness, hostility and loaded demands that people make of each other to 'be themselves'. But what Cassavetes essentially carries over is a tension between the hectic flux of experience, characters' need to rush from one experience to another, and a sense that the moment is already gone, the secret has been lost and the opportunity missed.

In the move from the city of New York to the country/suburban atmosphere of Los Angeles, Chekhovian rules still apply. The affluent home of business executive Richard Forst (John Marley) and his wife Maria (Lynn Carlin) is full enough of mirrors, glassed-in paintings, polished surfaces and objects that give off a dazzle of reflections. But the people themselves behave in a similar way, seeking reassurance in relationships that are self-reflecting and obsessively duplicated. In a rage of middle-aged, mid-life dissatisfaction, Richard abandons his wife to spend the night with a prostitute, Jeannie (Gena Rowlands), who offers – the question of paid sex being in the background – a simulation of domestic support. Maria meanwhile goes out for the night with some friends, returning with an amiable beach boy, Chet (Seymour Cassel), with whom she spends the night, but who then has to revive her from a suicide attempt in the morning.

Cassavetes compensates for the theatrical neatness of this construction – the action is confined to one night and morning – with an aggressive insistence on film in other ways. The story is framed as a film-within-a-film, Marley also playing a movie executive invited to a screening of something called *Faces* by a nervous gaggle of other executives: 'We call it the *Dolce vita* of the commercial field ...' *Faces* is also full of harsh variations in the film stock and lighting intensity, as the action moves from day to night and back again. Light and time seem to be cinematic gifts that can explode and explore the theatrical sameness of the setting.

If *Shadows* was Cassavetes' attempt to understand why he didn't feel free in film, Faces passes that challenge on to the characters, and to the performers playing them. The drives, the necessities and the limits of performance are what shape any Cassavetes film – and they feed as well into the poignancy of the subject, the sense of time passing, of age as a real component of what one is and can do, the fear of never being as good as one would like to be. In *Faces*, Jeannie and Chet are the performers, younger than the 'clients' they entertain, but they are coy about their age, feeling perhaps as the barely twenty-year-old Lelia does in *Shadows* that they should be further ahead.

In this respect, far from being marginal to Cassavetes' work, *Too Late Blues* is crucial, as deserving of revival as the five films being re-released now. It may be plotted conventionally enough as the fall and redemption of its hero, jazzman Ghost Wakefield (Bobby Darin), but within that its moods are anything but conventional. It happily evokes the frail camaraderie of a group of jazz musicians, young, but not as young as they could be: when they join in an impromptu game of baseball, one of them complains that, at thirtysomething, they're in danger of heart attacks. And they're at a point where the itch for success is beginning to overtake their satisfaction at playing the music they like for charity affairs or simply in the park 'for the trees'.

It's Ghost who eventually abandons the group and is promoted to a tawdry kind of success, more gigolo than jazzman. They're all reunited for a happy ending that has inevitably been scorned as a Hollywood cop-out. But the mood is singularly downbeat; the group is now playing, and grateful for the work, in a cheap dancehall. This is a 'happy ending' consistent enough with Cassavetes' careful distinction between different kinds of success, with self-respect and the recognition of certain realities.

The career – or lack of it – of Ghost Wakefield is a fascinating link between the Hugh Hurd character in *Shadows* and such later Cassavetes performers as Cosmo Vitelli (Ben Gazzara) in *The Killing of a Chinese Bookie* and Myrtle Gordon (Gena Rowlands) in *Opening Night*. Like Ghost's group, Cosmo has found a level of success – owning, operating and choreographing a 'sophisticated' strip show in Los Angeles – which doesn't satisfy his sense of where he should be, but expresses who and what he is well enough. Pretension to something else – a kind of high style – leads him into debt with the Mob and then, like Ghost, he is forced to fight his way *down* to a level he is comfortable with.

One of Cosmo's last acts, with a bullet hole in his side that may or may not be fatal, is to lecture the fractious members of his floor show on the necessity of being 'comfortable' with who or what you have chosen to be, that there are no absolute standards in life any more than there are any absolute standards of success or failure in show business. ('What's your truth is my falsehood, and what's your falsehood is my truth.')

It's a curious philosophy, at least with which to end a gangster film, but it's intimately connected with Cassavetes' own views on the sources of creativity, on finding one's level and on living with the pressures of time, the demands either to be or to become something: 'There are certain rules and regulations that I think are set specifically to destroy the actor and make him feel uncomfortable ...'; 'I gain energy by being comfortable, I get drained when I'm uncomfortable.'

Opening Night is an exploration of what it means to be uncomfortable in a part; Myrtle Gordon is finding it hard to play the role of an older woman in a play that has been written by a woman (Joan Blondell) who is somewhat older than she is. What complicates her rejection of the role is the fact that Myrtle, like every Cassavetes performer, is having to deal with her own ageing, with what it means in terms of her ability to feel passion in her private life, as well as her fear of being typecast professionally.

Like *Shadows*, *Opening Night* is full of scenes of auditions and rehearsals, try-outs and attempts to find a 'comfortable' reality. But stylistically, it is the least like *Shadows* of all Cassavetes' films; it is shot almost in tableaux, characters as masks isolated within the red plush depths of the stage, against the darkened background of the auditorium, or within the equally anonymous spaces of 'private' apartments. Not since *Too Late Blues*, in fact, had Cassavetes adopted a style which so strikingly framed and 'placed' the actor. In the earlier film, Hollywood cameraman Lionel Lindon (who also worked on Cassavetes' TV show *Johnny Staccato*) composed scenes in depth: a choreographed flux of faces, bodies, glances, shifting alliances and fluctuating attachments. Thematically, the link with *Shadows* is clear, but visually and dramatically the effect could be called Wellesian.

Other stylistic connections spring to mind. *Faces* is hysterical Antonioni; *Opening Night* Visconti in out-of-town try-outs. It is ironic – but in the end not surprising – that Cassavetes, who privileged the actor over cinema, who attacked the cinema with the tools of all his other trades, should have encompassed so much of it, should have made contact, consciously or not, with so many other practitioners. Apart from the growing list of directors who are now claimed as his beneficiaries, there are also those films in which Cassavetes appeared for other directors, which could all open out into unique examples of Cassavetes cinema. There is, for instance, his role as the husband in *Rosemary's Baby*, where he gives a particular reality to the witchcraft plot as he skulks, shamefacedly, on the edges of the coven, an actor trying to make himself comfortable with the fact that he has advanced his career by admitting the Devil to his wife's bed.

ALL THAT IS LIGHT – BRAKHAGE AT SIXTY

Suranjan Ganguly

When he's not in class lecturing on Méliès and the Sienese Renaissance painters, or drinking Irish coffee at Pearl's in downtown Boulder, or armed with crayons doing a very complicated squiggle with his two small children, Stan Brakhage is hard at work in his attic, carefully adding another layer of blue with his fingers to a celluloid strip thickly coated with reds, greens and yellows. The new film doesn't have a name, nor is Brakhage sure he wants to give it one. All he wants to talk about is that deep blue and the stained-glass windows which he has just seen at Chartres.

While most of his contemporaries with whom he forged the American avant-garde film movement have slowed down or stopped working, Brakhage, who turned sixty in January, is as prolific as ever, adding six to eight films a year to an *oeuvre* of nearly 250. Widely regarded as the world's foremost living experimental film-maker, he was recently honoured by the US Library of Congress, which selected his monumental four-part film *Dog Star Man* (1962–64) for inclusion in the National Film Registry. Earlier, Brakhage received the prestigious MacDowell Medal, whose previous recipients include Robert Frost, Georgia O'Keeffe and Aaron Copland.

Born in Kansas City, Missouri, in 1933, Brakhage made his first film, *Interim*, in 1952 when he was nineteen. Over the next few years, he met the key figures of the American avant-garde who were to influence him: poets such as Robert Duncan, Michael McClure, Louis Zukofsky and Kenneth Rexroth; film-makers such as Maya Deren, Jonas Mekas, Marie Menken, Kenneth Anger and Sidney Peterson; composers such as John Cage and Edgar Varèse, with whom he studied. Shortly after his marriage to Jane Collum in 1958, Brakhage set up home in the Colorado mountains near Boulder, where for the next thirty years he would live and make his films. From 1969 to 1981, he taught film history and aesthetics at the School of the Art Institute of Chicago, and from 1981 he has been teaching film at the University of Boulder. Divorced from Jane in 1986, Brakhage now lives in Boulder with his second wife, Marilyn, and their two children.

Described variously as a romantic, a visionary and a humanist, Brakhage has produced an astonishing range of work that includes psychodramas, autobiographical films, birth films, Freudian trance films, cosmological epics such as *Dog Star Man*, 'song' cycles inspired by lyric poetry, unphotographed films such as *Mothlight* (1963), and Abstract Expressionist hand-painted films such as *The Dante Quartet* (1987). In his book *Metaphors on Vision* (1963), he has defined his work in terms of 'birth, sex, death, and the search for God', but the ostensible subject of all his films is the act of seeing and its relationship to the world and to film, which becomes a corollary of that act.

* * *

Suranjan Ganguly: You've been involved with film for over forty years – as a maker, thinker, writer and academic. Has your sense of film as film changed?

Stan Brakhage: In one sense it hasn't changed: from the beginning I had a feeling for film as vision. I didn't think it was related to literature or theatre at all, nor had it anything to do with Renaissance perspective. I was struggling all the time against the flypaper of other arts harnessing film to their own usages, which means essentially as a recording device or within the long historical trap of 'picture' – by which I mean a collection of nameable shapes within a frame. I don't even think still photography, with few exceptions, has made any significant attempt to free itself from that. So I had certain instinctual feelings about film even before I made one.

Suranjan Ganguly: What do you mean by 'vision', and how is it related to film?

Stan Brakhage: For me vision is what you see, to the least extent related to picture. It is just seeing – it is a very simple word – and to be a visionary is to be a seer. The problem is that most people can't see. Children can – they have a much wider range of visual awareness – because their eyes haven't been tutored to death by man-made laws of perspective or compositional logic. Every semester I start out by telling my students that they have to see in order to experience film and that seeing is not just looking at pictures. This simple idea seems to be the hardest to get through to people.

Suranjan Ganguly: But is it really so simple? In your films, to see without picturing is a composite of many visual processes, only one of which is open-eye vision, or what we call normal everyday vision.

Stan Brakhage: Open-eye vision is what we are directly conscious of, but there's much more going on that we ignore. Seeing includes open-eye, peripheral and hypnagogic vision, along with moving visual thinking, dream vision and memory feedback – in short, whatever affects the eyes, the brain and the nervous system. I believe that all these have a right to be called seeing since they enable us to inherit the full spectrum of our optic and nervous system.

Suranjan Ganguly: Can you define them?

Stan Brakhage: Hypnagogic vision is what you see with your eyes closed – at first a field of grainy, shifting, multi-coloured sands that gradually assume various shapes. It's optic feedback: the nervous system projects what you have previously experienced – your visual memories – into the optic nerve endings. It's also called closed-eye vision. Moving visual thinking, on the other hand, occurs deeper in the synapsing of the brain. It's a streaming of shapes that are not nameable – a vast visual 'song' of the cells expressing their internal life. Peripheral vision is what you don't pay close attention to during the day and which surfaces at night in your dreams. And memory feedback consists of the editings of your remembrance. It's like a highly edited movie made from the real.

Suranjan Ganguly: How is film predisposed to embody these?

Stan Brakhage: Over the years, I have come to believe that every machine people invent is nothing more than an extension of their innards. The base rhythm of film – twenty-four frames per second – is sort of centred in its pulse to our brain waves. If you start a film at eight frames per second and with a variable speed motor slowly raise it to thirty-two, you put the audience in the first stage of hypnosis. So the natural pulse of film is a corollary to the brain's reception of everyday ordinary vision. Then film grain approximates the first stage of hypnagogic vision, which occurs at a pulse within the range of film's possibilities of projection. Also, during editing, film comes close to the way you remember. And finally, if you cut fast enough, you can reflect within twenty-four frames per second the saccadic movements of the eyes, which people aren't ordinarily aware of, but which are an intrinsic part of seeing.

Suranjan Ganguly: So virtually all your experiments were aimed at developing this relationship between film and seeing?

Stan Brakhage: My cutting has always tried to be true to the eyes, to the nervous system and to memory, and to capture these processes, which happen very rapidly. At one point I felt my montage – inspired by Griffith and Eisenstein – had to evolve to do justice to memory recall, so I began to use the single frame to suggest what the mind can do during a flashback. Then I began to use superimpositions because these occur constantly in the saccadic movements of the eyes and in memory feedback and input. I've done as many as seven superimpositions at one time – in *Christ Mass Sex Dance* (1990) – and I wish I could do more because there are more in vision itself. Then I shot out of focus to capture peripheral vision, which is always unfocused, or used flares to give a sense of the body when it has an overload in feedback and literally flares – something you can see with your eyes open. In *Loving* (1957), a couple make love in the sun and their optic system flares – it's really the nervous system's ecstasy – in oranges and yellows and whites. I had noticed that when film flares out at the end of a colour roll, you get those same colours, and I put them in because they are intrinsic to human vision as well.

Suranjan Ganguly: But of all these possible seeings, the hypnagogic has been the most important to you.

Stan Brakhage: Yes. I sometimes like just to sit and watch my closed eyes sparking, or the streamings of my mind. They're the best movies in town! But the flow is so rapid that to document it would call for a camera that would run 1,000 frames per second. All I can do on film is to grasp a little piece of it and then make a corollary. So my films don't reflect what I see when I close my eyes – only a symbol of that. The extent to which I accept that is the extent to which I can be true to what film can do.

Suranjan Ganguly: Since closed-eye vision is largely unfilmable, then, you had to find other means of representing it, and painting directly on to film became one way to do this.

Stan Brakhage: At the birth of my first child, I was acutely conscious of my hypnagogic vision whenever I blinked my eyes. But it didn't appear in the film I made of that birth – *Window Water Baby Moving* (1959) – so for the birth of my second child, which occurs in Part 2 of *Dog Star Man*, and of my third in *Thigh Line Lyre Triangular* (1961), I painted on film to include what I had seen. I became very excited when I realised that my closed-eye vision resembled the work of the Abstract Expressionist painters I admired so much – all very Pollock-like and Rothko-like.

Suranjan Ganguly: Did you sense that they were also doing the same thing – recording their optic feedback?

Stan Brakhage: When I was living in New York in the 1950s and 1960s, I became an avid gallery-goer. I discovered Turner, who is probably still the most pervasive influence on me because of his representations of light. I was also strongly drawn to the Abstract Expressionists – Pollock, Rothko, Kline – because of their interior vision. None of these so-called abstract painters – going back to Kandinsky and earlier – had made any reference to painting consciously out of their closed-eye vision, but I became certain that unconsciously many of them had. To me, they were all engaged in making icons of inner picturisation, literally mapping modes of non-verbal, non-symbolic, non-numerical thought. So I got interested in consciously and unconsciously attempting to represent this.

Suranjan Ganguly: But it wasn't enough to paint. To find as close a corollary to hypnagogic vision as possible, you had physically to manipulate the surface of the film strip.

Stan Brakhage: I tried a number of different things, including iron filings under magnets! I would bake film before and after photographing to bring out certain chemical changes in the grain so that it would correspond to certain stages of hypnagogic vision. I once even herded brine shrimp into a pack to capture the quality of their movements. And I worked with household chemicals and dyes, and placed coloured powders under vibrators and magnets. The making of *The Text of Light* (1974), which involved shooting through a glass ashtray, was another way of capturing certain forms of both closed- and open-eye envisionment of light.

Suranjan Ganguly: And you would scratch on film and write on it.

Stan Brakhage: Words appear on film throughout my work. By scratching them I try to be true to the way words vibrate and jiggle when they appear in closed-eye vision – which doesn't happen very often. Also, by scratching them I can at least make them more intrinsic to what film is – they become carriers of light. Photographed words relate more to memory recall or just to the open-eyed present.

Suranjan Ganguly: Hand-painted sections appear in your work as early as *Prelude* (1962), the first part of *Dog Star Man*, but in the past few years you've been making films such as *The Dante Quartet* and *Delicacies of Molten Horror Synapse* (1991) that are wholly hand-painted. You even claim this is all you want to do now.

Stan Brakhage: I now believe that film is much more predisposed to what you can do with paint and scratches than with anything else. My hand-painted films are my favourites – I look at them again and again and they always feel like film, not as if they're referring to something else.

Suranjan Ganguly: Do you see your work within a specific tradition of hand-painted film?

Stan Brakhage: I've always felt drawn to the hand-painted films of Méliès, which are an extraordinary phenomenon in their own right, and I've felt a kinship with film-makers such as Viking Eggeling, Walter Ruttman, Oscar Fischinger and Len Lye, who even batiked on film with his fingers. One of my main inspirations has been Marie Menken, and Harry Smith is often in my mind as I work. Many of them didn't paint on film, but their work has a hands-on quality that I admire.

Suranjan Ganguly: What do you mostly work with?

Stan Brakhage: Acrylics – mostly translucent acrylics – and India inks and a variety of dyes that are variously mixed with or not with acrylics. I have also made whole films with Magic Markers. I use brushes at times, but basically it's paint on fingers, a different colour on each finger. Usually I prepare the film first with chemicals, so that the paint can dry and form patterns, then during the drying process I use chemicals again to create organic shapes and forms. Finally, I go over it a frame at a time to stitch these patterns into a unified whole. If you watch me do it, it looks as though I'm playing the piano – it's very quick, very deft – but people forget that I have to paint twenty-four frames to get a second's worth of film. I have hand-painted films like *Eye Myth* (1972), which is nine seconds long, as well as *Interpolations* (1992) which runs for twelve minutes – the longest hand-painted film I have ever made.

Suranjan Ganguly: You've painted on all kinds of film stock, including 65mm Imax film. You also paint directly on footage you've found or shot yourself. What part of vision does that approximate?

Stan Brakhage: Let me say first that painting on Imax was very exciting – it was as if an easel painter had been given a wall, it was such a large space to work with. The model for painting on photographed film was closed-eye vision mixing with open-eye vision. Not very many people can see that, and it took me a long time before I could do both – see what I was looking at and also watch the nervous system's immediate shape-and-colour reaction to it.

Suranjan Ganguly: Are the recent hand-painted films a new involvement with the hypnagogic, or the beginning of a completely new phase in your work?

Stan Brakhage: No, that's over. I don't want to make corollaries of my closed-eye vision any more – not consciously – because it limits me in what I can be conscious of. I feel my consciousness is no longer a very good arbiter, that it could even be a limitation on my making, which is another way of saying I'm now more nearly at one with the painting I do on film.

Suranjan Ganguly: So what is the new hand-painted work going to be?

Stan Brakhage: What's new is that I don't have anything else as reference other than what the film itself is showing me. Every time film reflects something that's nameable, it limits what it can do. If I can make films that refer to things that can't be lived through, then I feel that I'm giving film a chance to be in the fullest possible sense, and that makes me feel good. Now I really just want to fool around with paint on film, hoping to do so in such an open way that whatever is deep inside me, past all prejudice and even all learning, can come out along my arms to my fingertips, and with the help of these smudges and dyes sing a song like birds on a normal day.

Suranjan Ganguly: From 1979 to 1990, you worked on an extraordinary series of films – *The Roman Numeral Series*, *The Arabic Numeral Series*, *The Egyptian Series* and *The Babylon Series* – where there's already a sense of leaving behind the hypnagogic for the electrical patterns of thought before it even becomes thought.

Stan Brakhage: I've been going in and out of the Egyptian *Book of the Dead* for the last fifteen years, and I've studied Hammurabi's code very closely. When I made those films I was trying to do two things: to get a sense of the moving visual thinking of those cultures, and to see how out of it rose the glyphs – hieroglyphs – that shape their language. I tried to represent pictorially what occurs during this 'seeing', and how within this flow of electrical colouration there are also bits of memory feedback that intermix with the hypnagogic and help shape the glyphs.

Suranjan Ganguly: So essentially you were trying to tap into a pre-natal, pre-verbal and pre-picture consciousness – the very womb of the image?

Stan Brakhage: Yes. We know that hieroglyphs are symbolic representations of the external world, but where do they come from? My sense is that they appear first as shapes in closed-eye vision. At the beginning of each film in *The Babylon Series*, I've scratched a particular Babylonian glyph, and then I go for the source of the thinking that produced it.

Suranjan Ganguly: So the films arose from a study of these written characters combined with explorations of your own moving visual thinking as a model?

Stan Brakhage: The first clear sense I had of these glyphs was when I was on a plane which was about to make a belly landing since its landing gear had malfunctioned. We were told to adopt the foetal position. It was then that I had a series of intense glyphs that was so powerful that even in that state I grabbed a pencil and piece of paper and drew them. Later, I scratched them onto film and interspersed them with appropriate colour flares that had also occurred at that time in my hypnagogic vision. The film was *he was born, he suffered, he died* (1974). As a result, I discovered how the mind can spark glyphs that seemed not pictures of events from my life, but compound symbols of those events.

Suranjan Ganguly: The films are also meditations on light, which is not new to your work, except that this light is different, situated deep within the pre-conscious.

Stan Brakhage: What is film, after all, but rhythmed light? I've always agreed with that line in Pound's cantos: 'All that is is light.' That's us and everything we're seeing, the dance of the light from the inside mixing with that coming from the outside in.

Suranjan Ganguly: How did you create the light patterns in these films?

Stan Brakhage: I didn't do any hand-painting or scratching, but photographed with various glasses, prisms, crystal balls, bits and pieces of tin foil and whatever else was handy. I manipulated these with my hands in front of the lens. If I was lucky, I would get an equivalent of the light streaming and would combine fragments of ordinary photographed material with this light to create a compound – little meaningful glyphs of a sort. I also used filters. In fact, often with at least two filters in my hands I would colour the streaks of light in various ways. And, of course, the prisms provided me with refraction colours, which I found intrinsic to moving visual thinking.

Suranjan Ganguly: One can enjoy these films on another level, as analogues to music. You've even called them 'visual music'.

Stan Brakhage: Of all the arts, music is closest to film, and I've had a long infatuation with music and film. I was very inspired by Charles Ives, who has several different sound sources going on simultaneously – a brass band on one side of the stage, a choir on the other and an orchestra in the middle – each playing their own music and it all interweaving. So I tried in combining sounds and visuals to push to the furthest possibility of a corollary between music and film, which is similar to Ives's combinations of different musical pieces, each retaining its own aesthetic integrity.

Suranjan Ganguly: At the same time, you've always held that sound in film is an aesthetic error. In fact, most of your films have been silent.

Stan Brakhage: Film is obviously visual and, from an aesthetic standpoint, I see no need for a film to be accompanied by sound any more than I would expect a painting to be. At first I did make sound films, but I felt sound limited seeing, so I gave it up. My films were complex enough and difficult enough to see without any distraction of the ear thinking. But if I felt a film needed sound, I always included it. In the last few years, I've even cut film to music – take *Passage Through: A Ritual* (1990) which I edited to a piece by Philip Corner – but that seems to be coming to an end. I believe now that you can only go so far with music, and then film is not music. It first became apparent to me fifteen years ago when I tried to cut exactly to the measures and shifts of a Bach fugue and the result was a mess. Since film clearly isn't music, I am now trying to find out what it is that film can do that's purely film. I really wish to open myself to that difference. I want to make films that are not even corollaries of music, that wouldn't even make you think of music.

Suranjan Ganguly: So a film that …

Stan Brakhage: … will not be about anything at all. I wish I could be more precise, but it's hard to describe this in words. It was in a chapel – the Rothko Chapel in Houston – that I had a sense of nothing. What I felt looking at those paintings was completely distinct from a religious experience, something purely organic and sensual but that drew me out to the very limits of my inner being. That's where I think it all begins – in the sense of the ineffable – and I want that to come through me into my work. I want that appreciation of nothing being everything.

Suranjan Ganguly: And anything that is referential deflects and limits that to some extent?

Stan Brakhage: Yes. A work which is too referential to things outside the aesthetic ecology, too dependent on something extrinsic, is not art. All this slavish mirroring of the human condition feels like a bird singing in front of mirrors. The less a work of art reflects the world, the more it is being in the world and having its natural life like anything else. Film must be free from all imitations, of which the most dangerous is the imitation of life.

Suranjan Ganguly: So when you speak of an 'aesthetic ecology', you're speaking of the artwork as a self-enclosed object?

Stan Brakhage: A work of art must be something with a world of its own in which everything that exists is interrelated so that it forms a whole, as do Rothko's paintings. And it must convey a sense of itself – for example, a film must show at all times some sense of it being an on-off projection of stills that flicker in the opening and closing of the shutter. The great films always do this – even narrative films have ways in which they do it. When I first scratched titles on film – in *Desistfilm* (1954) – I became conscious at once that they directed the eyes to what film is. Paint on film does that too with its irregularities and its rhythms.

Suranjan Ganguly: But isn't that too restrictive a definition? One of the complaints made about your work is that it fails to address the socio-political realities of the culture within which it exists.

Stan Brakhage: I think my films address that constantly. I don't think there has ever been a film that I wished to make that wasn't political in the broadest sense of the term, that wasn't about what I could feel or sense for better or worse from the conditionings of my times and from my rebellions against those conditionings.

Take *Scenes from Under Childhood* (1967–70) which I made out of disgust at the Shirley Temple representation of childhood which was utterly false and served only to aid and abet the abuse of children. Or take the childbirth films. It was appalling to me that childbirth was a taboo subject, excluded from human vision, and that women were often barbarously treated in child-bearing and ignored as mothers within this culture. So there were political motivations that led me to make the five childbirth films. At the same time, I would add that if in these films I had tried in some conscious way to present a political alternative, I would have falsified the art process. As an artist, I have to be very careful not to allow social and political impulses to dominate because then I would falsify the balances that are intrinsic and necessary to make an aesthetic ecology.

Suranjan Ganguly: The childbirth films are part of a long cycle you made about your first family. Although there is no implicit political subtext, these films resonate with the sense of a life lived in a specific place and time and according to a specific vision. In a way they are probably the most 'political' of all your films.

Stan Brakhage: I thought that if I photographed my daily life and photographed it as inspired by home movies or the amateur film, rather than from what I had learned from film theory and the work of film-makers such as Méliès, Griffith, Dreyer and Eisenstein, and if I could also take inspiration from errors which I read as significant Freudian slips in home movie-making, then I could avoid drama. But I didn't realise the extent to which people in their daily lives reflect the movies and what they read. We were plugged into the same literary/theatrical syndrome and our household to some extent was a template of what I wanted to avoid.

Suranjan Ganguly: How did you include Freudian slips in your films?

Stan Brakhage: I would study the raw footage so closely that it went beyond the average dream analysis in therapy. And I would find things in it that seemed very embarrassing, that I wanted to throw out, but by the time I was through, they would become the centre of the film. Also, while shooting I would sometimes consciously try to catch what seemed like a true slip – and then in the editing put it in a context where it would reveal itself fully.

Suranjan Ganguly: In almost all these films, there is a celebration of the trivia of daily life, a sense that the commonplace is itself sacred.

Stan Brakhage: For me, that's where we really live, that's what we really have. To stop the overwhelming influence of drama in film, I began to concentrate on the glories of an undramatic present, which is literally the tabletop. That is what peripheral vision is most involved with – the so-called mundane, which people use as a word of contempt when they really mean 'earth'. What they don't see is the potential for glory, for envisionment that's inherent in even doing the dishes, in the soap suds with their multiple rainbows, or in the dull edge of a plate that has to be scrubbed. If they could only see, only get involved with the wonders right under their noses – more specifically, if they could only see the movie playing on either side of their noses. All they have to do is close their eyes and look.

Suranjan Ganguly: Was there that hope behind the making of these films? Did you believe, like many of your contemporaries in the 1960s, that film could help change the world?

Stan Brakhage: Yes, we really believed we were going to change the world. One of my favourite jokes was that I was working on the 400-year plan. Well, I'm not any more. I have no world-saving ideas left in me. I would rather see my work as an attempt to clear aesthetic areas, to free film from previous arts and ideologies, to leave it clear to be of use to men and women to create formal integrities of various kinds which might help evolve human sensibility.

Suranjan Ganguly: Where is the avant-garde film movement that you helped to forge?

Stan Brakhage: There was no movement then and there is no movement now. What we shared was the uniqueness of each of us and that each of us was true to that uniqueness in his or her making, despite all attempts by society to pigeonhole us as a movement. But I must say that they succeeded, for the 'movement' became an aberration of the 60s – a drug-induced, sexually motivated movie-making tangent to pornography – and that's how it is seen today even in the academic community. Instead, we were a bunch of people who were dedicated to film and involved with the whole previous history of the arts in our concern to make an art. And this involvement we shared to some extent as 'moderns'. So you have a love of film, a love of art, a dedication to the arts. And one of the most vibrant ways to be dedicated to the arts is to be highly suspicious of every historical or inherited aspect of it.

Suranjan Ganguly: What about the current scene? Do you see anything in independent film-making today that you would consider innovative?

Stan Brakhage: There is much more uniqueness in film-making today than in the much-touted mid-60s. But the irony is that it is now truly 'underground'; in the 60s they said it was underground but it wasn't, now nobody says anything and it really is. It isn't affecting anybody; even the advertising agencies aren't renting their films to steal from them. And that's perhaps a good sign – that each of these film-makers is doing something so unique that there is no real way to pick up a trick. To that extent, the art of film is truly moving into a realm of its own, happily free from commercial usages.

Suranjan Ganguly: Looking back over forty years of film-making, what matters most now?

Stan Brakhage: That I believe in song. That's what I wanted to do and I did it quite selfishly, out of my own need to come through to a voice that is comparable with song and related to all animal life on earth. I believe in the beauty of the singing of the whale; I am moved deeply at the whole range of song that the wolf makes when the moon appears, or neighbourhood dogs make – that they make their song, and this is the wonder of life on Earth, and I in great humility wish to join this.

MY TIME IS NOT YOUR TIME

Amy Taubin

In 1963, several years after I'd become a devotee of underground cinema, I saw a film that showed me what my late-adolescent obsession was all about. Unannounced and untitled, Andy Warhol's *Kiss* (then dubbed *The Andy Warhol Serial* because it was shown in weekly four-minute instalments) flickered onto the screen of the Grammercy Arts Theater on West 27th Street. Its black and white was as deep and impenetrable as archival nitrate, its motion slower than life. Framed in tight close-up, two faces lunged at each other, mouth on mouth, sucking, nuzzling, merging, devouring. Some kisses were erotic, some comic, some verged on abstraction – less the oscillation of orifices than a play of light and shadow. Never in the history of the movies had the invitation to look but do not touch seemed quite so paradoxical.

During the months that followed, *Kiss* was succeeded by the meditative *Eat*, the torturous *Sleep*, the cock-teasing *Blow Job*, the vaguely threatening, flagrantly gay *Haircut*, and the monumental *Empire*. Nothing if not the measure of their own time, they needed to be seen to be believed. Like the best of his painting (the *Disaster* series, the *Marilyns*, and the *Elvises*), Warhol's silent films and some of the sound films that followed in 1965 and 1966 existed in the tension between presence and absence, assertion and denial. Fetishistic in the extreme, they allowed the receptive viewer access to the fundamentals of cinematic pleasure. Their surfaces opened on to the depths of your psyche.

Warhol's films were hardly *sui generis*. Their sources were in both Hollywood and the avant-garde. In the early 1960s, Warhol had trolled the underground from 'pasty' drag shows to minimalist dance/performances at the Judson Church. He had spent weeks at the Film-makers' Co-operative looking at films by Jack Smith, Ron Rice, Kenneth Anger, Stan Brakhage, Gregory Markopoulos, Willard Maas and Marie Menken. At some point, although it has never been mentioned in the reams of diaries and reminiscences of the period, he must have seen *Rose Hobart*, Joseph Cornell's collage film which had been discovered and was being presented (with significant alterations) by Ken Jacobs and Jack Smith. It's all there in *Rose Hobart*: the paring down of a mass-culture object to its fantasy essence (Cornell extracted from a print of the 1930s B picture *East of Borneo* all the shots in which the actress Rose Hobart appears and edited them together); the fetishisation of the female star; the single-minded title; the phantasmal effect that results when film shot at sound speed (twenty-four frames per second) is projected at the slightly slower speed of silence (sixteen frames per second).

More generally, Warhol learned from the avant-garde how to produce a (per)version of Hollywood in his own studio for little more than the costs of a roll of 16mm film and its developing. In 1964, I was introduced to Warhol's Factory (then on East 47th Street) by the rapidly fading, early superstar Naomi Levine. Like all newcomers, I was screen-tested. (I was escorted into a makeshift cubicle and positioned on a stool. Warhol looked through the lens, adjusted the framing, instructed me to sit still and try not to blink, turned on the camera and walked away.)

My screen test was included in one or another version of *The Thirteen Most Beautiful Women*. Later that day I was drafted into the ongoing 'Banana' series which was at some point incorporated into *Couch*. (Contrary to published description, *Couch* is not totally pornographic. I sat on a couch with superstars Levine, Baby Jane Holzer and Gerard Malanga, and for two-and-a-half minutes each of us masticated her/his/our own banana.) I was fascinated by Warhol's work process, but otherwise found the scene as unpleasant as high school – people with outlandish expectations all competing for a piece of the master. Although I made only one or two more visits to the Factory, I followed the films religiously until *The Chelsea Girls* and was a regular at The Exploding Plastic Inevitable (Warhol's presentation of the Velvet Underground, plus films, performance and dancing) when it took up residence in the Dom on St Mark's Place.

Framing time as it passes

In 1972, Warhol withdrew his films from distribution, leaving available only the Paul Morrissey-directed *Andy Warhol Productions*. The reasons (directly and obliquely stated at various times by various people, including Warhol himself) reveal the typical, perhaps irreconcilable Warholian oppositions between aesthetic and economic value, high and mass culture. There was the art-market notion that the films would gain in value from their unavailability. There was the Hollywood industry notion that the films depressed Warhol's potential value as a commercial film director. Hollywood types, it seemed, were incapable of the kind of selective vision practised by the art world, which managed to ignore the films entirely, although during the period of his greatest work (1961–68) Warhol devoted as much time to film as he did to painting. The only serious studies of Warhol as a film-maker are Peter Gidal's blind-sided *Andy Warhol* (1971), Stephen Koch's brilliant *Stargazer* (1973), and *Andy Warhol Film Factory* (1989), a collection of essays edited by Michael O'Pray which is all the more impressive considering how few of the writers had access to the films themselves. Left to moulder in the Factory and various laboratories, the films became merely an absence, a camp con job, until, in 1982, John Hardhardt, film and video curator of the Whitney Museum, convinced Warhol to turn all the existing material over to the Whitney and the Museum of Modern Art so it could be catalogued, preserved and rereleased.

To date, twenty-five films have been reissued; most of them are now available for non-theatrical distribution through the Museum of Modern Art. (Theatrical exhibition and electronic media licensing is handled by the Andy Warhol Foundation, which owns the films.) In the past six years, there have been three exhibitions of Warhol films in New York: two at the Whitney (in 1988 and 1994) and one at the Museum of Modern Art (in 1989, as part of a major Warhol retrospective). The confusion, defensiveness and outright hostility exhibited by most museum-goers towards the films are no less marked today than when they first appeared three decades ago.

At the Whitney screenings this spring, reverential silences quickly gave way to outraged heckling and noisy walkouts. Who knows what these viewers expected – the ones who expressly came to see a film by the notorious Andy Warhol, or the casual drop-ins from the main attraction (a Richard Avedon retrospective which coincidentally included his 1969 photograph of Warhol's scarred torso and his huge mural of Factory superstars, among them the transvestite Candy Darling with cascading platinum hair and penis in full view). Whatever it was they were looking for, it certainly wasn't this: a pudgy-faced man in a rumpled, buttoned-to-the-neck white shirt, self-consciously facing down the camera for ninety-nine minutes (*Henry Geldzahler*) or superstar Edie Sedgwick filmed for thirty-three minutes with a lens so severely out of focus one could barely distinguish the outlines of her lace bikini panties and bra (*Poor Little Rich Girl*).

'I'll be your mirror'

When asked in 1987, during the last interview of his life, if he was excited about his upcoming film exhibition at the Whitney, Warhol responded in the negative. 'They're better talked about than seen,' he said. It's terribly sad to think that Warhol had lost faith in the films as films, that he was unaware that the intervention he had made in the society of the spectacle was as profound as what Godard had done in roughly the same extended 1960s moment. But if Godard framed his psychosexual obsessions within a political analysis of global economic power, Warhol, the American anti-intellectual, transformed his psychosexual identity into a world view.

What Warhol threw up on the screen was basically a single shot removed from the editing language that facilitates narrative in the movies. And it's the absence of narrative that is so off-putting to viewers conditioned by Hollywood. Warhol's cinema frames time as it passes. (The films thus invert the strategy of the silkscreen *Disaster* series, in which time, stopped dead, is framed – over and over again.) Warhol described his silent films of the early 1960s in terms of their extraordinary duration: *Sleep*, intended as an eight-hour film of a man sleeping (which actually turned out to be only 5 hours 21 minutes at sixteen frames per second); *Empire*, an eight-hour film of the Empire State Building framed from a single camera position. The minimalists were making very large paintings and sculptures; Warhol made very long films.

It would be a mistake, however, to think that Warhol was interested in real time. 'My time is not your time' is the message of the silent films, from *Sleep* (1963) to *Henry Geldzahler* (1964). By being shot at sound speed and projected at silent speed (i.e. slowed by a third), the films unwind at a pace that is out of sync with the rhythms of the viewer. This disjunction – between the body clock of the person as image and the body clock of the person watching – heightens the viewer's alienation from the image. It makes us aware of the image as 'other' and therefore unknowable. Hollywood codes of realism elide the gap between seeing and knowing; Warhol's films reinforce it.

'My time is not your time' is also the message of the double-screen talkies, of which the best known is *The Chelsea Girls* (1966). Prior to making *The Chelsea Girls*, Warhol had begun to show most of the talkies from 1964 and 1965 (the Ronald Tavel–scripted films, the Edie Sedgwick films) as double-screen projections. Reels of thirty-three minutes that had been filmed sequentially (using a single-system sync-sound Auricon camera) and, indeed, in 'real time', were shown simultaneously. By splitting the viewer's attention between two shots, real time is effectively cancelled. Warhol's double-screen experiments climaxed with the 25-hour film **** (aka *Four Stars*), shown only once in 1968 and not yet reconstructed.

Most Warhol films open in stillness. Initially, one feels as disoriented by the image as when unexpectedly catching sight of one's reflection in a mirror on the street. The image seems both incomprehensible and strangely familiar, distanced and confrontational. Certain areas are too dark to read (notably in *Haircut #1*, *Vinyl* or *Beauty #2*); when a part of the body is framed in close-up, it's difficult to make out exactly what we're looking at (as in *Sleep* or *Lupe*). What's most disconcerting, however, is the marked frontality of the image, our sense that the performers, though operating in some radically different time zone, are directing their attention not at us, but at least towards us, or rather towards something that once occupied a place isomorphic with the place in which we are seated. In other words, the camera.

All Warhol's films celebrate the presence of the camera. The great Warhol 'superstars' – Mario Montez, Fred Herko, Edie Sedgwick, Nico, Viva – never concealed their awareness of the camera and often played directly to it, thus undermining a fundamental rule of Hollywood realism. The intensity of their relation to the camera – their unmistakable libidinal investment in the image they project for it – mirrors the viewer's libidinal investment in the image on the screen. In *Stargazer*, Koch analyses the profoundly narcissistic dynamics of Warhol's art: 'So narcissism means dividing the self to obviate the threat of needing others. All its energy, all its eros, all its sweetness, all its rage are directed toward this repressive end, which is almost never recognised as repression, because it is a repression that takes the form of desire ... it is desire as frustration.

'The narcissist yearns for wholeness because he feels himself divided, and his self-division finds its very image as he stands before the mirror. His divided autonomy is preferred to a wholeness of self. Yet that wholeness – obscurely intuited, loved as another is loved, mysteriously immanent in the mirror – is also his most dire image of self obliteration. That is his dilemma.'

'I'll be your mirror' sang the Velvet Underground and Nico in 1965, a decade before the Lacanian takeover of film theory. Warhol's camera was the mirror of the Warhol scene, but the scene also reflected on him. The scene was as much Warhol's product as were the films it inspired. It is still extraordinarily strange to imagine a person turning out some of the major works of twentieth-century art in a studio filled with people, most of them strangers to him. There was a core group of assistants, art-world powerbrokers, collectors, current and aspiring superstars. And then there were all these others coming and going – pop and underground celebrities, socialites, poets, photographers, models, drug dealers, hustlers, transvestites, beautiful boys and girls. 'Knock and announce yourself' read the sign on the door of the 47th Street Factory. People came to score sex, drugs, fame. The primary sexual orientation was gay; the drug of choice was speed. Some came to see the freaks, others to freak out. But primarily they came because the camera was always running. The camera inspired 'acting out'.

Death at work

Warhol presided over this alternative family like an inaccessible, inverse father figure: a father who in gesture and voice, as Victor Bockris notes in *The Life and Death of Andy Warhol*, was the incarnation of his childhood idol, the eight-year-old Shirley Temple; a father who licensed behaviours that were taboo, even to the imagination, in the conservative, working-class Catholic immigrant family of his 'real' childhood; a father who, despite his seeming passivity, was all-powerful. Warhol was the sole arbiter of whose concepts or scenarios were made into movies, of who became a star and who languished in the shadows. He almost never said no, but given the numbers of people clamouring for his attention, he seldom said yes. For those vying to be noticed, the scene was a perpetual audition. Most of them took out their frustration on one another, until Valerie Solanis, who couldn't get Warhol to commit to her screenplay, pumped the master himself full of lead. Warhol didn't die, but the scene did. He had exhausted it anyway; what came next was by invitation only.

In Koch's terms, Warhol became a star by being a 'stargazer'; which is not precisely the same as being an auteur, although the 1960s infatuation with auteurism contributed to Warhol's conflating of the artist with the film director. (It wasn't until the 1970s that he replaced both models with that of the producer. 'After I did the thing called "art" or whatever it's called, I went into business art.')

It's an oft-remarked-upon paradox that the most recognisable image Warhol produced was his own, that the star power of the shy voyeur eclipsed that of the under- and above-ground celebrities who were the ostensible subjects of his work. Appropriately, the first image one sees upon entering the new Andy Warhol Museum in Pittsburgh (the most ambitious single-artist museum in the world except perhaps the Picasso museum in Paris) is of Warhol himself. It's one of the death-head–like 1986 self-portraits: hair standing on end in petrified spikes, skull bones outlined through thin skin that glows as if radioactive, gaze frozen in bewildered horror before what it sees – which is nothing more or less than its own reflection in the lens of the camera. One thinks, of course, of Cocteau: 'The camera shows death at work.' But one is also struck by the historic specificity of the image; it's the face of someone trapped between Hiroshima and the age of AIDS, someone for whom death has the luminescence of the television screen. In any event, as Koch wrote in 1973 at the end of *Stargazer*: 'We are left with nothing but the works and their Theme … It is death alright, so let it be death, and I think we'd better take a good, long look.'

Awesome in their emptiness, the late self-portraits are less evocative than the occasional snapshots taken of, but not by, Warhol during the Factory film years. Peering through the viewfinder of his 16mm camera or sitting next to the projector during a screening, Warhol's face has the absorbed, disassociated look of a child sitting in front of a television set or a hacker contemplating the computer screen. 'The charm of the child lies to a great extent in his narcissism, his self-content and inaccessibility,' wrote Freud. 'Indeed, even the great criminals and humorists, as they are represented in literature compel our interest by the narcissistic consistency with which they manage to keep away from their ego anything that would diminish it.' How better to contain the danger immanent in the factory scene than to make it into an image – a virtual world, exciting but never threatening. Once the camera rolled, Warhol never intervened in the action taking place before it. He merely watched through the viewfinder, responding with an occasional zoom, tilt or pan. One imagines that if Warhol, for whom the telephone was a lifeline, were alive today, he'd be trolling the Internet, lurking in MUDS, enthralled by other people having virtual sex, absorbing on-line conferences about, say, the horror of Rwanda.

'In Warhol's view,' writes Callie Angell (who since 1991 has been working on a *catalogue raisonné* of the films) in her essay for *The Andy Warhol Museum* catalogue, 'television and his movies were "just one thing" – "a lot of pictures of cigarettes, cops, cowboys, kids, war, all cutting in and out of each other without stopping". Eventually, once the preservation of the Warhol film and video collection has been completed, it will be possible to consider Warhol's films and videotapes together as a single prodigious body of work, the results of three decades of non-stop effort in which the artist seemed to be laboring to create his own version of the omnipresent media culture.'

Crumbling masquerade

Unquestionably, the films are part of a project that's bigger – and longer – than any of them, but viewed individually, they prove singularly resistant to assimilation. There's something archaic about *Haircut*, or *Beauty #2*, or *Henry Geldzahler*. They reference a world before television, when the body, fetishised in celluloid, was projected larger than life. They're a response to the Hollywood films Warhol grew up on, the films that were available to every American, just like Campbell's soup. They're a camp send-up and furious attack on the Hollywood myth of sexual normality – that men are men and women are women, that sexual identity is naturally determined by genitalia, that men desire women (and act on their desires) and that women desire only to be desired by men (and therefore are allowed certain artifices to make their femininity more alluring and thus give men more pleasure).

Warhol's films, from *Sleep* to *The Chelsea Girls* (excluding the sexploitation films that begin with *My Hustler* and continue in collaboration with Paul Morrissey) are made from a deeply transvestite position, from the position of the boy who identified with Shirley Temple. Warhol understood that the distinction between identification and desire is not as clean-cut as Hollywood pretended. He took Hollywood's great subject – sexual identity – and destabilised it, turning it inside out and every which way. In Warhol's films, sexual identity is never naturalised. Constructed as masquerade, it is an imperfect shield for a terrible anxiety about sexual difference. The Warhol superstars are either drag queens (Mario Montez, Fred Herko, Candy Darling) or women who exaggerate their femininity out of the fear of being mistaken for boys (Edie Sedgwick, Viva), or studs (Gerard Malanga, Joe Dallesandro) whose obsessive focus on their own groins suggests a secret suspicion things might not be in order.

For all its seeming passivity, Warhol's camera is a weapon. Before its impassive gaze, the sexual masquerade crumbles, revealing raw narcissistic wounds and pathological insecurities as great as Warhol's own (and even greater when magnified by the projector). No one – not the most beautiful women nor the most beautiful boys, not the rich nor the famous – was immune from the fear that the camera would find something wrong. The would-be superstars flocked to the Factory to have their narcissistic investment in their own sexuality confirmed; the camera left them in shreds. One can remember no more than a dozen moments in all those hours of film when the performers are *not* in an agony of self-consciousness – though desperately pretending otherwise. Billy Linich and Fred Herko, co-conspirators in the castration metaphor implicit in *Haircut #1*, turning to the camera and laughing at the audience for being taken in; Viva cooking in *Blue Movie*, relaxed once her ordeal of fucking on camera is over, are among the exceptions.

The only subject to remain totally impervious to Warhol's camera was the Empire State Building. The most infamously conceptual of the films, *Empire* is actually one of the most visually subtle and richly reflexive. The longer one watches, the stronger the desire one feels to witness some structural collapse, some disturbance of that phallic monumentality. 'The Empire State Building is a star,' said Warhol, mocking the model to which no man can measure up.

Contagious boredom

Certainly not Henry Geldzahler. The morning after he shot *Empire*, Warhol used the rented camera and two leftover 1,200-foot magazines to shoot a silent, 99-minute portrait of the then Curator of Contemporary Art at the Metropolitan Museum – who was also a personal friend and power-broker for his art-world career. Like *Empire*, *Henry Geldzahler* is a silent, single-shot film. Geldzahler is positioned in medium shot at one end of a curving velvet couch facing the camera. His initial pose, as Callie Angell notes, 'bears a remarkable resemblance to Picasso's 1906 portrait of Gertrude Stein which was in display in the Metropolitan Museum. In both portraits the solid shape of the sitter, formally posed with hand on hip, is enthroned within the curve of an equally solid piece of furniture.' According to Angell, Warhol turned on the camera and left the room, returning some thirty-five minutes later to reload and then departing.

Left to his own devices, Geldzahler begins by nonchalantly staring down the camera. He has armed himself with sunglasses and a large cigar which is not, on this occasion, 'just a cigar' – Geldzahler is one of the few intellectuals to appear before Warhol's camera, and he makes sure that we know he means to outsmart it. For the first twenty minutes or so, it looks as if he is pondering the entire history of Modernist portraiture and the place of the motion picture within it. But no sooner does one impose this narrative on the film than one begins to question the basis for the assumption. Is it something in the way he flicks his cigar or tilts his head? Or is this imagined narrative suggested by what one knows about Geldzahler in the real world rather than what one perceives in the image? It's possible that Modernist aesthetics are nowhere in his mind. And yet...

Geldzahler passes his hand across his brow. Unlike his earlier magisterial gestures, this one is involuntary. It takes him by surprise. It upsets him. He carefully rearranges himself, takes off his glasses, puts them back on, as if to show he's in control of the image he's presenting. But the involuntary gestures keep coming. Now there's something decidedly swish about them. And Spanish. Is he following a train of associations that began with Picasso? Or has Geldzahler been inhabited by Mario Montez, the Factory's reigning drag queen?

In any event, he is beginning to look unnerved. He sinks onto the couch, feigns sleep, twitches, sweats – and then, suddenly, he seems to give up. He disengages from the power struggle with the camera and sits slumped over, an expression of total boredom on his face. The boredom is contagious. But how can that be? How can one feel empathy with an image that's so distant, so locked within its own time zone – 1964, flickering on the screen, eight frames per second slower than life?

Geldzahler starts to move around on the couch, more anxious than ever. He stubs out the last of the cigar. His hands move restlessly between his face and his lap. Then suddenly his arms fly up, he clasps his hands behind his head, he straightens his neck – and finds himself as Manet's *Olympia*. Could this indeed be his fantasy, or is it this viewer's projection? In any event, the brief moment of triumph fades. Geldzahler scrunches down into the couch, curled in foetal position, his hand over his face. A few minutes later, the film is over.

The antithesis of *cinéma vérité*, *Henry Geldzahler* demonstrates the power of the camera to transform its subject, to instigate a narcissistic splitting in which the self becomes totally invested in its own image, an image which is both excessive and never enough. Warhol pursued this line of attack the following year in the sound portraits of Edie Sedgwick (*Poor Little Rich Girl* and *Beauty #2*) and in *Paul Swan*, a portrait of an eighty-year-old former Isadora Duncan dancer who continued to perform the 'aesthetic' dances he'd choreographed at the turn of the century long after his limbs turned arthritic and his flesh spread through every gap in his costumes. Warhol filmed Swan's performance on a tiny, torn-tapestry–draped stage illuminated by four hardware store floodlights. As Swan plods through his atrophied routines, one imagines Warhol peering through the lens at his possible future, especially when Swan reveals a shoe fetish that Drella (Warhol's Factory nickname, a combination of Dracula and Cinderella) could relate to. At one point Swan leaves the stage to poke about for twenty minutes in the wings, looking for a shoe without which he can't continue.

If Swan seems painfully (or perhaps blissfully) unaware that the film unfolding in his head has nothing to do with the film Warhol is shooting ('You'll cut all this out anyway, won't you?' he queries when an on-stage costume change proves awkward), Sedgwick, in *Beauty #2*, drunk and stoned though she is, realises she is being set up and fights back. Seated on her bed, she is pulled in three directions at once. To her left on the bed is Gino, a dumb hustler type whom she has ostensibly brought home for a quick fuck. Facing her, but off-screen, is her former lover Chuck Wein, who keeps needling her about her looks, her voice, her mannerisms, her self-involvement – and anything else he can think of. And to her right is Warhol's envious camera, waiting for her to break. The camera is placed so that the tiny strip of Sedgwick's bikini is dead centre in the frame. Twisting nervously on the bed, she keeps her thighs pressed together as she shifts her legs from left to right and back again. As the film wears on, one realises that its objective is to destroy the upper-class social poise which is her only source of power and the only protection for her fragile sexual identity. Only if she loses herself completely will she spread her legs, and it's this sign of defeat that the camera waits to capture. It never comes.

These extended portraits are among the most extraordinary films in the history of cinema. And it's possible that there are other comparable films in Warhol's collection that haven't yet been restored. Considering that the collection comprises more than 4,000 reels of film, the preservation and cataloguing could take twenty years. Approximately one-third of the material is original (camera original or printing masters); the rest is prints and out-takes. Many of the films exist in multiple versions; some come with detailed notes that function as clues to Warhol's working methods.

Vested interests

In death, as in life, Warhol is surrounded by a number of vested interests: MoMA, the Whitney, the Warhol Foundation (all of which are involved in the preservation work); the Andy Warhol Museum (which has acquired about sixty film prints, but also plans to show videotape transfers of the films); and, of course, former collaborators and associates, all of whom want to preserve their place in the legend. The Warhol Foundation intends to generate income from the films by releasing them on video, laser discs and interactive media. The foundation recently licensed a version of *The Chelsea Girls*, which preserves the double-screen format by cropping half of each screen, to be shown on Channel 4 television.

Watching a film like *Henry Geldzahler* on video is like walking into a museum and seeing a 10x8 magazine reproduction hung in place of a painting (or whipping through the Prado on CD-ROM, a likely possibility in the near future). If there was anything Warhol understood, it was how 'presence' is medium-specific. Of course, 'presence' is an art issue. Unfortunately, what is still being debated is whether these films are art or business. That Warhol would have claimed to love the confusion is totally beside the point.

THE BIG WIG

Michael O'Pray

In Harmony Korine's recent no-budget, quasi-documentary feature film *Gummo*, there is a memorable head-and-shoulder shot – slowed down and fairly long-held – of 1990s chic icon Chloë Sevigny with her breasts black-taped, gazing into the camera. It is pure Warhol. Her narcissism, knowing sexiness and acknowledgement of the camera's gaze are all characteristic of a type of film-making first practised in early 1960s New York, film-making of a shocking audacity that attracted the fashionable yet repelled much of the art world.

Pop artist Andy Warhol's films are important because they influenced two kinds of cinema: Hollywood absorbed their gritty street-life realism, their sexual explicitness and on-the-edge performances; the avant-garde reworked his long-take, fixed-camera aesthetic into what came to be known as structural film – an austere, formalist project. When he started making films in 1963, however, Warhol knew nothing about the mechanics of film. Whatever he had gleaned about the contemporary underground film scene came from his friendship with Gerard Malanga, who introduced him to the veteran film-maker Marie Menken (one of the 'stars' of *The Chelsea Girls*, 1966) and took him to screenings at Jonas Mekas' Film-makers' Co-op. However, like any American of his generation he was brought up on classic Hollywood, and he was also familiar with gay porn films of the 1950s.

At that moment in the early 1960s, Warhol was on the crest of a wave as one of the most important artists on the New York scene, famous for his silk-screen paintings of iconic American figures (Marilyn Monroe), consumer objects (Campbell's soup cans) and dramatic images of death (lurid car accidents, the electric chair). He was an uncomfortable ally of fellow pop artists Robert Rauschenberg and Jasper Johns in their overthrowing of the abstract expressionist school of Pollock, De Kooning and co., who had dominated the art world throughout the 1950s. Like Rauschenberg and Johns, Warhol was gay, but unlike them he embraced the swish, camp images and attitudes of the gay world, especially when he turned to film. His stance would come to dominate 1960s popular culture. Cultivated camp soon became fashionable, notably in the theatricals of rock groups such as the Rolling Stones – in many ways Donald Cammell and Nicolas Roeg's use of Stones' singer Mick Jagger in *Performance* (1970) is a codicil to the Warholian moment.

Alone among major artists of the twentieth century Warhol committed himself seriously to film, so much so that in 1965 he stated that he was giving up painting. Warhol's prolific output, which ran to many hundreds of films, some only discovered after his death, was all produced between 1963 and 1968. These half-dozen years can be loosely divided into three phases. First, from 1963 to late 1964, there was a plethora of slow-projected (sixteen frames per second), silent, shortish black-and-white films shot on a Bolex – the favourite lightweight camera of avant-garde and documentary film-makers. The camera was static and the shooting unedited, the film's length determined by the length of the reel. Second, from 1964 Warhol used the Auricon camera with its built-in sound system (perversely, it was first used for the silent epic *Empire*). This was an intense, fertile period in which the slow-motion aesthetic gave way to a form of modernist 'theatre' aided and abetted by 'scriptwriter-collaborators' Chuck Wein and Ronald Tavel, the latter a dramatist associated with the Theatre of the Ridiculous. It was then that Warhol launched his 'superstars', including Edie Sedgwick, Gerard Malanga, Viva and the drag artist Mario Montez. These films were often seventy minutes in length, consisting of two single-take reels, each just over thirty minutes long — for instance, Wein's *Beauty #2* (1965) or Tavel's *Kitchen* (1966), both 'starring' Edie Sedgwick. Warhol told Tavel that he did not want plot, only 'incident'. The high point was probably reached with the commercially and critically successful *The Chelsea Girls*. The third phase is brief and not so distinctive, but it expresses a wider ambition and a realist clarity of narrative.

In many ways, it was an attempt to build on the commercial success of *The Chelsea Girls* under the driving force of the young Paul Morrissey, who disparaged the early 'art' films. The first step in this direction was *My Hustler* (1965); notable films of the period include *Nude Restaurant* and *Lonesome Cowboys* (both 1967). But after Valerie Solanas's bullets ripped into his body on 3 June 1968, Warhol's film involvement was much more at arm's length, although he continued to lend his imprimatur to films directed by Morrissey, such as *Flesh* (1968), *Trash* (1970) and *Heat* (1972).

As a film-maker, Warhol achieved international fame without showing many of his films more than once or twice to small art-house audiences in New York. Their word-of-mouth reputations sufficed. *Sleep* and *Empire*, both made in the early 1960s, were more talked about than seen. The regular description of them – a single image shown for hours on end (only really true of *Empire*) – was enough to evoke awe and disbelief. But these images of extreme passivity (a building, an unconscious man), made with extreme passivity, were unique in Warhol's *oeuvre*. Most of Warhol's films were of people, often doing very little – or a lot, ineptly. His reputation as an innovator rests in this fascinating combination of a simple shooting style with the 'performances' he elicited.

So what was so new and fresh about these early films? It has been argued that they resemble and were inspired by the early single-reel films of the Lumières and others, but they are quite different. For one thing Warhol's films are genuinely silent, unlike the so-called silent cinema which always had a musical accompaniment. For another their subject matter is not banal. To see *Sleep* (1963), *Eat* (1963), *Henry Geldzahler* (1964) or any of the hundreds of 'screen tests' Warhol shot is to experience something utterly different to anything offered by the early film pioneers. Lastly, in their provocative amateurishness, lack of skill and seeming effortlessness, they were an audacious challenge (and, for many, an insult) to both Hollywood and the avant-garde. Warhol seemed to switch on the camera and walk away. This was film's own Duchampian moment and film has never recovered from it.

The films were also made in a unique context: the Factory, a huge fifth-floor loft (about 100 feet by 40 feet) on East 47th Street. Billy Name had decorated it in silver foil, and opera played incessantly in the background. It became a parody of a Hollywood studio. According to Stephen Koch, Warhol, through Name, Malanga and the brilliant Ondine, gathered 'a-heads, street geniuses, poor little rich girls, the very chic, the desperately unknown, hustlers and call boys, prostitutes, museum curators, art dealers, rich collectors'. The Factory was classy and glamorous, chic and dangerous, and the door was always open. Drugs, sex and the pale presence of the ultra-hip Warhol provided the nexus for this volatile group, which seemed democratic, but was intensely not so. The sexuality was gay and the drugs were largely amphetamines.

As far as the films themselves were concerned, authorship was an anachronism. The camera was permanently placed ready for action in front of a large couch. Whoever visited the Factory, and was accepted into the circle, could perform on the couch for the 100-foot reel, while Warhol, Malanga, Name or whoever was available operated the camera. As Warhol confessed, film-making was so easy. A selection of these endless rolls of film was put together in 1964, entitled *Couch*. It showed various people, some famous, some not, doing this or that: hanging out, sleeping, hoovering, eating bananas, sucking cocks, fucking each other, cleaning a motorbike and so on. Silent, slowed down and shot in high-contrast black-and-white chiaroscuro, the work at times had a classic sculptural look – especially the sex scenes. Such narcissism and passivity were utterly new, and created a cinema of fantasies acted out, uncluttered by dialogue, storylines, stars, even – in its dream-like movement – time itself.

With the Bolex camera using 100-foot rolls of black-and-white film, Warhol also made portraits or what he called 'screen tests' of the New York literati, many of which were not seen until after his death. Almost in a Bazinian fashion, Warhol was interested in the surface of things. Art lies in the there-ness of things. They are fairly orthodox portraits: either head-and-shoulders or tight head shots with a single light, using chiaroscuro effects in the traditional photographic manner. The fame of his subjects – Allen Ginsberg, et al. – gives them an additional curiosity value. In his more elaborate, Hollywood-mimicking 'scripted' films, Warhol used such strong filmic personalities or physiognomies as Sedgwick, Malanga and Marie Menken. Never banal in the everyday sense of realism, these films are fantasy projections depicting a world both glamorous and dangerous. Warhol's decision to allow the length of reel itself to be the unifying factor was made in the face of the sophistication of post–Golden Age Hollywood. It was also a gob-smacking stance to take against the American avant-garde film tradition of Maya Deren, Stan Brakhage, Kenneth Anger and Jack Smith, who all clung with varying degrees of enthusiasm to editing as a shaping tool. In his bleak, relentless single takes, Warhol became, in an odd way, the ultimate Bazinian in an Eisensteinian montage-based film culture. His work was not simply a development in avant-garde tradition or a marginal snook at the mainstream, but a seismic shift not only of form, but also of subject matter. Warhol's intense and austere gaze on the supposedly obscene, the sexual and the perverse is now a cornerstone of our visual culture. On the surface he is not as outlandish as other film artists such as Brakhage. His films are not abstract, out of focus, or experimentally disorganised. But they are often very long – a celebration and exploration of boredom, as some have argued.

The later sound camera allowed Warhol to develop a more theatrical style of film-making using the exhibitionists and friends who gathered in the Factory – gays, druggies, transvestites, beautiful men and women, dangerous personalities. The 'superstar' was born: Edie Sedgwick, Mario Montez, Gerard Malanga, Ondine, and later Ingrid Superstar, Viva, Candy Darling – a move, however bizarre, towards Warhol's ambition to make 'real' films. Malanga and others have stated that Warhol always wanted to make such films. On the evidence of the years from 1963 until the Morrissey films, this intention seems ambiguous. To think that a film such as *Eat* – artist Robert Indiana languorously eating a mushroom and playing with a cat for thirty minutes – had anything much to do with Hollywood, you must believe either that Warhol was stupid or that he had some rather obscure game plan. Equally, the two-long-takes film *Beauty #2*, in which a half-naked Edie Sedgwick is on a bed being encouraged off-screen by Malanga and ex-boyfriend Chuck Wein to indulge in sex with a rather superfluous young man, hardly seems aimed at establishing a Hollywood career – except perhaps for its doomed 'star' with her easy upper-class ways and charismatic screen presence. *Beauty #2* was typical of many of the black-and-white sound films in its focus on sexuality, the ambiguities of 'performance' (people playing themselves) and the disjunction between image and sound. An early sound film was *Harlot*, shot in December 1964 and 'starring' transvestite Mario Montez in full drag, sprawled on the couch eating a banana with Carol Koshinskie. Behind them stood Malanga and Philip Fagan, Warhol's lover at the time. The sound comprises an off-shot discussion between Tavel and others about female movie stars. Characteristically, it is both an homage to Hollywood and a critique.

It was *The Chelsea Girls* that reached beyond the small New York scene to a wider international public. Seen by Hollywood directors and moguls, influential European art directors and movie stars, it had an impact rivalled in the same period only by Godard. Comprising twelve single-take reels, *The Chelsea Girls* was a novelty as a double-screen film, with sound only on one screen so that audiences never knew what was going on soundwise on the other screen. It ran for over three hours. Unlike *Empire* and *Sleep*, which were first shown in an installation context with people wandering in and out of the screening space, *The Chelsea Girls* played in a proper auditorium with big audiences soaking up the antics of Warhol's superstars.

The runaway success of *The Chelsea Girls* had a discernible effect on Hollywood, resulting in John Schlesinger's *Midnight Cowboy* (1969), which features a Factory party at which arty pretentiousness and decadence highlight the poverty of the two leads, Jon Voight's Joe Buck and Dustin Hoffman's Ratso Rizzo. Schlesinger's movie humanism owes little to Warhol's amorality. With its sentimentality, facile social conscience and deep cynicism about what Schlesinger saw as the self-indulgent elitism of the Warholian project, *Midnight Cowboy* can be seen as the establishment signposting the end of the 1960s and of the Warholian project.

The art critic Barbara Rose claims that Warhol was 'the inventor of the lifestyle of the 60s'. He did encapsulate all its idealism, experimentalism, arrogance (even, at times, its silliness) and most of what was understood as cool. Cool is precisely the hijacking of low and marginal culture into the mainstream – borrowing from the black ghettos, from the drug world of the streets, from gay clubs, from S&M dress. Warhol was an artist operating in a tiny elite avant-garde in New York, but only Picasso in the modern period has had such universal recognition.

In the late 1960s and the 1970s, Warhol's innovatory approach to sex, drugs and marginal lifestyles helped turn topics previously repressed by the Hollywood dream machine into commonplace subject matter for movies, formulating a new kind of gritty realism tinged by amorality. For the avant-garde, meanwhile, Warhol's process and formal concerns were what mattered – in Britain, for instance, in the work of structural film-makers such as Peter Gidal and Malcolm Le Grice, and, more recently, Young British Artists such as Sam Taylor Wood, Douglas Gordon and Gillian Wearing.

Crooklyn (Spike Lee, 1994)

Section 2: African Americans

HANGIN' WITH THE HOMEBOYS

USA 1991

Director: Joseph B. Vasquez

The South Bronx, New York. Willie and Tom, two African Americans, and Puerto Ricans Vinny and Johnny meet for their weekly boys' night out. Willie is unemployed, Tom is a telephone salesman with aspirations to becoming an actor, Johnny works in a store and Vinny lives off his various girlfriends. They cruise the neighbourhood in Tom's car looking for a good time, but with little success. After being thrown out of a Puerto Rican party for gatecrashing, they resolve to head south for Manhattan.

Opportunities are no better there and, after a series of mishaps, they decide to go home by subway (Tom has driven his car into a brick wall). They are arrested for jumping the subway barriers and before being released are lectured by policeman on the realities of life. With the help of a Rastaman they get into a racist night-club through the back entrance, only to find themselves socially out of their depth. They return home at daybreak having learned a few useful lessons.

* * *

Crudely but humorously, and to some extent unwittingly, young black/Puerto Rican director Joseph Vasquez's portrait of four 'homeboys' deals with aspects of masculinity played down in most other examples of new black cinema. To begin with, the characterisation is deceptively shallow; the boys seem to be concerned only with 'pussy' and having a good time. They are regular guys who want to escape from their restricted social circumstances in any way possible. For Johnny this means trying for a scholarship; Tom hopes to land a big acting role; Vinny has renounced his Hispanic name Fernando because he wants to impress women by passing as Italian; and Willie's ritual response to discrimination is the comic refrain, 'It's because I'm black, right?'

But Vasquez's four heroes journey into their own heart of darkness: Manhattan. Willie predicts disaster and asks to be dropped off in Harlem, the last safe outpost. Although the action takes place over one night, this is not the New York familiar from Scorsese's *After Hours*. When Willie is offered a job in Brooklyn he turns it down because, for him, Brooklyn is the other side of the world.

This emphasis on territory – 'home' – interacts with notions of race and gender to make *Hangin' with the Homeboys* more complex than it at first appears. The boys' derogatory attitude to women (the film is peppered with abusive language like 'ho', 'pussy', and 'bitch') is shown to be based on fear. All four have encounters in Manhattan that shatter their illusions about women and expose their illusions about themselves. When Johnny discovers that the innocent and virginal woman he idealises in the Bronx is in fact a porn queen in Manhattan, the real lesson is not this discovery, but Willie's challenging of his fantasy: 'You can't hate her for not being what you want her to be.'

Unlike Spike Lee, Vasquez does not claim to have answers to all the questions he raises. However, *Hangin' with the Homeboys* is not without problems. The racist stereotyping of Rastafarians recently in evidence in *Thelma & Louise* is unfortunately repeated here. More glaringly, this boys' own movie makes no effort to please the girls. The righteous woman who puts Willie straight about political commitment is no compensation for the female two-timers, lovesick idiots, sex kittens and whores who populate Vasquez's film. This said, the good performances, sharp dialogue and excellent cinematography are still something to savour.

Karen Alexander

GIRL N THE HOOD

Amy Taubin

About two years ago, the *New York Times Magazine*, in its role as cultural watchdog for the middlebrow, ran a story about 'the new African-American filmmaking'. Pictured on the cover were about half a dozen directors, all of them male. Although the photograph outraged a lot of people – all of them, as far as I know, female – it was hard to think of a single African-American woman director who had been unfairly omitted. Unless it was Julie Dash, whose *Daughters of the Dust* had attracted both critical and audience acclaim.

Daughters, because it was both an art film and a women's picture, was just a shade marginal for whatever it was the *Times* was after. More marginal, say, than Charles Burnett's *To Sleep with Anger*, which could satisfy a 'serious' audience of both sexes – meaning its dramatic conflict revolved around two men. Obviously the gender imbalance (Dash did receive a passing mention in the article) was a result not of a lack of talent, skill or drive on the part of African-American women, but rather of the structure of the film industry and its perceptions about film audiences. But try getting anyone who profits from the status quo to admit to that.

Despite denials that anything was wrong with the *Times*'s picture, there were signs from indie producers and distributors (and even from the studios) that the hunt was on for an African-American woman director who could deliver the goods to a popular film audience – the way a few women rap artists sell records (though no female rapper except the pop crossover Salt n Pepa has yet gone gold).

The first, and thus far the only woman to complete a film that even vaguely fills the bill, is Leslie Harris. Harris's ultra-low-budget *Just Another Girl on the I.R.T.*, a cautionary comedy about teenage pregnancy, opened in the United States in February. Miramax, its distributor, is expert at getting free publicity and *I.R.T.* had an even better talk-show hook than *The Crying Game*. There's an epidemic of 'babies having babies' in the United States: reports of newborns found dead or barely alive in the garbage are featured regularly on local New York television news. In most of these stories, the mother is written off as a drug addict or mentally impaired. Harris wanted to show that even the best and brightest kids can be pushed over the edge by an unwanted pregnancy.

Harris worked hard to get the audience she wanted – 'teenagers, mothers and feminists'. The week the film opened she was appearing on television (national and local, broadcast and cable) a couple of times a day. *I.R.T.* got mixed reviews: the *Times* was supportive, the *Voice* enthusiastic, the *New Yorker* vitriolic. The film played in about fifty theatres, hovered near the bottom of the *Variety* box-office chart, and disappeared after about a month.

It had been three years in production. Harris, who had made a couple of short films in college and then worked for some New York advertising agencies, started to look for the money to make *I.R.T.* in 1990. 'I hadn't seen realistic images of films made from an African-American male perspective about African-American males coming of age. The women in those films are just hanging off some guy's arm. I wanted to make a film from the perspective of a seventeen-year-old girl at the crossroads. I'd see these teenage women on the subway and I'd want to follow them home and show them as they are – with all their energy and all their faults and flaws.' The film, which cost less than $500,000, was shot with arts council grants and private money from relatives and friends. Shooting took seventeen days; editing about a year. Miramax saw the rough-cut and put up the money for post-production.

'The film Hollywood would never make' reads the title over the final fade. You'd better believe it. Thoroughly subversive in form and content, *Just Another Girl on the I.R.T.* is intentionally didactic – like a rap video crossed with Godard. Its adolescent hero, Chantel, tells her story in the first person with frequent direct-to-camera asides. 'Tomorrow you might be reading about this in the paper, or you might even see it on television. You might shake your head and say, "That girl must have been bummed out on crack..." But I'm going to tell you the real deal,' she confides over the opening image. Although we don't know it, the first thing we see – a night-time exterior with a young, worried black man carrying a plastic garbage bag – is a flash forward to the end of the narrative. Chantel tells her story in a mix of past and present, pointing out things as they happen but also explaining her actions from a position of hindsight. It's this first-person narration – the ironic view Chantel has of herself and events – that distinguishes *Just Another Girl on the I.R.T.* from American after-school television specials or from British social-realist drama of the early 1960s.

Smart, sassy and ambitious, Chantel lives in a crowded Brooklyn apartment 'in the projects', with her mother, father and two brothers. A working-class family, they're barely getting by on two full-time salaries. Chantel wants out; she's got her route mapped – she's going to become a doctor. A straight-A student, she knows she's 'not just any girl from the neighbourhood'. But just because she reads biology books doesn't mean she's all that clear about birth control. Or that in a compelling moment, she won't be persuaded to do without. Chantel gets pregnant, a situation so disruptive to the plans she's made for her life that she can't deal with it. She goes into deep denial. Harris shows us how Chantel's reaction to her pregnancy, which might seem implausible if outlined on paper, is, if anything, overdetermined, both psychologically and socially. Chantel knows what her choices are: to have an abortion; to have the baby and give it up for adoption; or to have it and keep it. In fact, she insists that the choice is hers alone to make. When her boyfriend gives her $500 for an abortion, she rebels against his 'pressure', spending the money on a clothes-buying spree.

Because all the options are terrifying, she refuses to do anything. Instead, she tells her friends that she's okay, takes elaborate measures to disguise her thickening body and acts as if she hasn't a care in the world. Sometimes she even convinces herself. (Be warned: what follows discloses the ending; if you prefer not to know what happens, this is the place to turn the page.)

While visiting her boyfriend, Chantel goes into premature labour. The scene is physiologically so inaccurate that it nearly tips the film into farce. Emotionally, however, it's right on the mark, a rollercoaster ride into hysteria. Harris manages to convince us that childbirth, especially when no one knows what they're doing, is painful and frightening enough to cause a derangement of the senses. In a state of what's sometimes called temporary insanity, Chantel tells her boyfriend to throw the baby she still refuses to believe she's carried into the garbage.

It's the film's most transgressive move – to suggest that the fabled maternal instinct is not infallible, that denial as desperate as Chantel's does not evaporate with the infant's first cry. Since *I.R.T.* is a comedy, however, it resolves in its hero's favour – in the nick of time, Chantel manages to do the right thing.

I.R.T. is engaging and moving only if you're thoroughly on Chantel's side. Harris could have cast an actor who looked young but was professionally adept at smoothing the edges of seventeen-year-old behaviour – making the voice less sing-song, the laughter less abrasive, the defences less impenetrable, the need for attention less irritating. Instead, she chose the relatively inexperienced but quite remarkable Ariyan Johnson. Johnson refuses to make Chantel merely likeable or to shy away from her contradictions. She can play mixed emotions; she's quick witted; her exuberance is irresistible. While the cinematography is merely serviceable, Harris's editing is lively, as surprising in its juxtapositions as her script. She cuts the film to Chantel's hip-hop rhythms (female rappers Nikki D. and Cee Asia back her on the track).

I have a couple of political differences with the film. There's a moment of knee-jerk anti-Semitism that panders to the worst in the current relationship between African Americans and Jews in New York City. And beneath Chantel's pro-choice insistence is an anti-abortion bias that Harris never confronts. The implication of *I.R.T.*'s decidedly 'up' ending is that Chantel's inability 'to make a choice was not such a bad thing, that although she winds up in community college rather than in medical school, it's only by having the baby that she "got her shit together"'.

These quarrels aside, *Just Another Girl on the I.R.T.* is as intelligent, moving and engaging as its hero. As the first African-American pop film about female subjectivity, it deserves, at the very least, the attention afforded Spike Lee's 1986 groundbreaking – though thoroughly misogynist – *She's Gotta Have It*. Instead (with few exceptions), it was dismissed by critics (almost all of them white and male) as 'inconsistent', 'didactic' and 'unbelievable'. Needless to say, these same critics would have had no problem with Harris's mix of realism and theatricality had it come from Godard or even Woody Allen. The reaction to Chantel as a character suggests the kind of unconscious racism that refuses to acknowledge that a girl from the hood could be intelligent, ambitious and vulnerable, let alone intelligent, ambitious, vulnerable and, though painfully confused, capable of saving her life.

In terms of audience appeal, *I.R.T.* falls between the cracks. It is too much of a teen film to attract the black middle-class female audience identified by Dash's *Daughters of the Dust*. On the other hand, it lacks the coding of the black teen genre: its violence has nothing to do with guns; its rap track is anything but hard; and, most problematic of all, it puts women, not men, front and centre.

In other words, it is not *Menace II Society*. The first feature by the 21-year-old Hughes twins, Allen and Albert, *Menace* grossed $20 million in the first five weeks of its US release (its soundtrack album is headed for platinum) and ignited a hotter critical debate than *Malcolm X*. Another cautionary tale, *Menace* is about young black men *not* coming of age in southern California ghettos, about dead-ending in Watts and South Central. As legend already has it, the Hughes brothers, who persuaded their mother to buy them a video camera when they were twelve and who had directed over a dozen music videos for major rap groups before they were twenty, were outraged by the Hollywood-style sentimentality of John Singleton's *Boyz N the Hood*. They convinced New Line Cinema to give them $2.5 million to report what really goes down in the ghetto – the self-destructive cycle of black on black violence, the pathological internalisation of the values of a racist society so that black men grow up believing their lives are worth nothing. New Line had the commercial smarts to realise that the extremity of the violence the Hughes brothers promised would be enough to outweigh the film's feel-bad ending.

Unlike *New Jack City*, *Menace II Society* is not merely a 1990s-style blaxploitation picture. As film-making, it is impassioned, ambitious and sophisticated. The Hughes brothers are enthralled with the gangster genre – with *Mean Streets* and *Scarface* (De Palma rather than Hawks). Thanks to Lisa Rinzler's cinematography, which combines hand-held *vérité* with lushly expressionist lighting (à la *Mean Streets*), and the directors' preference for mix-and-match set pieces (as opposed to seamless realism), *Menace* has enormous visual presence.

Menace II Society lays out the psychological dynamics of ghetto masculinity: where not to be a 'menace' is to admit that one is powerless, a victim, in other words feminine; where it's worth dying to prove that one is not a 'faggot' or a 'bitch'.

That the Hughes brothers fetishise the representation of the macho violence they critique is merely to place them in a worldwide tradition of great film-making. That the violence they fetishise has such an immediate and tragic referent in the world makes *Menace II Society* very painful to watch.

DAUGHTERS OF THE DUST

Karen Alexander

Two UK releases this year – Leslie Harris's *Just Another Girl on the I.R.T.* and Julie Dash's *Daughters of the Dust* – have challenged popular misconceptions about black cinema. Their respective distributors vied for the claim of 'first feature by an African-American woman to gain national distribution', and though Dash's film won that race, both movies speak loudly against the new black male hegemony of the HipHop or YoHo school. Leslie Harris fits the urban contemporary mould better and her challenge to it is simpler, pushing the boys aside to produce the first HipHop film where black women are not merely sexual sideshows or threats to black manhood. The difference Julie Dash makes in *Daughters of the Dust* is deeper, if harder to define, a difficulty unwelcome to journalists fond of cocktails like the 'God meets HipHop' tag applied to *I.R.T.*

Daughters of the Dust is set in the islands off the South Carolina coast at the turn of the century, where a Gullah family meets for a 'last supper' before most of its members leave for a new life on the mainland. The film is a tale of rootedness and migration, of a family's coming together and its dissolution – and women, as bearers of their culture's African heritage, are the focus of the dramas that unfold.

The matriarchal Nana Peazant uses spiritual means in her struggle to hold on to her departing family. Her rival for spiritual control is Haagar – a member of the Peazants by marriage who is leading the move north, away from the traditions and beliefs of the family's African past. Nana Peazant's granddaughter Eula is pregnant after being raped by a white landowner; her husband, Eli, is alienated from his wife because he believes that the child she is carrying is fathered by the white rapist. Nana's spiritual power is affirmed when she reconciles Eula and Eli through a ritual of communion with the family's ancestors, in which Eli is assured of his paternity of the unborn child. Meanwhile, Yellow Mary, who has returned to the islands with her lover Trula after both have worked in Cuba as prostitutes, is able to stake a claim for inclusion in the family's history. The film concludes with a ritual of spiritual regeneration designed by Nana Peazant to preserve the family from the dangers it will face in the cities of the north.

Daughters of the Dust is an extraordinarily seductive costume drama, on the surface far removed from the concern with contemporary urban life that has dominated the work of the latest wave of black film-makers. But we should remember that a costume drama – if viewed not simply as an excuse to dress up in Tuscany – is also a telling of history, and the retelling of history is a fundamental concern of almost all significant black cinema and culture. Spike Lee's *Malcolm X* and Isaac Julien's *Looking for Langston* could each be dismissed as a costume drama, but each is also a history lesson. The same is true of Lee's forthcoming *Crooklyn*, about growing up in Brooklyn in the 1970s, and of Julien's *Young Soul Rebels*, set in London in 1977. In both cases, visualising the past provides a much-needed historical context for the situation of black people in the present.

In Dash's film, the costumes, hairstyles and customs depicted are a corrective history lesson in a culture where nineteenth-century black people are usually shown dressed according to the codes of *Gone with the Wind* and the like. Hiding or distorting black people's history has denied us images of them, and *Daughters* works powerfully to recover these from the past, at the same time introducing the cinema-going public to an all-but-lost black aesthetic.

Before *Daughters of the Dust*, Dash was best known for *Illusions*, a forty-minute drama set in 1940s Hollywood and shot in glittering black and white. The film was acknowledged by Isaac Julien as an inspiration for *Looking for Langston*. Dash and Julien have both been accused of making films that are 'too beautiful', as if a 'black aesthetic' mustn't be too 'aesthetic'. *Illusions* and *Daughters of the Dust* are part of Dash's projected series of history pieces, each set at a pivotal moment in the lives of African-American women. The series is to end with a futuristic piece called *Bone, Ash and Rose*, set in 2050.

The Gullah people depicted in *Daughters of the Dust* are descendants of slaves who managed to survive on the sea islands and were able to retain close spiritual ties with the West African cultures from which they were stolen. The non-linear narrative evokes story-telling in the Griot manner of West African oral cultures, in which memories and objects are invested with meanings from which the story is woven: 'The Griot will come to a birth, wedding or funeral and over a period of days will recount the family's history, with the stories going off at a tangent, weaving in and out,' explains Dash. 'I decided that *Daughters of the Dust* should be told in that way.' This narrative structure evolved with the project: 'Originally, *Daughters of the Dust* was to be a silent film, but as American Playhouse became involved they insisted on dialogue, and, as I expanded the dialogue, I introduced the Unborn Child as a character and a narrative voice. So the story has two points of view: that of a child who has not yet been born, and that of a great-grandmother who has seen it all and who can see the coming of the child in the future. I realised that the story had to be told in a non-western way.'

Characters too reject western conventions. 'If this story is told in a non-western way,' says Dash, 'then my characters cannot be motivated by the Greek archetypes that are the foundation of western drama. The Unborn Child, for instance, is Elegba; one foot in this world, one in the other. Although Elegba is usually male, I made him female because I figured that he has the power to be anyone in his role as mediator between the sacred and secular worlds.'

The situation of this group of African-American women at the turn of one century resonates for African-American women at the turn of another, and we can measure the distance travelled over 100 years. There are also links and discrepancies across space, across the 'black Atlantic', between the roles assigned men and women in West African cultures and those assumed by the women Dash depicts. 'In this new world, it is the women who have become the Griots of their culture, even though in the old world it was a male thing,' says Dash. 'White sociologists look at it and say, "It's a matriarchal society," but there's more to it than that. It's as though in the desperate situation in which they found themselves, the women deliberately took on the role of oral historians, they took it upon themselves to be the ones who remember.'

Critical responses to *Daughters of the Dust* picked up on the visual qualities of its cinematography, but the film is also highly literary – perhaps unsurprisingly, a novel derived from it is in the pipeline. Dash's preoccupation with non-linear narrative structure, memory and voices from the past or from other worlds echoes the themes of several contemporary African-American women writers. The film uses fragments of Paule Marshall's *Praisesong for the Widow*, and other authors are an avowed influence. 'It was the literature of black women in the early 1970s that inspired me to become a film-maker of dramatic narratives,' explains Dash. 'Before that I made documentaries, but after reading Toni Cade Bambara, Alice Walker, Toni Morrison, I wanted to tell those kinds of stories. I see myself as a disciple of black women writers. They made me whole.'

Dash currently has a project to remake Michel Deville's *La Lectrice*, substituting a black heroine absorbed by the classics of black literature. 'This is something I can't get done in Hollywood. They love the project, but they say it's "too literary". I told them, "Just because it's about literature doesn't make it literary." And then they look at me with a blank stare.'

The current wooing of Julie Dash by Hollywood producers will be an interesting test of the adaptability of the independent sector to the marketplace. But Dash's determination to continue to work in the formats and genres which suit her means that it will never be a matter of assimilation. What we can hope for instead is the exposure of a sophisticated black cinema aesthetic to wider audiences.

* * *

Director Julie Dash reflects on images from her film

A The photographer Mr Snead represents the mainland, the future, science, technology and magic. I'm always amazed that no one asks 'Why is he using a flash in daylight?' He makes the smoke part of the spectacle, a puffy white cloud to match

those in the sky. The Chinese-style parasol the children are sitting in front of has been washed up on the beach and symbolises the flotsam and jetsam washed up from the mainland. The islanders may be isolated, but they are still influenced by objects from beyond. This shot starts out at normal speed then goes into slow motion, so when Snead snaps a picture, the puff from the flash is exaggerated and becomes like a memory.

A (above)   **B** (below)

B This is Mr Snead photographing the Peazant men on the beach. Through his lens he sees the Unborn Child posing next to her father, Eli, but when he looks at them without the lens he can't see her. She allows him a glimpse of her to suggest that there are things beyond the worldly science he and the magic of his camera represent.

C Yellow Mary, who has been away and knows from experience what awaits the Peazants on the mainland, kisses the talisman Nana Peazant has made – a Bible entwined with moss – to protect the family on their journey. Yellow Mary has returned from a more sophisticated life, but she still drops to her knees and kisses the talisman in homage to its strength.

C

D This is a Christian scene in a new context. A lot of African Americans became Baptists when they reached the new world because Baptism provided a camouflage for West African beliefs and religious practices, such as the worship of water gods. These characters are less focused than the Peazant family, who know their beliefs and where they came from.

D

E These are the hands of Daddy Mac holding a turtle inscribed with signs from the Kongo system of life and death. He is blessing the family before they eat. The symbols are visual proof of the persistence of a language, cosmology and a world view despite the confines of being an African captive into slavery.

E

F The actor playing Eli, in a genuine trance, is gazing at a figurehead floating on the water. He is balancing on a thin little bridge we built in very deep water; we had him walk it

F

through with scuba divers. The figurehead is a mock-up taken from the prow of a slave ship. It had a terrible power. Before seeing it I had never realised how cruel it was to have a figurehead of an African warrior guiding a slave ship.

G

H

G This is a flashback to an indigo-processing plant where the Unborn Child watches her ancestors at work. The colour, which is in the bow in her hair and on the hands of the ancestor, is my way of signifying slavery, as opposed to whip marks or scars, images which have lost their power. Processing the indigo plant was an African practice that became poisonous when transferred to the new world. The colour is a trace like a scar.

H Young Nana, with dust on her hands, is questioning the fertility of the land in what we assume is a flashback. But the scene is really in the present: the whole film is a flash forward. It starts with the hands, then you flash forward to what she means by the hands. Then you come back to the present and the question she asks. Then you go back to the future, and the rest of the story unfolds. The film starts out during the period of slavery. I dubbed the older woman's voice over the young actress, so when she says 'How can we plant in this dust?', you recognise the old Nana Peazant. The dust is the past, and 'Daughters of the Dust' means the daughters of the past.

BLACK IS... BLACK AIN'T

Kobena Mercer

When Marlon Riggs died on 5 April 1994, independent cinema lost the voice and vision of an important artist at the very moment when he was coming into his own. With three major documentary films behind him – *Ethnic Notions* (1986), *Tongues Untied* (1989) and *Color Adjustment* (1992) – Riggs was working on an investigation into the cultural diversity of black identities, *Black Is... Black Ain't*, when his life was cut short, at the age of thirty-seven, by AIDS. Like so many other influential black gay men of his generation – including critic James Snead, writer Joseph Beam and activist Craig Harris – Riggs's death bears witness to a bitter tragedy: that the 'talented tenth' of queer negro artists and intellectuals, who have been in the vanguard of the renaissance of black culture in the United States and United Kingdom during the

1980s and 1990s, have helped create new forms of collective identity among black lesbians and gay men and have achieved so much in displacing outmoded racial and sexual paradigms, are now menaced by the spectre of premature death.

But Riggs's legacy is very much alive and is fully part of the almost daily re-evaluation of the ethics of multicultural diversity in this volatile moment. In a climate of deepening uncertainty, in which the fragmentation of social identities has been dominated by a politics of resentment, Riggs held a crucial position as a multi-dimensional media activist. His roles of film-maker, lecturer, writer and advocate, pursued with prodigious energy, all contributed to the formation of a new politics of recognition which he sought to bring to public attention with urgency and passion. *Tongues Untied* remains his key work, not only because it was the first of its kind – a coming-out film for black gay men – nor because its struggle for self-representation was linked to the analysis of racial representation put forward in *Ethnic Notions* and *Color Adjustment*, but because its imperfections and rough edges offer fresh points of contact and contention. This is why the film retains its live and direct quality some five years after it was made.

Riggs came to film from journalism. He graduated *magna cum laude* from Harvard in 1978 and in 1981 received his master's degree from the Graduate School of Journalism at the University of California, Berkeley, where he subsequently became one of the youngest tenured professors. With broadcast-quality video as his medium, his first work on the urban blues music scene in his adopted city of Oakland located him within the black independent tradition of documentary realism established by African-American directors and producers such as William Greaves, Pearl Bowser, Henry Hampton, St Clair Bourne, Louis Massiah, and Carroll Parrot Blue. Equally influenced by the Bay Area tradition of lesbian and gay counter-information, exemplified by such classic documentaries as *Word Is Out: Stories of Some of Our Lives* and *The Times of Harvey Milk*, he found himself straining against the limits of the positive/negative images dichotomy common to black and gay counter-cinemas. What differentiated his project was his concern with the power of images *per se*.

Sermon to jazz

In the deconstruction of 150 years of racial stereotyping that he undertook in his Emmy award-winning *Ethnic Notions*, Riggs asked why the nineteenth-century repertoire of Sambo, Mammy, Uncle Tom and Pickaninnie remains so vivid in the American imagination. By dissecting the ambiguous emotional attachments that keep such stereotypes alive in the hearts and minds of those who would repudiate them, black and white alike, Riggs allowed for a deeper understanding of the way images unconsciously affect identities. In *Color Adjustment*, which examines primetime television portrayals of blacks, Riggs brought to light hidden continuities, from blackface minstrels to squeaky-clean sitcom respectability, in the fears and fantasies black images are made to represent. Advertisers boycotted *The Nat King Cole Show* in the late 1950s on the grounds that the sight of a charming and intelligent black man might alienate middle-class white families, who were precisely the target demographic sought by the neo-conservative *The Cosby Show* in the Reaganite 1980s. That *Color Adjustment* won US television's highest accolade, a George Foster Peabody Award, is an acknowledgment of the insight and impact of Riggs's analytical interventions.

Todd Gitlin, dean of UCB's School of Journalism, has said, 'Tongues Untied is extraordinary. To make a poetic, personal film in a culture that likes its documentaries matter-of-fact, that's a breakthrough.' Indeed, Tongues Untied also broke through the walls of silence by which oppressive norms and taboos erase any 'evidence of being' among black lesbians and gay men. But to be the first black or gay person to speak out is a dubious privilege. When so-called minorities are expected to speak as representatives of entire communities, such a burden of responsibility is sure to weigh heavily on your shoulders, give you an endless headache, and completely ruin your outfit. The real breakthrough Riggs achieved was to give expression to a marginalised group while steering clear of the pitfalls of the role of mega-minority spokesperson.

The video's montage of scenes and stories depicts aspects of black gay life from adolescent experiences of racism and homophobia, through coming out into a mostly white gay world, to moments of solidarity, pleasure and mutual recognition among black gay men. But such a linear description does little justice to the sass and authority with which Tongues Untied speaks as it taps into the African-American tradition of witness and testimony. A chorus of black gay voices – poets Essex Hemphill and Allan Miller, the music of Blackberri and the a cappella Lavender Light quartet, members of the Bay Area group Black Gay Men United – is woven around Riggs's autobiographical story. What results is not the impersonal, voice-of-God narrative that would set the director up as the authentic representative of a homogenous community, but rather a finely wrought medley of call and response which, as in a preacher's sermon or improvised jazz, produces a dynamic encounter between artists and audience in which truth is revealed through testimony.

Metaphors of being oppressed by silence or of the emancipatory power of speech may sound passé to postmodern cinemagoers who feel the politics of identity has had its day. But such a view misses the point that within the African-American cultural text, these figures of speech perform what literary critic Henry Louis Gates calls signifyin' – a term that encompasses a variety of verbal styles, from the dozens to louding, capping and snapping, which emerged in answer to the dilemma of how to name yourself in a language which has named you as its Other. Or, as Gates puts it, 'How can the black subject posit a fully and sufficient self in a language in which blackness is a sign of absence?'

Other queer black film-makers who grappled with the question of self-representation include Riggs's counterparts in Britain, such as Isaac Julien, director of The Attendant, Young Soul Rebels and Looking for Langston, and Pratibha Parmar, director of Warrior Marks, Khush and A Place of Rage, as well as his fellow African American Michelle Parkerson, director of Gotta Make This Journey: Sweet Honey in the Rock and Stormé: The Lady of the Jewel Box about a majestic black lesbian male impersonator and her club in Washington DC. What has emerged is not a uniform black queer cinema, but a shared aesthetic sensibility and ethical outlook which recognises the value of difference as an unmitigated good. In an age of postmodern and postcolonial globalisation, black lesbian and gay film-makers are contributing something of vital importance to world cinema, not simply because they feed the neglected needs of specialised audiences, but because they value the role cinema plays as an arena of cultural dialogue in which all sorts of audiences have the opportunity to adjust their images of themselves.

In this respect, the impact of *Tongues Untied* on audiences who are neither black nor gay, nor remotely interested in adjusting their image of themselves, should be acknowledged. *Tongues Untied* was funded in part by the National Endowment for the Arts and, when it was aired on US public television, this fact was exploited by New Right fundamentalists eager to fan the flames ignited by Senator Jesse Helms in his attack on a publicly funded retrospective of homoerotic photography by Robert Mapplethorpe. Far-right columnist Pat Buchanan even used a clip from the film in his television advertisement during the 1992 presidential campaign in order to accuse George Bush of misuse of tax-payers' money to fund a rainbow coalition. Seizing the editorial pages of the *New York Times*, Riggs met his enemies eye to eye and proceeded to 'read the riot act' to the political establishment, arguing that: 'Race-baiting has now been fused with a brazen display of anti-gay bigotry. The persecution of racial and sexual difference is becoming the litmus test of true Republican leadership.'

Black and white

In the culture wars of the early 1990s, Riggs stood more or less alone in defending everyone's right to representation. Yet his work provoked an equally fierce controversy in the black gay community. Taking up writer Joe Beam's call for solidarity expressed in the slogan 'Black men loving black men is the revolutionary act', *Tongues Untied* unleashed a heated debate on the subject of inter-racial relationships which turned on the apparent discrepancy between the video's concessions to cultural nationalism and the fact that Riggs's life partner of fifteen years, Jack Vincent, is white. While movies such as *Jungle Fever* and *The Bodyguard* show that this is a topic which upsets everyone, what was lost in the demand for a 'perfect' representation of black gay life was the opportunity for a broader debate, as B. Ruby Rich has argued, on why we remain tethered to ancient fears and fantasies about difference when it comes to sexuality and eroticism.

In the name of cultural decolonisation, Cuban film-maker Jose Garcia Espinosa called for an 'imperfect cinema', a cinema whose very gaps make it a living part of a public dialogue about the nature and direction of progressive social politics. This may sound deeply untrendy in the face of the shiny New Jack cinema of Spike Lee, Matty Rich, John Singleton et al. But the kind of cinema Riggs struggled to bring into being – in his passion for truth-telling and distaste for the hypocrisy that often characterises what Michael Eric Dyson has called 'the racial unity narrative' in African-American culture – is a cinema that is not afraid of difference or of being unpopular when it comes to speaking the truth.

'I am a black gay man living with AIDS. My work is expanding the way we use film and video to tell stories about our lives as black people.' In his commitment to an ethics of honesty that owed everything to the communal love and wisdom embodied in the Afro-Christian tradition in which he was raised (he once told me his parents thought he might become a preacher), Riggs created a rich legacy of work that is a valuable contribution to a fully inclusive cinematic vision of what our identities might be. Moving images are inherently about loss and memory. In the painful acknowledgment of his passing, there is a joyful obligation to treasure his memory in a way that Riggs's own words best reveal:

'At the end of *Tongues Untied*, I flash a number of photos of black men who have died of AIDS. These images initially signify death. Eventually, the photos start to turn into a number of ancestral figures that have been so important to my life: Harriet Tubman, Frederick Douglass, Martin Luther King Jr. For me, these faces have transcended death. We continually remember these people; they resonate in our lives from generation to generation. I believe in humanity, in our ability to connect over generations and even beyond death to move forward as black people. And this defines my spiritual perspective, too. My connection is not to some invisible, overbearing God – it is to other human beings. Through this, I believe, lies our ultimate possibility of redemption.'

CROOKLYN
USA 1994
Director: Spike Lee

Brooklyn, the early 1970s. The young Carmichael family – mother, father, five boys, one girl – live in a brownstone building that they own, renting out the top floor to a Vietnam veteran. The patriarch of the clan is Woody, a jazz musician who's seen better professional days; his wife Carolyn has recently returned to teaching. The cacophony of the street outside is matched by that of the dinner table, where Carolyn keeps order. When not arguing among themselves, the Carmichaels are plagued by their next-door neighbour Tony Eyes, a would-be composer and small-dog owner. Although Tony is white and the Carmichaels are black, their racial difference is less at issue than the condition of Tony's foul-smelling apartment.

More pressing yet are Carolyn's attempts to discipline her five rowdy kids. In a quiet moment, however, Carolyn tells her daughter Troy she will be sent down south to spend a few weeks with relatives. Later, Woody interferes with another of Carolyn's attempts to control the children. Instead of siding with her, Woody takes the kids' side, infuriating her. Carolyn consequently asks him to leave, which he does for a few days. When Woody returns, he disappoints again because he has failed to pay the electric bill, causing the power to be cut.

Shortly after, Troy is sent south. There she befriends her cousin Viola, but remains less than fond of her aunt Song. A Bible-thumper who dotes on her Pekinese, the aunt undoes Troy's braids and takes a hot comb to her hair. Troy pines for home and soon returns. At the airport in New York, she's met by another aunt and uncle who drive her to the hospital where the terminally ill Carolyn lies in wait. Soon afterwards, Carolyn dies.

Initially reluctant to attend her mother's funeral, Troy is convinced to go by her father. After the services, Clinton, the eldest Carmichael son, reaches out to his sister and takes her hand. Troy dreams that her mother is still alive, only to break down weeping in her mother's arms. Later, she imagines that Carolyn visits her. When the youngest son, Jimmy, asks Troy if he can play around outside, she consents. Troy follows him out, smiles, and gazes on a Brooklyn street full of children.

* * *

For a number of years now, Spike Lee has made more of a name for himself as an ideologue and entrepreneur than as a film-maker. Although he's one of the busiest directors – six features, in addition to TV commercials, music videos, a production company, a record business, retail stores – his off-screen words and deeds have often commanded as much if not more attention than his work in film. Whatever the personal gain, Lee's extracurricular activities have cost him dearly. Acclaimed by the black community (at least publicly), patronised, condemned and fetishised by the white media, the artist has been swamped by his own creation, a phenomenon otherwise known as Spike Lee.

Crooklyn is Lee's most personal work since his startling debut eight years ago with *She's Gotta Have It,* and decidedly his best to date. The semi-autobiographical film, which Lee co-wrote with his sister Joie and younger brother Cinqué, traces the emotional arc of the fictional Carmichael family over a few crucial months during the early 1970s, a sentimental interlude that closes in tragedy. Amy Taubin has called the film 'operatic', and it's not for nothing that in one scene the clan's patriarch and resident tortured artist Woody proclaims that he's writing a folk opera. Some twenty years after the fact, Lee has done just that.

Woody is a purist under siege. A composer and jazz musician, he's pressured by his wife Carolyn to compromise his art to put food on the table. Although clearly adoring, Carolyn is weary of playing the heavy for both her kids and husband. When Woody complains about her lack of support (he's just bounced his fifth cheque of the month), she reacts with fury, storming, 'I can't even take a piss without six people hanging off my tits,' and pointedly counting him into the equation.

Bristling with passion, Carolyn is by turns nurturing and punishing, a woman whose frustrations with her family are tempered by overwhelming love. She's also Lee's most complicated female character since his first feature, and her eventual departure goes a long way toward explaining the general failings of his other cinematic women. While Woody sneaks the kids sweets and spins out promises, Carolyn is the one who rises at dawn, conjures the meals, and does time from nine to five. Tougher than Woody, and demonstrably less sympathetic, she's the only parent who's keeping it together.

For all that, *Crooklyn* is a family melodrama, nearly as much time is devoted to the outside action as that rolling about inside the Carmichael brownstone. Lee launches his film with one of his characteristic flourishes, the camera sweeping over a riot of sounds and images, rushing to keep pace with all the children running, jumping and hurtling through these less than mean streets. This is Brooklyn as it used to be, a place where gossiping neighbours outnumber jiving glue sniffers, and racial unease simmers but rarely burns. More to the point, this is Brooklyn as remembered by its children.

One of the remarkable things about this remarkable film is that much of it is seen through the eyes of a nine-year-old African-American girl. Troy is both the film's conduit and its wellspring, the one for whom the world either slows down to a sensuous crawl, or squeezes together for a surreal kink. Devoted to her mother, enamoured with her daddy, Troy's gender makes her an outsider within the litter as well as, the script suggests, a keener witness to the family romance. For all that the boys of the Carmichael Five struggle to rock their world, it's Troy who signifies the loudest.

Shaped more by sensation than by narrative thrust, *Crooklyn* unfolds through a succession of shifting scenes, some little more than snapshots. With one striking exception (Troy's trip south, a sequence lasting roughly twenty minutes and related entirely through the use of an anamorphic lens), the mood is familiar, intimate, soulful. Arthur Jafa's camera keeps close to characters but doesn't crowd them, while the extraordinary soundtrack, as lush as that in *GoodFellas*, eases everyone on their way.

The original definition of melodrama is drama with music, and there's scarcely a moment in *Crooklyn* that isn't punctuated by either Terence Blanchard's plangent score or the wild style of over three dozen hot licks, pop hits, ballads, lamentations and sundry witless ditties. As much as the dialogue or lighting, it's music that shapes the film, filling in texture and building density. From Curtis Mayfield to the Partridge Family, the Carmichaels are awash in music, a fact that has as much to do with Woody's calling as with the cultural moment in which the director himself came of age. Long before he found his voice in film, Lee had discovered the pulse and pleasures of Brooklyn, New York.

Manohla Dargis

FRIDAY
USA 1995
Director: F. Gary Gray

It's Friday morning in South Central LA and Craig has been fired from his job for stealing. His friend Smokey joins him on the front porch. He is in trouble with Big Worm, the local drug dealer, for smoking his weed rather than selling it. Deebo, the neighbourhood thug, drops by and forces Smokey to help him break into the house next door. They return with $200, which Deebo pockets. Smokey convinces Lil' Chris to share a joint with him. While the two are stoned, Debbie, a friend of Chris's sister, drops by. Smokey convinces her to give him the number of a girl who he arranges a date with. Meanwhile, Craig has been harried on the phone all day by his jealous girlfriend, Joi. She arrives in time to see Debbie leaving the house.

Worm tells Smokey that unless he delivers $200 by 10 p.m. he'll shoot both him and Craig. Smokey and Craig desperately try to come up with the money. Joi is about to lend it to Craig when Debbie's sister buttonholes him, asking him for a favour; in a fit of jealousy, Joi drives off. Craig's mother, father and sister all refuse to lend him the money. Meanwhile, Smokey's date arrives – she turns out to be grossly overweight and bald. Smokey tries to steal the $200 from Deebo while he's asleep with Debbie's sister, but fails to find the cash.

At 10 p.m., Craig and Smokey still haven't got the money. Worm tries to gun them down in a drive-by hit; they survive, but the whole neighbourhood comes out to see who got shot. Deebo appears, followed by Debbie's sister who is badly bruised. Debbie yells at Deebo for hitting her sister and, when Deebo slaps her, an incensed Craig attacks him. The two men fight and at one point Craig pulls a gun, but his family persuades him to settle the fight without it. Craig finally knocks Deebo out, Smokey takes the $200 from Deebo's shirt and arranges to pay back Worm. Craig and Debbie make a date for Saturday.

* * *

As Republican Party *gauleiters* Bob Dole and Bill Bennett have shown by their recent attacks on Hollywood films and Interscope records, rap and the cinema have a singular place in the middle-American imagination: as bearers of a cultural form of nerve gas. *Friday* is a movie made by rappers, starring one-time gangsta rapper *extraordinaire* Ice Cube. Nothing much happens in the film, it doesn't have anything particular to say and such characterisation as there is seems propped up on a Zimmer frame of cultural stereotypes. Nonetheless, it is the sort of film that Republican commentators should be watching if they want to know what they're talking about.

Friday roughly approximates what you get if you take the Corner Men from Spike Lee's *Do The Right Thing* and give them ninety minutes to themselves. A good half of the film is taken up with Ice Cube and Chris Tucker sitting on the porch. They observe cute girls jogging past, a cuckolded husband throwing his wife out onto the street, the next-door neighbour's house being robbed. They never go anywhere except for a brief trip to the 'black-owned' grocery store (complete with a Korean counter boy – announced on the soundtrack by a gong). The film is content to describe the hermetic suburban universe that clusters around them.

The plot – such as it is – is pure stoop theatre. Cube and Tucker's dialogue is peppered with African-American suburban myths – the guy who mistook a PCP joint for weed and spent the night in a chicken coop, the philandering preacher who gets his just desserts and the paranoid girlfriend with five-inch blood-red talons for fingernails and braided hair like Medusa's locks. There's much fooling around and occasional contact with the neighbourhood thug, the local dealer and a stream of friends coming to visit Craig's sister. All the characters are standard models, with some idiosyncrasies. On the women's side, for example, you have crusty, foul-tongued old bats going door-to-door for the Jehovah's Witnesses, slutty suburban housewives, tut-tutting wise-ass mammies, pathologically persistent girlfriends, troublesome tramps and tough cuties. One might accuse the film-makers of misogyny – but the male characters are no less cut and dried.

Friday is therefore a comic-strip of a movie, a rogues' gallery of African-American folk figures, each one getting his or her just desserts. Yet it isn't quite a sitcom; more a shaggy dog story told visually out of corner gossip. Perhaps the movie's closest equivalent in form is rap itself. *Friday* was written by two rappers – Ice Cube and DJ Pooh. A former helmsman of the pioneer gangsta rap groups N.W.A., Ice Cube once argued that rap music doesn't exist to promote or reject, merely to report from the ghetto; to work as a broadcast for a black urban youth locked out of mainstream forms of communication. Equally, this would make a good justification of *Friday*.

Like freestyle rap, the stuff of the movie just pours out. Frequently, it makes no sense, but it is effortless to digest. Except for the brief climax of the film which advocates beating your opponent senseless rather than using a gun, *Friday* is mostly ephemeral stoop-side observation and front-porch philosophy. It shows a potted African-American universe with its own urban myths instead of the crack-addled gun-toting woman-beaters of Republican nightmares.

Olly Blackburn

CLOCKERS
USA 1995
Director: Spike Lee

In a drug-ridden Brooklyn housing project, Strike is a sixteen-year-old clocker (lowest level drug dealer). Troubled by ulcers so severe they cause him to spit blood, he is nevertheless the favourite of Rodney Little, the local crack kingpin. Rodney asks Strike to prove his loyalty by killing Darryl, a young pusher that Rodney claims has been cheating him.

Strike heads for Ahab's, a fast food joint where Darryl does his dealing. Trying to work up his nerve, he goes to the bar next door where he meets his older brother Victor, a model African-American citizen. Strike babbles some story about how Darryl deserves to die because he beat up a fourteen-year-old girl. When Victor says that he might know someone who could kill Darryl, Strike realises that his brother is drunk and splits. A short while later, someone pumps four bullets into Darryl.

The next day, Victor turns himself in, claiming he killed Darryl in self-defence. Veteran homicide detective Rocco Klein thinks Victor is protecting Strike. Rocco begins pursuing Strike with a vengeance. For Strike, Rocco is one too many among the people – narcotics cops, his mother, local black cop Andre and bright, idolising twelve-year-old Tyrone – who hassle him on a daily basis. Rocco arrests Rodney, suggesting that it's Strike who ratted on him. Strike realises he'd better get out of town. While packing his gear, he realises his gun is missing. He gives Victor's wife the money for Victor's bail, but Strike's mother refuses to make peace with him.

Errol, a stone killer in the last stages of AIDS dementia and Rudy's right-hand man, comes gunning for Strike. Tyrone sees him before Strike does, pulls out the gun he's 'borrowed' from Strike and shoots Errol dead. At the police station, Andre begs Rocco to help Tyrone get off with a minimum sentence. He then beats up Strike for getting Tyrone involved. Strike barely makes it back to his car when he spots Rodney coming after him. He takes refuge in the police station where Rocco presses him to confess to murdering Darryl. Suddenly, Strike's mother appears and tells Rocco that Victor came home that night acting crazy and that his story is true. Strike is set free, but, finding his car has been trashed by Rodney, he leaves on a train heading west.

*   *   *

Adapted from the Richard Price novel of the same name, Spike Lee's *Clockers* is about black-on-black violence. Lee shifts the focus from Price's central character Rocco Klein (a middle-aged white cop having an identity crisis) to Strike, the African-American teenage crack dealer who makes what he believes is a rational choice – to earn his living selling a product people want even though it kills them – and finds himself torn apart by the violence of the drug world and the unexpected revolt of his own conscience. The film shows that there are no positive choices for black men born into the under-class. Attempting to live an upstanding life, Strike's brother Victor is also driven crazy.

Clockers opens with a title sequence that's bravura even for Lee. The camera travels over a succession of grisly police photos of murder scenes – black male bodies torn apart by bullets. Behind a yellow police tape, crowds of black faces watch a nightly spectacle of bloodletting that's both too immediate and too removed to be comprehensible. At once didactic and operatic, this opening positions us for the film that follows. What's most startling about *Clockers* is its intimacy. Lee puts us inside the skin of a kid who seems morally reprehensible at the outset, making the agony of his experience inescapable.

Lee's choice of camera placement and movement has never been more brilliant. The camera's erratic rhythms and circular patterns articulate the extreme confinement of Strike's world and his panicky sense of being held in a vice. Similarly, the narrative, though dense with incident, seems to turn in on itself, covering the same ground over and over again. Everything in Strike's world – the repetitive riffs of rap music, the claustrophobic space of video games, his fetishised electric trains that circle a single track even as they testify to the existence of unknown and distance places – reinforces the feeling of confinement.

Given everything that comes before it, the final sequence – Strike's face pressed against the train window as it crosses a desert landscape that must seem to him as vast and charged with possibility as outer space – is, for a moment, wildly liberating. But Lee undercuts this feeling with a cutaway to one of Strike's crew, lying dead in a pool of blood on the concrete platform where we first saw Strike. Already the crowd is gathering around the corpse. Strike has escaped but he carried his past with him. Given what we know of American society today, why would we think there's a place for him that's different from where he's been?

In terms of form and content easily Lee's riskiest and most accomplished film to date, *Clockers* is not without its flaws. In focusing so much on Strike, Lee makes the other characters one-dimensional. Newcomer Mekhi Phifer makes an amazing Strike, so much like an ordinary kid it's hard to remember that he's acting. Yet such extraordinary actors as Isaiah Washington, Delroy Lindo, Harvey Keitel and John Turturro are straitjacketed by the script and direction.

Lee encourages cinematographer Malik Sayeed to extend the experiments with the cutting together of various types of film stock begun by Arthur Jafa in Lee's *Crooklyn*. Sometimes this method yields expressive results, as in the flashback sequences which have the texture of over-saturated 16mm Kodachrome. Just as often, the effect is purely decorative, as in the burnt-up look of the police interrogation scenes which seem borrowed from Oliver Stone's *J.F.K.*

The director's most serious mistake, however, is to toy with a whodunnit structure until the climactic and hopelessly stagy interrogation of Strike by Rocco reveals the truth about Darryl's death. Viewers who have read the novel will know that Strike is not a murderer (Price puts that issue to rest early on in his narrative), but newcomers will be led down paths that are irrelevant, if not downright destructive, to the sense of subjectivity that Lee wants to convey.

With the mystery out of the way, the film seems infinitely more powerful on the second viewing, and even more so on the third. Desolate, hallucinatory and fearlessly heartfelt, it is the 'hood movie to end all 'hood movies. In its violence, there is neither glamour nor pleasure, nor even release.

Amy Taubin

TALK NOW, PAY LATER

bell hooks

A page in the book *Her Tongue On My Theory* has a single photographic image of a woman's closed painted lips. Next to it, the caption raises the question: 'Stripped of history?' Desire has the power to do just that, to make us forget who we are. It both disrupts and deconstructs. It dismembers and disembodies. The power of desire to seduce, to lead us in dangerous directions, is explored in Spike Lee's moving film *Girl 6*. Offering audiences intense close-up shots of lips – closed, moving, talking – the passion of this film is there, in the mouth, the voice. Contrary to what most viewers may imagine before they see it, this is not a film that exploits the objectification of women. This is a film that explores the eroticisation of stardom, of attention. It is a long slow narrative about lack, about where the inability to feel pleasure can take one. It keeps telling us, over and over again, that there are spaces in our lives, spaces of longing where nothing matters but the quest to fulfil desire. The longing of the women and men in this film is not for sexual satisfaction but for undivided, unconditional attention. It is the desire to be seen, to not be erased or rendered invisible, that fuels individual longings.

Sometimes advertising can kill a movie, even as it makes everyone want to go out and see it. Before anybody sees *Girl 6* in the United States, the rumour is out that Lee is making a film about phone sex. The *Girl 6* previews we see at other movies aim to titillate. Exploiting hidden pornographic longings in the viewer, they imply that it will be shallow, light, all surface – just like your everyday run-of-the-mill heterosexual bad porn. Provocative advertising may lead audiences to the film, but most will not be satisfied with what they see on the screen. Of the nine films that Lee has made, this is the most serious, the one that really doesn't centrally focus on race and racism, the one that uses lots of technical experimentation in the cinematography.

Before I see *Girl 6*, everyone tells me that this film is 'Spike's answer to the feminists'. As a cultural critic and feminist thinker who began writing on film in response to *She's Gotta Have It*, I wondered what question it is that feminists have asked Spike. In my critical writings, I have called for a broader, more complex vision of womanhood in general, and black womanhood in particular, in Lee's work. And of course in the essay I wrote, 'Whose pussy is this?', I suggested that it might be great to have a film where, when asked that question, an empowered black woman would be seeking her own answer and speaking it with her own sexual voice. In many ways, Spike Lee's *Girl 6* shows that his artistic vision around the representation of female sexuality has expanded. This film is not an orgy of pornography/sexism. While audiences voyeuristically enter a world where men 'act out' their patriarchal fantasies, the women working in the sex industry whose job it is to respond to those fantasies are never portrayed as victims.

From the get-go, *Girl 6* lets audiences know that women working in this aspect of the sex industry, like so many other areas, are doing it for the money. And that sometimes it can even be pleasurable work, like any other job, and that at other times it is dehumanising, degrading labour. Headed by a sexy, powerful, full-figured black woman, the team of women Girl 6 joins are depicted as completely detached from their jobs, and fairly contemptuous of the men who are seeking phone sex. Everyone is clear that it is often boring, tedious work. Mostly they are doing other things while they talk to the guys on the phone – reading, drawing, eating. Even though undivided attention is what the callers seek, and appear to be getting, the truth is the operators are only pretending.

The lead character, Girl 6, seeks work in the sex industry only after she cannot find gainful employment as an actress. Ironically, it is her refusal to let her naked body be exploited for visual pornographic pleasure that leads her to lose jobs. In a masterfully satiric opening, film-maker/actor Quentin Tarantino – who plays the role of QT, the hottest director in Hollywood – humiliates Girl 6 when she tries out (in New York) for a role in his film. He silences her. Basically, he tells her to shut up and listen, to do as she is told. When she submits, exposing her gorgeous, full, rounded breasts, shame overwhelms her and she leaves. Later her agent admits that he had not informed her that she must audition and possibly work in the nude because he knows she would protest. His deceit and betrayal are part of the seduction. He attacks her principles, pointing out that Sharon Stone has had no such inhibitions. Again and again, Girl 6 gets the message that success depends on her willingness to exploit her body, her being. To be a film star she must be willing to go all the way. When she refuses, she ends up with no money, no skills, and turns to phone sex.

Girl 6 is utterly seduced by the magic of Hollywood. Her seduction begins in childhood, watching television and later movies. The filmic heroine whose footsteps she hopes to follow is Dorothy Dandridge, the first black woman ever to be nominated for an academy award for Best Actress. Dandridge broke down colour barriers, and tantalised audiences with her portrayal of a sexually liberated independent woman in *Carmen Jones*. She wanted to achieve stardom walking the same path as her white female contemporaries: Grace Kelly, Audrey Hepburn, Judy Garland, to name a few. She not only slept with white men, but when a newspaper reported that she had slept with more than a thousand men, she threatened to sue and received a public retraction.

Even though the film overtly deals with the issue of racism, everyone in the film understands that in the world of representations they are working with, whiteness is the essential ingredient necessary for ultimate fulfilment. This is true of both movie culture and the realm of phone sex. The head of the agency reminds all the women that they must all describe themselves as 'white' unless they are assuming a role in a requested fantasy. Sallie Tisdale's book *Talk Dirty To Me* documents the longing for young white, blonde flesh that abounds in the sex industry. The same holds true for Hollywood. At the very same time that critics are unable to see the deeper dimensions of Lee's film, *Casino* and *Leaving Las Vegas*, works by white male directors with female leads working in the sex industry who are white and blonde, receive critical acclaim. Lee's film subtly critiques the hegemony of white images of glamour, even as he explicitly shows the way black women enter a movie industry where their beauty marks them for roles as sexual servants.

Exposing how black female sexuality is imaged in television and movies in all black productions, Lee re-enacts a hilariously funny scene from the sitcom *The Jeffersons*, where the daughter is protected from the racy phone calls of a male admirer by her patriarchal dad, who literally shoots the phone. Nuclear family values intact, they dance to celebrate. Yet this image suggests that within the context of conservative black family values, sexual repression is the order of the day. This space is no more a location where a liberatory black female sexuality can emerge than the context of whiteness is.

The black woman who is Hollywood's representation of sexual power and agency is the private detective Foxy Brown, the hero of the 1970s black exploitation film of the same name, whom Girl 6 impersonates in a film within the film. In the 'clip' we see, Girl 6 as Foxy karate-chops down a posse of intruding bad guys. This suggests Girl 6 has power only by her destruction of black men. She becomes a pseudo male in drag, hence her ability to assert sexual agency. By relying on mass-media images to structure her sense of self and identity, Girl 6 can find no representation of liberatory sexuality. She must be victim, vamp or castrator. All of these roles still require that she shape her sexuality in response to the eroticism of the patriarchal phallic imaginary. For it is that imaginary that controls the world of media images, of representations.

Black males, the film suggests, can rely on the realm of sports to constitute a space where they can perform and shape an empowering identity. Jimmy, the friendly neighbour who lives in the same building as Girl 6, collects baseball cards with black players. While he borrows money from her to survive, he is able to use his childlike fantasies to ensure a future income. The imagery that he engages with does not require a negation of blackness. Whereas any black actress who wants to make it in Hollywood has to confront a world where glamour, beauty, sensuality and sexuality, and desirability are always coded as white. Therefore the black female who wishes to 'make it' in that cultural sphere must be prepared to dis-identify with her body and to be willing to make herself over. As the film progresses, we witness the myriad ways Girl 6 makes herself over to become the desired object. Her constant change of outfits, hairstyles and so on, remind viewers that femininity is constructed, not natural. Femininity, like phone sex, is invented to satisfy the male fantasy. It is there to affirm the realm of the masculine, of phallic power. The bodies of real women must be sacrificed on that altar.

But what unites black women and men in Girl 6 is that the heroine and the male friends who are her comrades (her ex-husband, her buddy Jimmy) are poor. They are physically damaged. The one black adult man who calls for fun-sex is as obsessed with baseball as Jimmy. His clinging to fantasies of phallic stardom contrasts with his flabby body and his lack of a real team. All the major black characters in the film are thwarted in their desire to achieve economic prosperity and stardom. Fantasy is the catalyst for their desire. Even if they cannot make it to the top, they can sustain themselves with fantasies of triumph – of stealing power back from the conquering forces of whiteness (the ex-husband bases his identity on Robin Hood). The white woman whom Girl 6 bonds with warns her not to become addicted to fantasy. She does not listen. All her dreams are rooted in fantasy. Addictively attached to the attention she receives from callers, she agrees to meet with Bob Regular, the well-to-do white male businessman who usually talks with her about his mother's impending death. Dressed as though she is starring in a movie, Girl 6 waits for him to show up, only he never comes. When a white male walks by not even noticing her, she calls out to him. He does not turn and look her way. Invisible within the realm of whiteness, Girl 6 is powerless to fulfil her fantasies.

Such rejection only intensifies the shame that has already been central to the formation of her identity. Philosopher Sandra Bartky in her insightful work *Femininity and Domination: Studies in the Phenomenology of Oppression* emphasises that 'shame is profoundly disempowering'; as 'the need for secrecy and concealment' it creates leads to isolation. Certainly, Girl 6 seems unable to share with anyone the extent to which she is trapped by her longings for stardom and her understanding that she cannot really fulfil those longings without destroying parts of herself. Both her shame and her sense of woundedness lead her to identify with the television image of the pretty little black girl growing up in Harlem who falls down the broken elevator shaft. Overidentified with the television image of this little girl, whose tragedy brings stardom, Girl 6 bandages her head as though she is also suffering.

Media images have so much power that they distort reality. They encourage children to seek solace in fantasy. Commenting on her relationship to them in an interview in *Essence* magazine, Theresa Randle (who plays Girl 6) remembers: 'I loved Shirley Temple movies. I used to watch this little girl go in and out of all these different experiences and I hoped to be able to do the same thing.' Throughout the film, Lee suggests that individuals who are psychically wounded are trapped in infantile states. Addiction to fantasies begins in childhood, to nurture the self when there is no real nurturance, when life is without substance or meaning. The mother and aunt of the little girl who is hurt use God as their solace. Whereas the wounded 'inner child' relies on fantasy – dreams of power and glory.

Yet corporate white men don't fare much better. No matter how powerful and materially successful they are in *Girl 6*, they are also emotionally wounded, stuck in infantile stages of development. Exploring the origin of male sexual fantasies in *Vogue* magazine a white male writer comments: 'It seems to me that many men fix on their object of desire at a place that is deep in the recesses of childhood; their libidos are coded at an early age. The childish aspect of lust is for most men the hardest to admit. It is the childishness that all prostitutes and role-players know. For many men, the mere fact that something regarded as infantile is a stimulus makes them reluctant to disclose it.' Anonymous phone sex enables these men to speak their desires, however strange or perverse. This discharging of the repressed emotion (culminating in jerking off) allows them to re-enter the space of real life.

Despite interventions made by the contemporary female movement, women are still struggling to find a sexual voice, to find places where our desires and fantasies can be articulated in all their strangeness and perversity. The powerful collection of feminist essays about sexuality *Pleasure and Danger* (edited by Carole Vance) contained work where women talked about the difficulty of naming what we desire sexually. In 'The Forbidden: Eroticism and Taboo', Paula Webster talked about the nature of female fear, the failure to find a sexual voice; 'Like strangers in a strange land, we ask ourselves these poignant questions when we admit our confusions to consciousness. The responsibility of creating a sexual life congruent with our often mute desires seems awesome and very likely impossible... Going beyond, the erotic territory that is family feels forbidden; we stop even our imaginings when confronted with taboo. Our hearts race, the world seems fragmented and threatening; we say "no" over and over again, convincing ourselves that to act or even to dream of new pleasure would be devastating. We meet the taboo head-on, and we are immobilised.' Girl 6 finds herself voyeuristically drawn to phone sex, getting deeper and deeper into the world of misogynist pornographic male fantasy. Following the lead of the female 'pimp' (played by none other than Madonna), she goes where the male imagination takes her. And it is only when the anonymous caller who is into 'snuff' fantasies threatens to actualise the fantasy, to really kill her, that she awakens from the seductive trance her erotic voyeurism has lured her into. Patriarchal fantasies require that female desirability be constructed in the space of self-negation, of lack. To be subordinated fully, Girl 6 (and all women) must die to her longings, and be willing to act as a mirror reflecting male desire. This is what Lee shows us.

When Girl 6 meets her ex-husband and demonstrates her 'sex roles', and finds that he then expects her to act the role of freak, she steps back into the conservative realm of family values, where repression is the sign of respectability. Acting like an outraged virgin, she sees no connection between her performance and his assumption that she will do anything to please him. Despite his addiction to stealing, he is the one person who constantly resists dehumanisation in the realm of the sexual. Valuing touch, connection, face-to-face encounters, he expresses emotions. He is the real romantic in the film, bringing her flowers, giving her the old magazine with Dorothy Dandridge on the cover. In the end he calls her by her name, Judy, reminding her of her real identity. Yet when she leaves for LA, even their farewell scene is life imitating the movies. In reality their marriage has failed. In the fantasy they can still be close. Like newlyweds dressed in white they reunite only to part. This is the culture movies create in real life. Jimmy carries the suitcase, looking on, genuinely disappointed that he is losing a friend, but pleased that she has awakened from her trance.

Girl 6 has no time for emotional feelings. She is stuck, unable to feel pleasure, swept away by her longings for attention, for stardom. Losing touch with caring black male friends, subtextually and symbolically she follows the path of Dandridge, who late in her career was repulsed by the touch of black men. White men matter more to Girl 6, because they have the power to give her the career she so desires (this too is a symbolic doubling with Dandridge, who was often sexually involved with the white men who helped advance her career). In the last black-and-white 'dream' sequence, Girl 6 is in Hollywood. This scene dramatises her desire to inhabit a visual universe where she can be centre stage, the glamorous star. She is led, in full diva garb, to the white male 'cinematic massa' by a fawning black female secretary. Enchanted by her presence, he lavishes her with attention. In this fantasy, racism does not exist and all is possible. Definitely the perfect actress for the part, Theresa Randle admits in *Interview* magazine that she is totally obsessed with 'old-style movie glamour': 'I want to be Dorothy Dandridge or Marilyn Monroe walking down a red carpet looking fabulous.' Willingly embracing fantasy, Randle, like her character, apparently finds it easy to look the other way when it comes to the fate of these two stars, whose lives ended tragically. They were glamour girls who made it and died young. They were women who wanted sexual agency and never found a way to have it. Even when their dreams of stardom were fulfilled it was not enough.

In many ways, *Girl 6* is a satiric comment on the theme of insatiable female sexual desire that Lee fixated on in *She's Gotta Have It*. As Nola Darling does, at the beginning and end of the film, Judy claims in voiceover that she is speaking to clear her name. At these moments she seems to be doubling for Lee, who is also clearing his name with this film, wiping away the charges that he can only create sexist representations of black women. With wry wit, his satiric comment is that he had it wrong in *She's Gotta Have It* by suggesting that sexual desire really mattered to the 'liberated' woman. Now he tells us that what sexy black women (and all women) really want is power and stardom, and that, if they have to, they will prostitute themselves to get it. And, of course, the white world of cinematic cool (quintessentially embodied in this film by Quentin Tarantino and Madonna) says, 'What's wrong with a little prostitution between friends?' It's all performance.

Like Nola Darling, Girl 6 is conflicted. She wants to go all the way to stardom, but she is not sure she is ready to make the sacrifice, especially if in the end, she must sacrifice her life. If she does not play the game, if she is not willing to go all the way, she can never be a big success. When Judy resists in Hollywood, this time refusing to take off her clothes, she leaves with her integrity intact, celebrating by dancing on Dorothy Dandridge's star. In the distance, we see that there is not a crowd outside to see the movie that is showing. The marquee gives its title: *Girl 6*.

Once again Lee reflects on the fate of his own work in Hollywood. Up to a point, he has played the game and made it, doing more feature films than any other black director to date. Yet he has refused to go all the way. *Girl 6* is his gesture of resistance. Combining strategies of experimental film-making, refusing to give us race as we conventionally see it at the movies – or sex, or class – he risks audiences being unable to appreciate the significance of this work. Working against the requirements of Hollywood, in *Girl 6* Lee offers viewers the most diverse images of black female identity ever to be seen in a Hollywood film. Represented as mothers, newscasters, business executives, phone sex operators, we *are* represented. Black women have centre stage in this film.

This does not mean that the story told is not sad. It is. When the movie ends, Judy's dreams are not fulfilled. They remain fantasy. Girl 6 never finds a sexual voice. We leave her as we find her, swept away by desire. It seems fitting that the soundtrack is created by the musical genius of the Artist Formerly Known as Prince: for he eroticises the voice in music, making a realm of sexual promise and possibility, of articulated anguish and unfulfilled desire. At times, this brings an operatic sensibility to *Girl 6*. Like the world of movies, from Hollywood to bad porn, the tradition of opera has given us a space of performance where women's longings are always betrayed, where negative representations of women abound. At the end of Catherine Clement's book *Opera, or the Undoing of Women*, she seduces readers with the promise of a world where women can live without betrayal: 'Singing there, scarcely audible, is a voice beyond opera, a voice of the future. A voice from before adulthood: the voice of tenderness and cuddling. The voice of a sweet body, one with no distance, one only a real body can make appear. Sleep will no longer awake to a little girl who is dead. Just as you always stretch your arms when you leave the darkness, these women will always sing.' There is this same spirit of hopefulness in Spike Lee's *Girl 6*. It lies not in the narrative, but in the representations.

The film acts as critical intervention, opening up a cinematic space where women can disinvest and disengage with old representations. Importantly, this exciting intervention will be overlooked if we see the film through the eyes of a narrowly formed feminism, one that clings to what Drucilla Cornell calls (in *The Imaginary Domain*) 'the configuration of the masculine imagery'. Another way to state this would simply be that, if audiences are so hung up about a black male representing female sexuality (using female nakedness and objectification), then they cannot see the whole picture. Often when the context of a film is the sex industry, that is all anyone sees. So far US reviews of *Girl 6* suggest that audiences are unwilling to look past the phallic cultural preoccupation with outlaw sex to see what is really happening in the movie. Surely some of this resistance has to do with the fact that audiences in our culture have yet to learn how to see race and sex while simultaneously looking beyond them. In other words, we still live in a culture where black female bodies are 'seen' in a sexual light, so that it becomes difficult for audiences of any race to see our image standing for universal themes of identity formation, sexual agency, feminist resistance, unrequited longing, and so on.

Drucilla Cornell reminds us that women are still struggling to create a space where our sexuality and our sexual voices can speak freely, where female sexual identity and performance can be represented in its diversity and difference. Those spaces have to be imagined and created by both visionary women and men. Affirming our need to make this cultural journey she writes: 'There is space for the woman with glory in her heart as long as we insist that we are already dwelling in it. We must write that dwelling into being as a space for us to "be" differently, to be beyond accommodation.' This is the cultural space Judy longs for, a world where she will not have to accommodate the desires of others. Spike Lee's *Girl 6* gives us a glimpse of glory. Don't look the other way.

MILLION MAN MOUTHPIECE

Paul Gilroy

The Million Man March, a protest rally organised in October 1995 by the Nation of Islam (NOI) in which an unprecedented mass of black males converged on Washington DC, will doubtless be remembered as a critical point in the development of African-American political culture. Less visible, but perhaps no less significant, was the announcement in December 1996 that Spike Lee would be taking on a new, unprecedentedly powerful role as 'Creative Director' of his own advertising agency, launched in conjunction with existing giant DDB Needham. The new set-up, christened Spike/DDB, will play an important double role. It will consolidate market access to America's 'urban consumers' (ad-industry code for blacks and Hispanics), and it will use Lee's own stardom, as well as his canny readings of this sector's styles, languages, sports, music and other creative innovations, to sell all sorts of products in an emergent global market. Against certain American expectations, African-American culture remains a prestigious, even glamorous phenomenon. Non-US multinationals may buy up the hardware and the mechanisms of distribution, but African Americans have defended their pre-eminence in the production of software. Often, they *are* the software: music-makers, sports stars, models and so on. Lee was characteristically candid at the launch: 'I really don't make a delineation between feature films, music videos and commercials… I try to tell a story in all those forms.' What sort of story is Spike telling these days?

In *Get on the Bus*, he has imaginatively annexed this March and employed it as a backdrop against which to explore the increasingly diverse, even discrepant components of present-day black American male identity. A twenty-strong posse of black men, young and old, wise and foolish, straight and gay, sets out from LA on the 3,000-mile journey across America to Washington DC. The principal players include the sports nut who wants to make films, the reformed gangbanger turned devout Muslim, the old patriarch whose life has come unglued, the father and son shackled together by a court order, the biracial son of a white mother and black father, the hip young actor – and the two gay men previously scheduled to feature in *Jungle Fever*, before disappearing so inexplicably from the final version. Breakdown, conflict with their not-so-liberal-after-all Jewish bus driver and encounters along the route supplement the drama of their revelatory self-discovery. And this didactic interaction is shot, it must be said, with a beauty that can be breathtaking. It is billed as an effective continuation of the positive spirit unleashed by the original event: we are proudly told that it was 'completely funded by fifteen African American men'. In the United States, the black audience at which it was primarily directed did not respond with enthusiasm. Whatever life it may subsequently win on video, the movie died at the box office.

This death expresses the same political mood of apparent disinterest that has made the momentum generated by the March hard to sustain. Why did those the March appealed to not respond in equal measure to Lee's reinvention of their experience? Perhaps in reaction against the sentimental mode in which he has chosen to project their lives? My own guess would be that the many self-made documentary videos of the event met any need among the target audience to see its hopes and dreams reflected on screen. And the non-black US audiences have been (understandably) unresponsive to Lee's affirmative presentation of the revolutionary conservatism associated with the March's controversial central figure, Minister Louis Farrakhan.

Though his name is regularly and repeatedly invoked, Farrakhan does not dominate Lee's movie as he did the real event. It is impossible to believe that Lee's feisty characters could have sat happily through the NOI leader's monomaniacal three-and-a-half-hour speech, replete with cryptic torrents of Masonic numerology. The film works to marginalise Farrakhan from the myth of the event he made possible, and 'to separate the message from the messenger' in just the way the NOI said would be impossible. Indeed, it's tempting to suggest that *Get on the Bus* is choreographed to confirm Lee – rather than Farrakhan – in the key role of mouthpiece for the Black Nation, a mouthpiece configured exclusively in the male gender.

As evidence of this, note how the sole uniformed NOI affiliate on Lee's bus, though visible, remains mute and peripheral. Lee silences him so his presence never emerges as a problem. And in the end, the bus in the film even fails to deliver its 'combustible' cargo of black male diversity to their political destination. Though footage of the event has been dropped in, history remains secondary to myth. To arrive (and thus to enter history) would be to stretch the field in which Lee's drama unfolds to accommodate the dimensions of a world he is only capable of addressing in the most trivial way. Arrival at the March would have necessitated the film's engaging with the political character of the event in more than the resolutely superficial manner Lee favours.

Yet politics has not been entirely erased by the careful and simplistic parochialism of Lee's film. Traces remain, and political dialogue has been carefully simulated between the characters in ways that are calculated to mislead. In this sense, *Get on the Bus* continues the pseudo-political tone established by the celebrated scene crowning *Jungle Fever* – the improvised conversation between black women about African-American male attitudes towards them. *Get on the Bus* is the belated antidote to the possibilities of representing black women that this earlier scene had inadvertently and clumsily opened up. The bus journey provides Lee with a legitimate means to exclude women so that he can do what he does best: explore the tortured contours of the black man's being in the modern world. The film thus owes something to that genre of military movies in which men can confidently become intimate with one another without the distractions women would represent. (Indeed, this mutual tenderness seems somehow to require the banishment of women.)

But *Get on the Bus* also conforms to the conventions of the road movie. We watch Lee's Brothers build a community-in-microcosm, through their rituals, through their shared joy in each other and in the righteous decision they have all made to join their Marching Brothers, and (of course) through their only-too-predictable conflicts. Here Lee brings to the surface many of the elements recurrent in all his movies: the place and significance of music in black life, the changing status of black masculinity, the bonds of family kinship – particularly between father and son. Above all, the film is shaped by Lee's gnawing, nostalgic hunger for a time when the rhythms of black life were more straightforward, and when the boundaries of the racial community were more clearly marked than they are today.

There are real pleasures to be had in the playful manipulation of the vernacular. The script (written by Reggie Rock Bythewood rather than Lee himself) is sometimes very funny. But, as ever in a Lee movie, there are also troubling features. His peculiar attachment to cardboard stereotypes seems undiminished, even as the script, together with some strong, improvised interactions, conjures up more realised characters than customary with Lee. Ossie Davis – Lee's alter ego so very often now – once again plays this role to perfection, as a 'reformed' Uncle Tom figure whose participation in the March offers a last chance to arrest his downward slide.

More sympathetic commentators will doubtless argue that this dialogue between plural voices – none of whom can claim a hotline to the essence of blackness – is a substantive attempt to articulate competing political and moral visions, to demonstrate that all black men are not exactly the same and that 'racial' unity, all the more precious from being wrought from diversity, is likely to be a priceless asset in the conflicts ahead. But if this were truly so, Lee's black men would have to become ciphers of genuine political choices – and we would then glimpse the creative work involved in forging a community not deformed by the cheap glamour of unanimity.

But the didactic conversations on the bus never achieve such glimpses, not least because Lee remains so frustratingly tied to tediously predictable stereotypes. To take just one instance: the biracial Brother is confused about his identity. He is also a cop following in the footsteps of his cop father, who was murdered in the line of duty by other blacks. He has no sense of humour – yet only he voices anything like a critique of masculinism and machismo, a critique which rapidly becomes a joke.

There's also a cynical, money-minded neocon, going to the march in order to network in the interest of his burgeoning Lexus dealership, whose rough expulsion from the bus *en route* serves the significant purpose of demarcating the ideological boundaries of this group; whatever these black men are, they are *not* Republicans heaping opprobrium on the underclass. And yet their conservatism (all the more plausible for emerging fitfully, unevenly and organically in the image of Lee's own) is perhaps of a deeper and more insidious variety. 'Work not welfare' and 'A chance not a handout' might be more compelling racial slogans were they not also chants that currently unify the US right.

This deeper conservatism is configured by an ideal of fraternity, jostling throughout with a more traditional patriarchal authority (of dwindling appeal). Lee is telling us that patriarchy – the power men enjoy through their roles as husbands and fathers – has manifestly not worked for black America. It has been destroyed by a combination of white supremacy, feminism and fecklessness. A rival collective maleness offers alternative patterns for restoring the 'natural' order of male domination over women – and, perhaps more significantly, over children. This shift of emphasis from patriarchal to fraternalistic power greatly stresses the transition between generations, and between phases in the life-course. These transitions emerge as the movie's second major theme, on the one hand via the weighty symbolism of the errant father shackled to his wayward son, and on the other through the redemptive power of patriarch Ossie Davis's fatal heart attack as the bus reaches DC, which prevents them from attending the March.

As in all Lee's films, music matters greatly – not least because it represents the kernel of the traditional black creativity which he is seeking to replace with film. His men sing, rhyme and drum together. Their improvised performances bond them into an organic collective. But while the same aspiration extends into Lee's use of incidental music, it is deployed too heavy-handedly to work this same bonding transformation on the audience. Tunes snatched from a distant period of black activism – by James Brown and particularly by Curtis Mayfield, that rightly revered custodian of black America's cultural conscience – are used to provide important emotional and moral frames for the action. Yet Curtis's twenty-year-old music in particular seems clangingly out of phase with the contemporary images to which Lee has linked it. It provides little more than a cheap gesture grabbing at moral authority and ethical gravity, dimensions conspicuously absent from this all-too one-dimensional drama. And hip hop – as with the official voice of NOI – is silenced, because to make it audible would be to precipitate a confrontation which Lee knows he cannot win.

Yet, though cynical and desperate, Lee's deployment of music is born of genuine appreciation. As a result, the mismatch between sound and image reaches its strange climax – with Stevie Wonder tackling Bob Marley's 'Redemption Song' – when the homophobic actor gets his physical comeuppance at the hands of the macho ex-marine whose gay sexuality he has been taunting. *Get on the Bus* has won some praise for its portrayal of gay characters, and does try to dramatise the destructive power of homophobia when it erupts, fracturing the fragile unity-in-diversity represented by this journey. But even this drama-within-a-drama seems out of all proportion, with the gay men the least developed of all Lee's characters, their sexual choice merely substituting for other personal attributes. What's more, their eventual re-admission to the happy collective is bought at a price: the homophobic is physically beaten, so as to establish these characters' necessary 'masculine' credentials – and so that male power is celebrated, rather than qualified, criticised, transcended or renounced.

In other words, gender is played out in the most tenaciously conventional way – and this is echoed by the way that Lee deals with the volatile issue of 'skin-colour', another of his routine pseudo-political preoccupations. Would the film not have been much more radical, useful and provocative if the characters' political stances were not so obviously co-ordinated with their skin shades, as with the biracial cop and the Muslim reformed gangbanger?

Elsewhere, some none-too-subtle product placement for Nike and Pepsi provides a jarring reminder of Lee's own complex trajectory and undiminished belief in the idea that black American popular culture sets significant patterns of consumption in the wider global markets for 'leisure' products. No doubt DDB Needham will be happy with this. In the meantime, the NOI is organising a Million Woman March for Philadelphia this October. It will be interesting to see whether Spike is as excited about this, and whether he finds a useful story to tell about it, on film, music video or commercial.

AIN'T NO METAPHOR

Leslie Felperin

Ray Joshua (Saul Williams), a lanky Washington DC rapper and dope dealer, is talking to some young kids in his neighbourhood. They ask him to recite some rhymes, he obliges, then coaxes one of them to do likewise. The scene, shot in a relaxed, handheld style, is suffused with dappled sunlight and human warmth. By the end of the day, Ray will be in jail.

* * *

This is the opening scene of *Slam*, the feature debut of Marc Levin, who started his career as an apprentice-editor on the Rolling Stones movie *Gimme Shelter* (1970) and went on to make issue-driven documentaries such as *Prisoners of the War on Drugs* (1996), which highlights the plight of petty drugs offenders in US prisons, and *Gang War: Bangin' in Little Rock* (1994). *Slam* has the grainy Super-16 image quality, improvisational dialogue, non-professional actors and leftist political message you might expect from a drama made by a documentarist. But what's surprising is its resemblance to a corny, fairytale musical in which gifted young things win success and self-esteem through performing. It's *42nd Street* with a quarter-pound of weed, or *Jailhouse Rock* with added syncopation.

Despite his sideline in Cyrano de Bergerac-style love poetry to order, Ray is no angel. His dealer is shot that same night and Ray is arrested while running from the scene with four ounces still in his pocket. After being taken into custody and lectured at by a judge (a cameo by former DC mayor Marion Barry Jr, who was notoriously caught taking drugs while still mayor), Ray finds himself in a DC jail – suspected of setting up his dealer – where he meets creative-writing teacher Lauren (Sonja Sohn). After she hears him defuse a potentially explosive confrontation in the prison yard by rapping out an imagistic poem, 'Amethyst Rock', she encourages his talent. Released on bail posted by fellow inmate Hopha (Bonz Malone, who has served time in New York City's Riker's Island prison), Ray 'slams' some of his poetry at a party of Lauren's. She wants him to perform at a slam competition the next night, but Ray is going to trial in a few days and is unsure whether to cop a plea (which would mean serving a minimum of two years), plead innocent (and face ten years if found guilty) or run.

Slam was shot in a real working prison, with real prisoners as extras and ex-offenders acting some roles. As with Ken Loach's films, it is unabashedly melodramatic, but at the same time refuses to soften rough edges or hard facts, using its realist arsenal to make sure we don't forget that such injustices do happen. (One of its most chilling moments is when a prison guard explains how Ray's ID number reflects the terrifying quantity of black men who have passed through DC's jails.) With its ending turning on an upbeat final performance, *The Full Monty* is another point of reference – and like watching people strip, there's something a trifle embarrassing about seeing people read poetry. In the United States, slams and spoken-word performances have gained significant audiences, though the movement hasn't quite achieved the 'new rock 'n' roll' status promised when profiles of such clubs as the Nuyorican Poets' Cafe in New York City started to appear in the style press a few years ago. *Slam* is right to point to the connections between slam poetry and street-rhyming, which has a distinguished tradition of its own in black culture, embracing such unrecognised art forms as 'the dozens' (a competitive, spontaneous word game, often involving insults to opponents' mothers) and the 'toasting' rap style of reggae. But where *Slam* gains energy from Saul Williams's passionate recitals of his own work, his poetry – highly literate and grad-school clever with references to Egyptian mythology and Thomas Pynchon – hardly fits with the implication that his character is a self-taught street kid.

The story Levin and producer Henri M. Kessler (both of whom are white, incidentally) tell about how the film came to be made involves another fairytale trajectory: Grand Jury Prize at the Sundance Film Festival, then a Camera d'or and Prix du Public at Cannes in 1998, where French audiences wept at screenings. And Williams has been deluged with offers of acting jobs after the film did fairly well in the US on its release – though most of the roles are drug dealers.

*   *   *

Leslie Felperin: How did you come to make this film?

Marc Levin: Henri and my writing partner Richard Stratton called me after they'd seen *Trainspotting* in Cannes two years ago and said, 'We've got to make a movie only we could make, in our style. Think of something you could do that we could get behind.' And that's where *Slam* was born. I was doing *Prisoners of the War on Drugs*, during which I'd been meeting talented people all over the country who'd been locked up on small bullshit drugs charges. Two days before I went to Cannes, I'd seen Saul Williams win the Grand Slam at the Nuyorican Poets' Cafe. I knew the slam world, but I'd never seen anyone quite like Saul. And so the idea was born: young black rapper gets busted on a small drugs charge, gets thrown in the criminal-justice system and that's where he finds his voice.

Henri Kessler: *Slam*'s the first film I've ever produced. I came out of the nightclub world, but I always had an ability to raise funds. Marc and I first came together for a film called *Acid Test* based on a true story about the CIA buying the world supply of LSD from Sandoz Pharmaceutical in 1952 and then drug-testing Americans with acid to try to create the ultimate Manchurian Candidate, the ultimate warrior. Hollywood didn't want anything to do with it, but not having been to film school, I didn't know what I couldn't do.

Marc Levin: In the nightclub business you're always dealing with people and crises, and you just get on with it. So in making the film there was no fear, just a combined, collective sense of joy, the purest collaborative team effort. We wanted to throw ourselves into the midst of chaos and create from that, working with real people who didn't have to be protected by fifteen handlers. And the people we worked with had never produced a feature before either, so they were open to doing it the way I'd been working for twenty years – 'gonzo' style. We only had a ten-page shooting script and the film shot itself in just two weeks, though all of us had rehearsed for it our whole lives. For instance, Richard was an international marijuana smuggler and has spent eight years in a federal penitentiary.

Leslie Felperin: Did you have a long rehearsal period?

Marc Levin: Nine months. We workshopped and videotaped, and had sessions from which we extracted key lines and images. I brought Saul down to DC and put him on the crew for *Thug Life* so he could see the jails with us. I've compared the whole process to jazz – the structure Richard and I worked out, that ten-page script, is the rhythm and then there were key lines, like the lyrics or the melody of a jazz standard. But what's magic about jazz is hearing someone improvise.

Leslie Felperin: Were there any films that were particular inspirations?

Marc Levin: Obviously the last shot, where Ray is staring up at the Washington Monument, is Kubrick-like. I consider his three films – *Dr Strangelove*, *2001: A Space Odyssey* and *A Clockwork Orange* – three of the all-time greatest. But in stylistic terms it's more inspired by the European New Wave, *The Battle of Algiers*, the neo-realists, and by Haskell Wexler's *Medium Cool*, Larry Clark's *kids* and Cassavetes.

Leslie Felperin: Some directors talk of how a film can almost be remade in the editing suite. Was that the case here?

Marc Levin: I wouldn't say so. This film could only have been made the way we made it. With all my editing experience I had the confidence I could get it to work, but I had to develop a style for it. We used montage sequences a lot, a technique that's amazingly underexploited in features though it's used extensively in music videos, commercials and documentaries. Because the film is a musical in some ways, instead of craning up and out to create transitions we wanted to go into the mind. And in any case we had no back-up shots from different angles – I think if a traditional editor had got this they would have given up.

Leslie Felperin: What kind of camera did you use?

Marc Levin: A handheld Super 16. Eighty per cent was shot on handheld by Mark Benjamin. It's a very rare skill. I told him that less is more, to dance with the characters. A lot was just his intuition.

Leslie Felperin: Which lines did you keep in from the rehearsals?

Marc Levin: In the alley scene, the line where he says, 'This is my life, this ain't no metaphor.' That was taken from the first audition where Sonja met Saul.

Leslie Felperin: Was it a challenge working with non-professional actors?

Marc Levin: Both Saul and Sonja are professionals – Saul is a graduate of Yale Drama School. But the real question was whether we were going to dumb down Saul's poetry. We thought it was a bit too intellectual, but my editor said there are lots of kids who grow up in tough situations but are self-educated or their mom's a teacher or whatever, so it's possible. What really turned the tide was bringing Saul down as a production assistant on *Thug Life*. On the last day we were in the yard with a bunch of juveniles who were facing homicide charges, and Saul did a minute-and-a-half piece. Mark Benjamin started filming the kids, who were looking at Saul. At first they were beaming, but then Saul's poetry started to lift off into transcendental and mythic imagery, and you could see them thinking, 'What the fuck is this guy saying? Is he trying to make fun of us, does he think we're stupid?' Then he landed back into some very hardcore street imagery, and they started cheering: 'South East!', 'South Side!', 'You're one of us!'

When we looked at that footage again it was the confusion on those kids' faces that became the reality we were going for. The struggle in those faces to understand became a touchstone. We conducted a workshop with the volunteers a few days before we started shooting, and one of them said that even if Saul's character was William Shakespeare, this was DC, and he was going to get his ass beat. Everybody laughed, and I suggested that Saul should do a bit of 'Amethyst Rock'. When he'd finished I turned to the guy who'd spoken and asked what he thought. He said, 'I forgot what the fuck I was thinking about' – which is a line we had Bonz Malone mouth in that yard scene. That was the key: the reaction.

Sonja's poem 'Run Free or Die' was the poem she recited on the first night we saw her and it was such a distillation of what the character was about we were stunned. We thought of calling the movie *Run Free or Die.*

The film's not preachy, but it does have a message about the conditions of life in South East.

Henri Kessler: It's a miserable situation that's going on there and if we can expose it through art and entertainment, maybe they'll wake up and listen.

Marc Levin: Obviously there's a social point of view, but there's a universality here as well. What was a revelation to me in Cannes was how a lot of Europeans seemed to be reacting to the very simple idea that we're all imprisoned, we're all trapped. A poet as a hero has universality built in. And Williams in his very body language looks otherworldly, which we played on by deliberately giving him no backstory – no Mom, no Dad, and so on. There are people who would say the film's naive, that poetry isn't going to save the world, but look at Richard, who became a novelist in prison, or Bonz, who was saved because somebody saw his talent when he was in Riker's Island and gave him a chance.

Leslie Felperin: How did you get to shoot in the prison?

Marc Levin: We were going to shoot on Riker's Island in New York and it was going to be a more multicultural movie – it wasn't conceived as a black movie. But the authorities were very uncooperative. I knew the warden of the DC jail, Pat Jackson, who was a great woman and a major character in *Thug Life*. I asked her if she thought we could ever shoot a dramatic movie in a jail, a real jail, and she said, 'Sure, but of course you'll have to get permission from Margaret Morrow, the head of the department of corrections, and she's a real tough cookie.'

So I went to Margaret, who was very angry at the time because it looked as if they were trying to close down the DC jails as part of taking home rule away from DC. I acted out the movie scene by scene for her up to the one where Ray talks to Lauren after the poetry class and maybe leans over and tries to kiss her. Margaret stopped me cold, and said, 'No way. A teacher in that situation might invest a little extra in her pupils, but if he ever stepped over that line like that she would be angry with him for putting her professional status at risk.' It had turned into a story conference. I said, 'Great idea,' and she said, 'It's going to be a great movie.'

She asked for three things: it couldn't be publicised while we were shooting; it had to be quick because she thought she might not even be there in three or four months; and if the movie ever succeeded it would be great if we could give something back. So we decided to start a small reading library. We shook hands and that was the agreement.

Leslie Felperin: How wide was the film's release in the US?

Henri Kessler: Nationwide, about seventy prints.

Leslie Felperin: Are people who live in the inner cities getting to see it?

Henri Kessler: I know it's at the Magic Johnson theatre in LA. But this is a big challenge with the movie, especially since it doesn't have a huge Hollywood distributor.

Marc Levin: I know in New York they've had record numbers for black audiences at the Angelica and Lincoln Plaza theatres, audiences who wouldn't normally be at those theatres. But in the inner cities it's right up hard against big Hollywood films such as *Blade*, so it's tough.

Leslie Felperin: Are you trying to get the film exposure through media targeted at black people?

Marc Levin: There's been a great critical reaction to the soundtrack album through those channels. But it's the box office that's the toughie.

BE BLACK AND BUY

Ed Guerrero

Today, the term 'black independent cinema' is elusive and tricky, hard to invoke with the cultural force and ideological certainty that characterised the debates of the late 1960s and 1970s. Just as black people have grappled with the unfixed, socially contested nature of race and group identity – moving from 'Negroes' to 'blacks' and now 'African Americans' – so, too, the term 'black independent cinema' has come to signal a complex and shifting phenomenon, an aggregate of overlapping practices that is pressing for redefinition. From commercial cinema's imperfect origins in the 1890s, the use of the term was driven by a historical irony. Since all aspects of black life in the United States were socially and institutionally segregated, this guaranteed a stable market and a unified spectatorship to feed the aspirations of a black independent cinema no matter how undeveloped or raw its production standards.

Nowadays one sees at least a foot wedging open the door of the Hollywood system, evidenced by a number of rising black film-makers feeding the 'new black film wave' and a series of broadly popular box-office successes ranging from *Do the Right Thing* (Spike Lee, 1989), *Boyz N the Hood* (John Singleton, 1991) and *Friday* (Gary F. Gray, 1995) to *Waiting to Exhale* (Forest Whitaker, 1995), *Eve's Bayou* (Kasi Lemmons, 1997) and *The Best Man* (Malcolm D. Lee, 1999). This opening is backed up by a rising number of black actors and outright movie stars finding work in the industry, including the likes of Denzel Washington, Halle Berry, Wesley Snipes, Samuel L. Jackson and Angela Bassett. Given the enormous influence of black cultural expressions, styles and ideas on consumer culture, America today finds itself a much more multiculturally integrated place. But perhaps most significantly, the parameters of the black audience have mutated. That sense of a monolithic, separate black audience fuelled by a fixed identity under siege no longer applies in quite the same way. African Americans now recognise themselves, even if still as an oppressed group, as a much more complex, heterogeneous, new world social formation, more openly engaging with pressing issues of colour, caste, class, interracial romance and sexual orientation. And, for better or worse, the black audience, at least as consumers, is just as enlightened and – problematically – as colonised as the white. The last aspect of this broad paradigm shift is succinctly marked by the popular updating of an old black aphorism as a contemporary joke: that all one really had to do in America was 'be black and die' has now shifted to 'be black and buy'.

Yet if there has been one common aim among black film-makers expressed in a divergent trajectory of works – from William Foster's *The Railroad Porter* (1912) and the early rebuttals of *The Birth of a Nation*'s white supremacy with such films as the loftily titled *The Realization of a Negro's Ambition* (1916) and *The Birth of a Race* (1918), through decades of race-building films such as Frank Peregini's *The Scar of Shame* (1926) and Spencer Williams's *The Blood of Jesus* (1941), to the 1970s revolt of university-educated black film-makers against Hollywood, Melvin Van Peebles and Gordon Parks's cagey infiltration of the system and the black film-makers of the present – it has been the wish to portray black humanity honestly in contrast with Hollywood's dehumanising stereotypes, box-office dictates and the sovereign optic of the industry-constructed white spectator/consumer.

Regardless of their widely varying views on politics, aesthetics and culture – from outright imitation of dominant styles in the Ebony Film Corporation's *A Black Sherlock Holmes* (1918) or the raw, exploitative 'coon comedy' of Michael Martin's *I Got the Hook-up* (1998), to the sardonic revelation of passing and double consciousness in *Chameleon Street* (Wendell Harris, 1989) or the female *bildungsroman* of *Alma's Rainbow* (Ayoka Chenzira, 1993) – black film-makers have consistently struggled to reveal the black world, and the world at large, through the discerning lens of the complexly varied African-American experience.

This ambition was vigorously taken up by the 1970s university-based LA School of film-makers, who struggled to create counter-current challenges to Hollywood's Eurocentric, discriminatory regime. As the survivors of this loosely gathered movement still argue, one of their main goals was to open up alternatives and oppositions to the monopoly of the Hollywood system and its blaxploitation wave. This is ironic, because blaxploitation was initiated by *Shaft* (1971), directed by Gordon Parks, the first black to helm a feature film for a major studio (*The Learning Tree*, 1968) and, more directly, by 'independent' black film-maker Melvin Van Peebles with *Sweet Sweetback's Baadasssss Song* (1971). The LA School's films absorbed many influences, from Italian neo-realism, through 'third' and 'imperfect' cinema concepts and Brazil's cinema novo, to social-statement films guided by the insights of Marx and Fanon in such productions as *Bush Mama* (Haile Gerima, 1975) or *Bless Their Little Hearts* (Billy Woodberry, 1983) emphasising black working-class struggles and a gritty poetic realism of the inner city. Rather than seeking financial and critical success within the framework and values of Hollywood, its mission was to initiate social change through black cultural production, to build an independent cinema and a 'conscious' black audience. The call for varying aspects of an 'independent separate system of production, distribution, exhibition and consumption of black films' is what still distinguishes the best known of the LA School – Haile Gerima, Julie Dash, Charles Burnett and Larry Clark – from the emergent young film-makers of the mid-1980s and the ongoing 'new black film wave'.

As many black film critics and scholars have pointed out, while the LA School produced an impressive, revolutionary vision that transformed camerawork and narrative style and delivered new revelations of black people at the centre of their own lives and stories, the movement's impulse was in many ways self-limiting and mostly confined to its historical moment. Because of the material and ideological obstacles the LA School encountered, it produced very few feature-length productions, a few classic examples of which still circulate in university classrooms and film archives, or pop up at odd hours on public television during Black History Month. When independent film-makers got beyond their first films, fund-raising strategies narrowed by circumstance and outlook meant they experienced paralysing lag times, in many cases amounting to gaps of six to eight years or more between productions.

Perhaps the LA School's most vexing problems were its contradictory relationship with the black popular audience and its ineffective conceptualisation of distribution and exhibition. In many instances ineptly made, didactic films were produced with the righteously proclaimed objective of 'educating' or raising the consciousness of black spectators. But vision and politics which are deemed liberating and progressive do not necessarily result in films that are watchable or compelling, any more than Hollywood productions can be automatically considered visually slick, sell-out expressions of a false consciousness alluring to all. Even if it is consumer oriented, the black audience has to be at least as sophisticated as any in the nation, and it could be argued that it's more sophisticated simply because blacks greatly overconsume film and television in proportion to their numbers. While the LA School offered a prescient and potent antidote to Hollywood's toxic stereotypes and racism, it failed to conceptualise film-making as capital- and technology-intensive, collaborative and on some level obliged to connect with a broad popular audience. In short, the LA School was unable to come up with a successful business model relevant to the national context. Consequently, its works and message never had popular impact or much circulation beyond the university and museum set or those of its stylistic insights Hollywood could openly steal for deployment in its own black-product line. Thus in the parallel universe of Hollywood's blaxploitation cycle there arose films with gritty urban environments, jazz-blues musical scores full of social meaning and some experimentation with the image and message, but most of all the realisation that there was a vast black audience thirsting to see themselves as fully-drawn human subjects winning the day on the big screen.

By the mid-1980s, the LA School had lost most of its momentum, and its film-makers' vision was distilled into three features that won some critical acclaim and art-house circulation – *To Sleep with Anger* (Charles Burnett, 1990), *Daughters of the Dust* (Julie Dash, 1991) and *Sankofa* (Haile Gerima, 1993). Nevertheless, black film-making continued to raise the issue of two loosely configured tendencies or camps grounded in cinema's commercial origins: those who wanted to mainstream their work and those who sought independence from the dominant system. The paradox of black cinema as articulated in the past had to do with the supposed corrupting effects of commercial success: how to maintain an uncompromised, justly honest vision of the black world's tales, predicaments and triumphs while simultaneously earning enough money at the box office to sustain one's vision over a long series of productions.

It is debatable whether this version of the paradox still applies. For one thing, the two polarities have always overlapped to some degree. Independents are always to some extent dependent in a collaborative business reliant on technology and capital. Conversely, because racism, sexism and homophobia at the institutional and business levels are such fundamental conditions of the nation, whatever one's difference, one must always swim in the mainstream with a sense of double consciousness and cynical opti-mism while remaining open to the independents in outlook, if not in strict practice.

But things did change in the mid- to late 1980s. The young film-makers of the emergent new black wave, with varying measures of individual success, started to work out their own solutions to the limitations and obstacles that had choked off past film movements. Responding to the conditions and opportunities of their time, these new film-makers began to alter the so-called paradox and the perception of two divergent approaches to black film-making. The new black wave differed in several respects from earlier movements, particularly in relation to goals and practice. While the LA School implicitly embraced varying degrees of 'by any means necessary' or 'guerrilla financing' to get their films made, for new black film-makers such as Spike Lee, Kasi Lemmons, Ice Cube, Darnell Martin, Rusty Cundieff, Robert Townsend, Hype Williams, the Hughes brothers, John Singleton and others, guerrilla financing to launch a first feature was only a beginning. Their goal has been to move quickly from feature to feature, increasing budgets, audiences, profits – in short, to make many movies, address popular audiences and 'to get paid', as Spike Lee famously put it, 'like the white boys do'. This was their practical response to the scarcity of marketable, quality black feature films and the limited circulation that proscribed the past practitioners of independence.

A major factor in this paradigm shift has been the way black entertainment, celebrity and stardom have now expanded, with rising movie stars, singers, entertainers and rappers such as Taye Diggs, Cuba Gooding Jr, Nina Long, Quincy Jones, Queen Latifah, Ice Cube, Vanessa Williams, Ice-T and the late Tupac Shakur all involved in various capacities – writing, producing, directing, acting – to extend the concept of black cinema. So the new black film-makers' biggest contribution has been to shift the thinking of all persuasions of black film-making to seeing black cinema as a more comprehensive practice, with a heightened awareness of its business dimensions, that addresses the representational and psychic needs of a popular black audience and its broadly based crossover adherents. Given the enormous influence of rap, hip-hop, jazz and blues styles and metaphors on all aspects of urban youth culture, at some future point even the term crossover will become irrelevant to America's increasing heterogeneity.

This shift has been most clearly confirmed by the young blacks now coming out of film school, the majority of whom no longer see black independent cinema as a separate practice or an ideological end in itself. 'Sundancing' is now in vogue. The graduating thesis film is no longer made only as a climactic philosophic, aesthetic and political statement, but is regarded more as a calling card to be put into circulation at Sundance, Milan's Festival Cinema Africano or LA's Pan African Film & Art Festival to hook up that industry reshoot and/or three-pic deal with one of the emergent mini-studios hungry for 'the new flavour'. This now seems increasingly to be the route for all independent film-making, whatever its orientation – everything from *El Mariachi* (Robert Rodriguez, 1993), *Drop Squad* (Clark Johnson, 1994) and *Smoke Signals* (Chris Eyre, 1998) to *The Blair Witch Project* (Daniel Myrick and Eduardo Sanchez, 1999) and *The Sixth Sense* (M. Night Shyamalan, 1999).

However, this does not mean that the film-makers of the new black wave casually dismiss the call for the ongoing liberation of the black image or that they are merely looking for a grudging entree to what is still a rigorously discriminatory system. Nor is it a naive call for more of the profiteering middlemen (only now, with black skins) camped outside the doors of the studios' executive suites, who are already too numerous. Rather, the new black film-makers are subtly shifting the terrain of the contest for the popular representation of blackness by taking their depictions of black life to higher levels in terms of funding, production standards and perhaps most importantly the broad circulation of their films among popular audiences. As Spike Lee has proclaimed in a recent *New York Times* article, 'There has never been a better time to be an African-American film-maker.' While the Hollywood situation is far from ideal, most of the young film-makers realise that if deeper structural changes are to come, they will come through the swift and diligent practice of all aspects of their craft. In short, it's time to get down to business, produce, let the work speak for itself – and make real connections with a broad, popular audience.

By whatever name, black independent cinema has never been a static affair but rather is an ongoing process determined by historical, political and economic forces and always subject to future reconfiguration. It is now shifting towards something more inclusive, perhaps more optimistic and ripe with possibility. While the two tendencies or camps will continue to exist in a dynamic tension, for the moment (and this might be a long oscillation) we may just be heading for a polycentric democracy of images on the screen that more accurately represents the rising multicultural demographics of the nation. Significantly, this would lead to the necessary inclusion of blacks and an array of difference(s) in what has always been a white male preserve: the executive, decision-making business of cinema. The paradigm shift is in process, as the term black independent cinema is subsumed in the larger expression the black film movement with – somewhere on the mid-horizon – the black film industry looming as a possibility.

Go Fish (Rose Troche, 1994)

Section 3: Queers

POISON

USA 1990

Director: Todd Haynes

Hero. An American suburb: interviews with neighbours and acquaintances investigate the story of seven-year-old Richie Beacon, who killed his father and then, according to his mother Felicia, flew away. Richie's schoolmates and teachers express their bewilderment at the boy and his way of arousing instant animosity. Felicia says that her son was 'an angel of judgment', and tells how the boy came home one day to find her in bed with the family gardener. Later, discovering her affair, her husband attacked her, and Richie took his father's gun and shot him, before flying out the window.

Homo. As a boy, John Broom is caught stealing. As an adult prison inmate, he recalls idyllic scenes of homosexual love in the reformatory where he spent his youth. A new inmate in Broom's tough prison is Jack Bolton, whom he knew earlier, and for whom he feels a renewed passion. Broom and Bolton develop a tender relationship, but Broom begins to feel jealous about the attentions shown Bolton by other prisoners (including the tough convict Rass), and they argue. A fight between them culminates in Broom raping Bolton. Broom remembers watching a scene in the reformatory in which Bolton was spat at and humiliated by other boys. One night, Bolton is killed as he makes an escape attempt with Rass.

Horror. Dr Graves is researching the mysteries of the sex drive, but his theories are rejected by an angry scientific establishment. Having isolated the sex drive as a serum in his laboratory, he is visited by Nancy Olsen, a young colleague; distracted, he accidentally drinks the serum. His body beginning to mutate, Graves kills a woman he meets in a bar; a police hunt for the 'Leper Sex Killer' begins. Nancy is at first horrified by Graves's transformation, but accepts him and offers her love. Outside, she tries to pretend that all is normal, but bystanders flee the now horribly mutated Graves. A television story announces that an epidemic has started, and Nancy realises that she too has been affected. She subsequently dies, and Graves is pursued by the police. Besieged at his flat, he addresses the waiting crowd before jumping to his death.

* * *

Conceived in tribute to the writings of Jean Genet, *Poison* is a film about deviance, with deviance encoded in its structure. Its three stories are interwoven, but without any apparent overlap or connection between them. Each has a visual style and a clear narrative of its own; and each takes place in its own separate fictional world. The 'Hero' section is set in an archetypal mid-American suburb, recorded *vérité* fashion, at least until its final primal confrontation; the black-and-white 'Horror' section takes place in a stylised urban setting that seems anachronistically stuck between the present and a remembered B-movie 1950s; and the supposedly American setting of 'Homo' seems a direct translation of Genet's Europe, switching between a medievally grim prison and a 1920s pastoral of innocent sexuality. The three fictional worlds have little in common except their varying degrees of indeterminacy; together, they define an imaginative non-space, an atopia of desire and transgression.

Despite the invocation of Genet, only the prison story seems to relate directly to his work. Caught stealing as a boy, Broom – like Genet in his autobiographical *Thief's Journal* – accepts the name 'thief' and makes rejection his very *raison d'être*. Broom's is a world defined by exclusion on many levels – the gay criminal's from the legalistic order, and the exclusion that exists within the prison itself, with its distinctions between 'masculine' and 'feminine' sexuality at once fixed and open to slippage. Thus, Broom, apparently the very image of the hardened macho lag, is thrown off-balance by the change in the formerly delicate Bolton, whose new hard-man stature and highly charged sexuality threaten to destabilise Broom's sense of self. A desire based on role-playing and role-exchanging within the prison's rigidly codified world is beset with traps; in this respect, Todd Haynes does more justice to Genet's perverse slippages than Fassbinder did in his burlesque *Querelle*.

The film's most accessible section is its gruesome skit on 1950s horror which, in its command of pop-culture clichés, echoes Haynes's short *Superstar*, in which Barbie dolls enacted the life of anorexic singer Karen Carpenter. As well as the 1950s horror genre in general, the story refers explicitly to David Cronenberg's re-reading of it in *The Fly*, and the body of criticism that took that film as an AIDS parable. But 'Horror' is less about AIDS than about the tendency – both of the media in general, and of the horror genre in particular – to stigmatise illness as an object of horror. This is a narrative not about sex as disease, but about popular culture's reinforcement of the myth of sex as disease. The fact that it operates as very broad parody allows it to deflate those assumptions that Cronenberg's *The Fly* tended to reinforce even while questioning them.

'Hero' is perhaps the most fascinating section by virtue of its elusiveness. Even though it is cast in the language of the TV news report, it effectively resists reading. How does this domestic anecdote relate to the two other stories of sexuality, and what is the mystery surrounding Richie? His function as missing piece in the narrative jigsaw that refuses to cohere around him, is to reveal the hesitations of others, drawing out their bewilderment (like that of the horrified neighbour in whose yard he defecates), and their unarticulated desires (of the schoolmate he has apparently 'seduced' into a spanking game, and of his mother, whose religious fervour is fuelled by a mythomania that draws on Richie's own ability to generate narratives). In the context of a 'healthy' suburbia, Richie is 'poisonous', a purgative influence.

The film's construction tends to encourage a reading of the three narratives as being separate, and it is only towards the end that a faster cutting speed between them encourages a stronger sense of parallelism. But the film fosters this sense of separateness in order to maintain a *suspended* possibility of comparison between the three. The narratives are only conflated at the beginning and the end, and the initial links are far from self-evident. In the opening subjective shot, the police raid a house and pursue someone out of the window (subsequent events reveal this to be Graves); the story of Richie is then recounted; then, in the title sequence, a boy's hand explores various objects in the dark, before threatening adults appear to accuse him of theft.

Although these scenes belong to three different narratives, they are initially perceived as one – all three heroes are caught at the moment they are named as object of pursuit (Graves), of investigation (Richie), of justice (Broom). *Poison* contents itself with suggesting that the three are one, but refuses to comment further on that insight. It is left to the viewer's desire for meaning – a desire that would perhaps be as perverse as those which Haynes's three stories address – to establish exactly what their relationship might be.

Jonathan Romney

OBJECTS OF DESIRE

Amy Taubin

At the opening of Gus Van Sant's *My Own Private Idaho*, we look down a very long stretch of two-lane highway, bisecting the desert scrubland, curving upwards as it disappears into the distant mountain haze. Like a shot, River Phoenix skids into view. His cheek, with its ragged blond sideburns and faint tracing of acne, is disorientingly close. It's like waking up with a stranger's head shoved against your own. Phoenix coughs; you can feel his breath in your ear.

Phoenix plays Mike, a narcoleptic gay hustler whose parentage is as incestuous as that of Faye Dunaway's sister/daughter's in *Chinatown* (1974). But since Mike's origins are below the poverty line, this is no Greek tragedy, just an extra Oedipal wrinkle in an already disenfranchised existence.

Mike looks down the road and decides he's been here before. 'I know this road. It's one kind of face. Like someone's face. Like a fucked-up face.' Just in case the viewer is not yet in touch with Mike's way of seeing, Van Sant irises down around the relevant features: the eyes are two bushes; the smile, a depression in the blacktop highway. Suddenly Mike falls down in the middle of the road in a narcoleptic stupor. He dreams a faded home movie of himself as a child, safe in the arms of his mother, a bottle blonde with a Mona Lisa mouth seated on the porch of a wood-frame house. Clouds rush across the sky, salmon leap slow motion upriver towards their spawning ground, and Mike wakes in a Seattle hotel room, being sucked off by a balding beer-bellied john. As in *Blow Job* (1964), Andy Warhol's notorious porn send-up, genitals are safely out of frame. Mike reaches orgasm and a wooden house comes crashing out of the sky, splintering on the highway.

My Own Private Idaho shifts fluidly between close-up and panorama, intimacy and distance, symbiosis and alienation. While there is something of Godard in Van Sant's depiction of sex as labour and/or theatrics, his films are associative rather than didactic, closer to Pasolini's in their blend of neo-realism and poetic lyricism. The influence of the European art cinema notwithstanding, Van Sant is a distinctly American film-maker with an extraordinary sense of place. Like the David Lynch of *Eraserhead* (1976) and

Blue Velvet (1986), Van Sant uses elements of Hollywood psychodrama and American avant-garde trance film to explore the subjectivity of young men coming of age.

In the past six years, Van Sant has made three features: *Mala Noche* (1985), a $25,000 black-and-white stunner about a gay skidrow store clerk's sexual obsession with a Mexican illegal migrant worker; *Drugstore Cowboy* (1989), a £6 million Hollywood indie production starring Matt Dillon as the leader of a quartet of junkies who rob pharmacies to feed their habit; and *My Own Private Idaho*, starring teen idols River Phoenix and Keanu Reeves, about the unrequited love of a teenage gay hustler for the slumming preppie prince who briefly acts as his protector. Set in and around Portland, Oregon, where Van Sant spent his adolescence and where he lives today, all three films identify with the subcultures they depict, whether gay, junkie or both.

Profiles of Van Sant treat as axiomatic the facts that he was born into an affluent family and that he is openly gay. Van Sant is 'openly gay', but he questions the usefulness of the term. 'A person's sexuality is so much more than one word, "gay". No one refers to anyone as just "hetero" because that doesn't say anything. Sexual identity is broader than a label.'

The son of a corporate fashion executive, Van Sant grew up in the wealthy suburbs of New York City, moving to Portland when he was in high school. 'I was a preppie wannabe, but my parents wouldn't let me go away to school. They didn't want to miss me that much. I was all they had,' he says jokingly, and then qualifies, 'Well, I have a sister.' Van Sant's first talkie, made in high school, is reported to be about a brother and sister who go on a trip; the sister is killed in a car accident.

Van Sant attended the Rhode Island School of Design from 1971 to 1975, along with David Byrne and the other members of Talking Heads. It was a few years after David Lynch had graduated from the Philadelphia College of Art. Like Lynch, Van Sant shifted his focus from painting to film part way through college. The explosion of the 1960s underground film scene was over, but Warhol was still an influence.

'I'd seen *Trash* (1970) and I knew the Velvet Underground, but I really didn't know Warhol's aesthetic,' Van Sant recalls. 'In 1974, there was a party on St Valentine's Day. It was the first time Talking Heads played, but they called themselves the Artistics at the time. They did pop songs and then David Byrne would take over and he'd do his stuff. He did "Psycho Killer" and there were no words, just psycho killer, psycho killer, over and over. They were also doing covers for Velvet Underground songs and I remember thinking, "Man, it's so clichéd, I mean we're obsessed by Warhol because he's a painter like we are." I remember being too nervous to dance so I pretended I was watching the band, but it felt like there was nothing to watch so I was there for no reason. At RISD, everyone was into fame, that was a Warholian thing. Art was beside the point, but everyone was really a good artist.'

'It felt like there was nothing to watch so I was there for no reason.' Warhol himself could not have said it better. Like Warhol, Van Sant has the charismatically absent presence of the obsessive voyeur. He also shares the slightly hunched, arms wrapped, self-protective stance of the 'pale master' and a reputation for silence, notwithstanding a gift for the gab. 'Everyone has a crush on Gus,' commented a woman who briefly worked with him. (Warhol held a similar fascination for the regulars who hung out in his Factory.)

After the success of *Drugstore Cowboy*, Van Sant bought a large Tudoresque house in Portland Heights, the quietly moneyed section of the city where his family had lived. During the production of *My Own Private Idaho*, members of both the cast and crew, including River Phoenix and Keanu Reeves, moved in. So Idaho's alternative family had an off-screen life as well.

Where Warhol, the son of working-class Polish immigrants, fixed his gaze on glamour, wealth and fame, the upper-middle-class Van Sant is fascinated by adolescent drifters, naive and vulnerable. And unlike Warhol, whose distance from his subjects was palpable in his work, Van Sant connects with his characters through a shared sense of alienation. He once described his method of working with actors as slipping inside them, like a hand in a glove. Such an empathetic collaboration would have been outside Warhol's psychological capacities.

After graduating from RISD, Van Sant spent a brief time in the film industry as an assistant to Ken Shapiro, director of *The Groove Tube* (1974). His first attempt at feature film-making, *Alice in Hollywood*, was never completed. He moved back to the East Coast and worked in an advertising agency. One of his short films, *The Discipline of D.E.*, adapted from a Burroughs's story, got some attention at the New York Film Festival in 1977. About seven years later, he read *Mala Noche*, a novel by a gay Portland writer, Walt Curtis. He moved back to Portland and, using his own savings, made it into a film. *Mala Noche* is remarkable for its richly textured black-and-white imagery, the evocativeness of its crudely recorded soundtrack, its matter-of-fact, explicit depiction of gay sex, the connections it makes between sexuality and power, and the absence of sentimentality in the performance of its leading actor, Tim Streeter. Streeter lets us see how the character's racism – his contempt for the Mexican who is the object of his desire – feeds his obsession.

Mala Noche won the 1987 LA Film Critics award for best independent feature. By then, Van Sant had co-written the script for *Drugstore Cowboy*, based on an unpublished autobiographical novel by James Fogle, a convicted felon. The script caught the interest of Laurie Parker, a production executive at Avenue. *Drugstore Cowboy* was a critical success *and* made money at the box office. As a result, Van Sant was offered big-budget films to direct. Instead, with Parker producing, he opted to make *My Own Private Idaho*. He says he sent the script to Phoenix and Reeves, never dreaming that they'd accept. Given the performance Van Sant got from Matt Dillon in *Drugstore Cowboy*, how could they refuse?

In more ways than one, *Drugstore Cowboy* is Van Sant's straightest film. The narrative is less associative, the visual style less improvisatory than in either *Mala Noche* or *Idaho*. The film's strengths lie in its detailed depiction of lower-middle-class suburbia and its non-judgmental and non-romanticised attitude towards drugs. With Nancy Reagan's hypocritical 'just say no' campaign in full swing, Dillon's speech about how heroin made it possible for him to tie his shoes every morning without going nuts was as subversive as it was honest.

Despite *Drugstore Cowboy*'s putatively heterosexual orientation (junk precluding much libidinal investment of any kind) and the conventional linearity of its narrative, its image of an alternative family unit prefigures *Idaho*'s band of outsiders. Bob (Dillon) and his long-term girlfriend (the dry-spoken Kelly Lynch) act as dad and mom to the novices, Rick and Nadine. In a twist that anticipates Mike's confused parentage in *Idaho*, mom beds down with her son when dad tries to go straight.

Drugstore Cowboy is about dropping out of middle-class tedium; the more surreal *Idaho* juxtaposes the societal extremes of haves and have-nots. For the first time in his films, Van Sant uses a lead character, Scott Favor (Reeves), the son of a mayor, whose class origins correspond to his own. But, unlike Van Sant, who chose to make *Idaho* rather than any of the big-budget films he was offered, and to make it on less than half the budget he had for *Drugstore Cowboy*, Scott betrays not only his friends, but also his own sexuality for money and power.

If Scott is both the villain and the object of desire of *My Own Private Idaho*, Mike is its governing consciousness. The irony here is that the narcoleptic Mike is literally the most unconscious character ever to hit the screen. In terms of Van Sant's beat romanticism, Mike's absence of consciousness is what saves his soul. It's also what makes *Idaho*, for all its black humour, politically less tough than *Mala Noche*. On the other hand, the oneiric structure – the filtering of the narrative through Mike's snoozing subjectivity – gives coherence to the film's remarkable heterogeneity, its split-second shifts between the burlesque and the heartfelt, Rudy Vallee and the Pogues.

Mike and Scott are part of a gang of street prostitutes who hang out in a derelict hotel. Their leader is Bob Pigeon (William Richert), a fat, beer-guzzling chicken hawk who's got a thing for the narcissistic Scott. Bob and Scott act out their relationship as Shakespeare's Falstaff and Prince Hal, challenging each other to ever greater heights of bowdlerised verse. Scott has also fallen into the habit of taking care of vulnerable Mike, whose narcolepsy endangers not only his income, but also his life.

As a final fling, before cleaning up his act so he can inherit his father's political mantle, Scott goes on a trip with Mike, who's in search of his long-lost mother. Huddled beside a campfire in the desert, Mike risks, or perhaps courts, a repetition of his primal loss by confessing his love to Scott. 'I just want to kiss you, man,' he says softly, hugging his arms around his chest. Phoenix fills the moment with an absolute, naked need that blasts through easy tags of homo/hetero/bi. (That sexuality in Van Sant's films is too complex for labels doesn't make his work any less gay.)

It's a bit too much for the self-protective Scott. After a terrifying encounter with Mike's alcoholic brother/father (James Russo) and an acrobatic bedroom threesome with the ubiquitous Hans (Warhol superstar Udo Kier), whose impromptu cabaret performance rivals Dean Stockwell's in *Blue Velvet*, they wind up in Rome, where Scott, in a homophobic panic, falls in love with an Italian beauty. Her wordless adoration makes him feel that he's really a 'man'.

'I'm sorry we didn't find your mother, Mike,' Scott mumbles guiltily as he presses money and a plane ticket into Mike's hand and rushes out of the door with his bride-to-be. It's a permanent parting of the ways. Back in Portland, Scott comes into his inheritance and Mike is out in the cold.

My Own Private Idaho ends with a double funeral. Scott's two fathers – Mayor Favor and Bob Pigeon – have both died and are being buried in the same graveyard. The schizoid structure is, for once, not a projection of Mike's fragmented psyche, but a mini-allegory of the polarisation of Reagan/Bush America. Eyes front, spines stiffened, the properly heterosexual Favor clan, now led by Scott and his wife, is desperately trying to ignore the carnivalesque spectacle taking place a few hundred metres away, where Mike and his fellow-outcasts are dancing on Bob Pigeon's grave. One close-up is enough to suggest that Mike's first eruption of anger is also his first taste of liberation.

Threaded with home movie images (no film-maker has ever been better than Van Sant at forging and integrating these), *My Own Private Idaho* is a crazy quilt of family romances. Everybody is either looking for or escaping from their families, organising new families, or poring over photographs of other people's families. Mike's sadistic brother/father has a mail-order portrait business in which people send him their family snapshots to be copied. 'I like to have them around. They keep me company,' he laughs, waving his bottle at the grotesque array. And in the campfire scene, Mike prefaces his lovelorn confession with the agonised question: 'Do you think I'd be different if I'd had a normal Dad?' 'What's a normal Dad?' shrugs Scott, the sophisticate.

Deeply regressive, Mike's desire for family is for the safety of the mother's body; his narcolepsy is his defence against the agony of his childhood abandonment. Anything that reminds him of his lost mother triggers a violent psychosomatic reaction. He shakes so much he looks as though he might explode, and then keels over in a stupor. Because he short-circuits before he can connect past and present, he remains as asocial as an infant, and in that sense, innocent. *Idaho*'s fragmented editing style – its heterogeneous visual associations and dense layering of spoken word, concrete sound and music – evokes Mike's confusion of inside and outside, past and present.

And what cannot be said can sometimes he sung. Songs such as 'Deep Night' and the Pogues' 'The Old Main Drag' can both punch up an irony and cut to the quick. This is certainly the effect of the lyric 'Locked in the arms of love', the last line of the 1920s ballad 'Deep Night' and of *Idaho*'s soundtrack, crooned by Rudy Vallee over the closing credits. Its irony at this point is compounded by the fact that Van Sant has used the song earlier – as an accompaniment to Mike's date with a kinky john who fetishises Little Dutch Boy household cleanser.

Even more interesting is Van Sant's use of instrumental arrangements of songs like 'Home on the Range' and 'America, the Beautiful' that are, at least in the US, part of a collective cultural consciousness. What happens here is that the viewer silently sings along with the film. And I suspect that Van Sant is counting on that process, both to trigger memory of the lyrics and of what the songs meant when we sang them as children and teenagers.

The best-known patriotic hymn, 'America, the Beautiful', is oddly elegiac, a quality emphasised in the film's hushed-pedal steel guitar arrangement. Van Sant uses the song twice. The first time – in conjunction with Scott telling Mike about his conflict with his father – it functions ironically to connect the betrayal of familial love with the betrayal of the American dream. The second time the song is heard is in the enigmatic coda that follows the funeral scene.

Mike is alone again, back on the road. 'This road will never end, it probably goes all around the world,' he says, and then promptly collapses in a stupor. A car pulls up. Two men get out. Mike does not even stir as they strip him of his shoes. The opening chords of the song are heard as the car roars away. The camera cranes up to an eye-of-god angle and we look down on Mike's fragile, sprawled-out body and, in the distance, the 'spacious skies' and 'purple mountains' majesty' that the song refers to. The camera doesn't move. The song continues. A second car drives up, a man gets out, picks up Mike's sleeping body, puts it in the back seat, and drives on. Given the narrative of the film, we have reason to suspect that this is no rescue, but a prelude to some horror down the road. But what tips the tone of the scene – and the meaning of the film – towards some possibility of affirmation is the fact that as the man carries Mike to the car, the line we're singing in our heads is about crowning America's good 'with brotherhood'. At that moment one wants to believe in the possibility of brotherhood as one did when one was twelve – to say nothing of the particular charge the word has in a gay context.

Van Sant's *Private Idaho* is a place where one can hold fast to the desire for 'brotherhood' and to be 'locked in the arms of love'. Betrayed countless times, the desire is never vanquished. For the surrealist beat, 'A throw of the dice does not abolish chance' (Mallarmé).

* * *

Amy Taubin: Do you like *My Own Private Idaho*? Do you go back to see your movies?

Gus Van Sant: I love this movie. It's my favourite. I've seen it probably ten times and it's much better if you see it more than once. There are all sorts of things that become apparent on multiple viewings – I still see stuff that I didn't know was there; serendipitous things that are there for a purpose, that are put in, ultimately, by my subconscious. Because when we're making the film, we're not doing it intellectually, or at least, I'm not.

The other day I got a fax from Simon Turner, who does Derek Jarman's soundtracks. It was in a kind of child's handwriting – I guess that's how he writes. He had written 'My' and then 'OPI' and then the next sentence started with a 'C', which is like 'myopic'. That's exactly how the character of Mike is seeing things – myopically, and I had never noticed. I had some rub-on letters from when I was a kid and I had made a cover for the script with different-sized letters. It came out 'My Own Private Idaho'. And I started thinking that the character's id was part of his insatiable need to be loved, the beast within him that he doesn't really know about, but that drives him.

A certain contingent of street hustlers I met, boys of his age, were looking for guidance and attention from men. Sex was something they did, but it was unimportant. What was really important was sometimes control and sometimes attention and focus from somebody who could be like their dad. That sort of thing, I guess, would come from the id.

Amy Taubin: I read in an interview with you that the campfire scene was rewritten by the actor, River Phoenix.

Gus Van Sant: The character wasn't originally like that; originally, he was more asexual. I mean sex was something he traded in, so he had no real sexual identity. But because he's bored and they're in the desert, he makes a pass at his friend. And it just sort of goes by, but his friend also notices that he needs something, so he says we can be friends and he hugs him. But River makes it more like he's attracted to his friend…

Amy Taubin: That he's really in love with him.

Gus Van Sant: Yes, that he's in love with him. He made the whole character that way, whereas I wrote the character as more out of it, more myopic.

Amy Taubin: Now, it's all about unrequited love.

Gus Van Sant: It's about abandonment, yes.

Amy Taubin: What about the Shakespeare? I have a feeling that people who can't deal with what the film's about go straight to the Shakespeare and say it doesn't work. What do you think it does to the film?

Gus Van Sant: I had three different screenplays and segments of each were mixed and cut together. There was one whole screenplay that was just a modernised version of *Henry IV*. I thought it was interesting that Shakespeare was writing about similar characters to the ones I was writing about – I realised that while I was watching Orson Welles's *Chimes at Midnight*.

Then I also had a short story I had written about Ray, who played Pepper in *Mala Noche*, and his cousin, Little George, who was like Angelo in *Angelo My Love*. Little George was thirteen, but he acted thirty – like he tried to make passes at ladies who were forty. He had this mouth that was really funny and he never stopped talking or moving. Ray was a hustler but Little George was just on the street. The story was told through Little George's eyes; he had narcolepsy and a dog who helped him, so it was part a dog story, too, which was pretty funny. And they went to Mexico and Ray fell in love with a girl and had to ditch Little George. The film was also called *My Own Private Idaho* and the two lead parts were Chicanos.

And then there was a third script. It was called *In a Blue Funk* and it was about Mike and Scott, but with less of Scott – he was Mike's friend, but he wasn't a rich kid and I don't think they went on a trip and there wasn't Shakespeare. And I think Mike had narcolepsy – that was the blue funk part.

So the three scripts were put together and I thought we'd cast street kids and see if they could connect with the Shakespearean words and make any sense of them. At the time, of course, I assumed my films were still going to be in the $50,000 category.

Amy Taubin: You were writing all this before *Drugstore Cowboy*?

Gus Van Sant: Yes. So the final version still had one foot in Shakespeare, but now I'm casting Keanu Reeves. I thought he'd be able to do it; for one thing in *Bill and Ted* they had their eloquent way of speaking – a false eloquence, their own valleyspeak. So I thought of it as characters who are speaking in their own secret language when they're together – it's their way of having fun. I figured that when we got to the set, we'd find out if it was ridiculous or if it was working. So that's what we did, and I thought it was fine. I don't think it's pretentious, but some critics react badly to it.

Amy Taubin: I think it's just postmodernist. I'm sure the critics who don't like it wouldn't mind having a David Salle painting in their living room.

Gus Van Sant: Yes, it's a postmodernist move. It's like being in a plane where there are six different channels: it's all *Awakenings*, but you can switch to whatever language you want. So in the movie the characters are the same, but suddenly they're doing Shakespeare, as if they're travelling back to another time, yet where there were characters like them. Time is often used like that in the film – the lead character has lapses in time. And then when they travel to another country, to an ancient city (Rome), the boys hanging out on the piazza are also like them.

Amy Taubin: The PR people in 'Idaho' got upset when I referred to it as a gay film.

Gus Van Sant: Do you think it makes a gay statement?

Amy Taubin: I don't know what it means to make a gay statement, but I think it's a gay film.

Gus Van Sant: It's not that it's *not* a gay film, but it doesn't play into any obvious gay politics. I've been noticing that when people write about me, they say I'm 'openly gay'. John Waters and I were talking about it and he said, 'in a list of forty things that I am, gay is not the first thing'.

Amy Taubin: So if you got to choose your label, what kind of things would you choose?

Gus Van Sant: Well, impressionistic, or postmodernist, which is a term that applies to what goes on today. I guess I'm a postmodernist, in the way that people like David Salle are. He talked in an interview about how when he was a kid he would watch the same movie over and over because on *Million Dollar Movie* on TV you could watch it four times a day. And that's just what I did, too. I'm not exactly aware of a postmodernist movement, but if I do things like David Salle or Michael Graves, it's a natural conclusion from having the same sources of, for example, education – a combination of things that led to your development as an artist. Like you watched Chiller Theater on Sandy Becker in 1961, but you also got immersed in *Naked Lunch* in 1968.

TOM KALIN

Seun Okewole

Each year, New York's Independent Feature Film Market provides a necessary platform for film-makers at varying levels of independence to exhibit their films to the industry at large. In an informal atmosphere, writers, directors and producers meet buyers, exhibitors and schedulers potentially interested in funding or purchasing their work. Unique in that it admits both shorts and features as well as specially prepared versions of unfinished work, the Market has been responsible for providing early public exposure for films such as Louis Malle's *My Dinner with André* (1981) and Jim Jarmusch's *Down by Law* (1986). Norman Rene's *Longtime Companion* (1990) also received an early outing, as did *Poison* (1991), Todd Haynes and Christine Vachon's delinquent take on American society.

Vachon and Haynes's company Apparatus, one of too few such organisations in New York, was set up to fund short films, offering up to $20,000 per production. Later it became a re-granting organisation, awarding less cash, but increasing the volume of projects in which it became involved. At the 1991 IFFM, Vachon was back with yet another film – a five-minute edit of Tom Kalin's debut feature: *Swoon.*

Kalin, a Chicago-born New Yorker, made a name for himself on the art-house movie scene through the sheer outrage and inventiveness of his video short, *They Are Lost to Vision Altogether*, an experimental thirteen-minute black-and-white and colour observation of the treatment of AIDS information by the US government and media. Before this, the thirty-year-old director had been an associate producer at AIDSFilms, an AIDS education company, working on films on issues surrounding AIDS prevention and education made by four separate communities in New York.

In 1989, Kalin approached Vachon, through Apparatus. To make the feature-length *Swoon*, he had written to 'every possible granting organisation in the US' and managed to raise $100,000, awarded on the merit of *They Are Lost to Vision*. Vachon agreed to produce, leaving Kalin free to concentrate on the script, an account of how, in 1924, eighteen-year-old Nathan Freudenthal Leopold Jr and Richard A. Loeb, sons of wealthy Jewish Chicago families, kidnapped and murdered fourteen-year-old Bobby Franks, purely for the intellectual stimulation afforded by the crime. The young men were soon apprehended, brought to trial and sentenced, each receiving ninety-nine years plus life. Their cold, hard, Nietzsche-driven reasoning somehow led them to neglect the more banal details of their actions: indelible traces were left at the scene of the crime, evidence compounded by their final, pressured mutual denunciation.

If this sounds familiar, it's because it is not the first time the Leopold/Loeb story has made it on to the screen. It already exists in altered form, as Alfred Hitchcock's one-take wonder *Rope* (1948), in which Farley Granger plays Leopold, the sensitive half of the murderous duo. Eleven years later in Richard Fleischer's *Compulsion* (1959), Orson Welles appears as the defence attorney Clarence Darrow in a version marginally closer to the truth. Unsurprisingly, neither film addresses the certain existence of the pair's homosexual relationship, and to set that record straight is Kalin's primary motive for making another film on the subject. Disregarding protests about negative imaging, Kalin maintains that the sexual relationship between Leopold and Loeb was an important reason for their behaviour.

At last year's IFFM, American Playhouse, having viewed a rough cut, offered to carry the film to completion. US distribution rights were secured with Fineline, so helping to lay a number of Kalin's and Vachon's independent film-maker anxieties to rest. Shortly after this, I met Kalin in a deli on Lafayette Street, on the same block as Apparatus and his own Intolerance Pictures, formed specifically for the film. He had been editing round the clock, his head was buzzing, his heart was racing.

*   *   *

Seun Okewole: How did you start to raise funding for *Swoon*?

Tom Kalin: I applied with a treatment called *Intolerance*, written with Hilton Als. I was originally going to do an ambitious piece that took the structure of D. W. Griffith's story and produced a reading of lesbian and gay marginalisation in twentieth-century culture by taking specific historical episodes – the Leopold/Loeb case was going to be just one – and attempting to link them up; how what happened in 1913 related to 1924, related to the mid-1950s, related to now.

Seun Okewole: Why did that concept change?

Tom Kalin: To make a film of that scale with the level of funding and access I had was impossible. And then what I was really compelled by was the Leopold/Loeb case. There was also the English case of the silent twins – June and Jennifer Gibbons – which Hilton had become involved in; they literally refused language and invented their own, totally metaphoric and very beautiful, an interesting idea of twinness and couples. We related Leopold and Loeb to them.

Seun Okewole: How did you begin to research the story?

Tom Kalin: I started in 1988, though most of what I know I know intuitively. My grandmother was obsessed by the case; she was a little older than Leopold and Loeb and kept a Leopold and Loeb scrapbook.

Seun Okewole: What struck you about the legend?

Tom Kalin: The gay aspect was always reduced to innuendo in Chicago history. I'd see the photographs of these two beautiful boys from the 1920s; there was something in the photographs about the relationship, I could tell, but it was always very hushed. In fact, they weren't gay as we understand it. Homosexual identity in 1920s Chicago was different from what we think of now.

Seun Okewole: After two quite competent films about the case, *Rope* and *Compulsion*, why make another?

Tom Kalin: To state publicly, once and for all, in an unabashed and direct fashion the facts of the case. That's why the script is very close to the research; almost all the confession speeches and courtroom material is either literally transcribed or condensed, though obviously it's interpreted.

Seun Okewole: What's your theory?

Tom Kalin: The case is murky and tangled. They did kill a boy, they had a sexual relationship, and they were also involved in an exchange of crime for sex. Nathan Leopold was very much in love with Richard Loeb in a 'homosexual' way; Richard was a sociopath, able to seduce people to his point of view, but not very sexually motivated. He used his sexual charm to say to Nathan, 'if you'll go along with me in these criminal activities, I'll allow you to use me sexually'. In a way it was a classic SM configuration of power and submission, but not so simple as Richard being in control of Nathan, as they both were both the master and the slave. I don't think the crime came directly out of sexuality, but it was linked to it.

* * *

Visually Kalin opts for a contemporary veneer; his acknowledgment of the style of Bruce Weber's photographs relays what he calls a 'revisionist aesthetic'. There is also reference to the Nazi photographer, Herbert List, and to Leni Riefenstahl: 'very over-laboured, you can't miss it'. To communicate the atmosphere of the period he has reproduced it with a similar extravagance – retro style: 'All the original photographs of Leopold and Loeb have that glamour; the Valentino hairstyles, the good suits, smoking cigarettes, sitting just so... I wanted to pay tribute to that element of it.'

The film opens with elegant creatures gliding across the screen in expansive, romantic, monochrome milieux – it could be Montauk or the Hamptons, but it's not. Rather it's a scene within a scene, and Kalin widens the film from a narrow homogeneous elite to embrace a humanscape of minorities that includes a selection of fabulous, enigmatic drag queens.

* * *

Seun Okewole: Why are the drag queens included?

Tom Kalin: Gender is not innate, it's a performance. We learn gender through a series of codes, and in a subtle way I wanted to gender-fuck, to propose disarray. I don't believe drag queens are always degrading to women. Later, in the courtroom, there's a stenographer who is very compelling because she's played by a black woman wearing a bob wig. She looks like a lot of the drag creatures. I intentionally cast an impossible person in that role: in Chicago in the 1920s a black man would never have been a stenographer.

Seun Okewole: I love the way you have her leaving when the courtroom is cleared of women.

Tom Kalin: It sets up a paradox: how can you send out the stenographer – you would have no court record. It was assumed that women would be horrified by what was being said, that the discovery of gay sexuality would pollute their ears. But what does it mean on the level of who's allowed to listen, who's allowed to speak?

Seun Okewole: How do you feel about the film's general representation of homosexuality?

Tom Kalin: I want us to take to task the feeling in the gay community that representation is instrumental. Certainly heterosexual pornography has a strong role in denigrating women and objectifying them, but an unquestioned link from degradation to rape is presumptive. We're in a sorry state if we can't afford to look at 'unwholesome' lesbian or gay people. It's the same thing in the emerging African-American (mainly male) wave of film-making in the US – where are the black women, the gay black men? It's dangerous if we can't speak from within our own communities about issues that are politically problematic.

Seun Okewole: But positive representation does have its place?

Tom Kalin: It has its place because it represents many lives, but it doesn't represent my desires. I'm not going to make myself a slave to a political programme that doesn't benefit me. I think the solution is to make more images rather than less; if someone hates this movie, they should make something that counters it.

BEYOND THE SONS OF SCORSESE

Amy Taubin

Rooted in Cocteau and Warhol, Fassbinder and Kenneth Anger, Genet and Jack Smith, American queer cinema has achieved critical mass. Encouraged by twenty-five years of gay activism made urgent by the AIDS crisis and a right-wing homophobic backlash, queer film-makers have fought back through production of images.

In the past three years, gay-themed films have garnered the kind of attention that makes Hollywood want a slice of the action. Warners is following up its Malcolm X biopic with a film about Harvey Milk, to be directed by Gus Van Sant. And TriStar has

People Like Us (working title), a Jonathan Demme movie about a gay lawyer who's sacked when his firm discovers that he's HIV positive, ready to shoot in autumn.

Demme and Van Sant are no strangers to the contradictions of gay cultural politics. Demme's *The Silence of the Lambs* was attacked as homophobic because its serial killer Buffalo Bill was read as a negative gay stereotype. And Van Sant's *My Own Private Idaho* was attacked by some of the same critics for its lack of positive images of gay life. But it's Van Sant's depiction of marginality – the teenage male hustler hopelessly in love with a slumming preppie prince in *Idaho*, the grocery clerk obsessed by an illegal Mexican migrant worker in *Mala Noche* (1985) – coupled with his non-linear, associative film-making strategies, that make him one of the leaders of American queer cinema.

Budgeted at $2 million, *Idaho* is the priciest queer movie to date. The $20,000 *Mala Noche* is a more pertinent model for a queer cinema that is subversive in content, form and methods of production, but maintains just enough of a narrative spine to win it theatrical or television prime-time release. In 1991, the emblematic US queer films – Todd Haynes's *Poison*, Jennie Livingston's *Paris Is Burning* and Marlon Riggs's *Tongues Untied* – each cost less than $200,000. So did the most interesting and visible of 1991: Tom Kalin's *Swoon*, Christopher Münch's *The Hours and Times* and Gregg Araki's *The Living End*. These last three shared so many festival spotlights that it became impossible not to think of them as part of a single impulse. A quick look at their similarities and differences might provide some sense of the range and limitations of queer cinema.

A visually spare and emotionally intricate chamber film (sixty minutes, black and white) about what might have happened between Brian Epstein and John Lennon during a weekend the two spent together in Barcelona in 1963, Münch's *The Hours and Times* is so far removed from biopic, docudrama or *cinéma vérité* as to seem *sui generis*. Münch is a pomo humanist – a rare combination – raiding the image bank for the purpose of constructing empathetic characters. He told me in an interview that what was missing from the material he researched was 'a sense of what it was like to be Epstein'.

Aided by David Angus's selfless performance, *The Hours and Times* shows precisely what it was like to be the intelligent, physically awkward, emotionally vulnerable, self-deprecating Epstein – the gay Jewish aesthete hopelessly in love with a working-class tough whose genius was his spontaneity and intuitive grasp of 'the hours and times' in which he came of age. The film flies in the face of the hetero culture of *Rolling Stone* by suggesting that Lennon was capable of a homoerotic involvement. And it defies simplistic gay identity politics by representing a deep affinity between two men that is not defined by the sexual act. That the film doesn't specify what, if anything, happens when Lennon and Epstein share a bed, is exactly the point. Because, either way, it didn't change the relationship.

Although *The Hours and Times* is about a relationship between two men, women figure prominently in its narrative. In addition to the off-screen presences of Epstein's mother and Lennon's wife, there's the stewardess who visits Lennon's hotel room. 'What would you do if I said I wanted to make love to you?' he asks. 'I might agree or I might not,' is her self-possessed reply.

Like *The Hours and Times*, Kalin's *Swoon* uses black and white as a sign of history and memory. But unlike Münch, who evokes our identification with Epstein in terms of what Epstein says and does vis-à-vis his object of desire, Kalin wants us to admit the eroticism of protagonist Nathan Leopold's *fantasies*, which he suggests through fragmentary sounds and images and slip/sliding camera moves. Tony Rayns nailed it when he wrote: 'The film uncovers an orgasmic truth between the flutter of bird wings and the sound of a whip lash'.

Kalin makes a pretty clear case for the process by which internalised homophobia and anti-Semitism are transformed into sadomasochistic fantasies and a fascination with criminality. The first half of the film unabashedly identifies with Leopold, with his equation of glamour and deviance. If his homosexuality places him outside the law, it's also his connection to Chicago's underworld.

Swoon falters when it attempts the leap from erotic fantasy to the actuality of child murder. Abandoning Leopold's subjectivity, it perfunctorily filters the crime through various institutional perspectives – psychoanalytic, criminological, legalistic – all of them homophobic. At this point, I began to have the sense that Kalin was less interested in Leopold and Loeb than in the way their myth was formative in terms of his own sexuality. Failing to make that connection explicit and failing to illuminate the crime itself (in the way, for example, that Fassbinder illuminates the patricide in *Wild Game*), the film ends up as conceptually muddled as it's visually elegant. One should not underestimate, however, its importance in proclaiming a desire that is anything but 'politically correct'.

Gregg Araki's *The Living End* treats the queer-as-criminal theme from a contemporary perspective. An angry young drifter and an anxious young film critic, both HIV positive, fall in love, and, with nothing to lose, crash through to the other side of the law. The sex between the men is sweet, hot and extremely moving; *The Living End* is best when Araki sets aside his California cool and risks the aching romanticism of *Pierrot le fou* combined with the melodramatics of *Duel in the Sun.*

If one accepts these three films, along with *Poison, Paris Is Burning* and *Tongues Untied,* as the effective queer films of the 1990s, then the limitation of that cinema is obvious: queer cinema is figured in terms of sexual desire and the desire it constructs is exclusively male. (Jennie Livingston is a lesbian director, but *Paris is Burning* is about black and Hispanic male transvestites.) Indeed, women are even more marginalised in 'queer' than in heterosexual film; at least in the latter they function as objects of desire. (Which is why the pre-feminist stewardess who comes between Epstein and Lennon is such a powerful figure.) Worse still, *Tongues Untied* and *The Living End* are heedlessly misogynistic. Where does the politics of *Tongues Untied* – that 'black men loving black men is the revolutionary act' – leave lesbians of any colour? I'd say high and dry. As for *The Living End*'s inept lesbian serial killers and the woman who kills her lover when she discovers he's bisexual, a case could be made that they are no more or less stereotypical than their nerdy hetero male counterparts: all of them function as comic relief. But then what is one to make of Araki's claim that the woman whose symbiotic attachment to the gay hero defines her entire emotional life is a feminist character?

In fact, this queer cinema has much more in common with the current crop of male violence films (with Quentin Tarantino's *Reservoir Dogs* or Nick Gomez's *Laws of Gravity*, for example) than it does with any feminist cinema. Like Tarantino and Gomez, Araki and Kalin are also the sons of Scorsese, whose films define and critique masculinity through violence, but also make Robert De Niro a homoerotic object of desire.

To find a cinema that is queer and feminist, one must look further into the margins, where Sadie Benning is using a toy Pixelvision video camera to monitor and exhibit her adolescent lesbian identity. Ten years younger than any of the queer male film-makers above (most of whom are under thirty), Benning shares with them the pleasure of flaunting the fact that she's 'as queer as queer can be'. Unlike the women film-makers produced by the feminist film theory of the 1970s, she doesn't have a problem about defining herself in terms of her sexuality.

Benning's work is easily as powerful as any of the queer films I've mentioned. In terms of form, however, she's making something radically different – a hybrid of video and solo performance in the tradition of gallery artists such as Vito Acconci. Benning hasn't made the transition that Chantal Akerman made before our eyes in *Je tu il elle*, when she redirected her attention from the self to the other, thereby acknowledging the narrative standard for theatrical release.

Like Akerman, Haynes, Kalin, Münch, Livingston, Riggs and Araki incorporate the formal and sexual transgressions of the avant-garde within a narrative of queer desire. As long as that desire remains exclusively male, however, it's only queer by half.

GOINGS AND COMINGS

B. Ruby Rich

This is a fish story about not the one that got away, but the one that got caught and won the trophy. Caught big time, in other words. But it's also a cautionary tale, one about marketing, identity and innocence. *Go Fish* – the movie, the trailer, the legend – wasn't always such. It was once just like its title – derived, presumably, from the beloved children's card game that uses 'Go fish' as a command, but also, more pointedly, from the corny classic sign (gone fishin') hung on office doors throughout America when spring fever, that most uncapitalistic and anti-entrepreneurial syndrome, struck. It's probably fitting, then, that a little, low-budget, black-and-white independent film with a title signifying 'play' at its least hip, almost provincial best, should have evolved so immediately into a festival hit and legendary deal. This kind of success, after all, is the other kind of American fantasy. But in the process, care has to be taken that the fragile innocence and labour-of-love sincerity of the original doesn't evaporate on its way to the bank. If this article has a hidden agenda, it's the attempt to head off the backlash and argue that this film is far more than any mainstream distributor's fishing expedition.

Go Fish started life as a little film called *Max & Ely*. It was written in Chicago in 1991 by Rose Troche and Guinevere Turner, a couple of twenty-somethings smitten with each other and their project. It was a lesbian film, by and about and for lesbians. As Turner says, it was 'the little film that could'. For a while, though, it couldn't.

In 1992, Roche and Turner ran out of money. Their all-volunteer crew began to lose faith. Everybody had been working for free because they shared the dream of bringing a lesbian cinema into existence. Troche says, 'If you don't think that you can walk up to any lesbian and say, "Hey, do you want to make a film because look at the shit that's out there?" and they're, like, "I'm with ya"' – well, the consequences go without saying. So when they found themselves with little money, fewer friends and a film only partly made, they sent a letter to Christine Vachon in New York. As bad as things were, there was now a lesbian producer in the US helping independent films (*Poison, Swoon*) to get made. And her production partner, Tom Kalin, was a Chicago boy. Vachon read the letter, saw their twenty minutes of film, read the script and signed on. They were back in business.

By 1992, John Pierson's Islet Films came up with completion money and shooting could be finished. By 1993, ex-lovers Turner and Troche were working and playing in New York. Troche was editing the footage, Turner was fine-tuning the voiceovers, and the Sundance Film Festival would soon decide to show the film. As soon as I saw it, fine-cut on an editing table, I was enchanted and started composing catalogue copy in my head: '*Go Fish* begins just about where coming-out films used to end.' I wasn't particularly restrained in my choice of adjectives: wistful, lyrical, seriocomic, fanciful, plus 'an assured cinematic ability to confer grace'.

Go Fish came to Park City, Utah, with high hopes and lots of fears. By the opening day, director/co-screenwriter Rose Troche and actor/co-screenwriter Guinevere Turner had arrived. A box of nail clippers to be distributed as promo hadn't. Troche and Turner wondered if anyone would like their film in boytown – until its first screening. The crowd went nuts. 'God, are they hot,' said the straight women about the lesbians on screen. 'Give her money to make another one quick,' said the straight man about the lesbian on stage. Goldwyn made festival history by signing them to a distribution contract on opening weekend.

Then came the marketing. Unprecedented ads matched two women kissing (except that when it's printed too dark, one looks like a man, intentionally or not) with quirky hand-written copy. Trailers were in the theatres by May, playing back-up to other big-time quality product. Then the press kicked in. Turner, her hair arranged in front of her face like a beaded curtain, had a whole page in *Interview* touting her as a writer to watch; Rose, all pierced and intense-looking, got a pitch in *Rolling Stone* as the hot director for 1994; the two together got the number-two slot in the *New Yorker* Talk of the Town section, which would be a major status symbol even if the writer (anonymous, as is customary for Talk contributors, even when Jacqueline Kennedy wrote an item) hadn't gone on and on about what a good flirt Turner is and how much all the adulation was pleasing Troche and, well, how charmingly full of themselves and hand-rolled cigarettes and beautiful women and Café Tabac these two were. It's unprecedented respect for a lesbian movie. And bear in mind that *Go Fish* hadn't even opened.

Go Fish, then, offers up a lovely fable: the little film that is saved from extinction, hits the bull's-eye and is swept into the marketplace leaving its hardcore fans to worry that the hype might backfire, that the innocence and fervour that are the film's finest qualities will be mistaken for mere artifice once the context changes. If *Go Fish* is to get the respect it deserves – and to get it on its own terms, undistorted by the context of reception – it's important to understand the film's birthright. Consider these ten origin myths as a start.

Origin 1: 'A Comedy in Six Unnatural Acts'   In 1975, Jan Oxenberg made *A Comedy in Six Unnatural Acts*, the first (and nearly last) lesbian comedy. As a send-up of both political correctness and homophobic stereotypes, it was ahead of its time. Technically raw and politically sophisticated, it was shot on a shoestring and went on to play for years at women's film festivals and cultural women's evenings. For me, *Go Fish* is the daughter of *Comedy*, the living proof that lesbian camp does exist and even has a lineage. Except that Troche and Turner have never seen it.

Origin 2: Puerto Rican rhythm   Rose Troche's parents are Puerto Rican, from the island. She says that they couldn't understand why moving to the US didn't make them automatically able to pump out blue-eyed, blonde-haired babies instead of the kids they got. They moved all over the country, thereby obliging her to change schools mid-year to comply with the moves; she learned to fight and/or make people laugh. With no vocabulary for racism, Troche could never understand why their house was egged in the white neighbourhoods her parents favoured or why her mother's accent on the telephone was a cause of social ostracism for her. She looks around the room, points out how differently she'd be treated at Sundance if she had a heavy-duty accent herself instead of assimilation speech. Moving around and switching communities became a theme. She went to a public university where students commuted and never really knew each other. She had lots of time to study lots of things in the nine years she spent at the University of Illinois. Industrial design, for instance, which was her major for several years. 'Can you imagine anything more shallow than designing the *outside* of things?' jokes Troche, who clearly moved on to designing the guts.

Origin 3: Commune crisis   Guinevere Turner doesn't like to talk about her past or her childhood, though she finally admits she was a commune kid. 'That's the book I want to write: the children of the flower children.' I ask if she was radiantly happy or damaged and she indicates the latter. Her college experience at Sarah Lawrence continued the commune theme: in other words an isolated and mutually dependent group, sure of themselves, with cultish tendencies. Probably great boot camp for the lesbian nation. She moved to Chicago to get away from scrutiny and to try to write. She was afraid her long-haired straight-girl look would make it hard to find dykes. So she went to an ACT-UP meeting, where she met Troche. The rest is history.

Origin 4: The bars, negative   Turner and Troche did what any young self-respecting dyke couple in love would do: they went clubbing. And what did they see? 'Oh no, not the rain scene from *Desert Hearts* again. Not *Personal Best!* Oh, *The Hunger* again.' Video clips are the entertainment staple of lesbian bars all over the United States. The trouble is that there's so little to clip. The pair didn't have anything against most of these films:

in fact, Turner saw *Desert Hearts* when she was eighteen and was totally fixated, as much by the lesbian couple in front of her as by the movie. No, it was the paucity that got to them. Then that hideous Blake Edwards vehicle came out: *Switch.* Troche remembers: 'We thought, well, if they can do it, we can.' Vows were taken. They stopped making T-shirts and staging ACT-UP benefit performances and making lesbian safer-sex erotic photographs, and got themselves a new concept. They'd make a film. 'We loved having a project. It wasn't even a labour of love. It wasn't a labour.'

Origin 5: The bars, positive   They loved what they found in the bars; the energy and camaraderie, the fierce commitment to a life choice. And, I venture to add, the video. Not the video clips of mainstream movies featuring historical or farcical lesbians, but the alternative videotapes that were being produced, starting in the late 1980s, in and for the community. Just as disco music fuelled gay male culture in the 1970s, I'd argue, so has the bar video explosion fuelled lesbian identity in the 1990s. Turner and Troche see their allegiances to this sector very clearly. Troche says: 'I really hope the connection between our work and the work of people like Cheryl Dunye and Sadie Benning is recognised. It would be terrible if *Go Fish* were to be put up on a pedestal just because it's a feature.' Film critics, though, tend to live outside this subculture: to them, *Go Fish* must look as though it dropped, unique, out of the sky, instead of out of a community with a shared aesthetic voice.

Origin 6: Happy writers write happy characters   'No, we were miserable.' Turner and Troche insist that they fought like cats and dogs when they were together and that *Go Fish* was a very deliberate attempt to imagine lesbian happiness. They wanted to make a feel-good movie in spite of themselves. 'Yes, yes, this is so excellent' was their mantra for being a lesbian. 'We need a jolt in our lives to remember: girl, don't hold your head down.' Pride, you might say, was on their minds. Once there was a car accident in their script, and a suicide, and a confrontation with some violently homophobic men. But they got over it. Despite charming everyone who crosses their path, they continue to insist that their characters are much nicer than they are. And vice versa. When Turner tries to claim that she's not obnoxious like Max, Troche counters that it's more that she wears a different hat off-screen.

Origin 7: Chicago   Rose Troche is a product of the Chicago avant-garde tradition and is proud to say that she wants her audience to know that what they're watching is a fiction. Hence the eloquent bridges between scenes that link emotion and gesture in a series of tops, games, hands. She studied at the University of Illinois with Hans Schall, her hero. 'I owe it all to Hans,' she insists, in tribute to the man who taught her that, given three minutes of footage and an optical printer, you could make a feature. 'I like to see film grain.' She prides herself on doing all her own opticals and freely admits her avant-garde training. 'My negative cutter hated me because there are so many cuts in the film.' She remembers struggling to find a film analogue for the scratch in hip-hop music when she was cutting to 'Feel That Love' at the end. She thinks it's a question of rhythm, wanting to get the groove. She jokes that, being Puerto Rican, she ought to have rhythm. 'But I'm so white-washed, it's like: excuse me, could

I have some of my culture back now?' Of course, the University of Illinois wasn't all a piece of cake. Wayne Boyer, the resident authoritarian, would never let her near the 'good' optical printer, to this day.

Origin 8: Literary and filmic formation   They, uh, vary. For Turner studying fiction writing at Sarah Lawrence, the major influence was Jeanette Winterson's writing. She's still her hero. Turner writes short – very, very short – pieces of fiction and great one-liners. That's why *Go Fish* has such a coherent sense of vignette. Since the pair virtually finish each other's sentences, Troche immediately launches into a polemic about her desire to find a way to put the passion, the intensity of a love story such as Winterson's *Written on the Body* into a film that can taste and smell and breathe like books do. For Troche, some of the influence was counter. She bemoans the way that Lizzie Borden and Chantal Akerman switched from their core lesbian audience to mainstream ones where heterosexuality has to rule on screen, but stops herself from 'dissing' the sisters. 'Go girl' is more their style. She loved *I've Heard the Mermaids Singing*. Patricia Rozema is another hero, unmet so far, like the rest.

Origin 9: The lesbian community   When Troche and Turner rounded up their lesbian company for the years-long *Go Fish* shoot, they still had a euphoric view of lesbianism and lesbians. In the beginning, the crew was all women, and Roche can still recall the energy field produced by that gathering. 'Some days you'd see fifteen women laying down the track for the camera.' It was a fantastic experience. 'There's just so much strength in this community,' says Troche, bemoaning how little it is mobilised. When the tide turned and the gang got haircuts, got attitude, took off, well that's the lesbian community too. 'They won't believe this is happening.' Now Troche and Turner have a philosophical view of the film: 'Even if lesbians who see it say: "Damn that *Go Fish*", then that's a success.' If they swear they can top it, and they go off to make their own, great, let it spur successors and oppositions and debate, so long as it generates more films. In this sense, their film is something of a Molotov cocktail, tossed, like a bridal bouquet, to the waiting throng.

Origin 10: Genre traditions   The original press kit for *Go Fish* has a fascinating statement from its director. She tries to talk in one and the same breath about the need to build a tradition of lesbian film-making and her desire to be recognised as a film-maker, period. She bemoans the fact that reaction so far is so fixated on content that comments on the film's complex structure and associative image-cutting go unexpressed. She argues that the genre need is so great that *Go Fish* is moved into the new slot 'regardless of its merit' and earns its place 'purely because of lesbian content'. She talks wisely about how a starved market is asked to prove its loyalty over and over. She finally ends as follows, reconciled: 'I believe I should deal with a subject I have a relationship with, and be able to make my art without taking a political vacation, and hope that with the fulfilment of these beliefs I will gain the momentum to see me through the tasks ahead.' Go girls.

Decade of the dyke

This text goes to press on the eve of the *Go Fish* premiere at the 18th San Francisco International Lesbian and Gay Film Festival. Playing the massive 1,500-seat Castro Theatre on opening night, the film sold out on the first day of ticket sales. (But then, the festival itself sold out all its season passes on day one, too.) When Troche and Turner come to San Francisco for their fix of adoration, they'll alternate interviews with the mainstream press with an informal lesbian discussion at the Bearded Lady Cafe. It's a symptomatic juxtaposition.

Today, there's a locomotion to lesbian and gay film work that's undeniable. Two years into the 'New Queer Cinema', film and video are still taking off, driven by the fuel of political passion and aesthetic urgency. The queers have staked out this historical moment, making sure it doesn't erode. And the new film-makers and video artisans are producing their work without compromising stylistic rigour. Who can resist, when there's a huge audience willing and waiting to respond to less traditional work? There's nothing like a political movement to make artists responsive and interactive and full of mandates, while audiences full of their own sense of empower-ment can be counted on to swell the ranks of the ticket line and bring their own serious demands to the screening (and, sometimes even to the film-makers themselves).

Finally, critically, not incidentally, a lesbian feature cinema is emerging alongside lesbian video. After years of boys-only film-making, *Go Fish* is a lesbian dramatic film to cheer. It's the flagship for a season already sporting Shu Lea Cheang's new *Fresh Kill* and Midi Onodera's just completed *Sadness of the Moon.* If the papers are to be believed, there are already more than a dozen mainstream lesbian films in production or pre-production in Hollywood. If this keeps up, then the 1990s may just be the decade of the dyke after all.

*TOTALLY F***ED UP*
USA 1993
Director: Gregg Araki

The film opens with a newspaper clipping, reporting that gay kids form a disproportionately high percentage of teenage suicides. In fifteen numbered chapters, the film presents a group portrait of six gay/lesbian teenagers in present-day Los Angeles.

1: Film school student Steven is making a video documentary about the lives of his friends: Andy, who describes himself as 'totally fucked up' and thinks he may be bisexual; Tommy, a boyish skateboarder; Deric (Steven's steady boyfriend), who paints and plans to start college soon; and the lesbian couple Michele and Patricia. All of them find life boring. 2: The six talk about their experiences of sex in the age of AIDS. Tommy is the only one relaxed about casual sex. 3: Everyone in the group enjoys getting high. 4: While Michele shops for Patricia's birthday, Steven confides his fear of settling down with Deric. Patricia longs to have a fatherless child.

5: Most of the six want to believe in love; Andy is adamant that it is a non-existent fantasy. After another dull evening, the boys head home discussing the sexuality of well-known movie and rock stars. For his video, Steven asks them about masturbation. 6: The girls ask the boys to pool specimens of their sperm, in an attempt to artificially inseminate Patricia. 7: The six feel alienated from both society and mainstream gay culture. One night Andy is cruised by Ian, who aspires to write like novelist Dennis Cooper. They agree to meet for a date.

8: Tommy has one-off sex in a car with Everett. Steven comes home from casual sex with Brendan to find a note from his mother that Deric called twice. At the end of a relaxed evening together, Andy allows Ian to seduce him. 9: Andy asks Tommy about submitting to sodomy. Steven confides to Michele that he was unfaithful to Deric, but starts lying to Deric to fob him off. 10: Andy feels a growing attachment to Ian, unaware that Ian has other boyfriends. Deric watches Steven's unedited tapes and comes across his confession of infidelity; enraged and deeply hurt, Deric storms out. Tommy's parents discover that he is gay and throw him out of the house; he moves in to stay with Deric.

11: Steven sends Deric a videotaped apology, but Deric can't forgive him. Andy is stood up by Ian, and gets his answerphone when he calls. 12: Deric, thinking of cruising the night streets, is beaten up by queer-bashers. He calls Steven, who rushes him to hospital and fetches the others. Andy visits Ian's apartment in the small hours and finds that he has company already. 13: Andy feels mentally broken. 14: Deric convalesces at home, but still refuses to take calls from Steven. Andy visits him, reporting that his 'love affair' is over. At night, Andy cruises and has casual sex with a stranger. 15: Steven picks a fight with Tommy. Andy totters home and tries to phone his friends, getting either no answer or busy tones. He downs a tumbler of liquor, and then brews himself a cocktail of household chemicals and swallows it. He is found floating face down in his family's pool.

* * *

As many critics have discovered, it's often hard to keep the solipsistic airhead act that Gregg Araki puts on when he presents his films in public separate from rational appraisal of the films themselves. But the effort has to be made, not least because the films are in some ways getting better. *Totally F***ed Up* (the title is not written but spoken by Andy in the opening moments) announces itself as 'another homo movie by Gregg Araki', but it's actually quite different in stance, style and structure from *The Living End*, Araki's first agit-queer movie. In some ways it revisits the manic, depressed LA soulscapes of his first two features, *Three Bewildered People in the Night* (1987) and *The Long Weekend (o' Despair)* (1989); however the protagonists this time are not failed performance and video artists but relatively cheerful and resilient kids in their late teens. And this time the film is framed as an explicit homage to Godard.

For *Masculin Féminin*'s '15 Precise Acts', Araki substitutes '15 random celluloid fragments'. Each chapter is a mini collage: Araki's observational and storytelling footage is intercut with video material supposedly from Steven's documentary, and the whole is interspersed with Araki's attempts at sardonic, Godardian captions. The first six-and-a-half chapters are organised around themes such as sex and dope, and designed to establish the characters, their preoccupations and problems; the caption 'START NARRATIVE HERE' midway through chapter 7 heralds the somewhat half-hearted shift to storytelling mode and the subsequent chronicling of Andy's heartbreak, Deric's split from Steven and Tommy's expulsion from his family home. Very little of this is authentically 'random' except for the Godardian composition of shots (there's a lot of tight framing that makes very inexpert reference to off-screen space) and the role of the lesbian couple Michele and Patricia. The girls are all too clearly present for PC reasons of balance and solidarity, but the only problems Araki can think of giving them are those of shopping and prospective lesbian parenting; most of the time they are there only as confidantes for the screwed-up boys.

As the film goes on, its purported randomness looks more and more like a cop-out, a mask for an underlying (and decidedly un-Godardian) sentimentality. Aside from a couple of anecdotal references to homophobia on television and in the press, nothing here addresses the sociological questions raised by the newspaper clipping on which the film opens. Showing Tommy (apparently the only working-class kid in the group) being thrown out by his parents and having Deric being beaten up (off-screen) by queer-bashers do not amount to an analysis of society's homophobia. Leaving all the parents off-screen is not an adequate answer to the obvious questions about the presence or absence of parental support. And showing Andy's suicide does nothing to explain why more gay kids than straight kids will kill themselves. Andy drinks Drano on impulse and drowns in the family swimming pool because he gave his anal virginity to a guy who subsequently two-timed him and because he couldn't get any of his friends on the phone when he needed to; sad, but not much sadder than spending a late adolescence holed up in your room with your Jesus and Mary Chain records, a habit by no means exclusive to gay teenagers. Araki, himself no spring chicken at the age of thirty-five, may pride himself on getting so close to emotionally inarticulate teenagers, but he ought to be experienced enough to know that empathy alone gets you nowhere.

And yet the film has cherishable qualities. Its observation of the gay, teen and gay-teen subcultures in LA is spot on: a bootleg tape of Nine Inch Nails in concert used as an aid to seduction, an AIDS patient begging on the sidewalk, a relationship forged in the toilet of a theatre screening *My Beautiful Laundrette*, lousy re-run tapes on the phone-sex lines. It's both admirable and believable that no one inside or outside the core group ever draws attention to the group's variegated racial mix. The sex scenes involving Andy – particularly his seduction by Ian in chapter 8, but also his failure to agree on a mutually pleasurable act with a casual pick-up in chapter 2 – are models of 1990s safe-sex realism. Best of all is the casting: all six principals are new to movies, but Araki makes up for the shortcomings of his scripting by guiding them into performances of great naturalness and charm. All of which suggests that Araki may yet make a terrific film. Maybe next time.

Tony Rayns

NOWHERE TO HIDE

Amy Taubin

Todd Haynes makes experimental films. He admits it openly and without hesitation. *Superstar: The Karen Carpenter Story* (1987), his 43-minute biopic of the 1970s pop star who died young of anorexia, was shot on miniature cardboard and contact-paper sets with a cast of Barbie dolls. *Poison* (1991) is a stubbornly structuralist feature: three stylistically dissimilar fables of 'transgression and punishment', intercut and glued together with much spit, blood and semen. *Dottie Gets Spanked* (1993), for a PBS series innocuously titled 'TV Families', is a lucid and tender portrait of the artist as a gay seven-year-old obsessed with a Lucille Ball-like sitcom star and fascinated by spanking.

That the establishment's wrath quickly descended on Haynes only enhanced his position at the forefront of gay film-making. When A&M Records (the Carpenters' label) won an injunction to keep *Superstar* from being screened publicly, bootleg VHS copies became fetish objects. And when the religious right used *Poison* to mount an attack on the National Endowment for the Arts which had partly funded the film, the publicity boosted box-office grosses to unexpected heights.

Compared to these three earlier films, *[Safe]* (1995) seems almost conventional: it has linear narrative; a name actress (Julianne Moore) plays the leading role, Carol White; it's shot in 35mm and, although produced for a mere $1 million, has the glistening look and sound of films costing ten times more. But it introduces Hollywood conventions only to throw them coolly into disarray. It's the most subversive of his films, a subtle match of radical form and radical political content.

Its material is similar to *Superstar*'s. Set in upper-middle-class Southern California suburbia, it's the story of a woman with a mysterious wasting ailment without a cure. Even more than Karen Carpenter's anorexia, this environmental illness (or multiple chemical sensitivity) can be read as an AIDS metaphor because, like AIDS, it is an immune deficiency disease.

The film opens with an extended travelling shot; the point of view is from the passenger seat and through the front windshield of a Mercedes cruising through the SoCal night. Street lamps cast a greenish glow, throwing into silhouette the meticulously landscaped houses on either side of the road. The music under the image swells ominously, as in an upscale horror or sci-fi film, adding to the sense of free-floating anxiety. The car passes through a wrought-iron gate, up a driveway and into a garage. A man and a woman get out, backs to the camera, and we hear the sound of a discreet, half-stifled sneeze. 'It's freezing in here,' says the woman in a breathy, childlike, apologetic voice. There's a cut to an overhead, medium shot of her opalescent face. She's lying on her back amid peach and aqua sheets, a passive participant in the act of marital sex. Above her, the man pounds and grunts, oblivious to faint flickers of confusion and pain in her eyes. Freezing indeed.

This is Carol White, the not-quite Stepford wife saved from banality by her inchoate sense that all is not right in her perfect world. For the next forty-five minutes, the film follows her through her daily routine: exercise class; the dry cleaners; lunch with a woman friend; the hairdresser. Driving on the freeway behind a fume-spewing truck, Carol begins coughing uncontrollably. She pulls into a deserted underground parking garage. The car spirals wildly and finally stops. From a distance, the camera watches as Carol coughs and coughs. From then on, her symptoms worsen rapidly. Looking in the mirror at her newly permed hair, she panics as she sees blood slowly dripping from her nose. The sequence teeters on the edge of camp, loaded with horror-film tropes. In fact, the entire first act follows the form of a horror film. The protagonist knows that the monster is on the loose, that the plague has descended. But no one believes her. Carol's husband, friends and doctors prefer to think that the problem is only in her head. After a brief middle section where Carol attempts to investigate and take charge of her illness, she winds up at Wrenwood, a New Age retreat where she's once again isolated – as in her suburban cocoon.

Keeping Carol at a distance, a fragile, almost paralysed figure in repressive, chill environments, Haynes nevertheless locates the film within her subjectivity. Rather than alienating us from her, the measured, wide-angle, hyperreal *mise en scène* becomes an expression of the alienation she experiences. From the moment Carol has her coughing fit, we begin to read everything in her environment (which is our own environment) – and the very fabric of her identity (which is not very different from the fabric of our identity) – as lethal. 'It's scary,' Haynes has said, 'for me to think about how much I identify with Carol White.' This tension, between identification and remove, gives *[Safe]* (or at least the first half) an extraordinary gravity. Every frame in the LA section seems simultaneously charged with the push/pull of desire and loathing.

The Wrenwood section is stylistically quite different, with an almost casual documentary look. Meaning is located (or undermined) in the dialogue rather than the images. The similarities between Wrenwood's repressive and disengaged culture and that of LA suburbia are suggested but not quite realised on-screen.

Nevertheless, from beginning to end, *[Safe]* is a film that demands to be read by the viewer. There are signs in abundance but no answers or messages. Nothing could be further from Haynes's own politics than the New Age platitudes of Wrenwood. *[Safe]* is above all a critique of a passive society in which people ignore the ecological disaster all around them, or else, if they can't, wait helplessly for someone else to tell them what to do about it. Haynes is not interested in being that someone else. *Do you smell fumes?* is the headline on a flyer that catches Carol's eye and that leads her to a meeting of Environmental Illness activists, a fledgling resistance movement against the disease of the twenty-first century. *[Safe]* alerts us to the fumes and that no one is immune to them; the rest is up to us.

Haynes grew up privileged in various LA suburbs. With his blond hair and snub nose, he could have passed for the all-American boy, but in fact he was Jewish and gay. At eighteen, he fled to the more congenial East Coast environment of Brown University where he studied semiotics, read Freud and made *Assassins*, a super-8 film about Rimbaud and Verlaine. After graduating in 1985, he moved to New York where, with classmates Christine Vachon and Barry Ellsworth, he set up Apparatus, a low-budget production company that was a linchpin in the indie film movement. *Superstar* put him on the downtown map; *Poison* made him the gay film-maker to be reckoned with. [Safe], a box-office disappointment, had more critical success than expected, though less than deserved. Haynes is currently working on a Glam Rock movie set in 1970s London and New York.

* * *

Amy Taubin: I remember you saying that all your films are about illness. Why is that?

Todd Haynes: AIDS. Though none of my films are specifically about AIDS. It's too easy for people to separate themselves from AIDS, to compartmentalise it as a gay disease. So I wanted to make films about these end-of-the-twentieth-century diseases without limiting those vulnerable to gay men and junkies. Instead, I located them in the safest, most protected places on the planet.

Amy Taubin: The San Fernando Valley you grew up in is the setting for both [Safe] and Superstar.

Todd Haynes: Yes, although Superstar was made in New York. After I graduated from Brown, I came to New York and wrote the Superstar script with my friend Cynthia Schneider. I enrolled in the MFA summer programme at Bard College and we shot it there. I knew I wanted to make a film using dolls. I didn't know what it would be about, but I wanted it to follow a certain narrative form, a particular genre closely enough, only with dolls instead of actors. It would be a kind of experiment about identification. I was pretty certain people would identify with dolls as if they were actors, but on some level, you would become aware that you were cathecting onto this plastic object.

Amy Taubin: Did you play with dolls as a child?

Todd Haynes: Not really with Barbies. My sister didn't get into Barbies; she had (toy) horses. We were very close and still are; she's three years younger than I am. So she had horses and a lot of international dolls that my parents bought on trips. We would do little shows for each other under her bedroom table with a blanket on top and a desk lamp for the light source. Mine always would be really sad stories about girls and their horses and the horse would die and come back to life and she'd cry. And so we'd play with dolls in that way. And I also had a friend, who was more of a femme girl. She had a Barbie and a Ken doll so I got to play with them. So I knew the film had to be with dolls. And then I heard a Karen Carpenter song on a lite-FM station one day and I said, 'Oh, my God, we have to do the Karen Carpenter story.' At the time, there was no glimmer of a 1970s re-examination; you weren't hearing that music or seeing those images as you do now everywhere. It felt truly like something I hadn't thought about in a long time.

Amy Taubin: When were you born?

Todd Haynes: In 1961. But I remember the last time my parents and I agreed on popular culture, when we shared the same love of a pop song on the radio. I was in the bath and I remember my Dad walking in, and he said, 'Oh Todd, I've just heard this groovy new song on the radio,' and he started singing 'We've Only Just Begun' [the Carpenters' song]. And I remember in 1970 going on vacation with my family and meeting a teenage brother and sister at the resort in Laguna Beach. The girl had long dark hair and bangs and wore a crocheted bikini and she loved Karen Carpenter. I thought she was so cool, that she was Karen Carpenter. But there's also this funny thing: I was close to my sister – she was the star of all my productions – and the Carpenters, as a brother/sister team, had this weirdly sexual asexuality, this weirdly romantic but pure quality about them. They were like all the great fantasies about brothers and sisters. And when I did research on them later, I discovered that journalists actually questioned them very aggressively about the incestuous element.

Amy Taubin: But did you do the Karen Carpenter story, in part, because of her anorexia?

Todd Haynes: Oh yes. I thought about what had happened to her since the early 1970s, mainly her anorexia, and how that early moment in the 1970s was changed a few years later with Watergate. There had been all these pure images of America – the Brady Bunch, the Partridge Family and the Carpenters – that had been almost aggressively fostered onto youth culture in an attempt to get out of that nightmare of the late 1960s. It was very closely aligned with Nixon's revisionist view of America. Not that my parents ever supported Nixon, but nevertheless, that stuff was all around. But it was turned inside out by Watergate. And what I loved about Karen Carpenter's lyrics and that quality in her voice was exactly what, at that time, made people roll their eyes and ask what does this nineteen-year-old girl with a deep voice really know about love and pain. So it seemed like rich material to explore in film.

Amy Taubin: And it's easy to see the connection between Carpenter and Carol White, women who have these inexplicable illnesses.

Todd Haynes: That you think, in both cases, they brought on themselves.

Amy Taubin: Do you think they brought it on themselves?

Todd Haynes: That's one of the questions that haunts *[Safe]*. There's no easy way for me to answer that. No, I don't think Carol brought it on herself simply to get attention or in some false way. I think, if it was self-induced, it was at a completely unconscious level. Or that there's a susceptibility to being made vulnerable by the world that she carries with her, that some people carry with them. But I do think that the illness in *[Safe]* is the best thing that happens to her. It's the thing that kicks her out of unconsciousness, out of this unexamined life, and makes her begin to think about things in a completely different way and take some steps toward changing her life. And I'm interested in how disease can do that, can force you to look at things in a completely different way.

Amy Taubin: When you talk about her susceptibility, do you mean something along the lines of the way some people would claim schizophrenia is a logical response to an insane world?

Todd Haynes: Yeah, I do. And that's why in both films (*[Safe]* and *Superstar*) they're women. There's a history of inexplicable illnesses, that established medicine can't confirm as absolutely physiological, that have affected women. I think they are diseases of identity that force you to see that identity is a fragile and basically an imaginary construct that we pretend to carry around. The more unexamined it is, the more vulnerable you are.

Amy Taubin: I'm still trying to understand the level of responsibility you place on her. You are not, I think, saying what Peter, the Wrenwood guru, says: that she could cure herself by loving herself more.

Todd Haynes: Definitely not. Peter's cure is to adhere completely to these very basic ideas about self that affirm the society as it is. His kind of New Age philosophy comes out of a 1960s ideology, using Eastern traditions to re-examine the West. It claims to change the world through self-esteem or a softening of basic structures of resistance, but I see it as a reiteration of basic conservative arguments about the self, which are closely aligned with masculinity and patriarchy. Postmodern gay theory has tried to chip away at them; the cyborg generation is looking at less Freudian models and claiming those models are already in us. But I'm not sure I agree with that either. So that's why ultimately the illness and its chaos is where hope lies in the film, not where it's tied up and organised by Wrenwood philosophy in the end.

So while I don't think she's responsible for being ill, I don't think the illness just came from chemicals in the world. I can't turn it into a simply materialist explanation for the illness. And in a way when I think about whether it was chemicals that make her ill, or living the kind of insulated life she lives as a woman in the world, both are cultural not psychological problems. They're not internal problems that can be solved by loving yourself more. You have to look out in the world to solve them, and that's the big difference between the Wrenwood perspective and mine.

The popular view of anorexia says it's about women trying to look like models and being really sexy and really thin. But that didn't account for the extremes to which this diet takes them and the profound misrecognition of the body – how anorexics look in the mirror and think they're fatter than someone next to them who weighs thirty pounds more. So we were more interested in the theories that claimed anorexia was a resistance against femininity and a denial of one's breasts and menstruation and those sexualised aspects of the body. Why else would it hit women so often at adolescence when their bodies are changing? So I found the most poignant and interesting way to approach Karen Carpenter's anorexia was as a kind of unconscious resistance. Disease as a kind of resistance to notions of healthy identities and selves is what recurs in my films.

I think what [Safe] is really about is the infiltration of New Age language into institutions. And about the failure of the left; how it imploded into these notions of self and self-esteem and the ability to articulate and share emotions in the workplace or whatever. And it's such a loss because what was once a critical perspective looking out, hoping to change the culture, is turning inward and losing all of its gumption and power. It's time for the left to look at itself and how it's losing any effective voice politically or culturally.

Amy Taubin: Do you think someone seeing [Safe] would conclude that because Carol's insularity – at the beginning in rich SoCal suburbia and at the end inside her plastic bubble in Wrenwood – doesn't work for her, the only thing is for her to be more directed outward toward changing her situation in the world?

Todd Haynes: No, I don't. I've made a film that gives you that answer. But it's particularly sneaky in that it is a film directed toward the left, maybe because I know that's the constituency that will go to a Todd Haynes film. So it plays with your leftist expectations, making you think that Wrenwood has got to be the answer. After all, it's at Wrenwood that you see a black woman character for the first time in the movie. And because the Peter character has AIDS, it's implied that he's gay, so how could he possibly not be telling the truth or not be a sympathetic character? These are little internal messages I think we look to: 'Oh, it's a film by Todd Haynes so the gay character can't be a jerk, he has to be reliable.' So the film purposefully draws you in only to pull the rug out from under you slowly. It tries to trick you into thinking it has an answer.

Until Wrenwood, you haven't had the kind of character that most movies give you. So it's like, wow, Peter has a whole philosophy. He's engaging, manipulative, charismatic, all the things you expect from characters in the movies. So I think you are kind of lured into believing what they're saying. What I really to do is frustrate your narrative expectations. You want her to be healed, and you want to have some understanding of the illness, and those narrative desires drive you to wanting her to be in a place that you also know is wrong and cruel. Your narrative expectations commit her to oppression. I think that happens in almost every movie you see, but it's painted as some sort of personal victory and affirmation of identity and you walk out of the movie thinking, 'Yeah, everything's just fine.' But how could it be fine to be closed up in that plastic bubble? The Wrenwood answer to Carol's damaged immune system is quarantine – no newspapers, no books, no television, no sex, no contact with the world. How could that be someone's idea of a happy ending?

Amy Taubin: The characters in the first part – the husband, the doctors, her women friends, even the guy telling the dirty joke in the restaurant – are much more familiar to me, and complicated. Their confusion is right on the surface. They can't articulate what's going on but they haven't learned to do the Wrenwood denial thing. I don't know who the Wrenwood characters are except that they're the people who turn up on *Oprah.*

Todd Haynes: I didn't really care to do the story of the people who dominate these movements. I don't really care who the character of Peter is. I remember trying to get funding from Zenith for *[Safe].* The script wasn't getting through to the people there. But then one of them said, 'One project we're really interested in doing is the L. Ron Hubbard story.' And like, wait a minute, it's exactly the same theme, but about the powerful side. I'm interested in the people drawn in.

One of the things that initiated *[Safe]* was my own questions about AIDS therapy and recovery treatments. I read the Louise Hay book (*The AIDS Book: Creating a Positive Approach*) and I still don't have the answer to why people with AIDS would want to turn to that. I know it's about control, some sense of control, but to be told you wouldn't be sick if you had loved yourself right and if you learned to love yourself right you'll be cured – it puts the person in this impossible situation where they're continually blaming themselves for their illness which just won't go away no matter how much they love themselves, whatever the hell that means. There's this beautiful quote I found from this cancer patient who said, 'We humans would rather accept culpability than chaos.' That's why people are drawn to places like Wrenwood.

Amy Taubin: And yet I know intelligent gay men who saw the film and came out thinking you believed in Louise Hay. Do you think that's because they can only identify with the gay character? I don't have that problem because I'm totally identified with Carol.

Todd Haynes: I don't get it. When Peter says things like 'I've stopped reading the newspaper,' I mean, especially in such an understated film, it shouldn't take a sledgehammer to get the point across. I always look for those moments in movies when there are messages to disagree with. Even when they're unintended, when they think they're saying one thing and they're saying the complete opposite. I love those moments. They give me a way into things that otherwise would be too horrifying to deal with. I would be excited to see a film where they're trying to show you this negative philosophy not by attaching a villainous handlebar moustache, but showing it in a subtle way, the way these things are in the world.

I know it's hard and mean to make a movie where there's no escape, but just walk around. But there are markers of resistance. There's Nell and Lester [two of the characters at Wrenwood]. And there are the women in the middle of the film who are talking around the table about their illness without all this bullshit. That's when Carol seems the most alive – when she's talking with them, and then when she's telling her friend everything she's discovered. And it is all about this illness. And yes, people do take on illness as an alternate identity. And it does give them the sense of who they are for a time, and there's a sadness about that, but it's also the first time Carol is motivated to look around and take some action in her life. She acts independently, and sadly that takes her to Wrenwood where all the lines are cut and she's sealed up. So it's not as if the film is completely without the indication that there are other ways of dealing with it.

Amy Taubin: Why did you set it in 1987?

Todd Haynes: I wanted to set it at the height of the Reagan/Bush 1980s. Now it doesn't matter because we're back in it with a vengeance, but there was a slight moment when Clinton was elected, when it seemed a little less necessary to make the film, but God, that was a fantasy, a mirage.

Amy Taubin: Can we talk about your directorial choices? The film was made for only $1 million.

Todd Haynes: Yes and it was very difficult. I could never do it again.

Amy Taubin: How did you choose the locations?

Todd Haynes: Most of the LA interiors were shot in my grandfather's and my uncle's houses. The exterior of Carol's house, where we shot the garden scenes, doesn't belong to anyone I know, but it's in my parents' neighbourhood. It wasn't there when I was growing up, but when I was writing *[Safe]* I would smoke a little pot and get in the car and drive up to the top of the hill overlooking this house. And I'd put on a Sonic Youth tape and picture this movie about this woman who'd be getting sicker and sicker in this huge house, this bizarre fake Tudor manor. And we ended up getting that exact house for the exterior.

I was looking for these single-level expansive houses. I was trying to force architecture into every frame and always show Carol in relation to her environment. And certain architecture gave us a way to divide up the frame and segregate different characters into different boxes. I wanted there always to be this empty frame and she'd enter it and be this little figure in the corner. I wanted the frame very wide, with very little movement, and this enormous sense of off-screen activity – vacuum cleaners and Spanish television shows and lite-FM – like the house was alive but that Fulvia [the housekeeper] was running it and Carol was just one of the objects inside it.

Amy Taubin: You mentioned Kubrick.

Todd Haynes: I saw *2001* again while we were raising money. And I thought that's what I want. We should feel we're in a world where nature has been completely overcome by man and there's no trace of it. It should feel like space, but it's really LA. It should feel like an airport where you never touch real ground. You're just in this carpeted, air-controlled systems world where people just glide by.

Amy Taubin: The isolation also reminds me of Antonioni's *Red Desert.*

Todd Haynes: I hadn't seen it when I wrote *[Safe]*, but Alex [Nepomniaschy, Director of Photography] talked about it. I just loved the way Alex shot *Poltergeist III*. The lighting he did – it wasn't just 'turn on the green gels'. He looks like he was using real light and real reflections and allowing them to be green naturally. He uses muslin and mirrors. He has his own system of diffusion that's soft, but not pretty. We used a very restrained palette and camera, so, in a way, it's about what we're not doing. I was thinking about the way the film literally obliterates Carol, blanks her out.

Amy Taubin: How did you decide on Julianne Moore? Her performance is fantastic; she deserved to win every best actress award and, instead, she's been almost entirely overlooked.

Todd Haynes: Julianne does something that few actors do. She disappears before your eyes. It becomes a 'Can you find the woman in the picture?' puzzle. It's an amazingly selfless performance.

A lot of very talented name actors read for the part. But they loved the dialogue, so they indulged in all these naturalistic tics, that made you just hate the character. I got really worried because Carol seemed like Little Orphan Annie. Then my casting director persuaded me to read Julianne. I knew the part had to be played in a very restrained way. And Julianne understood that instinctively and intellectually. Unlike actors who are trained to show you every nuance of emotion, Carol can't do that. Julianne understood Carol was more limited than most people. So her performance is exactly the opposite of what a personality actor like Jennifer Jason Leigh's or Meryl Streep's would have been. But paradoxically, you're drawn into her blankness. You want to know more. I don't think she was having fun doing what she was doing. It's a denial of the actor's pleasure, especially the method actor. But we both knew that *[Safe]* was somehow about refusing pleasure.

THE DOOM GENERATION
USA/France 1995
Director: Gregg Araki

Jordan White and Amy Blue are two bored Los Angeles teenagers. One evening, after a party, they're attempting to have sex in the back of a car when there's a brawl in front of them. Handsome young drifter Xavier Red, wounded in the fight, jumps in beside them and tells them to drive away. Amy takes an immediate dislike to Xavier. She drops him off by the side of the road. Amy and Jordan stop a short distance away at a local Quickie Mart to get something to eat. When they're unable to pay, the Korean store clerk trains a shotgun on them. Xavier suddenly appears and jumps him. There's a struggle and the Korean's head is blown off. The trio hole up in a motel. Jordan and Amy have sex in the bath. Later that night, Xavier seduces Amy. They're having sex in the car when a lovesick burger store attendant turns up with a gun, threatening to kill Amy. Xavier wrestles with him and shoots off his arm.

As they wind their way across America, the three have various other bizarre and bloody encounters with barmaids, liquor store clerks and fast-food salesmen. Between times, they stop off in gaudy roadside motels. Television shows monitor their progress. The FBI ponder how to deal with them. In one small town, they set up bed for the night in a huge shed. They're all having sex together when they're interrupted by a group of crazed rednecks, brandishing the American flag. These naked neo-Nazis accuse Jordan and Xavier of being faggots, rape Amy, and murder Jordan by emasculating him with a pair of scissors. Amy escapes her bonds, grabs a gun, and shoots her captors. Xavier and Amy are last seen heading off down the open road.

*   *   *

Early on in *The Doom Generation*, there is a grotesque but comic little incident which sums up the picture's expressionist, cartoon-style approach to violence in a nutshell: after a scuffle in a Quickie Mart, a Korean clerk's head is blown off. It somersaults through the air in slow motion, and lands on a tray of half-eaten fast food. Relish is seen oozing from its mouth. The three narcissistic slacker heroes react to the event with typical Californian cool, as if decapitations were a daily event. Nothing fazes them. Nothing much, outside of sex, food and music, intrigues them very much either. Writer/director Gregg Araki claims that he likes making films about teenagers because 'there's something monumental and heightened about their hormone-mad lives – like they get a zit and the world ends; they live and die ten times a day.' What is most striking about these heroes, though, is their world-weariness, the sense that they've seen it all before. Only when they accidentally run over a dog on the highway do they show the slightest flicker of emotion. 'Do you ever wonder what life means?' dreamy adolescent Jordan Blue (James Duval) asks from time to time. His question is barely heeded. This is a road movie, but it isn't one with any kind of existential undertow. Nor, despite frequent cut-aways to absurd television news shows, does it seem especially concerned with making satirical points about violence and the media. The America it depicts, a surreal expanse of fast-food outlets, bars and derelict cars, is too kitsch to bear easy comparison with the landscapes of *Natural Born Killers*. If anything, it recalls the hyper-animated world of Jim Carrey.

This is Araki's fifth feature, but his first with a significant budget. Much of the $1 million he was given by his French backers seems to have gone on production and costume design; on the absurd uniforms which the various burger and liquor store attendants wear, and on the gaudy backdrops. The three lads are named after colours. (By calling them White, Blue and Red, Araki may even be having a little joke at the expense of Kieślowski's Trilogy, as well as Tarantino's bank heist gang in *Reservoir Dogs*.) Casting seems to follow the John Waters principle: there are several clean-cut faces from American sitcoms lurking in the minor roles and there's even a part for real-life Hollywood Madame, Heidi Fleiss.

The various motel rooms where the three teenage runaways hole up are decorated like bordellos, all chequered wallpaper and fluorescent light. Dialogue, too, is stylised: Araki takes Californian 'surfer speak' and pushes it to extremes. Amy Blue (Rose McGowan), who is made up to look like Louise Brooks's nymphet teenage sister, rattles out her invective in breathless, but sardonic fashion. 'God, when will you take a reality pill?' she yawns when Xavier Red (Johnathon Schaech) spins her an outlandish yarn about killing a traffic cop. Jordan comes up with more cryptic remarks. 'I feel like a gerbil smothered in Richard Gere's butt-hole,' is a typically gnomic one-liner.

The sex sequences are frenetic and played for laughs, all humping and pumping. Gregg Araki has labelled *The Doom Generation* as his 'first heterosexual movie'. He suggests that it's a 'straight movie for gay people' in the way that *Philadelphia* and *Longtime Companion* were 'gay films for straight people'. However, there's a clear sense that the relationship which most interests him is the one between Jordan and Xavier. They're the ones who are in each other's arms just before the bloody finale. It sometimes seems that Amy Blue is just along for the ride. Whenever she makes love to one of the boys, the other is sure to be watching from the sidelines.

It's a moot point whether the increased budget helps or hinders Araki. His last effort, *Totally F***ed Up*, had a rough, anarchic energy in keeping with the way it was shot. (It used camcorders as well as 16mm to tell the stories of six different characters.) *The Doom Generation*, by contrast, is all surface 35mm gloss. The fervour here is displaced into the narrative. As if to counter the relative conservatism of the shooting style, Araki packs the soundtrack with hardcore indie music, and lays on the sex and violence with a trowel. Much of the comedy comes from the sheer hyperbolic zest with which he tackles the material. At one moment, during a bar room brawl, Xavier is stabbed in the genitals. Blood spurts out in profusion. But the scene is wilfully exaggerated. We know he can't really be hurt.

It's this sense that nothing is for real that makes the film's denouement disquieting. With the sudden arrival of a gang of fascist homophobes, the mood of fey surrealism is shattered. The sequence certainly satirises gung-ho patriotism (the rednecks rape and murder to the accompaniment of 'The Land of the Free and the Brave') but is so wantonly gruesome that it seems utterly out of keeping with the comic book-style antics that have preceded it. This time, the dead stay dead. It's no wonder that even Xavier and Amy, sole survivors of the massacre, look a little chastened as they drive off into the sunset, munching nachos. Audiences are likely to be similarly disoriented by Araki's shock tactics.

Geoffrey Macnab

BOY WONDER

Danny Leigh

It sounds like supermarket tabloids and Jerry Springer, salaciousness and tragedy neatly wrapped and headed for Movie of the Week. In late 1993, petty criminal Brandon Teena, then twenty-one years old, was found dead in a decrepit farmhouse just outside Falls City, Nebraska. The killers, John Lotter and Thomas Nissen, turned out to be ex-con acquaintances of Teena's girlfriend, a factory worker two years his junior named Lana Tisdel.

Except that wasn't quite the whole story, and it's certainly not what inspired the front-page delirium. What became clear only after the event was that Brandon Teena was actually Teena Brandon, a young woman who for most of her brief adult life had passed as male. Lotter and Nissen, it transpired, raped Brandon upon discovering his real gender then killed him days later to prevent being testified against. Sex, death and transgression in the Midwestern dustbowl: flawless hard copy.

Which makes it all the more remarkable that *Boys Don't Cry*, feature debutante Kimberly Peirce's account of the events leading up to Brandon's death, manages to avoid both macabre sensationalism and the dutiful prosaics of Susan Muska and Gréta Ólafsdóttir's 1994 documentary *The Brandon Teena Story*. Instead, intercutting a pacy semi-fictionalised narrative with bursts of hazily somnambulant cinematography, Peirce revels in the Brandon she admits to 'falling in love with' and the at once barren and dreamlike landscape of powerlines and Qwik Stops that surrounded his life and framed his death. In doing so her film becomes less a biopic and more the latest entry in the distinguished line of acute paeans to rural America's nihilism and violence. While *Boys Don't Cry* is no *Badlands*, it isn't such a leap of faith to mention them in the same sentence. Moreover, in coaxing a slew of arresting performances from her cast (most notably Hilary Swank, whose touching, utterly poised portrayal of Brandon belies a professional track record that includes *Beverly Hills 90210* and *The Next Karate Kid*) she proves herself as adept with actors as with a chimerical pan across a series of electricity pylons.

Sitting in the Soho offices of her UK distributor's PR firm, Peirce, schooled in film at Columbia and the Sundance Directors' Lab, makes for a fiercely articulate inter-viewee, her words delivered with clipped self-assurance and a great deal of eye contact. The only potential cloud on her professional horizon – an ill-fated defamation-of-character lawsuit from a disgruntled Lana Tisdel – recently behind her, she explained her longstanding interest in transvestism and transsexuality ('I've always been interested in women dressed as men, because that was how I grew up, as a tomboy swinging from trees') before moving on to discuss the film which would win her the London Film Festival's FIPRESCI award and Swank a Golden Globe for Best Actress.

* * *

Danny Leigh: How did you hear about Brandon Teena?

Kimberly Peirce: In April 1994, I opened up the *Village Voice* and there was the story. And it blew me away. Here was this girl, living in a trailer park, with limited economic means and few if any role models for what she was about to do. She puts on a cowboy hat, puts a sock in her pants, transforms herself into a boy and goes out for the night. That in itself was enough. But Brandon asked girls out and girls bought him as a boy, and if he failed he'd try again the next night and commit petty crimes if that failed too. It made him totally charismatic to me. It wasn't the crime but the fact that he was so terrible at it, like Woody Allen in *Take the Money and Run.*

Danny Leigh: Was part of the project's appeal reclaiming the story from the tabloids?

Kimberly Peirce: Absolutely. The coverage was focused almost exclusively on the spectacle of a girl passing as a boy, without any understanding of why a girl would want to pass. And I thought that was dangerous.

Danny Leigh: What were your initial steps in researching the story?

Kimberly Peirce: I interviewed a number of butch lesbians and pre-op transsexuals about their histories, because I wanted to understand why they dressed as boys. And I started seeing wonderful divisions within the queer community where you get transsexuals who pass as boys to align their bodies with their true selves and butch lesbians who pass as performance. I learned Brandon was all that and neither, and what I didn't want to do was characterise him in any way he wouldn't have characterised himself. I wanted to get in touch with Brandon and his desire. Because desire is the one truth – if someone walks in and you desire them, that at least is true.

Danny Leigh: How did that intention translate in practice?

Kimberly Peirce: First it meant going wherever Brandon went, so I went with a group of fifteen transsexuals back to Falls City where we staged a vigil on Brandon's behalf. I went to Tom Nissen's murder trial and watched him give evidence against John, watched the dynamic between them, watched the dynamic with Lana. And I went to the farmhouse where Brandon was killed because to understand his life I felt it was necessary to understand his death. There was still blood on the wall, bullet holes in the window, clothing scattered around – I don't know why – and I realised my job was to get to the epicentre of this.

Danny Leigh: In the way you put the narrative together, the film almost seems like an anti-biopic – there's no 'explanation' of Brandon's transgenderism.

Kimberly Peirce: To me, movies are about great main characters and one event. I welcome anybody changing the form, but for me anything that gets in the way of the story shouldn't be there. And knowing Brandon was destroyed for not being understood, I needed to bring him to life in a way that was universally understandable. How could I do that? Not through a biopic. You do that by creating a unified event, by having him stand in front of the mirror getting ready to go out. Gay or straight, male or female, you understand that.

Danny Leigh: You never wanted to show Teena's life pre-Brandon?

Kimberly Peirce: There were a million different openings – the first cut was three hours long and started with Teena in her trailer, Teena at her dishwashing job, Teena at the skating rink. And people were fascinated, but two feelings emerged: 'Can we know more about Teena?', which sent me backwards when I needed to go forwards, and 'I didn't realise until half way this was a love story.' So the question was whether this was a film about transformation, a *Pinocchio*, or a tragic love story, a *Romeo and Juliet*. It was both.

Danny Leigh: How much attention was devoted to structure? There's a real momentum to the way certain sequences segue into one another.

Kimberly Peirce: I studied structure a lot. I love structure. I have a dream sequence very early on. The sequence where Jake La Motta is in the ring in *Raging Bull*, for example, is one of those liminal periods where you can do anything. And because you meet Jake in a dream, as his idealised self, in beautiful slo-mo, you can also reach the nadir with him. Then I looked at *GoodFellas* and saw there's a period right after where you can do a set-up, though you have to be quick. So here you have the dream then you move into a title sequence because in a title sequence the possibilities are also wide open, however briefly.

Danny Leigh: Were you worried audiences would demand a clearer line between fact and interpretation?

Kimberly Peirce: How could you ever tell the audience what is and isn't true? All you can do is make the character accessible and push the story forward. In any case, I'd say it's all emotionally true. I interviewed Lana, I interviewed her mom, I interviewed the cops, I read the trial transcripts. I spent years creating chronologies from the day Brandon was born, event by event, and then from the rape, hour by hour. But if I have to collapse a year into a night to get the story where it needs to be, I'll do it. Because if I show the audience every detail, they're going to hate me. The minute you tell it like a fairy tale, they're so happy.

Danny Leigh: Were you expecting Lana's legal action?

Kimberly Peirce: I wasn't, and that was naive. The first time we heard she was against the movie was before she saw it and, without going too deeply into it, somebody got to her. This wasn't Lana. So I insisted Fox fly her out, I watched the movie with her, and she was fine. But they continued the action, and guess what? First, the story's in the public domain, so I have a right to tell it. Second, I had her sign a release, so I could have defamed her if I'd wanted. Third, I didn't defame her, I spent five years bringing Lana to the screen in a way people could love.

Danny Leigh: She's probably more sympathetic than Brandon.

Kimberly Peirce: And probably more than she is in real life. Maybe I amplified Brandon's life in Falls City to create a love story that worked within a movie. Anyway, the judge said there isn't even a case here, so what does that say about Lana? She had sufficiently poor judgment to align herself with John and Tom and Brandon got killed, and look what's happened now.

Danny Leigh: How difficult was it to cast Brandon?

Kimberly Peirce: I started looking in 1995, so it was three years' worth of difficult. And I saw so many wonderful girls, but none of them could pass. We needed a girl who could pass on-screen and someone with enough experience to carry a feature. And a fight background was crucial – I didn't have time to train someone to make fight moves, we had to hit our marks and go. And we also needed someone who wasn't a star, because if it's hard to transcend class, then gender's even harder, and if she was famous she wouldn't shake free of either. So she had to be on that weird threshold of being totally brilliant and experienced without being famous [*laughter*]. Then by 1996 agents wouldn't send anybody to play Brandon because of the stigma attached to the role. So eventually at four weeks away from shooting we're having open calls. I told my producer Christine Vachon I didn't think I could make the movie unless Brandon was perfectly cast, it would just be a waste of everybody's time, so we pulled out all the stops and late one night a tape arrived. Beautiful androgynous person floats across the screen, cowboy hat, sock in her pants, Adam's apple, boy jaw, boy eyes. She had everything. And more than that, she smiled. Hilary loved being Brandon, just as Brandon loved being Brandon. So I told her she could have the role if, like De Niro in *Raging Bull*, she made a full transformation.

Danny Leigh: What did that involve?

Kimberly Peirce: I gave her Brandon's psychological history, I played her the tape of him being interviewed by the cops – which is terrible, you can hear how scared he is – and she absorbed all that. We took her up to Astor Place in New York where the boys get their hair cut – halfway through the woman says, 'She's too beautiful, I can't do it': get another hairdresser, buzz cut, powder the neck, and I saw a boy emerge before my eyes. She looked like Leonardo DiCaprio. We had a voice trainer, a physical trainer. I told her to live as a boy for four weeks and keep a journal. I wanted to ensure it wasn't an on-set creation.

Danny Leigh: The later scenes must have been traumatic to shoot.

Kimberly Peirce: It was terrible. The hardest thing was the stripping scene, because it was in wideshot, which meant everyone was in the room together. It was claustrophobic – Pete Sarsgaard, who played John Lotter, was throwing up between takes. I'd lived with this person for so long and here was the destruction of their spirit. It was painful for everyone.

Danny Leigh: Visually, it's very striking how you move between the bleak and the near hallucinatory.

Kimberly Peirce: The neo-realists were a definite influence on me, guys who shot the world as they saw it, but with poetry. I didn't use handheld all the time but I knew there was a place for it because I wanted it to look rough the way those kids' lives were rough. And the story was supposed to be reflected in the film-making – for instance in the rape scene there are four frame flashes viscerally knocking into you, like memory knocking on consciousness. Also, those kids escape into their imaginations – so the influences were Gus Van Sant certainly, Michael Powell, that kind of dream-life opulence. But it needed finessing – I got complaints from people saying the landscape shots were a distraction.

Danny Leigh: Certain moments reminded me of *River's Edge*.

Kimberly Peirce: *River's Edge* illustrated how to make a film about kids hanging out without boring the audience with endless scenes of kids hanging out [*laughter*]. And I love Frederick Elmes's work there – the greens, the blues, the body, and that beautiful, grainy pull out from the river at the opening.

Danny Leigh: Were you worried these influences might overshadow your film's identity?

Kimberly Peirce: Not at all. I love those movie-makers because they changed my life. So when I fell in love with Brandon and wanted to tell my Brandon story, I thought that when you're in a hard place you go back to the films you love and you find the answers. So it's not a question of being derivative, it's a question of learning.

QUEER AND PRESENT DANGER

B. Ruby Rich

Almost a decade ago, the biggest independent-film news was the arrival of a phenomenon dubbed (by this writer, in this publication) the 'New Queer Cinema' (*Sight & Sound*, September 1992). That was then, this is now. As this issue went to press, the most recent film that would seem to qualify for that moniker, *Boys Don't Cry*, had become one of the most acclaimed films of 1999. Based on the best made-for-the-movies true-crime story since *In Cold Blood*, *Boys Don't Cry* tells the tale of a small-town boy from the land of country-western music who transgressed the rules of gender and finance and paid with his life. The fact that he turned out to have been a biological female who had changed names and cities to pass as male was central to the case and, by now, the legend; the fact that he'd forged cheques, less so. Not only had Brandon Teena started life as Teena Brandon, but he'd won girls over with a special brand of romantic charm lacking in the male of the species in the backwaters of America. For sure, the story had possibilities.

Critical raves have poured in, from the FIPRESCI award at the 1999 London Film Festival to the breathlessly awaited Oscar nominations, where *Boys Don't Cry* looks to stand a chance of snagging at least one – for its luminous star Hilary Swank, who has already picked up a Golden Globe for her trouble. The coveted Independent Spirit Award nominations have already been announced, with first-time director Kimberly Peirce as well as her star and co-star Chlöe Sevigny qualifying, while critics' associations throughout the US have bestowed honours on director and cast. Peirce even picked up a Five Continents Award at the European Film Awards. Recently PopcornQ, the pioneering and immensely popular queer-film website, completed a poll of its visitors and named *Boys Don't Cry* one of the top queer films of 1999.

In so far as Peirce's true-life saga of Brandon Teena, a woman murdered for passing as a man, can be counted as the full-fledged flowering of the New Queer Cinema's early shoots, then the movement may really have arrived, hitting the big time at last. But not so fast: the story is more complicated than that, its conclusions less clear-cut, the movement itself in question, if not in total meltdown.

First of all, from the beginning, the New Queer Cinema was a more successful term for a moment than a movement. It was meant to catch the beat of a new kind of film- and video-making that was fresh, edgy, low-budget, inventive, unapologetic, sexy and stylistically daring. The godfather of the movement was the late great Derek Jarman, who pronounced himself finally able to connect with an audience thanks to the critical mass of the new films and videos that burned a clearing in the brush and attracted attention from the media as well as audiences. This was an exciting moment, but hardly due purely to cinematic developments. The era was defined by two other major but utterly unrelated events: the survival of the AIDS virus (but few of its victims) past the original crisis into a second decade and the proliferation of small-format video as a medium for both production and distribution. To these should be added the new alliances forged between lesbians and gay men in the wake of AIDS organising, along with an exponential growth in gay and lesbian film festivals servicing emotionally spent communities in need of relief and inspiration. A new generation was growing up and old genres were wearing out. Clearly there was now fertile ground in which something new and powerful could take root.

Creation is never explicable, really. Elements can be identified, but not how they came together, or why, or when. And even when we see something happen, there's rarely an explanation that satisfies. Why me? Why now? Even those caught up in the maelstrom are unlikely to know the answer. Similarly, when it's all over, there's never an adequate reason for why it had to end so soon. So it was with the New Queer Cinema and its short sweet climb from radical impulse to niche market.

In the late 1980s, Hollywood was too busy manufacturing blockbusters to take much notice of the independent world. But that changed, famously, in 1989 when *sex, lies and videotape* won the audience award at Sundance and proceeded to fill the bank accounts of an upstart distribution company by the name of Miramax. The queer moment for independent film owes its genesis not to money but to repression, namely the savage attacks by US right-wing politicians on government funding for such films as Todd Haynes's *Poison* (1990). The bad press, though, made for good reviews and decent box office. More dramatic features followed, laying claim to the same category: *Young Soul Rebels* (1991), *Swoon* (1992), *Go Fish* (1994), *All Over Me* (1996), *Beautiful Thing* (1996), *Lilies* (1996), *Watermelon Woman* (1997), and dozens and dozens more. The work spawned a whole sector of queer filmdom, not just genres but viewers and distributors and venues. By the late 1990s, there were well over 100 film festivals billed as queer; according to one survey, a full 80 per cent of the work shown there was never seen outside the queer circuit.

There were downsides, too, and they came along fast. First, the sheer volume diluted the quality. For critics the consequences could be dispiriting, as queer audiences flocked to films every bit as mediocre as those pulling in heterosexual dollars at multiplexes down the road. Soon enough the draw of the queer dollar and the aura of a queer fashion began to attract heterosexual directors eager to make their mark and skilled enough to do it well. Remember *Heavenly Creatures? Bound*, anyone? If imitation truly is the sincerest form of flattery, then *Chasing Amy* (1996) was probably the most sincere product of its season. Not only did Kevin Smith manage a career comeback, but also his film managed to draw all the attention in a year when numerous lesbian independent features languished for lack of publicity and audience. Queerer than thou? Identity politics doesn't meld well with market considerations. Soon enough the glut of product began to be blamed by distributors for the receding public: lesbian and gay ticket-buyers were no longer reliable and could no longer be counted on to rush to the box office in support of 'queer' work. The problem had become so acute by 1999 that PopcornQ started up a first-weekend club to try to fill the seats for queer films.

But what's a queer film? The films and their receptions over the past few years have rearranged all such definitions. *Gods and Monsters* (1998), for instance, was such a crossover hit (i.e. beyond queer audiences to straight ones) that it propelled Sir Ian McKellen into an Oscar nomination and won writer/director Bill Condon a best adapted screenplay Oscar. The film, which beautifully excavates the life of James Whale (creator of the *Frankenstein* movies), crossed over in part because of its Hollywood-history theme. I suspect it was also helped by the homophobia of the Brendan Fraser character, who provided an identificatory figure for audience members suffering from the same ailment, and by the participation of such a class act as McKellen (stand by for more about actors and the New Queer Cinema). Finally, though, I'd wager that *Gods and Monsters*, a film I dearly love, could achieve success beyond the previous run of queer films not only for these reasons, but also because it's set in a particular corner of the modern edition of Brideshead-land, a place in the not-so-distant past where British accents of the proper vintage can be heard and money is still required for entry (except, à la Sirk, for the gardener). The same American affection for upstairs-downstairs dramas helped John Maybury's exquisite *Love Is the Devil: Study for a Portrait of Francis Bacon* (1998); the box-office triad of high art, rough trade and a tragic death never fails, however queer the particular application.

Two other films might be seen, in retrospect, to have both gilded the lily and sounded the death knell of the New Queer Cinema. One is Wong Kar-Wai's *Happy Together* (1997); the other Lisa Cholodenko's *High Art* (1998). Both could tear your heart out with one hand tied behind their respective backs. (Indeed, tragedy seems paradoxically to have been the favoured tone of much of the New Queer Cinema.) *Happy Together* illustrated how brilliantly a heterosexual director could capture the essence and nuance of queer romance, lust, jealousy and rage; in so doing, it also pointed up how cowardly many of the certified-queer films had been in dealing with the realities of queer relationships. So, you see, it seemed to be saying, it all comes down to genius after all, despite all your labels of sexual identity.

As for *High Art*, well, that's a bit different. Lisa Cholodenko very much fitted the mould of the New Queer Cinema film-maker. Not only was she a certified lesbian, but she'd even been inspired to quit her career in Hollywood and move to New York to enrol in film-making at Columbia University after reading an article about these new films. Cholodenko's *High Art* defied all the prior taboos of contemporary lesbian cinema by showing the dark side of lesbian society: cut-throat ambition and opportunism, infidelity, drug addiction. The film charted new territory and did so brilliantly. It even had the nerve to go for an unhappy ending. But it also did something else: it made stars of its actresses. Ally Sheedy launched a much deserved 'comeback' after winning awards and praise for her daring role, while Radha Mitchell showed she could play American and Patricia Clarkson, who played German so well, expanded a cult following into more widespread admiration.

With such films, it could be a moment of triumphant consolidation for the New Queer Cinema. Yet the opposite would seem to suggest itself: that it has become so successful as to have dispersed itself in any number of elsewheres. Lacking the concentrated creative presence and focused community responsiveness of the past, the New Queer Cinema has become just another niche market, another product line pitched at one particular type of discerning consumer. At a time when casting has become essential to getting independent films financed and produced, it's clear why actors have to be involved. On the other hand, it's the runaway success of the New Queer Cinema works that has turned them into such welcome vehicles for actors, reversing the trend that in the past saw them turn away from films that would push sexual identity into a zone of ambiguity. Suddenly, queer directors can get actors. 'We actually got to cast this film,' said one producer in reference to *Boys Don't Cry*.

And cast it they did! Hilary Swank's performance as Brandon Teena has the film working overtime. It is Swank who makes the audience hold its collective breath at the magnificent, fine-tuned cockiness of the performance, capturing the exact feel of a young guy in the full flush of puberty. And it is Swank who makes the awards audiences hold their breath once more: the boyish Brandon transmutes back again into sexy babe as Swank shows up in form-hugging dresses, batting her eyes and thanking her husband. The good news? That was all acting. The bad news? The same. In the old days the New Queer Cinema tended to be peopled by friends or lovers of the director, or sympathetic actors who wanted to help put the picture over. Now it's turned out that starring in a gay- or lesbian-themed film can be a career-making move. (This can, of course, be a huge advantage for queer film-makers. Most recently, Ana Kokkinos benefited from the trend when she was able to cast an Australian television idol as the star of her passionate coming-of-age tale and gut-wrenching family drama *Head On.*)

Boys Don't Cry has another problem fitting into any imaginary New Queer Cinema canon: it's not about a lesbian at all. When the real-life Brandon Teena murder took place, a slew of stories followed in the gay press. One, by US journalist Donna Minkowitz, took a lot of heat for presenting Brandon as a butch lesbian – an identity roundly rejected by the transgender community that turned out for the murder trial. As an earlier documentary, *The Brandon Teena Story* (1994), made clear, Brandon saw himself as a transgendered person (even though at the time of his death he hadn't yet had any surgery) not as a lesbian or as a woman. Gender confusion haunts the reviews of the film and even showed up at its big premiere bash at the Toronto International Film Festival, where Lindsay Law, then head of its distributor Fox Searchlight, rose to offer a toast to Brandon and 'her bravery' only to be followed by director Peirce toasting Brandon for letting them film 'his story'.

It's the murder at the centre of *Boys Don't Cry* that links it, perhaps perversely, with the other hot film of 1999, *The Talented Mr. Ripley*, another lethal cocktail of covert queerness and killing. Back to back, the two make a new sort of sense. Step out of the cosmopolitan world of big cities at the turn of the millennium, switch the time zones into the lockstep past or redneck present, switch identity into attraction to the same sex without the baggage of modern queer identity, wander into the land where the US military policy under Clinton (don't ask, don't tell) becomes instead a social habit, and *voilà*, there's a perfect set-up for a new cinematic code of conduct: kill or be killed. Ripley kills, Brandon is killed. Both of them were invented: one by a writer, one by himself. Both based their lives on a driving need to be something they were not (wealthy, male). And both inventions depended on not being found out, lest the price be death, spilling either one's own blood or someone else's. Ripley becomes, in this scenario, the mirror image of Brandon. Is either one a New Queer Cinema product? I think not. If only because no such thing can exist any more.

If it did, though, I can think of another film entirely that I'd have to nominate for the honour: *Being John Malkovich*. Here's a movie that's all about gender confusion, gender trading and the kind of identity destabilisation brought about by celebrity worship. Its characters are deeply implicated in the whole project of gender positioning, a crisis precipitated by the now-familiar device of discovering a portal leading into John Malkovich's brain. As a result Lotte (Cameron Diaz) is bowled over by her unexpected attraction to another woman and immediately assumes she's going to need gender-reassignment surgery, as though lesbianism were beyond the pale, a lesser alternative. *Malkovich* is just the sort of cheeky and original film that first made the New Queer Cinema possible. And it's got something none of these other films can offer, apart from its box-office numbers: it offers a lesbian happy ending, though somehow none of the newspaper reviews ever mentions it.

I think of *Being John Malkovich* as a mainstream movie made possible by the advances of the New Queer Cinema. I like to imagine one of those television voiceovers accompanying any awards ceremony in which it figures. I can just about hear the stentorian tone, acknowledging the debt as rewards are bestowed, as though movies followed the traditions of science, rock music or pharmaceuticals. For truly, madly, deeply, without all that groundbreaking and heart-stopping work of the early days, it's impossible to imagine the existence of the more mainstream films coming along now to play with the same concepts, cast bigger stars and shuffle the deck for fresh strategies. Don't get me wrong. I'm happy to have them. I'm happy to be part of a new niche market. And, yes, I'm working on my ability to synthesise current fashion with memories of the good ole days. I think of it as a millennial strategy.

Night on Earth (Jim Jarmusch, 1991)

Section 4: Miniaturists and Minimalists

ROADSIDE ATTRACTIONS

J. Hoberman

Jim Jarmusch may be the hottest American independent on the international film circuit, but he's scarcely a prophet without honour in his adopted hometown. On the contrary, his film *Night on Earth*, which has been holding for months at two Manhattan first-run cinemas, received rave reviews from all four of New York's dailies, not to mention the *Wall Street Journal*.

Indeed, it would not be too much to say that Jarmusch is adored in New York – as much a local hero as Woody Allen or Martin Scorsese or, more controversially, Brooklyn's Spike Lee. Each of Jarmusch's last four features has had its American premiere at the New York Film Festival (the packed press previews have been events in themselves) and, with Jonathan Demme relocated to exurbia, Jarmusch is the best-known film-maker associated with the downtown bohemia. For some, he *is* that bohemia.

Night on Earth, hailed in the *New York Times* as Jarmusch's 'most effervescent work to date', was heralded by a *Times* profile as warm and gushing as the film-maker himself is cool and taciturn – a portrait of the artist as a one-man fount of gentrification. 'Jim Jarmusch's planet is the Lower East Side, its bars, bodegas and its pavement make up his home, his office, and his hangout,' the piece began, going on to describe an evening on 'planet Jarmusch' that consisted mainly of a brief stroll around the director's neighbourhood (noting such landmarks as Martin Scorsese's school) and a few quick drinks at a watering-hole populated by 'old Italians playing Vic Damone'.

What's striking is that Jarmusch has in fact done relatively little filming on his 'planet'. Only his first (and weakest) feature, *Permanent Vacation* (1980), is set entirely in New York. *Stranger than Paradise* (1984) opens in Lower Manhattan, but soon takes to the road; *Down by Law* (1986) and *Mystery Train* (1989) unfold in a mythical South. What is distinctively New York is Jarmusch's attitude – his cultivated immigrant-eye-view, highly developed taste for urban detritus, studied minimalism, beat disdain, fondness for roadside attractions and fascination with chance encounters. 'Why movies? Why don't we just go outside and watch real life instead,' he invited the *Times*, propounding the basic tenet of the Warholian aesthetic.

Jarmusch is always in danger of being overrated. Despite the cosmic perspective implicit in its title, *Night on Earth* is the work of a miniaturist. Less overtly stylised and more performer-oriented than previous Jarmusch efforts, this anthology of five stories, each the drama of a cabdriver and a fare, set in five cities (LA, New York, Paris, Rome, Helsinki) is less guided tour than *tour de force* – the logistical complexity of shooting in the quintet of cities is dwarfed by the ingenuity required to shoot in five different cabs. The taxi is a vehicle – literally – and each actor in Jarmusch's splendidly eccentric cast is some sort of text. (There hasn't been a film since Godard's *King Lear* in which the performers' mere presence carried so much cross-referential baggage.)

Night on Earth opens, at twilight, in LA with one-and-a-half genuine movie stars, Winona Ryder and Gena Rowlands, as the first combination. With her backwards baseball cap and oversized shirt, Ryder is the ultimate teenager, while Rowlands, in an eye-catching yin-yang suit, plays a high-powered casting agent. It's a mother/daughter riff (one sucks her cheeks, the other rolls her eyes), but the explicit, almost hackneyed rejection of the Hollywood ethos with which the episode ends articulates the Jarmusch credo – albeit, having outsider Rowlands playing would-be Svengali to the near-bankable Ryder is given a further (and perhaps unintentional) twist by the kabuki 'naturalism' of Ryder's performance.

Jarmusch prospers in the realm of diminished expectations, and if I found *Night on Earth* a more enjoyable movie on second viewing – far from the hoopla that unavoidably surrounded its world premiere at the NYFF – it's because I was prepared to savour its small, sometimes cornball, pleasures. The brief illuminations – Ryder working her bubble gum in the frame's foreground while Rowlands works her cellular phone in the seat behind – are matched by the smoggy montage of deserted swimming pools and decrepit fast-food joints that introduces LA, the edgy glamour of the New York City locations, the discordant hurdy-gurdy of Tom Waits's spare, jazzy nocturne, the velvet richness of Frederick Elmes's night photography. (Elmes, of course, is a reference point himself – having shot Cassavetes' *The Killing of a Chinese Bookie*, as well as David Lynch's *Blue Velvet*.)

To the degree that *Night on Earth* is a movie about acting, Jarmusch's least likely ensemble is his most memorable. The New York sequence has a Brooklyn-bound B-boy named YoYo (Giancarlo Esposito at his most manic) trying to hail a taxi in Times Square. He is reduced to waving money when a yellow cab, tortuously driven by an affable East German (Armin Mueller-Stahl), arrives as if by magic. The interaction is pure Jarmusch: the two men wear matching aviator hats, both with the ear-flaps out; the German is a former circus clown ('Get the fuck outta here,' the astonished YoYo enthuses), while the New Yorker is no mean schoolyard performer.

The group is made complete when YoYo spots his sister-in-law Angela (Rosie Perez) striding through the deserted Lower East Side. Working in tandem with Esposito's ebullience, Perez's patented head-bob – emphasising the fastest mouth in American movies – generates enough exoticism to warm the wide-eyed driver (not to mention Jarmusch), as the movie heads deeper into night, an other-worldly Fassbinder survivor piloting two savvy denizens of planet Spike Lee.

If Paris at 4 a.m. is necessarily more picturesque than Brooklyn, another immigrant driver (African actor Isaach de Bankolé) is having an even rougher night – the Band-Aid applied to his sullen brow is the bright pink signifier of some recent, if unspecified, mishap. After dumping two obnoxious African diplomats, he's close to tears – the darkness coalescing in the form of a blind woman (Béatrice Dalle, the eponymous, self-mutilated heroine of *Betty Blue*). Eyes rolling in her head, head swivelling on her neck, Dalle is beautiful and monstrous; the driver's fascination with his sightless fare is matched by her prickly conceit. His questions squelched by her contempt, his charity confounded by her self-sufficiency, he drops her off by the Seine.

In a final sound gag, she hears his car crash and her downturned smear of a mouth twists into a smile.

Meanwhile, in a grungier Rome, Roberto Benigni cruises for a fare. Dalle's self-regard is nothing compared to Benigni's, as blinded by a pair of wraparound shades, he careers around piazzas and down alleys, singing, ranting, gesticulating – a manic monologue in search of an audience. Midway through he picks up a priest and, although initially put out ('bad luck, touch my balls'), soon turns his cab into a freewheeling confessional – regaling the priest with descriptions of his affairs with pumpkins, sheep and sisters-in-law. In the end, *Night on Earth* moves from an agitated depression to an actual one. The final episode not only features Aki Kaurismäki regular Matti Pellonpää as the stoic driver with the tragic story, it invites allegory by naming him Mika (after the other Kaurismäki) and his drunken fare Aki.

True, Jarmusch has to fight a sentimental streak the way his drivers have to buck traffic. And yes, *Night on Earth* starts running out of gas well before dawn breaks like a wino's bottle on the Helsinki pavement. Yet the movie is something more than a linear ride. It has the feeling of an endless loop, filled with surprising echoes and unexpected cross-references. The gigantic Rocky and Bullwinkle and the LA Coliseum glimpsed in the opening sequence reappear after a fashion in subsequent episodes – and they're only the most traditional of archetypes.

Whether by chance or design, *Night on Earth* has a kind of overarching narrative, based on the evolution of cabbie and fare from one chance encounter to the next – one immigrant driver melting into another as Rosie Perez mutates into Béatrice Dalle, Benigni's confession segues into Pellonpää's – as though they were a single pair speeding through some vast celestial city on the road to eternity. *Night on Earth* may not mean any more than it is, but in it Jarmusch (and Elmes) have created a new constellation, call it the Cabdriver, and populated its stars with transmigrated souls.

HOME AND AWAY

Peter Keogh

Peter Keogh: Is this your neighbourhood?

Jim Jarmusch: I live a little east of here. I've lived here for fifteen years.

Peter Keogh: It seems that each of your films moves further out of town. First to more distant American cities, and now this one is international. Is this a conscious trend?

Jim Jarmusch: Not really. Though perhaps it has something to do with the fact that making my first film, *Permanent Vacation*, enabled me to travel. I got invited to different film festivals and travelled to promote my films and as a result I met a lot of people outside New York. And I tend to write things for specific people. This film is a good example of that.

Peter Keogh: Your films are inspired by the characters?

Jim Jarmusch: Usually I write for specific actors and have an idea of a character I want to collaborate with them on. The story is suggested by those characters.

Peter Keogh: Does the gestation process take a long time?

Jim Jarmusch: It differs. I carry them around for a long time, thinking about the actors and the characters to make for them. But then I usually write them pretty fast – for example, I wrote this one in eight or ten days.

Peter Keogh: I'm sure the production was more complicated than usual.

Jim Jarmusch: Just shooting in cars was complicated. Also shooting episodes in this way. Usually when you make a film it takes the first two weeks or so to understand how to work with your crew, but in this case, we prepared each story for about a week and shot for ten days and were out of there and on to the next place. And shooting at night outdoors in the winter and shooting with crews that didn't always speak English were complicated. But we had very good crews because we hired people in different cities based on their enthusiasm rather than on their experience. So we had enthusiastic people – they had to be to stand outside at night, all night.

Peter Keogh: This could be described as a low-rent version of Wenders's *Until the End of the World*. Did you know he was making his film at the same time?

Jim Jarmusch: I knew he was making a project that was taking him to cities around the world. But the films are very different in that his plot crisscrosses through all the locations, whereas ours is simultaneous stories that take place solely in each place rather than intercutting.

Peter Keogh: Blindness seems to be a motif in each episode.

Jim Jarmusch: On a lot of different levels. Although I'm perhaps not the best person to be analytical about that, it's in there. I was more aware of it while editing the film than while writing or directing it.

Peter Keogh: Could you analyse it a bit?

Jim Jarmusch: Well, a lot of people have talked to me about the idea that people don't see what's right in front of them. In the Paris story, the girl is actually blind, but in a way it's the driver who's blind because he thinks her blindness must be a weakness, a flaw she has to deal with, a handicap. So he spends most of the conversation trying to find that weakness to support his preconception of her. And really she doesn't have a weakness. She's blind. That's it. It's who she is. In other stories people are also blind to each other and to their own situations.

Peter Keogh: Is any allusion to Béatrice Dalle's poking her eye out in *Betty Blue* intended?

Jim Jarmusch: No, I had forgotten that she had done that in *Betty Blue* until after making the film, when I saw *Betty Blue* again.

Peter Keogh: Another motif in your films, beginning with *Permanent Vacation*, in which the character leaves and an emigré from France replaces him, is that of immigrants and rootlessness. Why is this an obsession?

Jim Jarmusch: People ask me about that a lot. I don't know. When I was a student I lived in Paris for a year. It was the first time I'd been outside the United States and it really changed the way I thought about the world. It also inspired me to make films because I saw a lot of movies I hadn't seen in New York and I became fascinated by the form of cinema.

Peter Keogh: Do you see your own style growing more complicated since *Stranger than Paradise*, which consists of several long takes barely disrupted by a camera movement?

Jim Jarmusch: It changes depending on what the story needs. This film is much more dialogue-oriented. Because we're in an enclosed space, I didn't have room for characters to express themselves physically or in moments when there is no dialogue as I could in *Stranger than Paradise*. That's what I like most about that film: the moments between dialogue when you understand what's happening between people without them saying anything. If you think about taking a taxi, it's something insignificant in your daily life; in a film when someone takes a taxi, you see them get in, then there's a cut, then you see them get out. So in a way the content of this film is made up of things that would usually be taken out. It's similar to what I like about *Stranger than Paradise* or *Down by Law*: the moments between what we think of as significant.

Peter Keogh: Your first film was very solipsistic and was focused on one character. This one deals with several characters and many points of view. It seems that each film has more characters, their stories are more episodic, people bounce off each other. Do you feel your scope is expanding in this way?

Jim Jarmusch: No. In fact, it's accidental. After *Mystery Train*, I never intended to make another film that was episodic, or whatever you want to call this form; I had another script I had written which was about a single character. But for reasons too complicated to go into, that film was postponed and so I wrote this one very fast, out of frustration.

Peter Keogh: It probably has the most impressive cast of any of your films, with Gena Rowlands, Armin Mueller-Stahl, Winona Ryder...

Jim Jarmusch: Gena and Winona arrived through a very strange set of circumstances. I had just finished the first draft of the script and had written the LA story for two male characters. But I wasn't satisfied with it. I had written it for a specific actor who found just as I finished the script that he would not be available. And then in a two-day period I met Winona and Gena separately – completely by accident. Gena is one of my favourite actors, and Winona is one of my favourite young, American, female actors. In the course of my conversation with each I described the project and they both seemed interested. And then I rewrote the story for them and gave them scripts and they both said yes. I wrote specifically for other actors too: Rosie Perez, Isaach de Bankolé, Béatrice Dalle, Roberto Benigni and three of the four actors in Finland. So I already had about 70 per cent of the actors in my head while writing and 30 per cent were due to circumstances.

Peter Keogh: Do you improvise once you start shooting?

Jim Jarmusch: We do a lot of improvisation in the rehearsal process; in fact, we rehearse a lot of scenes that are not in the film, but are the characters in character. They are scenes I play around with and out of that I get a lot of new ideas. Then while we're shooting, how much improvising we do depends on the actors. Obviously I prefer to improvise in rehearsals because you're not burning money. But some actors need a longer leash. Giancarlo Esposito improvises a lot, too. The guys in Finland stayed much closer to the script once we'd rehearsed it. To me, the essence of each scene is what is important, not the exact dialogue. I like to find dialogue that I like and that the actors like, but there is an infinite number of ways of expressing something, so as long as the idea remains the same, the language can change. What's most important is that it seems natural and in character.

Peter Keogh: Has this always been your procedure or has it developed over time?

Jim Jarmusch: It's always been my procedure, though I've become better at playing in the rehearsals and gradually focusing towards the script. In a way, I do everything backwards. Most directors get a script that they didn't write and then someone casts that. I start with the characters, the actors themselves. I'm much more a film-maker than a film director, in the sense that a director can go in and take over a project, get it going, whereas for me it starts from a basic perception, sometimes not even accurate, of a person, an actor, a quality of that personality, and I want to grow a character on it. It's more organic.

Peter Keogh: Do you feel a kinship to Cassavetes, Scorsese and other directors who proceed in this organic fashion?

Jim Jarmusch: I admire that way of working. Scorsese is from this neighbourhood. The way people talk in his films is so realistic and strong, you never doubt that they are those characters. Language is very important to me. I love the way language takes on slang, gets mixed up by different influences, different cultures. And I like working in other languages. In *Mystery Train*, I got the chance to direct actors in Japanese, which I don't speak. And I don't speak Finnish and I don't really speak Italian, though I understand it somewhat.

Peter Keogh: How do you write the dialogue in other languages – do you give the actors the idea and then let them work it out?

Jim Jarmusch: I write the script in English and then I work with translators, or friends, or the actors themselves to find the right way to translate it. Language is just a kind of code we use, so as long as I know that the actors and I translate the script together and are very attentive to what kind of people these are, for example working-class Finnish guys and how they would talk, it's okay. In the Paris episode of *Night on Earth*, for example, the African driver speaks in a very different way from the girl, who speaks a kind of street French, slang, tough, rough French. His French is more like that of an immigrant. These things are important so that it feels real.

Peter Keogh: You're often referred to as a minimalist. Do you agree with that label?

Jim Jarmusch: I think of minimalist as a label stuck on certain visual artists. But I don't really feel associated with them.

Peter Keogh: There are also literary minimalists – Raymond Carver, Annie Beatty.

Jim Jarmusch: I think maybe what they're saying is that the films are very light on plot and therefore minimal stylistically as well. My style is certainly not Byzantine or florid or elaborate. It's pretty simple. Reduced.

Peter Keogh: Would you say that your use of film language is very minimal, but is growing in vocabulary?

Jim Jarmusch: There are more cuts in it, but we're still limited as to what camera positions we can have. We also don't see nearly as much of the city from the point of view of the cab as I shot because when I was editing I couldn't find places to stick it in – it seemed superficial to go away from moments with the characters, which is what the film is about, just for the sake of other visual input.

Peter Keogh: Since *Stranger than Paradise*, your sensibility and style seem to have been dominant in American independent film-making, and also in film-making around the world, such as the Kaurismäki brothers. How do you account for it?

Jim Jarmusch: It's hard to respond to that. I don't know if my early films have influenced those people or whether it's a simultaneous reaction to things being glossy and quick cut – you know, using montage sequences à la *Miami Vice*, slap a music cue over a sequence in which the characters don't hear the music, the whole MTV aesthetic. Aki Kaurismäki is one of my favourite directors; I'm excited to see his new film, *La Vie de bohème*.

Peter Keogh: Do you see your films and those like yours as an alternative to a Hollywood that's encroaching on all independent cinema?

Jim Jarmusch: I'm interested in types of film. In films there's such a wide scope – from porno films to Kung Fu to Michael Snow to Stan Brakhage and Scorsese. Yet at the moment it seems that in Hollywood the idea is to saturate markets and release films wider and wider, so the margins get smaller.

Peter Keogh: Do you read reviews?

Jim Jarmusch: With my last film, *Mystery Train*, I reached a point where I was hardly reading anything, except when people told me about negative reviews, which I found more interesting. I respect other people's opinions of my films more than my own because I'm so inside – I don't even know if I like my own films, sometimes. I certainly never look at them again after I'm done with them. I'm at a point with this film where I don't need to see it again. I've been watching it for video transfers – so I'm only seeing the surface now; I've reached that point where I'm not seeing the film.

Peter Keogh: You like making the films, I imagine.

Jim Jarmusch: My favourite part is shooting; collaborating with all those different people and everybody working together towards one thing.

Peter Keogh: What are you working on now?

Jim Jarmusch: I have two scripts in the works which are very different from each other. I've never written two things at once before, but I've been making notes back and forth and carrying them around for a while. I haven't had time to start writing them because I've been travelling and promoting this film, getting prints ready and so on.

Peter Keogh: Which is your favourite of your movies?

Jim Jarmusch: *Down by Law*, I think, because shooting it was so much fun. Being in New Orleans was great and we had a really wild time. In retrospect I don't know how we got through it – it seemed as if we had a celebration after each night of shooting and I don't know physically how we got the film made. I tend to see my films in retrospect like home movies – I don't see the film any more, but I remember the experience of making it.

Peter Keogh: You have a mythic structure to that film: I remember the scene where they come to the crossroads. And with this film the basic structure is the rotation of Earth.

Jim Jarmusch: I have a very classical way of thinking about telling stories; I still cling to that need to order things in a classical way. Like *Stranger than Paradise* is three acts with a coda, as is *Down by Law*; before prison, in prison and their escape from prison, with a coda at the end. So formally, I use that even though the acts don't necessarily follow the classical form where there is a conflict presented and resolved. In *Night on Earth*, the crossing time zones, being on the planet at the same time and the sun going down at the beginning and coming up at the end helped me give an overall form.

Peter Keogh: Bentley College invited me to be in a panel to discuss one of your films; I was wondering if they asked you, too?

Jim Jarmusch: Yes they did... when is that?

Peter Keogh: It's tonight.

SLACKER
USA 1991
Director: Richard Linklater

A young man arrives by long-distance bus in Austin, Texas. Hailing a cab, he tells the driver his theory of alternative realities. After leaving the cab, he crosses a road where, a moment later, a middle-aged woman is knocked down and killed by a hit-and-run driver. The driver, her son, goes home and is subsequently arrested. Two neighbours comment on his arrest before going their separate ways. One of them, who carries a guitar, encounters a young blonde woman...

Continuing this relay-team pattern, the film follows a succession of the inhabitants of Austin (many, though not all of them, young), moving from one to the next as their paths intersect. They include a man with a conspiracy theory about people being abducted by NASA; a woman who wants to sell what she claims is Madonna's pap smear; a bunch of children into voyeurism and stealing Diet Coke from machines; a would-be writer obsessed with Kennedy assassination theories; a man returning from the funeral of his hated stepfather; a young man who tries to hold up a bookshop, but is gently disarmed by the elderly, anarchist owner; a woman making an outdoor model of her menstrual cycle; and a hippy who believes the Smurfs are a form of religious indoctrination.

Finally, a man broadcasting a litany of violence from a loudspeaker van is filmed by a laughing group of young people in a convertible. This gang, all equipped with cameras and busily filming each other, drive out into the country and climb to the summit of a rock high above a river. One of them hurls his camera down into the river. The film's viewpoint spirals down with it and the film blacks out.

* * *

With *Slacker*, Richard Linklater crosses *The Phantom of Liberty* with David Byrne's *True Stories* – but comes up with something less detached, and even more inconsequential, than either. And where Byrne's narrator remained the quizzical outsider, inviting our superior amusement at his small-town freakshow, Linklater signals identification with his compulsive verbalisers by becoming one of them, playing the taxi-fare hung up on alternative realities who initiates the narrative chain reaction. Not only that, but Linklater's character, with his belief that 'every thought you have creates its own reality', sets the tone of the film, since more than one of his fellow citizens is evidently far gone into parallel universe.

Slacker shares its constituency of fringe dwellers with Douglas Coupland's recent novel *Generation X*: young no-hopers doing nothing much, or at most 'McJobs' – short-term, dead-end, mindless labour. But while Coupland, for all his modishly lax narrative, sticks largely to a recurrent group of characters, Linklater never follows the same person twice. Like a dog distracted by a new and more promising scent, he meanders from one digression to the next, always interested but without urgency. Vignettes may last a few seconds, or five minutes. Now and then we get short snatches of almost-plot – the hit-and-run matricide, the old anarchist fantasising about Orwell – at other times a brief gag line. As a woman is pulled in for shoplifting, an older couple walk past: 'She's in my ethics class,' one observes.

Slackers, for Linklater, are people who 'spend their whole lives in their own heads' – where they evidently generate no shortage of paranoid conspiracy theories. (Though maybe no more so than in America as a whole.) So we get the JFK-assassination freak, the guy who believes 'the Masons control history', another who ties together NASA, the CIA, the greenhouse effect and an undisclosed Mars landing in 1962 – and, most engaging of all, the pot-head who claims the Smurfs are designed to 'get kids used to seeing blue people' in preparation for the coming of Krishna.

What is absent from *Slacker* is any significant political dimension. Though one irascible man snarls, 'I may live badly – but at least I don't have to work to do it,' there's little sense of serious deprivation, nor any suggestion that these marginal characters are the victims of callous economic policy. Which isn't necessarily a fault. Linklater has chosen to present his 'slackers' (most of whom seem to be busily, if not gainfully, employed) on their own terms, neither pitying nor patronising them. The result is a film of quirky, unpredictable and oddly poetic charm.

Philip Kemp

SURE FIRE
USA 1990
Director: Jon Jost

Circleville, Utah. In a cafe, Wes and his friend Larry talk about a local woman, Sandra Jean, who has disappeared. Wes asks Larry to pick up a rifle for him in the neighbouring town. As Wes is about to leave, the sheriff takes a phone call: Sandra Jean's body has been found. Wes calls on Dick Blackwell, a banker, to get backing for a property scheme, and tells him to transfer funds from Wes's own account to cover interest payments due on Larry's overdraft.

Wes's wife Bobbi visits Larry's wife, Ellen, who is missing her daughter, away at college. Bobbi relates a distressing dream about a bird caught on barbed wire. When Larry gets home, the news that Wes has paid the interest causes a row between Larry and Ellen. Wes arrives home, shows his son Phillip how to trampoline, and gives Bobbi elaborate instructions on various tasks. She reacts coldly.

On the way to a deer hunt, Wes patronisingly offers Larry a job, which he turns down. At the camp, in front of Larry and another friend, Dennis, Wes presents Phillip with his first rifle and delivers a long lecture on how to use it. Later, alone with Phillip, Wes attempts a man-to-man talk about sex. Phillip reveals Bobbi is planning to leave for California, adding that if she does he will go with her. Wes is furious.

The hunting party splits into pairs, and Wes accompanies Phillip. In the woods, Larry and Dennis hear two distant shots, and come upon Wes and Phillip dead, apparently both shot by Wes. With Larry and Ellen, the sheriff goes to break the news to Bobbi.

*　*　*

It is fourteen years since the last UK release of a Jon Jost fiction feature. That film, *Last Chants for a Slow Dance*, also had Tom Blair playing a rampant egomaniac who ends up committing an act of senseless violence. But where Tom Bates in the earlier film was aggressively nihilistic, an unrepentant destroyer, the Wes of *Sure Fire* is a more ambivalent, even pitiable, figure. Far better integrated into his community than Bates, from one angle he could even be seen as an ideal citizen – supportive husband, solicitous father, generous friend and keen entrepreneur. Which is clearly how he wants to see himself.

It's his desperate need to have everyone else go along with his self-image that turns Wes into a monster of control, unable to relax his grip on those around him. At one point we see him pumping bullets into a target, each time hitting closer to the centre, exercising over his gun the kind of mastery he longs to exercise over people. Soon afterwards, telling his wife Bobbi how to handle a young man working for them, he lays down a long, manically detailed scenario of what she should say and do, right down to the exact words, gestures and tone of voice. Conventional film grammar would punctuate such a monologue with occasional cutaway shots of Bobbi; Jost instead holds steadily on Wes, tracking slowly in, giving us no clue how his wife's reacting or even if she's still in the room. Only at the very end of the spiel do we see her exasperated glare, as her 'Are you done, Wes?' comes with the force of a slap.

Here as elsewhere the film's pared-down economy (not just financial, though that too) serves to clinch the impact of the scene. Jost can do more with less than almost any other film-maker around, and there are passages in *Sure Fire* whose austerity would make Bresson look fidgety. The camera moves very little, often not at all, yet there's no feeling of stasis – rather of poised stillness, an unwavering gaze that takes in, and enhances, the emotional intensity of the action.

Naturalism has never been Jost's aim, but his stylised, even minimalist technique can create an exceptionally rich sense of place. *Sure Fire* was shot entirely on location, using only four professional players (the rest of the cast were local people) and allowing the story to develop out of 'the opportunities at hand'. The stern, beautiful landscape of Utah becomes as much a character as any of the actors, and Jost uses it to enlarge and comment on what happens. In the final scene, rather than follow the sheriff into Bobbi's house – since we can predict just what he's likely to say – the camera leaves him on the porch and rises to execute a slow 360° pan around the treetops and the distant mountains. As it circles, blood-red letters appear along the bottom of the screen: the last of three quotes from the Book of Mormon that punctuate the film.

Jost has long since sloughed off the Godardian didacticism that encumbered early works such as *Angel City*, and these Mormon texts hardly feel like the film's 'message'. Instead the effect of their lapidary certainties ('The works, and the designs, and the purposes of God cannot be frustrated'), set against the stark outlines of trees and mountains, is of a meditation on the landscape and all the national myths tied up with it – Manifest Destiny, the frontier, go-getting, men in a man's world, and so on – that could give rise to someone like Wes.

Sure Fire is dedicated to Jost's father, a professional soldier, and the film is partly 'a kind of self-therapeutic, highly metaphoric working out of a bad relationship with my father', which no doubt accounts for its insight into the pathos of Wes, the loneliness behind his non-stop bluster. But Wes also stands for something Jost hates and vehemently opposes in his film-making career: 'the American Way [that] has no place or time for smallness, because it is all too desperately busy trying to mask its emptiness with bombast'. In a *Film Comment* article last year, Jost likened Hollywood movies to the fleshy magnitudes of Rubens, and his own determinedly small-scale work to the quiet subtlety of Vermeer. The comparison might sound pretentious; but it's one that the richness and poetic complexity of *Sure Fire* go a long way towards justifying.

Philip Kemp

THE FIRST KISS TAKES SO LONG

Ben Thompson

In 1989, Richard Linklater met a woman in a toyshop in Philadelphia. They walked around the city together, conversing intimately, deep into the night. For Linklater, the only thing holding him back from complete immersion in this brief encounter was the nagging suspicion that it 'could be a movie'. Now it is. *Before Sunrise* shares the less-than-24-hour timespan of his two previous films. But whereas Linklater's groundbreaking mid-twenties lifestyle epic *Slacker* (1991) could boast not far short of a hundred characters, and his hazy but perspicacious high-school memoir *Dazed and Confused* (1993) had between twenty and thirty, *Before Sunrise* puts just two characters 'under a microscope to see what would happen'.

Set in Vienna, which Linklater describes as being 'a lot like Austin – full of smart people in coffee shops at a loss for what to do next', *Before Sunrise* pursues his theme of roads not taken. Jesse – a rangy American Euro-railer, played by Ethan Hawke – persuades Julie Delpy's smart French student Céline to get off a train with him on the grounds that this will forestall the moment in twenty years time when she will wonder what might have happened if she had. With the same capriciousness that led it to constantly hare off to meet new people in *Slacker*, Linklater's camera opts to stay with them, even when potential distractions – an arguing couple on the train, a German avant-garde theatre troupe – seem to offer more in the way of dramatic reward.

Slowing down the traditionally accelerated screen romance to something which at least feels like real time proves to be a productive device, allowing compelling ambiguities to open up, not only in the characters' relationship with each other but also in the audience's relationship with the actors who play them and the genre they inhabit. A series of romantic set pieces – a chance initial meeting, subsequent encounters with a gypsy palm-reader or a street poet – prove to be not quite as set as might have been imagined. When Céline and Jesse part, the camera revisits all the places they have been, and finds them diminished by their absence.

Before Sunrise opened the Sundance festival, confirming Linklater's standing as a leading American independent film-maker, even though this film is actually – like its predecessor *Dazed and Confused* – a studio presentation (the studios being, respectively, a supportive and hands-off Castle Rock and a somewhat less sympathetic Universal). From the voice of Generation X to the Texan Eric Rohmer, the conventional wisdoms about Linklater do scant justice to the distinctiveness of his work. He is habitually discussed in terms of disconnection and disengagement, but it is for connecting and engaging that he should be most celebrated. Cinematically self-educated (excepting a term at a community college film history course: 'they'd ask for two-page assignments, I'd deliver eight') Linklater founded and is still artistic director of the nine-year-old Austin film society. His life's work is 'trying to serve the movie-making process in ways that aren't being done much', and straight after this interview he was jetting off to Berlin to collect a Silver Bear.

* * *

Ben Thompson: Do you think not having any formal training helped you to find your own cinematic voice more easily?

Richard Linklater: It's hard to say why you do stuff, but I think my instinct in not going to film school was basically that I didn't want anyone telling me what to do. It's that authority thing – some teacher saying [*assumes ridiculous quavery voice*] 'Where's the close-up of the hands?' Or, 'This story won't work, there's no dramatic tension.'

Ben Thompson: 'This story won't work, there's no dramatic tension,' would have caused a few problems for *Slacker*.

Richard Linklater: Exactly. I would never have been able even to conceive of that movie if I had been in some programme whose job was to churn out people for the industry. And also I guess I was just too shy – I didn't want to make films before I was ready.

Ben Thompson: You worked on offshore oil rigs for a couple of years. Was it your ambition to make films even then?

Richard Linklater: It kind of came about during that period. Because we worked out in the Gulf of Mexico, when I was on land I had a lot of time. At that point I was mostly interested in writing and reading, but when I was ashore I began seeing two or three films a day at least. I was living in Houston which still had a big repertory theatre which had double features: *The Magnificent Ambersons* and *Citizen Kane*, *Badlands* and *Days of Heaven*. I had this book, *The Technical Aspects of Film-making*. It sat on my shelf. I'd look at it every day and think, 'Some day I'm gonna open that.'

Ben Thompson: It must have been frustrating going back on the rig.

Richard Linklater: Not really, because I would just read. At sea it was all literature – Dostoevsky, whatever – but on land it was all film.

Ben Thompson: Was there a corresponding conflict for you between ambitions to write or become a film-maker?

Richard Linklater: I think I wanted to be a writer at first – growing up in Texas that seemed the only option, though I played music a little bit, too. It took me a while, and seeing a lot of movies, to realise that I wasn't really a writer: I had a visual thing, I could see films in my head, and cinema is really my calling. If I couldn't make films any more I would try and get them seen, or write about them, or own a theatre, something like that – I think of it as all the same anyway.

Ben Thompson: How did you set about training yourself to make films?

Richard Linklater: My offshore period should have been my second two years of college, so by the time I was twenty-two I had all this money saved up. I moved to Austin and bought a Super-8 camera, a projector and some editing equipment, and started studying that book. A lot of film-making – the finer points of lighting for example – is a real craft which it takes years to perfect, but the basic stuff is easy. Anyone can set some lights and shoot a scene. And I found I loved the technical aspects of it: I would blacken my windows and edit some film I just shot for twenty-four hours straight. I spent several years doing shorts which were really just technical experiments. Looking back I'm amazed at how methodical I was – I would do a whole film just to work on a different lighting technique. I knew it was important not to try to say anything in my first couple of years, as I would probably get really frustrated and quit, because I wouldn't have the formal skill to achieve that thought. Finally, as a kind of culmination of all this work, I did an 89-minute Super-8 feature.

Ben Thompson: What was it called?

Richard Linklater: *It's Impossible to Learn to Plow by Reading Books*. I spent two years on it: shooting for a year and editing for a year – I've never had that schedule since [*laughs*].

Ben Thompson: Has it ever been shown?

Richard Linklater: We had a little film festival in Austin recently, where I showed it for the first time. A lot of people say it's their favourite film of mine, but it's so personal it's kind of painful to watch.

Ben Thompson: What is the film about?

Richard Linklater: It's kind of a prequel to *Slacker* and a forerunner of *Before Sunrise*, in that it's actually all about the mind-set of travel. It's about a trip around the US on Amtrak: more than half the film takes place on a train, the rest is just getting off in a town and walking around. It's like one guy – me – I would put the camera on trip, push the button, then go and be in the scene. It's very formal, the camera never moves, but there's hardly any dialogue in the whole movie, and what there is is just kind of mumbling because the microphone is at a distance. In a way it's the opposite of *Slacker*, where everybody says exactly what is going on inside their heads.

Ben Thompson: In all your films there seems to be a very exact sense of history, in terms of both your own personal place in it and observing things culturally with a high degree of accuracy. It must have been very galling for you to have *Slacker* so widely thought of as the epitome of something that it wasn't.

Richard Linklater: You have to make your peace with a film when you finish it, as whatever happens to it then is beyond your control, but it has been a little irritating. I have found myself somewhat detached from the whole Generation X/Slacker conversation – kind of bemused by it. President Clinton is using the word! He did this graduate address at UCLA and he was saying 'I don't think you're a generation of slackers, I think you're a generation of seekers,' but to me that's what slackers were: seekers. All these people in the film had their own projects going – the guy's JFK assassination book, or the woman's menstrual cycle sculpture – but they were outside the consumer culture. That's the cardinal sin: not basing your life around working or buying things. And it does bother me when people who should know better project negativity onto that.

Ben Thompson: It's a neat irony that something which starts out as a rejection of life lived as a marketing category should then become a marketing category in itself – a means of selling stuff to all these kids that don't want to be part of a capitalist process!

Richard Linklater: I know, I know. It's a really evil circle. I think that's why I didn't want to get into that whole thought too much, because it's my worst nightmare. People look at the characters in *Slacker* and ask what's wrong with them? They're white, semi-middle-class kids – what have they got to complain about? And I say, well, it's kind of a malaise in this culture where the enemy, the idea that money is everything and we should all capitalise on the new trend, is so subterranean, so entirely in all of us. I think that's what they're complaining about: they're complaining about what's going to happen to them before it's even a deal!

Ben Thompson: So with *Dazed and Confused*, did you have a sense of trying to supply historical perspective?

Richard Linklater: That was really important, because I don't think people have changed, which is why all this generational talk is ultimately ridiculous. It's just demographics: you have to make people feel special when you're trying to sell them stuff. No one's going to get anywhere saying, 'You know, people don't really change that much.' People were like this in the 1970s too, and probably even in the 1950s. It's only the drugs that changed. So there was definitely an idea of a continuum with *Slacker*. *Dazed and Confused* is set in 1976 – the hair is long, the music is kind of the same.

Ben Thompson: It's funny that people were rebelling against that whole FM rock thing then, and now it sounds great.

Richard Linklater: Right. It was all, 'What is this corporate garbage they're shoving down our throats!' Retrospectively, I found an energy there, and I used that to drive the movie. That's the major character in the movie – the music.

Ben Thompson: How did you make that work? Did you plot the soundtrack as you plotted the film?

Richard Linklater: Sometimes, yes. It was very intuitive: I'd wake up every morning with a new idea of what song would work where. About half of them I had before shooting began, and the other half came as it went along. I knew it would open with 'Sweet Emotion'; 'Hurricane' would be when they walked into the pool hall; and when Mitch was getting spanked it would be 'No More Mr Nice Guy'. I liked the irony of the lyrics, even if some of them – 'School's Out', for example – are a bit obvious.

Ben Thompson: That's how it should be though, isn't it? You don't get many teenagers saying 'I'm not going to like that song – its relevance to my life is too readily apparent.' I suppose it's the same with films. Presumably, in making *Dazed and Confused*, you gave the odd thought to the proud heritage of bad high-school movies?

Richard Linklater: It was probably seeing all of them that made me think I had a teenage movie to make. I wanted to make a film that captured the energy of what I remember: driving around, not much happening but everything happening at once. It was fun to be in a genre that I knew pretty well – there are a lot of good high-school movies, too.

Ben Thompson: What sort do you like?

Richard Linklater: My favourite ones are really the edge movies, *Over the Edge, River's Edge*. I like *If…* a lot – the true way to end a teenage movie is complete apocalypse, whether it's imagined or real. Like in *Over the Edge*, they're fire-bombing the school – that's the ultimate teen thing.

Ben Thompson: *Dazed and Confused* ends more on a plateau though.

Richard Linklater: My movie's a little more ambiguous I guess. It just wasn't a good enough set-up: the oppressive force wasn't so clearly defined.

Ben Thompson: Are you worried that you might have made this generation's *Animal House*?

Richard Linklater: If I have, I didn't mean to! There are teenagers who've seen *Dazed and Confused* fifty times and have parties to it. They all think the 1970s were a great time, even though there is plenty of evidence to the contrary in the film.

Ben Thompson: Were the two characters in *Before Sunrise* set in stone in your mind before you knew who would play them?

Richard Linklater: I had a script, and there were two people I was looking for, but I wasn't really aware of who until I found them. If say an American woman and an Italian man had been right then it could have easily swapped over. It was always vague. It was the same with the city.

Ben Thompson: Once you'd settled on Vienna, did you have to work hard to avoid homages to *The Third Man*?

Richard Linklater: Well, we did film on a Ferris wheel, but only because it was the sort of touristic – I love that word – thing the two characters would do.

Ben Thompson: I like the way the film's structure echoes the trajectory of their relationship: it's as if the characters are deciding when and how to move things on.

Richard Linklater: The film's only agenda is to go onto the next interaction – all it propels you to is the next thing. The fact is they won't know until they're apart how much they really care about each other. We all create these romantic ideals, even if they don't exist. It's kind of an endearing thing about the species that we do that.

Ben Thompson: There's an unusually forthright quote in the production notes. Julie Delpy says, 'I knew unless I was tough with these two American men, Céline could have possibly disappeared into some cliché-ridden feminine mass.' Then there's the line in the film where she describes the scenario as being 'like a male fantasy: meet a French girl on a train, fuck her and never see her again'. Was it this that led you to seek out a female co-writer [Kim Krizan, 'Cynic Questions Happiness' in *Slacker* and the teacher in *Dazed and Confused* who says, 'The 1968 democratic convention was probably the most bitchin' time of my entire life'] for *Before Sunrise*?

Richard Linklater: I certainly thought that since the film is so much a dialogue between a man and a woman, it was important to have a strong woman co-writer and a strong woman in the production. But I feel equally close to both characters – I think a lot of me actually goes through Julie.

Ben Thompson: *Slacker* was very much a shot in the dark, but with a high-school comedy and now a romance, you seem to be picking out ever better-ploughed furrows. Isn't charted territory more perilous than uncharted?

Richard Linklater: It kind of is, but at the same time it's kind of neat. It's like going into an old goldmine with a new process. I can't say that I'm a big fan of the genre *Before Sunrise* might be said to belong to, but these films answer a huge need in people, and I was wondering if I could still answer that need, but with my own interpretation of how things really are. I think that what throws people about the film is that the first kiss takes so long: they're used to it being couple meets/couple immediately all over each other in bed/now we can get on with the story.

Ben Thompson: There's a scene I really like where they're in a record shop listening booth, listening to some awful romantic song, and you can see Hawke's character thinking, 'Am I corny enough to take advantage of this, or should I respect how bad a song it is?'

Richard Linklater: Right. In most films they would have kissed there, but no one wants to make the first move, so there's that wonderful awkwardness. That's how life is, but you don't tend to see it that much in the movies.

Ben Thompson: Can you imagine making a film compressed within a 24-hour timespan?

Richard Linklater: The next one covers about eighty-five years! It's a true story, based on an oral history (Claude Stanush's *The Newton Boys – Portrait of an Outlaw Gang*) of these four 1920s Texas share-croppers who become bank robbers. It'll obviously be much more epic in structure, but I hope it'll have the same feel of hanging out with these guys in the moment. Epic storytelling can be really distancing and boring; there's this strange idea that things become grander the further you go back, but I really want to show the 1920s as I imagine they might have been.

Ben Thompson: All your films seem to have a strong autobiographical element, but presumably you didn't rob that many banks in the 1920s, so this must be a bit of a leap.

Richard Linklater: Not really, because I've always found it is very easy to think of myself as a criminal. I don't know what I would have done had I not been a film-maker, but

I wouldn't have had any trouble justifying crime in my mind. So on the surface it looks like complete departure, and it is in a certain way, but in another it isn't. *Before Sunrise* was a big departure, too – I hope every film is. It keeps you curious.

LIVING IN OBLIVION
USA 1995
Director: Tom DiCillo

In New York, director Nick Reve struggles to make a low-budget film. His lead actress, Nicole Springer, is nervous about a very difficult scene in which she confronts her mother with her feelings about traumatic events in her childhood. This is because this scene echoes one in real life that her real mother died too soon for her to play out. A complex mix of characters are at work on the shoot – among them bossy assistant director Wanda and temperamental cinematographer Wolf – and a series of mishaps frustrate them; a sound boom keeps dropping into the frame, focus is lost, a light explodes. The actresses run through their lines again to collect themselves, and achieve the perfect take with no film in the camera. A persistent beeping noise sends Nick into a tantrum. It's the noise of his alarm clock. He wakes from his nightmare.

Nicole wakes up after an ill-advised one-night stand with her moronic leading man, Chad Palomino. The next day's filming goes very badly. Palomino's macho antics distract the crew and his increasingly absurd suggestions for the big love scene plunge the whole set into chaos. When Nicole overhears him complaining about her to Nick, and boasting about their sexual liaison, she humiliates him in front of the camera and a fist fight develops which Nick joins in with. As a battered Palomino limps off the set, Nick tells Nicole the whole film is really about her and they kiss. She wakes from her dream.

On the real set, the filming of a dream sequence becomes the stuff of nightmares. Nick's mother (who bears an uncanny resemblance to the mother actress in his dream) turns up, having escaped from her old people's home by walking through walls. The smoke machine explodes and the dwarf hired to lend a sinister quality to the dream sequence takes umbrage at his stereotypical role and marches off the set. Nick is about to throw in the towel when his mother steps into the dwarf-shaped breach and – to universal sighs of relief – a suitable dream sequence is completed.

* * *

Tom DiCillo's second feature (after 1992's widely praised but disappointingly soulless *Johnny Suede*), *Living in Oblivion* has been a long time coming, but it turns out to be richer and more entertaining than anyone had a right to expect. At first glance, the subject matter looks alarmingly self-indulgent – the opening shot is a slowly looming close-up on a well-used movie camera – and how much mileage can possibly be left in that old 'It was only a dream' device? Quite a lot, as things turn out.

There's a whiff of self-referential flannel about the writer/director's insistence that the stuff going on behind the camera is often a lot more interesting than the stuff going on in front of it, but it only takes a few moments of *Living in Oblivion* to realise that something authentic and intriguing is going on. The grainy black-and-white opening segment sucks the viewer into the film-making process with consummate skill. The sequence in which Catherine Keener's performance progressively deteriorates through seven retakes is not only superbly acted, it also invites the audience to make the kind of judgments about what constitutes a convincing characterisation that they routinely entrust to the director. The fine gradations that divide success and failure are compellingly hard to discern under this kind of intense analysis.

The opening third of *Living in Oblivion* – the director's dream sequence – was originally shot as a complete short with a view to possible expansion to full feature length. It would have been easy for the completed film to lose its way from there on in, but the characters and their interconnecting tensions expand happily to fill the available space. The atmosphere broadens and gets progressively more comic, with accrued complexity. The scenes in which Chad Palomino lets his creative juices flow with ever more ridiculous suggestions are hilarious, even without remembering that DiCillo is the man whose debut film gave the mighty talent of Brad Pitt its first significant cinematic exposure.

All the actors appear to be enjoying themselves. If Catherine Keener resents the fact that a film which was originally conceived as a showcase for her eventually becomes one for the rat-like loveability of Steve Buscemi, she does not show it. This is the second film in the past couple of years (the first was the excellent *In the Soup*) in which Buscemi has shone in the potentially irritating role of struggling film-maker. Someone somewhere has got the message, because he is currently shooting his debut feature.

Tom DiCillo's greatest achievement here is to demystify the film-making process without robbing it of its thrill, its beauty or even, in the end, of its mystery. The man still best known as Jim Jarmusch's one-time cinematographer has given a beguilingly human face to the dreams and nightmares of American independent cinema.

Ben Thompson

WALKING AND TALKING
United Kingdom/USA 1996
Director: Nicole Holofcener

New York, the 1970s. Two small girls, Amelia and Laura, giggle over a copy of *The Joy of Sex*. New York, the present. The two friends, now in their twenties, meet at a café and arrange to take Amelia's cat to the vet. They shared the cat when they were roommates, but Laura, a trainee therapist, now lives with her jewellery-designer boyfriend, Frank. Amelia bumps into Andrew, her ex-boyfriend, who is carrying a porn video. She suggests to her therapist that it's time to end her sessions. That evening, Laura and Frank announce their engagement. The next day, Amelia tells her therapist that she wants to continue, but her slot has already been filled.

Amelia decides to date Bill, the 'ugly' video store clerk. Laura fantasises about kissing a good-looking client. At the vet's, the two girls learn that the cat has cancer; Amelia opts for expensive chemotherapy for her. Despite her reservations about his looks and his revolting taste in horror videos, Amelia sleeps with Bill. While she is in the bathroom, Bill overhears a phone message from Laura asking about Amelia's date with 'the ugly guy'. He wipes the message and leaves. In bed with Frank, Laura notices a mole on his chest, and tells him he should have it removed. Having heard nothing from Bill, Amelia follows him to the video store where he snubs her.

Amelia goes with Andrew to meet his father, stricken with Alzheimer's disease, but Andrew avoids talking to him. When they next meet, Andrew asks to borrow money to pay his phone bill. Remembering his new phone-sex relationship with a Californian girl, Amelia refuses him. Amelia, Laura and Frank travel to Amelia's house in the country to make plans for the wedding. That night, Laura becomes hysterical about Frank's mole. He becomes angry and leaves. After receiving obscene phone calls, Amelia asks Andrew over. They get drunk and discuss the breakdown of their relationship.

Back in New York, Amelia discovers that her cat has fallen out of the window and died. Andrew's phone-sex partner turns up and he reluctantly has a date with her. At a conciliatory lunch, Frank presents Laura with a jewellery box containing his excised mole. Disgusted, Laura walks out. At the video store, Amelia confronts Bill, who tells her about the answerphone message. Amelia sleeps with Andrew. She and Laura argue about the changing nature of their friendship, but make up. Laura and Frank get married. Amelia attends Andrew's father's birthday party where Andrew talks to his father.

* * *

Walking and Talking is a welcome example of that rare hybrid: the independent cinema chick movie. This debut feature from Nicole Holofcener is a quick-witted study of female friendship, which conveys warmth and emotion without resorting either to *Oprah*-like confessional or melodrama. Much of its time is spent analysing the anxieties surrounding dating and commitment from a female perspective. In this analysis, as well as in its low-budget aesthetic and episodic structure, *Walking and Talking* could be a sister film to *The Brothers McMullen* (they were both made by the same production company, Ted Hope and James Schamus's Good Machine), except that it's smarter and in many ways more winning.

The film's two sharply contrasted female protagonists have their differences signalled early on when we find out that Amelia is in therapy, while Laura hopes to make therapy her profession. One of the most engaging things about these women is that they retain their autonomy despite admitting the importance of men in their lives. In another film, such a preoccupation with finding the right partner might be read as a weakness, but Holofcener's direction of her own, sharply funny script makes their emotional honesty a strength.

Holofcener's 1992 short *Angry* saw her labelled as a female Woody Allen and there is much here to support the comparison. Inhabiting a middle-class New York of small apartments, coffee shops and video stores, Amelia and Laura are no more than usually confused denizens of that city, but Holofcener brings them to vivid life with a wealth of idiosyncratic detail. The vicissitudes of Amelia's love life are particularly well drawn. Sartorially and emotionally disarranged, she frets about being 'out there' in the singles market, while lending money to Andrew, her ex-boyfriend, and reassuring him that his newfound porn addiction 'isn't hurting anybody'. Her disastrous relationship with Bill, the clerk from the video store, meanwhile, is a superbly comic combination of self-deception and achingly familiar hypocrisy. Desperate for attention, she 'dates down', humouring her new partner's love of horror flicks while dismissing him in private as 'the ugly guy'. Yet she is upset when he dumps her after one date.

A blonde, prettily poised control-freak, Laura is Amelia's physical and temperamental opposite. Still, her trim life occasionally capsizes into wild fantasies, seamlessly manifested on-screen in a manner reminiscent of Allen's subjective projections. She is also fixated about a new mole on her fiancé Frank's chest. At one point this small mole fills the screen, looking wildly malignant. Laura screams, the mole reverts to normal size, and she is left trying to placate her offended partner. When he eventually offers her the excised mole in a velveteen jewellery box as a joke, she yells at him: 'That's not a joke. That's the most passive-aggressive thing you've ever done.'

Reprising his sleeveless nerd from *Living in Oblivion*, Kevin Corrigan, as Bill, a good-egg horror nerd, has a great moment when he rises into the frame after his sexual conquest of Amelia, anaemic chest puffed out with pride. When the phone rings (to deliver a devastating answerphone message from Laura asking Amelia about her date with the 'ugly guy') he moves from indecision about answering it, to guilty nosiness, to utter deflation in one shot. But it is Catherine Keener who holds the eye throughout *Walking and Talking*, supplementing her own great performance as the lead actress in *Living in Oblivion* with another subtle piece of acting. She invests Amelia with a barely controlled panic, achieving pathos without sentimentality.

After her bridal makeover, Anne Heche as a tearful Laura cries: 'She just kept spraying and curling, spraying and curling. I look like a drag queen.' This is just one of many moments female viewers will empathise with, one characteristic of a really enjoyable film which analyses the minutiae of contemporary relationships, while never forgetting the continuing importance of cats, dresses and make-up to the modern woman.

Liese Spencer

PULLING THE PIN ON HAL HARTLEY

Ryan Gilbey

It's almost a decade since Hal Hartley made his first feature, *The Unbelievable Truth*. Now *Henry Fool*, his sixth, is upon us, and the extent to which it violates the pristine, antiseptic surface of his earlier films is the one thing that prevents me from dismissing Hartley as vapid and obsolete. *Henry Fool* offers a hopeful flourish in the director's artistic development: for the first time Hartley accommodates emotions that exist outside the inverted commas within which his movies have always been bracketed. For the first time, he concedes events can hurt, really hurt. And not in a funny way either.

It's what happens when you find your mother making love with the man you were about to take to bed, or when you get scalded with boiling water: it can hurt and not stop hurting for a long time. These events happen respectively to Fay (Parker Posey) and Simon (James Urbaniak), the siblings at the heart of *Henry Fool.* Their small-town lives are changed irrevocably by the arrival of mystery man Henry Fool (Thomas Jay Ryan) – a scenario that echoes throughout Hartley's work and particularly in *The Unbelievable Truth* – but the pain doesn't go away. The shock of watching reality penetrate Hartley's introspective universe is palpable. It's like a Tom and Jerry cartoon where the injuries Tom sustains from having a vase broken on his head last well beyond the punchline.

All of which may not be good news for Hartley fans, a group to which I let my membership lapse a long time ago. It is wise to acknowledge that our own biases and prejudices affect the extent to which we engage with particular directors, films or even genres. Hal Hartley films figure on a long list of things I consider myself to have outgrown – and the fact that I've consciously discarded these movies which I once adored accounts for some of my hostility towards them: they are old flames; we all have them, and lie about them.

Stories your parents like

When I first saw *Trust* (1990), Hartley's second picture, I can remember being tickled by the way a story more suited to daytime soap opera had been given an irreverent spin. It was a second-generation *Pygmalion* in trendy clothing. And I think most young viewers – and make no mistake about it, a passion for Hartley was virtually a prerequisite of undergraduate life in the early 1990s – initially respond to this ironic tang: the lilt of the voice, not the weight of the words. The flip, ice-cool glaze with which Hartley coats his tales of romantic imbroglios and domestic breakdowns provides an insurance policy – a way of getting close to emotion but never so close you might lose yourself. Eric Rohmer more than Douglas Sirk; stories your parents might like, if only they weren't told in a style to suit your hip younger brother.

Hartley's films hinged on a number of components: arch, stilted dialogue peppered with comic non-sequiturs – carefully crafted language thriving on its own artificiality in the manner of Samuel Beckett, Harold Pinter or Whit Stillman (whose own debut, *Metropolitan*, was released in the same year as Hartley's); watchful camerawork and rigid compositions; and an arrangement of actors that draws attention to the mechanics of choreography. And unlike Woody Allen or Fassbinder, who occasionally went out on a limb when it came to casting, Hartley depended on the same anonymous actors, never chancing anyone who might introduce baggage from other roles. (The exception to this rule – Isabelle Huppert in *Amateur* – comes across largely as a scientific experiment along the lines of: can a renowned actress shed all traces of personality and be absorbed into homogeneous territory? The answer being: yes, but so what?)

A harsher reality

The films – *The Unbelievable Truth* (1989), *Trust, Simple Men* (1992), the short *Surviving Desire* (1993), *Amateur* and *Flirt* (both 1995) – were throwing up the same themes, too.

The struggle to forge an identity in the shadow of oppressive or infamous parents depicted in *Trust* and *Simple Men* became in *Amateur* simply the struggle to forge an identity. The curse of perceiving yourself to be an intellectual, or worse an intellectual who had fallen in love despite believing the world to be full of pain and punishment, was arbitrarily bestowed. Such concerns were usually prevalent in the characters played by Martin Donovan. If I had a pound for everyone I met who thought they were Martin Donovan in *Trust* – brooding, cynical, impossibly witty, carrying a live grenade in his coat pocket to symbolise he is just an accident waiting to happen – I could outdo the Royal Mint. And they were all out to capture their own Adrienne Shelly, their own baby doll.

The same actors, the same themes. So Hartley has made his mark as an auteur. But where is the progress in this body of work? I discern some in *Henry Fool*, which is a lot of things you wouldn't expect a Hal Hartley film to be: painful, challenging, self-referential. In many ways it feels as though Hartley is returning to familiar ground and making amends for the flippancy of his earlier work.

Henry, a pretentious, self-absorbed and possibly deprived writer fresh out of prison, seems a typical Hartley kook. But he's a paedophile. His victim was thirteen, like Jack Nicholson's conquest in *One Flew over the Cuckoo's Nest* – an age young enough to suggest the perpetrator's immorality, yet not too young to preclude an audience's sympathies. Hartley is very perceptive in the way he constructs Henry's justification of his crime, and indeed all his embittered reactions to a world he feels has wronged him. 'She knew how to play on my weaknesses,' he tells Simon, a garbage man he encourages to write. Later, when Simon becomes the successful writer his tutor never was, Henry argues that his own failure is emblematic of uniqueness, yet he offers to compromise his writing to get into print. He drifts numbly through life, misreading situations to his own advantage or bluffing. Near the end of the film, he rescues a teenage girl and her battered mother from the mother's partner by (accidentally) murdering the man, but there is no John Grisham–style triumph to the act, and Hartley's traditional final scene promising escape and a new life feels bleak and hopeless, in stark contrast to the climaxes of *Trust* and *Simple Men.*

Like those films, *Henry Fool* is populated by dropouts and abusive or irresponsible parents. But there is a new rawness here. Hartley has always filmed violence as though it was part of a Gary Larson cartoon – the father and son fighting in *Trust*, the nun wrestling the cop in *Simple Men*, the torture scenes in *Amateur*. Now it isn't so funny. People suffer; a woman and her daughter endure years of physical abuse from the woman's new husband who could formerly be relied on to take out his rage on Simon. Even the graphically scatological scenes are played more or less straight: Simon projectile-vomiting over a woman's naked buttocks, Henry losing control of his bowels in a scene that would have the Farrelly brothers fighting peristalsis.

Hal and Woody grow up

The collision between Hartley's vacuum-packed writing and this new, harsher reality creates some intriguing tensions. Only when the film introduces laptop computers, pony-tailed publishers and a cameo from Camille Paglia does it hit you how completely Hartley has always retreated from reflecting an era-specific world. Only when Fay lets out a scorching scream on finding Henry having sex with her mother are you struck by Hartley's sudden capacity to sacrifice dramatic control for genuine anguish, something he was incapable of in a similar scene in *Trust.*

It's coincidental that both Hartley and Woody Allen should have entered a new phase of maturity at the same time by displaying more or less the same urge. That after a whole career (or in Allen's case twelve years, the length of time between his last great work *The Purple Rose of Cairo* and last year's *Deconstructing Harry*) of sealing themselves off from society in a hermetic shell of their own constructing they should both apparently wake up.

The most telling evidence of Hartley's burgeoning maturity comes when the battered wife screws her eyes shut and clamps her hands over her ears as her brutal husband kicks Henry to the floor. What Hartley shows us is a close-up of the attacker's gnarled face. But the sound has been removed, so though we are seeing more than the wife, we are hearing what she hears, stranded in her perspective, with no irony or cutaways for relief. Hartley has rarely been so generous to one of his creations, and I think a lot of people are attracted to the relationship of superiority he establishes between the audience and his characters. In *Henry Fool*, you can't bank on that luxury. A brief scene shows Henry approaching a man who is watching television. 'Who's winning?' he asks. 'Nobody,' the man replies. For once you feel the gloomy irony of this exchange is not lost on the characters: for the first time you might be chuckling with them rather than just at them.

HAPPINESS
USA 1998
Director: Todd Solondz

The New Jersey suburbs. Thirty-year-old Joy breaks up with her boyfriend Andy at a local restaurant. Overweight loner Allen tells his psychiatrist Bill of his lust for Helen, a successful poet who lives in Allen's apartment block. Unable to approach Helen directly, he plagues her with obscene phone calls. Helen has two sisters: the now-single Joy, and Trish, who is happily married to Bill the psychiatrist. The sisters' parents, Mona and Lenny, have retired to Florida and are separating.

Andy commits suicide and Joy quits her job. She takes a post filling in for striking teachers at a language school. This leads to a one-night stand with Vlad, a Russian cab driver who steals her stereo. Bill becomes obsessed with Johnny Grasso, an eleven-year-old friend of his eldest son Billy. When Johnny stays the night, Bill drugs the child then molests him. Later, Bill visits another schoolmate of Billy's (whom he knows is at home alone) and molests him, too.

Helen decides she needs to live more dangerously and invites her mystery caller to visit her home. Allen, in turn, is bothered by his neighbour Kristina, who tells him she has killed the apartment block's porter and hidden his body parts in her freezer. Allen eventually calls at Helen's apartment but, disappointed, she sends him away. Bill is caught by the police and confesses his crimes to Billy. Kristina is also arrested. Joy,

Trish and Helen visit their reunited parents in Florida. Billy masturbates and runs in to tell his family that he's had an orgasm for the first time.

* * *

The first scene in *Happiness* details a forlorn break-up in a New Jersey restaurant; the second a turgid therapy session where the analyst's mind wanders off to checklist his plans for the afternoon. Suburban life, it is implied, is drab, uniform and quietly despairing. But its semi-formal etiquette and chintz masks real runaway psychosis. We subsequently learn that, having finished his dinner, the dumped boyfriend goes home and kills himself. The man on the psychiatrist's couch makes dirty phone calls. The shrink himself is a child molester. Writer-director Todd Solondz (as with his earlier indie hit *Welcome to the Dollhouse*) presents suburbia as a type of peripheral hell, a moral darkness on the edge of town where, in the words of Wallace Stevens, 'the pure products of America go crazy'.

All of which is nothing new. Contemporary film-makers – from Hal Hartley in the United States to Alain Berliner (*Ma vie en rose*) in France and Mike Leigh in the United Kingdom – have found suburbia such a fertile creative territory that there's a danger it's become a kind of comic shorthand, a knee-jerk symbol for a certain strain of middle-class pretension and hypocrisy. *Happiness* certainly doesn't shirk from hitting these buttons, but it hits them with such bravery and abandon as to conjure up a landscape at once blandly familiar and almost surreal. A perpetual, at times unbearable tension – between normalcy and deviance, between comedy and tragedy – is the fuel driving *Happiness*. Sex (the getting of it, the mastering of it, the getting rid of it) is the currency for all its inhabitants. Its genial caricatures turn abruptly black as pitch.

At the heart of Solondz's intersecting train-wreck of lifelines sits psychiatrist Bill (an astonishing, no-safety-net performance from Dylan Baker), an outwardly upstanding suburban dad who masturbates to pre-teen magazines and romps off in dogged pursuit of his son's classmates. The portrayal of Bill is central to the success or otherwise of *Happiness*. On the one hand, Solondz has undeniable fun with the character. Bill's interactions with little Billy view like a paedophilic pastiche of the father–son chats in *Leave It to Beaver*; his attempts to dope the 'girlish' Johnny Grasso are played as farce. Moreover, Solondz forces us to identify with this man. The dramatic medium favours his character; for all his faults, Bill is at least an active protagonist, a take-charge contrast to the insipid Joy who is dumped on by others, or the impotent Allen who can only release his desires by phone. Most crucially and problematically of all, the grim consequences of Bill's crimes are either lightly glossed over or omitted entirely.

By rights, such hurdles should be insurmountable. But *Happiness* conspires to get over them, and ultimately there is more to Solondz's film than shock tactics. It's undeniable that *Happiness* relies extensively on queasy comedy and the zap of the audience gross-out. Yet these extreme flights of fancy finally take on a quality that hoists it far above the level of the supermarket tabloid. *Happiness* stretches its taboo subject matter to the limits, using a freak-show explicitness to attain a rarefied altitude that other, supposedly 'brave' pictures (Adrian Lyne's *Lolita*, Roberto Benigni's *Life Is*

Beautiful) perhaps dream of, but are finally too dramatically conservative, too compromised, too burdened by perceived audience reactions to reach. By the time Bill has his last painful conversation with Billy, *Happiness* has come to rest in a dreamscape where alienation dovetails into shocking recognition, where disgust and delighted laughter exist side by side. We wouldn't want to live in the place where Solondz takes us, but somehow, we suspect, we do.

Xan Brooks

POSTCARDS FROM MARS

Shawn Levy

Professional assassin Ghost Dog (Forest Whitaker) lives alone on the rooftop of a New York apartment building where he gets his orders to kill from Italian mobsters by carrier pigeon. He keeps himself attuned to the task by following the samurai warrior code. Having pulled off twelve perfect hits for Louie, the mobster who once saved his life, he is ordered to commit a murder that backfires on his masters. They must now atone by sacrificing Ghost Dog. However, the mobsters have reckoned without Ghost Dog's phenomenal powers of survival, which can withstand anything except his own sense of loyalty.

* * *

Nothing could be more American than being an outsider – except, maybe, hating outsiders. We are, after all, a nation of immigrants who banded together to slaughter a native people who were themselves hostile to aliens; who imported a race as slave labour and fought a ghastly internecine war over the right to keep up the practice; who became a superpower through bloody conflicts on remote continents and the scapegoating of an Other during a prolonged non-shooting war.

And yet, perversely, obstinately, we identify ourselves with external origins via grotesque hyphenates (I'm an Italo-Irish-Hebrew-American, myself); our celebrations of St Patrick's Day, Cinco de Mayo and Hanukkah are more vigorous than those in Dublin, Mexico City or Tel Aviv; our biggest cities have their Little Italies and their Chinatowns; our national fast food, the hamburger, is named for a German city and the runner-up in popularity, the pizza, is Italian. We are, in short, a mess of mixed bloodlines and contradictory impulses, simultaneously revelling in our genetic distinctions and suspicious of them.

Surprisingly few of our major film-makers, however, have bothered to chew over this oddity of our national character. D. W. Griffith and Howard Hawks, to name a pair of well-bred WASPs, espied the ethnic and racial minorities around the margins of the culture and were frankly discomfited by them. Modern directors such as Spike Lee, Martin Scorsese, Francis Ford Coppola and Barry Levinson have worked from inside the perspective of the individual groups disenfranchised by the majority, but haven't, generally, considered them as dynamic parts of the greater whole.

Only two American directors have dealt openly and repeatedly with questions of ethnic, racial and religious heterogeneity, assimilation and mistrust: the great classicist John Ford and the postmodern groove master Jim Jarmusch – and if you can name a stranger pair of kindred spirits, then you could make a living as an ecumenical matchmaker on the West Bank. For Ford, America was truly the proverbial melting pot of Swedish, German, Irish, Mexican, black, and, yes, native blood; he recognised and perhaps shared the inherent suspicions of and biases against aliens in the American character, but he seemed, too, to respect the unique traditions cultural minorities brought into the whole. He made one great film about bigotry (*The Searchers*), but then tried to apologise, after a fashion, in his late career with a series of lesser works celebrating (though he'd despise the thought) diversity: *Sergeant Rutledge*, *Cheyenne Autumn*, *7 Women*.

Jarmusch, on the other hand, has been explicitly fascinated since his first major release *Stranger than Paradise* (1984) with the notion of America not as melting pot but as salad bowl – a collection of independent and distinct ingredients, endemic, imported and idiosyncratically hybrid. Far less determined than Ford to see America's ideals and manifest destiny fulfilled, Jarmusch has the late twentieth-century ironist's taste for irreconcilables juxtaposed. Travel in his films is less a means to an end than a process in and of itself; speech in languages other than English isn't always translated with subtitles; beginnings and ends seem arbitrary (indeed, they don't always come at the beginning and end); regular Americans seem just as odd and ill suited to their surroundings as aliens.

Jarmusch's first five mature features deal explicitly with immigrants – the troika of Hungarians in *Stranger than Paradise*; the Italian jailbird (and his lover) in *Down by Law* (1986); a pair of Elvis-seeking Japanese hajis, an Italian widow and a Chinese hothead in *Mystery Train* (1989); the taxis filled with out-of-towners and out-of-sortsers in *Night on Earth* (1991); a displaced eastern city slicker and a Native American educated in England in *Dead Man* (1995). (For clarity, let's leave out discussion of his quasi-autobiographical student film *Permanent Vacation*, 1980, though its story of a young man's adventures in the big, bohemian city incorporates themes and images of tourism and escape; also, let's skip his one feature-length work of non-fiction *Year of the Horse*, 1997, even though it is explicitly about a foreigner – Canadian rocker Neil Young.)

Unalienated aliens

In his new film *Ghost Dog: The Way of the Samurai*, Jarmusch shifts the thematic focus of his lens slightly to consider not people living in a land other than that of their birth (though there is one of those) but people whose adherence to subcultures – hip-hop, the Mafia and the code of the samurai, principally – marks them as alien to the American mainstream. In this vision, as much a deconstruction of the mob film as *Dead Man* is of the Western, gangsters sing along with Public Enemy instead of Dean Martin, black hitmen study Yukio Mishima instead of Malcolm X, and a taciturn American can be best friends with a garrulous Haitian even though neither speaks a lick of the other's language.

Ghost Dog is decidedly darker than Jarmusch's earlier works and utterly sincere, possessed of a dignified sadness rather than the slightly rueful irony of his youth. (He was thirty-one and still playing in a punk rock band when *Stranger than Paradise* debuted.) The director retains his respect and affection for his characters, but treats them more tenderly now, perhaps because he can sense the mortality he shares with them. In this light, his fondness for aliens is, touchingly, a form of altruism: we shall pass this way but once, he seems to be telling us, and all that jazz.

Reading through his biography, it's tempting (and perhaps not altogether incorrect) to surmise that Jarmusch comes to his love of unalienated aliens for purely personal reasons. With his high-punk wardrobe and trademark shock of white hair, he stands out even in his adopted hometown of New York City. Jarmusch hails initially from Akron, Ohio, a small industrial city so well known for its production of rubber it was long considered a likely target for Soviet nuclear weapons during the Cold War. (Maybe this is why it was, in the 1970s, a noted hotbed of both underground rock – Devo, The Cramps – and despair: at least one notorious survey listed the town as America's suicide capital.)

By his late teens, Jarmusch was attending Manhattan's Columbia University and taking a semester in Paris, where he haunted the Cinemathèque Française. He then pursued a graduate degree in film-making at New York University, during which time he worked as an assistant to Nicholas Ray and Wim Wenders on their collaboration *Lightning over Water*. As his graduation project he used some leftover film stock Wenders gave him to make a short film called *The New World* – which would evolve into the first chapter of *Stranger than Paradise*.

After nearly two decades of increasingly tedious and familiar American independent films, it's hard to recall just what a thunderclap *Stranger* felt like in 1984. Shot in a creamy black and white, populated almost entirely by non-actors and first-time actors, sketchy in its narrative, frightfully deadpan in its jokes, it was the sort of movie that changed the way other movies looked – and which no other movie dared to imitate. Spare, comic, droll and, somehow, heartfelt, it answered only to its own sense of rhythm and technique; it was so unignorably idiosyncratic it won both the Caméra d'Or for best first feature at Cannes and the National Socitey of Film Critic's award for best picture.

With the very first frames of *Stranger*, Jarmusch immersed his audience in what would become recognisable as obsessive images and themes: an immigrant arrives in the United States and encounters not the Statue of Liberty, but taxiing aeroplanes and a run-down neighbourhood of walk-up apartments. Much of what followed would become equally familiar as Jarmusch continued to release films: the themes of immigration, road trips and wry hopefulness; the reliance on non-actors (especially such musician friends as John Lurie, Tom Waits, Screaming Jay Hawkins, Joe Strummer and Iggy Pop); the little webs of coincidence that passed as plotting; the eye for emptiness and post-industrial waste that made the cityscapes of New York, Cleveland, Memphis, Los Angeles, Paris, Rome and Helsinki look scarily alike.

Blank generation

Most idiosyncratically, *Stranger* introduced Jarmusch's chief cinematographic tic; the little black spaces between the scenes that punctuate and give rhythmic shape to all his films. No American film-maker of the talking-picture era has made such hay of the interstices that film affords. Jarmusch's movies characteristically slip in and out of consciousness – and not always at times that coincide with important (or, for that matter, trivial) moments in the plot. In all his films he gives the screen over to scenes of utter blankness – characters reading, sitting, staring, walking, playing solitaire, listening to music. Yet at the same time vitally important material sometimes goes missing: the jailbreak in *Down by Law* for instance, or the Hungarian girl's decision not to return to Budapest at the end of *Stranger*. In each case, the plot hangs crucially in the balance of a moment Jarmusch has chosen not to render visually.

If, on one hand, this is a sly way of making do with low budgets, it's also a critique of cinematic literalness. Nobody, it could be argued, makes movies so bald-facedly as Jarmusch, yet he demonstrates time and again that one needn't show – or have your characters discuss – everything that happens in order to convey to the audience that it has occurred. This above all marked *Stranger* as the work of an artist with a singular grasp of his medium. And over the course of the three features that followed, Jarmusch continued to explore the themes and tics introduced in that groundbreaking work.

In *Down by Law* there were, once again, three travellers, two more or less native (Waits and Lurie) and an immigrant (Roberto Benigni) whose presence catalyses and liberates his comrades. Like *Stranger*, it had a three-part structure (events leading up to jail; jail; events after escape) and a penchant for strangely lowbrow yet highly conceptual comedy. *Mystery Train* was another three-parter, with a brief coda, about what happens one night in a cheap Memphis hotel. A formal experiment in simultaneity, it mixed the most American of signifiers – Elvis Presley – with, in turn, a couple from Yokohama who've journeyed to see Graceland and Sun Studios; a Roman widow visited by the ghost of the King; an English yobbo (Strummer) whom everyone calls Elvis because of his retro hairstyle. The stories are united by a gunshot and a passing train, but the real unifying element is the increasing corporeality of Elvis, from spoor to vision to in-the-flesh imitator, of a kind. Like *Stranger*, *Mystery Train* begins and ends with images of locomotion – quite literally in this case, as trains are the chief means of transportation. And it's as much a valentine to the allure of the American way of pop culture as it is a cheeky bit of structural legerdemain without terribly much resonating significance. (It, too, went over big at Cannes.)

In 1991, Jarmusch finally hit the far limits of the form he had devised. *Night on Earth* is the story of five taxicab rides taken simultaneously in five different cities in Europe and North America. In each story, the driver and passengers interact in ways that change one or the other's view of his or her self: sins are confessed; a terrible wound is revealed; a woman discovers the finite charm of her supposedly infinitely alluring world; another woman reveals that her apparent disability is in fact a potent weapon; and, in the slightest and most ironic episode, an immigrant cab driver in New York City is so ill suited to his job he allows a passenger to drive, through which process both men discover their shared humanity.

It's a virtuosic film and a maddening one at the same time, filled with comic and empathetic high points yet lacquered with an overall sense of purposelessness. In a sense, everyone in the film is an equal – passengers and drivers alike are like aliens in their own hometowns – so the immigrant theme, while inescapable, doesn't carry the same weight or poignancy it bore in Jarmusch's other films. It's also the first film in which he seems to have dissipated his restless inventiveness by doing things he'd done before. Too closely imitating the interstitial passage in which clocks set to the time zones of the five cities spin backwards to the minute when all the stories begin, Jarmusch seems to be running in place on a treadmill.

A plausible witness

Perhaps not coincidentally, the period after *Night on Earth* was the longest to date that Jarmusch would go without releasing a feature – four years. When he re-emerged, it was with a film astonishing in its strangeness, originality, wit, craft, energy and refiguring of his essential fetishes. *Dead Man* is a Western John Ford wouldn't recognise, yet one which thoroughly honours and reinvents some of the great poetry Ford forged in his own depictions of the American past. It's a damning revision of the great theme of manifest destiny – the presumptive fate of the white race to conquer and settle the North American continent. And it's a gorgeous film celebrating the raw beauty of the land, the beneficent wisdom if its natives, and the visceral gratification of plain storytelling.

The journey to the West is undertaken by the whitest of white men, a ghostly Johnny Depp playing a Cleveland accountant named William Blake who possesses none of the skills by which the wilderness or its feral inhabitants (native or immigrant) might be tamed. Fleeing from the town of Machine, a ghastly final outpost of colonial industry, Blake is protected and preserved by Nobody, a hulking Native American of mixed blood and European education (played with enormous good humour by Gary Farmer). Together – and sometimes apart – the two journey through a surreal landscape to a seacoast village where Nobody sends Blake towards a final destination where all men are aliens and natives both.

The film isn't a complete break with Jarmusch's earlier praxis: there's the theme of the immigrant and the aboriginal, the theme of restless travel and cyclical return, the sumptuous black-and-white cinematography, the mordant japery, the celebrity cameos (including, God bless him, Robert Mitchum in his very last role), the soundtrack that churns like fugal chamber music (but is actually Neil Young playing a solo electric guitar with piercing eeriness). But it opened up his possibilities as a film-maker in ways even an ardent fan couldn't have foreseen. Its structure is fluid and open-ended. It embraces its genre (it *has* a genre) and its lead character. Its narrative takes place in comprehensible and unified space-time and it comes to a full-stop ending. Sure, it's weird and post-hip and, at least in some of its technique, terribly arch: it's a *Jim Jarmusch* picture, after all. But it's a bracing leap away from the early films – not so much a repudiation of their innovations and concerns as an application of them, as if by another artist digging around for fresh inspiration, to new material.

So, too, does *Ghost Dog* feel a new tack, with its obeisance to at least some of the laws of action films, its generally straight-ahead narration, and even the physique of its leading man Forest Whitaker, who uniquely among Jarmusch protagonists looks as though he's eaten at least once during the last month. And there are important resemblances to other films of its genre. Whitaker, always a disarming presence, makes for a thoroughly plausible and particularly menacing hitman (à la *Get Carter*, *Point Blank* or *The Limey*), brandishing his pistols like swords and all but silent save for voiceovers in which he reads from a seventeenth-century philosophy of the samurai; the gangsters who hire and then pursue him are delicious gargoyles save for the one (Louie, played by dog-faced John Tormey) to whom the hitman owes allegiance; the killings (killings in a Jarmusch film!) are beautifully staged (in particular the one that involves plumbing).

Playing for keeps

But there are elements here unique in the annals of mob stories. The key Jarmuschian ellipsis that impels the plot, for instance, isn't, as usual, a lacuna of space-time, but rather a jarringly disparate account of a crucial event in the lives of the hitman and his mob master: whereas both men recall that the gangster rescued Ghost Dog from a racially charged and potentially lethal beating, Louie remembers that he killed the attackers because they pointed a gun at *him*, while Ghost Dog (who was, we must remember, dazed from the thrashing) thought *he* was the target of the pistol. It's an explicit invocation of *Rashomon*, yes, and one of several in the film, but the disharmony of the accounts is particularly shimmery because Ghost Dog's entire life of subservience to Louie is based on what may very well be a complete misapprehension – one with, finally, irreversible results.

As in Jarmusch's early works, the outsider in *Ghost Dog* is recompensed for his alienness with suspicion, mistrust, persecution, nullification. But where the first films were steeped in a playful irony that made their knavish conclusions equivalent to pushing a kind of existential reset button, *Ghost Dog*, like *Dead Man*, is a game played vitally and for keeps. Jarmusch still loves his aliens, but as he nears middle age he seems less inclined to indulge their strangeness with whimsical, noncommittal plotting. His New World is coming to look more and more like the Old one – a place where the only way to reinvent or redefine yourself is to leave. Trouble is, he's starting to tell us, all the good places to start fresh are full up.

CALIFORNIA SPLIT

Xan Brooks

Like a series of lights coming on in an uncurtained building, Mike Figgis's *Timecode* opens at quarter-strength and then builds to full illumination. With the bulk of the screen's physical space still black (though abstracted light sources occasionally streak through or flicker), a window pops up filling the upper right-hand corner. Inside, a young woman (Saffron Burrows) is recounting a dream to her therapist. Midway through their exchange, an adjacent window at the top left-hand comes alive and the viewer sees a power-dressed vixen (Jeanne Tripplehorn) storm down the steps of a Beverly Hills residence and hurriedly let down the tyre of a nearby car. And we're torn. Do we continue to eavesdrop on the low, murmurous confessional in the shrink's sanctum or switch our attention to the more nakedly subversive actions next door? Or do we attempt to keep tabs on both: snooping on the top-right square while playing peeping Tom on top-left. A moment later, two more windows of opportunity have opened up on the picture's bottom storey and we're torn again. Four frames, four narratives. A quartet of options for the discerning voyeur to choose between.

Played out on a quartered screen, in real time, with no edits, *Timecode* is an ongoing fascination. As an exercise in parallel plotting, it's endlessly inventive. As a filmic experiment, it's gloriously audacious. If the closing credits neglect to acknowledge an editor, that's in part because the viewer is implicitly encouraged to fill that role for him or herself: concentrating on the dramas and characters that grab his or her attention and tuning out the others. Admittedly *Timecode* falls some way short of attaining the Holy Grail that is the first truly interactive feature film, but it at least has its nose pointed in the right direction.

It also hits something of a high-water mark in Figgis's push towards a more formally ambitious mode of movie-making; a push that began with 1995's award-winning, low-budget *Leaving Las Vegas* and continued through last year's floridly experimental *The Loss of Sexual Innocence*. In preparing *Timecode*, Figgis (a keen musician) composed his film on music sheets, as though scoring a string quartet. He then proceeded to shoot the picture in one continuous 93-minute take. The film's four digital-video cameras (operated by Figgis, James O'Keeffe, Tony Cucchiari and director of photography Patrick Alexander Stewart) were all turned on simultaneously and run on a common timecode, the electronic counter encoded on the tapes. There was no formal script and the blocking was largely improvised. The dangers, of course, in such a no-nets mode of working are manifest. At one stage a telltale hand can be glimpsed holding open the door as we trail Salma Hayek's starlet into the washroom, while on several occasions where the narratives overlap two frames move into such close proximity that the cameras must be mere inches away from clashing. But, on the whole, *Timecode* synchronises its high-wire act with aplomb: technically, this is a virtuoso piece of work.

More crucially, the film succeeds on a dramatic level. Figgis has admitted suffering initial qualms over the viability of his split-screen, parallel-plotting device, fretting that Timecode's constant four-way dialogue of sound and visual information would swamp the viewer. He concluded, however, that a diet of channel-surfing and multi-media has made sophisticates of modern-day filmgoers, equipping them to process a bombardment of information thrown at them on various frequencies. Where MTV would sate its audience through frenzied editing, Figgis reasoned, *Timecode* would do so through simultaneous, real-time narratives. Formally separate, these two modes of communication are spiritual cousins. The difference is that while the dominant MTV style is traditionally accused of spoonfeeding its public, *Timecode* empowers them. It serves up four dishes and invites us to sample instances of drama from each one.

Undeniably this makes for a tart and appealing diet. *Timecode* revolves around the Hollywood offices of Red Mullet films (the name of Figgis's own production company) and juggles a roster of semi-crazed *Day of the Locust* types with lots of satirical potshots at the movie industry. So we get comedic script pitches ('It's like *Shine* except the guy has a lot more problems'), forlorn mantras ('I am always in the right place at the right time') and duff green-lit projects (a director is auditioning actresses for the star role of a girl 'who's sleeping her way to the top of a public-relations firm in Missouri'). The largely improvised acting is sharp and convincing (particularly from Stellan Skarsgård and Salma Hayek) and the quartet of stories feed smartly into one another. But while *Timecode* provides some measure of viewer freedom, this is finally a freedom within limits. Throughout it all, one can never quite escape the godlike hand of Figgis (credited as writer, director, producer and composer) at work behind the scenes. In structuring the film as a piece of music, its creator shrewdly allows some frames to idle while the others combust. In overseeing the sound edit (with no room for a boom, a plethora of hidden microphones were used, following techniques pioneered by Robert Altman on *California Split*, 1974, and *Nashville*, 1975), Figgis elects to keep certain tracks low down in the mix and emphasise the dialogue elsewhere.

He even throws in a mission statement. Near the end of the film, Mia Maestro pops up as Ana, a glacial teenage prodigy who wants to throw out the trusty Eisensteinian montage in favour of a new form of cinematic language. 'Montage has created a false reality,' she proclaims. 'Digital is demanding new expressions.' Her proposed film will be played out in real time, on four cameras, in one continuous take. To Ana, the proposal is revolutionary. To Skarsgård's anguished executive, it sounds like 'the most pretentious crap I've ever heard'.

In the end, *Timecode* is never pretentious – it's too witty, too sure-footed, too infectiously exuberant for that. But it's not quite revolutionary either. In dispensing with montage, *Timecode* liberates the medium up to a point, but is still constrained by the simple need (perhaps inherent in all drama) to order its material and tell a story. Ergo, *Timecode*'s structure nudges the viewer subtly towards what Figgis regards as the important frames.

Timecode unfolds like a fantastically textured stretch of contemporary jazz. Its segmented interior is maddening, involving, often exhilarating. But there is a strict methodology behind its madness, and what sounds like free-form chaos in the opening bars soon swings into orbit around a central, unifying structure. In attempting to reconfigure the language of film, *Timecode* bends the rules beautifully. Yet it never quite breaks them.

PARALLEL LINES

Murray Smith

Among the things we might look for in an independent American movie – or at least might have looked for before the idea was reduced to the status of a marketing pitch – are weird-looking actors and eccentric performers, a simplicity, directness or freshness of style, and a willingness to stretch the thematic boundaries and moral proprieties characteristic of most studio fare. A particularly striking feature of late 1980s and 1990s American independent cinema, however, was an exploration of the formal possibilities, and in a few cases the limits, of narrative film, in particular by elaborating parallel structures – films based around several parallel storylines rather than a single, linear path.

The elaborate money-switch at the heart of Quentin Tarantino's *Jackie Brown* (1997) can stand as an example of one variant of the tendency in miniature. The switch – involving an exchange of shopping bags in the changing rooms of a clothing store in a mall – is not narrated to us in a linear fashion, tracking the actions of a particular character or set of characters. Nor is the action related to us through crosscutting, flicking back and forth between the various parties – Jackie (Pam Grier), Melanie (Bridget Fonda) and Louis Gara (Robert De Niro), the cops (Michael Keaton and Michael Bowen), and the bond bailsman, Max Cherry (Robert Forster) – as they pursue their goals. Instead, the action is played out a full three times, on each occasion from the perspective of a different key figure in the switch – first Jackie, then Melanie and Louis, and finally Max – laying the parallel sequences out in succession, end on end as it were. This is a curious and striking choice; the much more common way of structuring a scene of this sort, through crosscutting, ensures suspense by moving among the various characters moment to moment, so that (to imagine this example crosscut) as we watch Jackie in the changing room, we wonder about the exact whereabouts of Melanie, a speculation which is quickly rewarded when we cut to see that she and Louis are running late. The effect of crosscutting is to build suspense cumulatively, by revealing the progress of each set of characters more or less simultaneously. What, then, is Tarantino up to by revealing the action in this curiously repetitive fashion – by showing us twice over what we'd already been shown once?

In fact, the construction of the scene in this elongated fashion doesn't dissipate suspense per se, but it does scatter the focus of the suspense, so that each time we see the action, new dimensions are revealed, different aspects become salient, and the interests of different characters come to the fore. More importantly for the purposes of this essay, the successive revelation of the same action witnessed from different viewpoints creates a kind of formal fascination, heightening our sense of the way the various lines of action interweave with one another. By placing the temporally parallel sequences in succession, their parallel existence is, paradoxically, underlined. The sequence certainly doesn't distance us from the thrill of the action itself, but it does bring to it an additional pleasure derived from the way that the story is being told to us. This 'architectural' pleasure – in the form and manner of the story as much as the story itself – is emphasised further in the style of the sequence, which uses prolonged tracking shots alternately following the main characters from behind, or moving rapidly backwards as the characters stride towards the camera, as they flee the scene of the switch. In sum, the scene is given a parallelistic articulation in terms of both the story and its stylistic treatment.

Before *Jackie Brown*, there was *Pulp Fiction* (1994), and, before *Pulp Fiction*, there was... yes, *Reservoir Dogs* (1991), but also *Mystery Train* (1989). *Mystery Train*? At first glance, there might seem to be little in common between Tarantino's motor-mouthed hyper-ironised crime caper movies and the self-consciously artful minimalism of Jim Jarmusch. But a closer look reveals some surprising similarities. Both directors ally themselves, through the style and allusions of their films as well as the identity and taste of many of their characters, with black culture (especially music). Both directors invite the viewer at certain moments to sit back and appreciate the distinctive speech patterns of their characters, holding our attention in long takes on characters who 'talk the talk', or endlessly 'riff', to use Richard Williams's apt analogy (think of the Sun Studio guide in *Mystery Train*, or the Roberto Benigni and Rosie Perez characters in *Night on Earth*, and then think of the opening of *Reservoir Dogs*). And both directors share an interest in the elaborate, formal shaping of their narratives, and it is in this respect that *Mystery Train* adumbrates key features of the money-switch scene in *Jackie Brown*, and the entire structure of *Pulp Fiction*.

Jarmusch's interest in multiple parallel stories was already evident in *Stranger than Paradise* (1984) and is still present in somewhat subdued fashion in *Dead Man* (1996); however, it is in *Mystery Train* and *Night on Earth* (1993) that it is most explicit. *Mystery Train* is comprised of three intersecting sub-stories: 'Far From Yokohama', depicting the visit by Jun (Masatoshi Nagase) and Mitzuko (Youki Kudoh), a pair of Japanese rockabillies, to Memphis; 'A Ghost', which dwells on the tragic-comic travails of Luisa (Nicoletta Braschi), an Italian woman whose husband of one week dies unexpectedly, leaving her stranded in Memphis; and 'Lost in Space', which focuses on disgruntled Englishman Johnny (played by Joe Strummer and nicknamed 'Elvis') – laid off work and jilted by his girlfriend – along with his girlfriend's brother Charlie (Steve Buscemi) and his black friend Will Robinson (Rick Aviles). The action of all three stories takes place within a period of roughly twenty-four hours, between the time of the arrival of the train that delivers Jun and Mitzuko to Memphis, and their departure on another train the following morning. The three stories intersect with one another most crucially at a hotel where all three sets of characters find themselves overnight, the hotel night clerk (Screaming Jay Hawkins) and bellboy (Cinqué Lee) forming another pair of characters and a fourth story. The three major stories are both temporally and thematically parallel (all three involve the presence of foreigners in one of America's most famous cities). As with the sequence in *Jackie Brown*, however, the stories are told successively rather than simultaneously, and a great part of the interest of the film derives from our gradual realisation that the stories are temporally (and not simply thematically) parallel – and from our progressively greater understanding of just how and when the stories traverse one another. (It is this dimension of the film's structure that *Pulp Fiction* closely resembles.) The intersection of the three storylines is given graphic expression in a single shot – the last shot of the film before the credit sequence – in which we see a train (carrying Jun and Mitzuko) moving left to right over a bridge, the truck driven by Johnny and company driving under the bridge and off to the top right of the screen, and seconds later a police car moving right to left on a street parallel with the train track. The shot thus gathers together in a single image three trajectories, at once parallel and perpendicular, intersecting briefly and then disappearing into off-screen space.

Retrospectively, we can see that the process of intersection begins early on: Jun and Mitzuko pass by Charlie as he opens up his barber shop in the morning (apparently using a fishing rod to pull down the awning), an event paralleled at the end of the film when they find themselves on the same train leaving Memphis as Charlie's sister Dee Dee (Elizabeth Bracco). They also pass by several locations which will become import-ant in the subsequent stories, though at this point in the film they are important mostly as landscapes of a run-down Memphis (their impact in this regard heightened by the incongruous presence of the two Japanese rockabillies, the contemplative rhythm established by the extended tracking shots which follow them, and the slow, spare blues which accompanies them). In general, the film establishes a kind of 'circuit' of streets and locations within Memphis, with the hotel at the heart, through which the various stories will circulate. But our understanding of this is one that gradually accrues over the course of the film, and among the most important ways that this occurs is through a number of linking moments which relate the stories to one another in temporal terms. In the first two of the three stories, at some point in the evening a character (Mitzuko and Dee Dee, respectively) stares out from their hotel room window and sees a train – the mystery train? – passing over a bridge in the distance. In the third story, the truck that the three characters are driving is shown passing under the bridge as a train crosses it, and we see this from roughly the same position – from the hotel, although in this case the shot is not ascribed to a character. Precisely because these simultaneous stories are *told* successively, however, we have to be alert to spot the link, and even if we spot it, we can't be sure that this is the same train at the same time in the evening, as the distant sound of trains moving through the city echoes throughout the film.

The absence of precise temporal markers in the film ensures that we have to put the jigsaw of the three stories together on the basis of less overt clues (contrast this with the use of clock subtitles in the sequence from *Jackie Brown*, or the exact temporal indications provided by the voiceover in Stanley Kubrick's *The Killing* (1956), a film Tarantino has cited as an influence). These clues come in the form of more unique events which are repeated and which consolidate the link: in the second story, Luisa and Dee Dee hear Jun and Mitzuko making love through the wall later in the evening; all four sets of characters listen to the radio at the same moment, during a transition from a Roy Orbison song to Elvis's 'Blue Moon'; and, the following morning, Jun and Mitzuko, Luisa and Dee Dee, the clerk and the bellboy all hear from their respective locations the gunshot which wounds Charlie in the leg. The most exquisite linking device, however, is a brief scene involving the clerk and the bellboy, which threads through all three major stories. Bored to distraction, the bellboy slips on a pair of sunglasses (an absurd gesture given that it is the middle of the night), and then takes them off when the gesture fails to draw the attention of the clerk. Trying another tack, he complains about the state of his uniform, but only provokes the clerk into a brief homily on the importance of sartorial style ('You know what they say – the clothes make the man.'), followed by the abrupt exclamation that the bellboy looks like 'a damn mosquito-legged chimpanzee!'. Quite aside from the intrinsic performative and comic value of this moment, it is also distinctive because the core of the scene is represented in an identical fashion in all three stories. In the first story, we see the stretch of action as I've described it; in the second story, the action begins fractionally sooner, but ends with the bellboy still wearing the sunglasses; the third story picks the scene up from the moment where the second leaves off, and extends the sequence beyond the dialogue concerning clothes, to an announcement on the radio concerning a new restaurant in town called 'Jiffy Squid'. But, unlike the three variations in *Jackie Brown*, and the other examples of linking moments in *Mystery Train* (the lovemaking, the gunshot), in this case the place from which we perceive the action (a static frontal two-shot on the two characters) remains constant. Instead, what varies is the size of the durational slice of the action in each story.

The turn of the decade – from the 1980s to the 1990s – delivered not only *Mystery Train*, but also another modern classic of parallelism, Richard Linklater's *Slacker* (1991). In some ways, *Slacker* is as spare as a Jarmusch film, but it is also a densely populated film. Instead of teasing out a small number of rather slight comic stories and creating an intricate, slowly-unfolding series of connections, Linklater piles up a vast of array of microstories – some of them little more than monologues – which intersect only at the apparently chance moment when they meet spatially, and the camera moves from the characters it has been following to those that it will follow next. Thus, a pair of characters wander along a street, one of whom complains about the futility of travelling, claiming that everywhere looks the same anyway (a most Jarmuschian theme, by the way: Mitzuko reckons that Memphis looks pretty much like Yokohama). The camera then picks up a pair of women who pass by the first pair of characters, walking in the opposite direction and discussing a sensual epiphany one of them experienced on holiday, as the scent of flowers wafted in from the sea to the shore. *Slacker* is filled with these random encounters, by turns mundane, ironic and surreal. All the action takes place in Austin, Texas – almost all of it in its bohemian district – and, as in *Mystery Train*, there is the sense of a closed circuit of landscape through which all the characters move. And, again as in *Mystery Train*, there is a graphically emblematic shot of the film's structure – in this case a sequence shot near the beginning of the film, which tracks around a complete city block in the course of establishing an incident involving a young man running over and murdering his mother. However, while just about all the characters are 'slackers' of various ages, no specific character or event ever recurs in the manner of *Mystery Train*'s tripartite repetitions. Rather, the structure is one of endlessly forking narrative pathways, an idea given explicit expression in Linklater's opening monologue, in which he talks about a Borgesian world of endlessly proliferating parallel universes, every choice resulting in at least two new possible worlds. Here, as in *Mystery Train*, there is a faintly mystic quality to *Slacker*.

Did the parallel narrative spring from nowhere in American independent cinema from the 1980s onwards? Certainly not. Setting aside literary forebears, the cinematic precursors of this trend are many and various, and to be found in many national cinemas. Most immediately, there are the contemporary cousins of the films discussed here, from geographically immediate neighbours such as *Poison* (1991), *Thirty-two Short Films About Glenn Gould* (1993) and *The Red Violin* (1998), to far-flung kin such as the early Jane Campion short *Passionless Moments* (1983), based on a succession of miniature neighbourhood vignettes, and Wong Kar-Wai's *Chongqing senlin* (*Chungking Express*, 1994), with its juxtaposition of the stories of two lonely cops whose lives overlap for a fleeting moment in the course of the film, but resonate with each other in a host of ways – it is no coincidence that Tarantino has been an advocate of Kar-Wai. *Run Lola Run* (Tom Tykwer, 1998) provides another contemporary variant, focusing on the large consequences of minute differences in timing in a story told three times. Widening the circle a little further, there are those older independent American directors, chiefly John Sayles and especially Robert Altman, who have used parallelistic forms (Sayles in *City of Hope* (1991), Altman in many films, including *Nashville* (1975), *A Wedding* (1978), *Short Cuts* (1993) and *Prêt-à-Porter* (1994)). Other directors of the movie-brat generation dipped their toes into the water with collaborative anthology films such as *Twilight Zone: The Movie* (Joe Dante, John Landis, George Miller, Steven Spielberg, 1983) and *New York Stories* (Woody Allen, Francis Ford Coppola, Martin Scorsese, 1989) – a practice revived by the current generation of indie directors with *Four Rooms* (Allison Anders, Alexandre Rockwell, Robert Rodriguez, Quentin Tarantino, 1995). Further back still, Kubrick's *The Killing* contains the pattern of repeated, identical slices of action in distinct but overlapping storylines so important to *Mystery Train*, though in less elaborate form.

Moving out (and back) still further, there is a significant lineage within international art cinema, including Chantal Akerman's *Toute une nuit* (1982), Greenaway's *The Falls* (1980), Ophuls's *La Ronde* (1950), the tradition of 'portmanteau' films such as Ealing's *Dead of Night* (1945), all the way back to Jean Epstein's *La Glace à trois faces* (1927), which narrates successively the stories of three women simultaneously in love with the same man who spurns them all. We should not overlook another branch of the family tree, which uses parallelism as a way of raising questions about the objectivity of any particular account of a person or event, most famously in *Citizen Kane* (1941) and *Rashomon* (1950), as well as – less famously but more proximately given the focus of this essay – in Amos Poe's *Triple Bogey on a Par Five Hole* (1991). And in the first decade of cinema, as film-makers grappled with the way in which stories could be told using the new medium, some films pursued the option of repeating action from different perspectives, creating a temporality which 'is staggered, stuttered, [and] repeats itself', to use Tom Gunning's words. In Thomas Edison and Edwin Porter's *Life of an American Fireman* (1903), for example, a fireman enters the room of a burning house and rescues a woman and then her child. We see this first from within the room, and then again from the front of the house. As often happens in art, what we might take to be a 'primitive' technique is revealed as a form of great sophistication.

And a few years back there was Hal Hartley's *Flirt* (1995) – in some respects the purest and most extreme manifestation of the principle of parallelism of all those discussed here, insofar as the three stories in this film are not just similar thematically and temporally parallel (as in *Mystery Train*, *Slacker* and *Pulp Fiction*), but variations on an identical core story. Along with Jarmusch, of all the directors discussed here Hartley is the director whose general sensibility is most suited to this form of film-making – the 'stilted', repetitive dialogue, muted acting, and compositional simplicity and precision of his earlier films always pointing towards what I have called here 'architectural' pleasure. Indeed, the triadic structure of *Flirt* was presaged in Hartley's own work by *Surviving Desire* (1991), a compilation of three shorts originally released separately, but clearly paralleling and resonating with one another when set side by side. In *Flirt*, the underlying parallels are so marked – one lover leaving town, the 'flirt' staying in town, both in doubt over the future of the relationship, the flirt receiving advice from a chorus of his or her gender peers, the flirt flirting with both a friend and another lover who has left their partner for the flirt, and so on – that it is the differences that become more salient. For example, in the final (and most elaborate) version of the story, set in Japan, the fact that the flirt is a woman (rather than a man, as in the previous two versions) changes the way we think about the facial scar that this character will be left with as a result of the gunshot wound (underlined by the appalled reaction of the surgeon in this version of the story, in contrast to the more phlegmatic reactions of his peers in the earlier two versions). As the chorus of three builders tell us in the middle story, 'the film-maker's project is to explore the changing dynamics of the same situation in different milieux' – as well as, we should add, changes in the gender and sexual orientation of the main characters. Many critics viewed *Flirt* as at best a kind of diversion, and at worst a dead end, for Hartley, but it seems to me to be one of his most fully realised works – precisely because it elaborates the kind of formal play that the parallel structure supports so well, and that has always been a strong, perhaps the dominant, element in Hartley's work. From this point of view, the real dead end for Hartley is the sloppy comic absurdism of *Amateur* (1994) or the heavy-handed grotesquery of *Henry Fool* (1997). The latter especially seems like a forced attempt to escape the charge of 'formalism', without any real sense of what will take its place other than gestures which violate it.

Whatever its history, it might seem from the examples I've focused on here that after a brief efflorescence as the twentieth century closed the parallel narrative is dying out. Maybe so, but it's always been a rare bird, and it is just as likely that there will continue to be occasional sightings of this unusual species. And – to stick with evolutionary metaphors, but to shift from nature to culture – now that the 'meme' has successfully been transplanted into the meme pool of American film-making, it is fair to assume that it will reappear. Linklater's particular spin on the form was evident again in *Dazed and Confused* (1993) (though with a mere seventy-eight, as compared with *Slacker*'s ninety-seven, characters), and even in *Before Sunrise* (1995), where we are taken on a *Slacker*-like tour of Vienna's eccentrics, this time though in the company of two very central characters who are present in every scene. The narrative meme of the repeated scene which acts as the tie between three parallel tales successively told, first appearing in *Mystery Train* and picked up by *Pulp Fiction*, has more recently been replicated in Doug Liman's *Go* (1999). Paul Thomas Anderson has emerged, with *Boogie Nights* (1997) and *Magnolia* (1999), as a director eager to work with epic, multiple storyline structures, though with a stylistic exuberance quite distinct from Jarmusch's carefully measured rhythms or Altman's comic realism. Last but not least, Errol Morris's *Fast, Cheap and Out of Control* (1997) reveals how creatively parallelism can be used in a non-fiction context, in a film which tests and teases our ability to discern the kinship among four distinct documentary strands concerning robots, topiary, wild animal training, and mole-rats! Keep watching for (parallel) developments...

Bad Lieutenant (Abel Ferrara, 1992)

Section 5: Mavericks

Robert Altman

IN THE TIME OF EARTHQUAKES

Jonathan Romney

The last word spoken in Robert Altman's film *Short Cuts* is 'lemonade'. We hear it as the camera tracks out over a briefly shaken Los Angeles, as two partying couples toast to survival in the face of a minor apocalypse. As so often happens with Altman, who is famous for his habit of scrambling soundtracks to the limit of comprehensibility, the word is audible but not entirely noticeable, certainly not impressing itself on you as central to the film's meaning. Yet, in an oblique fashion, that is precisely what it is – an operational password for the entire film. For 'Lemonade' is the title of a poem by Raymond Carver, and the poem's subject is also the film's real subject, as well as its structural principle.

Short Cuts is based on nine stories by Carver, who died in 1988 aged fifty, having established himself as the poet laureate of small, desolate, claustrophobic middle American lives. 'Lemonade' itself is not directly adapted in the film, although its theme – What if this had happened, rather than that? What then? – is foregrounded in the episode involving Jack Lemmon, and runs throughout the film, both in the narratives themselves, and in the way they interlock. In the poem, a man ponders on his son's drowning: he is convinced he would still be alive if only he had not gone to fetch lemonade that day. The lemonade, he reasons, would not have been there if only there had not been lemons in the shops. So he tries to pick his way back causally to a prelapsarian moment: 'It all harks back to first causes, back to the first lemon cultivated on earth.'

Carver knows there is no first lemon, and Altman knows it, too. There is no way of untangling the mesh of cause and effect, hence the gloriously unruly tangle of chance that governs *Short Cuts*. The credits divide the cast list conveniently into nine family sets of characters, plus supporting players, but in reality the groups are not separated neatly from one another; rather, they intermingle, meeting, playing, straying with seismic effect into each others' lives. Each group has its own story, but no story belongs solely to one group. Altman plays with an illusion of order by framing the narratives between two urban catastrophes during which all the characters are effectively united simply by virtue of being in the same boat. The sense of unity is illusory, though, imposed as it is by narrative contingency. There is no start or finish, no first or last lemon, only the all-pervasive smell of lemonade. Savour it, or baulk at its bitterness, that's all you get in life, and you have to drink it.

There is no first lemon in Robert Altman's career, either. Looking back on the director's exceptionally diverse history, no clear thread is immediately apparent. We can impose an overall narrative on it, but only if we give in to the temptation continually to ask, 'what if?'. There is the fact that after the international success of his 1969 film *M∗A∗S∗H*, Altman went on to make a number of movies whose eccentricity wilfully flew in the face of box-office logic – the flight fantasy *Brewster McCloud* (1970), the dream-like *3 Women* (1977), the bleak science-fiction vision *Quintet* (1979). He also made some that worked over genres in a way that seemed to tap in directly to the sceptical Zeitgeist of the 1970s – notably his brutal demystifications of the frontier Western and the Philip Marlowe myth in *McCabe and Mrs Miller* (1971) and *The Long Goodbye* (1973), respectively.

But *what if* Altman's career had been more coherent? *What if* his 1980 shot at a grandly fanciful comic-book epic, *Popeye*, had been the intended box-office smash? (Indeed, *what if* its star Robin Williams had actually been audible at any point in the film?) And *what if* the administration at Fox had not suddenly changed just in time to scupper the commercial hopes of his 1980 satire *Health*?

Pure speculation, of course, but all these factors contributed to one of the exemplary adventures in American cinema – the strange situation in which the most ambitious, wayward director of his generation (Altman, remember, preceded the Class of Movie Brats) suddenly found himself having to reinvent his career on a shoestring, having blown his luck not only with the major studios, but also with his own ill-fated production company Lion's Gate. Hence an extraordinary spate of low-budget ventures into chamber cinema, often drawn from theatre: the remarkable one-hander for Richard Milhous Nixon, *Secret Honor* (1984), which did for Tricky Dicky what Syberberg did for Hitler; *Fool for Love* (1985), *Come Back to the Five & Dime Jimmy Dean, Jimmy Dean* (1982). There were other off-the-cuff projects for television, such as the adaptations of Pinter's *The Dumb Waiter* and *The Room* (1987), and a version of that creaky tub-thumper *The Caine Mutiny Court-Martial* (1988), a small miracle of a film which testily jump-started that somnolent genre, the courtroom drama.

It's tempting to consider that had Altman's Hollywood fortunes been more consistent, this whole daredevil chapter might not have happened. Altman himself is sanguine about his whole story and aware of just how random can be the elements that impinge on his progress. Visiting Britain for *Short Cuts*'s screening at last November's London Film Festival, he cited the example of his *Buffalo Bill and the Indians* (1976), co-written with his protégé Alan Rudolph and, after *McCabe and Mrs Miller*, his second scathing debunking of the legends of the Wild West.

'*Buffalo Bill* was released on Independence Day 1976, which was the Bicentennial of the country. Nixon had just resigned in disgrace, and the whole country was licking its wounds, and I come out with this picture and say, "Hi, folks, here I am, let me tell you what assholes you are and how America's myths are blah blah blah blah..." Nobody wanted it. At a different time in history, that film could have been a big hit.'

Short Cuts, too, falls wonderfully into this schema of apparent randomness. Altman first read Raymond Carver's stories on a plane journey. Inspired by them, he started planning a Carver film, and got as far as selecting the locations and signing up a number of actors, including Tim Robbins, Peter Gallagher and Fred Ward. But finally the finance was not available. While pondering his next move, he was offered a project called *The Player*. Those same actors found their way into that film, which in 1992 turned out to be Altman's first commercial and critical success in years – as well as a modish *succès de scandale* among the Hollywood mandarins, at once outraged and flattered to see their world lampooned. *Short Cuts* was financed on the strength of that film.

The Player was notable for playing an extreme version of a trick that Altman had used before, and fully intends to use again – the interweaving of real and fictional universes. In *The Player*, a host of familiar Hollywood faces played themselves, raising the interesting question of what being 'oneself' might mean in a city predicated entirely on performance. But the most cunning variation of this effect came in Altman's television series *Tanner '88: The Dark Horse* (1988), in which real-life US politicos including Robert Dole and Pat Robertson were drafted in to be encountered by Michael Murphy's fictional Democrat presidential hopeful. Altman intends to push the method further in his next production, *Prêt-à-Porter*, which he is filming this year in the Paris fashion world.

'In *Prêt-à-Porter*, we're using much more reality. There's not much reality in *Short Cuts*, except the presence of the game show host Alex Trebek [who appears early on in a concert scene]. In *Prêt-à-Porter*, I will probably push the mix between reality and fiction as far as I've ever pushed it. I'm dependent on it, because I can't recreate the amount of people in that world – especially when you get into the fashion shows, the press, the photographers. So I have to use a lot of reality.'

Unlike *The Player*, *Short Cuts* plays less on reality per se than on the real. Carver's low-key, minimally stylised portrayals of the doldrums and zero moments in blue-collar living led him to be counted as a leading exponent of that amorphous school known as 'Dirty Realism'. He wrote about dead marriages, dead-end jobs, typhoons in teacups, minor misunderstandings that blow up into little household apocalypses – but apocalypses in aspic. What's remarkable about these stories is the way they merge explosiveness with absolute stillness. A typical story, one of those in *Short Cuts*, is 'Jerry and Molly and Sam', in which a fatigued father contrives to lose the family dog, then has to retrieve it. When he finally finds the dog, he simply contemplates it, and the story ends on a suspended moment: 'He sat there. He thought he didn't feel so bad, all things considered. The world was full of dogs. There were dogs and there were dogs. Some dogs you just couldn't do anything with.'

Altman and his co-writer Frank Barhydt take a very different approach. The episode becomes a source of high farce, the dog a benign comic focus for the chaotic rage of Tim Robbins's blustering cop. There's clearly more meeting the eye – more energy, more incident – in Altman's version than the moments of cold, clear deadness that Carver's original stories are imbued with. Yet Altman claims that he leaves out everything that Carver leaves out – and precisely what that is, he says, is 'judgment, in most cases. I make a little bit more judgment than Carver made. I have a tougher task in a way. It's very hard to do films as minimalism, because the audience is there and they see every square inch of that screen. They see wallpaper and they see rugs and they see shirts and expressions and weather – until all of the descriptive passages that you have in a book are *there*.

'Carver uses no descriptive passages, so I don't believe a Raymond Carver story can be literally translated to a visual medium. So I just tried to take the feeling from Carver, the type of incident he dealt with, and express that in a way that tells the same story for an audience. I don't think that I could take any one of his stories and make a film out of it.'

How did Altman and Barhydt decide which stories to use, and which ones would lead into which others?

'They do it themselves automatically. You take one base story, you throw it up on the wall, and it's like vines – they grow where there's space to grow in and out of one another.' The image of vines perhaps expresses what's most peculiar to the film. It's certainly true that, as some Carver specialists have pointed out, the film does not strictly adhere to the writer's spirit; it's at once too upbeat and too cynical for that. It only rarely displays the stoic empathy that the stories solicit for their characters; instead, Altman's characters redeem the claustrophobic quality of their lives by the energy and charisma with which they *perform* (to the extent that some of these lives look somewhat glamorous *because* they're incarnated by the likes of Tom Waits or Frances McDormand). But it is the connections between the episodes that make the film – the sense that they're all bunches of event growing on the same tangled vine. And it's when we become aware of the incongruity of these connections that the film transcends its merely anecdotal base.

There are moments of sublime embarrassment in *Short Cuts*, notably in the sequence where Jack Lemmon, as the estranged father of the son that he hasn't seen for years, turns up at the hospital where his young grandson is in casualty. It's a painful situation in itself, but the film pushes it further by having the father deliver a monologue recounting the banal indiscretion that years ago led to his banishment from the family. Here most of all, the spirit of 'Lemonade' (could Lemmon have been cast purely for a conceptual pun?) makes itself felt. The father's reminiscence represents a crisis in itself, but one that is totally inappropriate to the crisis happening in the hospital ward. It's as if he has wandered from one story into another, suggesting that life's most dramatic moments are the result of inadequate separation between different narratives.

'This is what happens every day of your life,' says Altman, 'but we don't recognise it so much because we can't take the involvement. Somebody gets hit by a car and you stop and look in the street, and you think, "I don't want to see that," so you go the other way. But people who *don't* go the other way see more of that story, and the people who are actually involved in that story have *another* story. These things go on all the time, and it's the juxtaposition of these lives that makes *Short Cuts* interesting.'

The Carver stories operate on two levels. Each one is very much like a closed box, a miniature in which a single core of event, or lack of event, is to be contemplated – in the tradition of modernist short story narrative since Chekhov, Joyce, Mansfield. At the same time, however, the stories taken together, and the regularity of the themes and styles, make an overall human comedy made up of small mosaic pieces. *Short Cuts*, though, functions only through the concatenation of parts – the clash of micro-narratives sparking ironic parallels and negations off each other.

It's a technique that has formed the basis of what is probably the most celebrated strand of Altman's work. The idea of sprawling ensemble pieces made of varying, decentred dramas is one he famously perfected in *Nashville* (1975). At one point he planned a follow-up, *Nashville, Nashville*, with some of the same characters, and *Short Cuts* could be seen as the pay-off of that aborted project (Altman plans eventually to make *More Short Cuts*). But there are variations to this approach. *Nashville* derived its unity from having different characters doing different business in one setting – a place that in its iconic status as an anti-Hollywood, America's great *other* dream factory, opened the film up to an allegorical state-of-the-nation reading. *A Wedding* (1978) similarly used a single setting, this time to follow the conventions of situation comedy to their extreme conclusion.

Short Cuts differs from *Nashville* in its relation to place – it is not primarily the portrait of a specific city, but simply uses Los Angeles as a convenient, anonymous venue to bring its various protagonists together. (As Frank Barhydt points out, 'apart from the palm trees and the weather, there's nothing indigenous to LA, nothing in the characters of the people.') However, the city's anonymity brings its own meaning to the film. Where the city of Nashville forms an arena in which individuals intermingle, with politics and country music as the uniting factor, *Short Cuts* captures the cellular essence of LA, a city in which separate zones, separate homes, are linked by highways. You can imagine each segment to be equivalent to a family cell – and things start happening when characters step out of their own territory into other people's. The theme is seen in undiluted form in the episode based on the story 'Neighbors'. In the film, there is no life-transforming catastrophe as there is in Carver's story. A couple simply make free with the apartment they're caretaking; but our sense of unease is no less powerful, just because we expect the worst – we know they should not be there. As with the Jack Lemmon episode, we receive a sense of *trespass*: lines have been crossed.

Despite the sense of impending chaos that is perhaps inevitable in a film that juggles twenty-two lead parts, there are plenty of guide rails in *Short Cuts* to ensure that we know where we are. One is the use of familiar faces in the cast. ('I don't have to tell you too much about these people,' says Altman. 'You do the work for me by recognising them.') Another is the use of a nightclub singer, played by Annie Ross, to act as a chorus, casting a sardonic torch-song commentary throughout the film. And another is the way the diversity of incident is framed between the two minor apocalypses.

At the beginning of the film, the city is sprayed against medfly, a pest which leaves harmless blemishes on fruit (what could be more suggestive of the Californian obsession with cosmetic surfaces?). The end of the film – which, beware, this paragraph reveals in full – is rather more violent. At the very second that Chris Penn's repressed, brooding character Jerry unexpectedly smashes a rock down on a young girl's head, an earthquake erupts. It's a horribly suggestive moment. Perhaps Jerry's pent-up rage is the entire city's; perhaps, because of him, heavenly wrath is being visited on the community. But you could read it more cynically as a self-conscious sleight of hand, a playfully apocalyptic gesture in which Altman plays God and brings all the film's diffuse threads together, packing all his characters back in the narrative toy box.

'That's just coincidence,' Altman says of the ending. 'I'm sure that for every earthquake that's ever happened, some very strong, acute dramatic event has happened in somebody's life – I just happened to be there at this particular incident. I needed to polarise the beginning and end of the film – these people's lives never really came together, they just occasionally crossed in a very haphazard way, so that's something that was a common experience. I wouldn't be surprised if in *More Short Cuts* there'll be another two events. One of them might be the Californian fires.'

This closing image of the all-powerful narrative deity suggests a director who likes to keep a tight rein on his creation. But, Altman says, only one type of control interests him: 'the control to be able to change and let ideas come in from my collaborators. To have the ability to say "Yeah" and turn the piece this way or that. Not say, "Wait a minute, you said you were going to do this and you'd better stick to it."'

Altman's list of recent and future projects may suggest a sense of multi-directional crazy-paving, but there's a flexibility and ambition there that he's always had, and that directors a third his age rarely evidence. Already chalked up: a stage opera version of the novel *McTeague* (the source of Von Stroheim's *Greed*), with composer William Bolcom; a short documentary recording the hoofers' musical *Black and Blue*; producing Alan Rudolph's new film *Dorothy Parker*, itself a multi-character sprawler in the Altman tradition. Planned after *Prêt-à-Porter*: a Mata Hari project; another collaboration with Frank Barhydt about Kansas City's boomtown years during the Depression; a two-film version of playwright Tony Kushner's Aids diptych *Angels in America*; a film called *Cork* with Harry Belafonte, 'about blackface and entertainment from the turn of the century'. Altman admits, 'I'll never do all of those. It's like *pommes frites* – you throw the potatoes in and then whichever one pops to the surface is done first.'

Altman also offers another, perhaps more apposite analogy, that applies just as well to his career as a whole – reckless, unruly, wilfully patchy – as it does to particular films like *Short Cuts*. 'It comes down to what occurs to me. It's like doing art – I'm not doing Rembrandts or Corots. I'm doing Rauschenbergs. I'm doing collages. If suddenly I want to stick into my painting a photograph of a flat-iron, it just goes in.'

Paul Thomas Anderson

NIGHT FEVER

Gavin Smith

The opening shot of Paul Thomas Anderson's second feature film begins with its name in lights: *Boogie Nights*, immediately revealed, as the camera cranes back, on a San Fernando Valley movie marquee. Even before the viewer can wonder when last they saw a movie's title appear actually in the movie's own physical world, let alone at its head, the shot descends in one uninterrupted movement to a night-time boulevard and then over and into a bustling nightclub. Here the steadicam insinuates its promiscuous way from dance floor to table booth to dance floor, introducing all the main characters and much of its supporting cast, before coming to a halt at the protagonist, a busboy named Eddie whose unique talent is about to be spotted and put to use. Anderson will bring us back to marquees more than once, for this is a movie about showbusiness in all its tawdry pathos, about the high price talent pays to play, and about the schizophrenic self-reinvention, compulsive longings and dread-filled narcissism of show people, a breed apart.

This three- or four-minute opening shot is neither unique nor exemplary, even if film history begins for you with *GoodFellas* in 1990, but its uninhibited exuberance and will to cinematic mastery allow you to glimpse something we can't get enough of at the movies: the erotic abandon of cinematic form, pure or impure as it gets. It's precisely this that announces the advent of a new stylist, one young enough to make an old device seem brand new. If you were lucky enough to have seen Anderson's first film, premiered at Sundance two years ago under its 'true' title *Sydney*, but only belatedly released this year as *Hard Eight*, this may not be news.

Both films feature enigmatic, benignly corrupting fathers and the sons who become attached to them, and both inhabit closed, alienated worlds defined by vice – gambling in the first, pornography in the second. Yet the cool distance and cryptic intrigue of the first film and the overheated, reckless acceleration and emotional turmoil of the second both emanate from an unsentimental sense of human weakness. Anderson gives every character their due, clarifies the emotional stakes that underwrite the action and doesn't moralise. *Hard Eight* tells of an ultra-precise professional gambler, played with unforgettable restraint by Philip Baker Hall, who becomes mentor to John C. Reilly's young man who's just hit rock bottom. Following the logic of character with relentless post-Mamet discipline, *Hard Eight*'s style took its cue from its cerebral main character: spare, controlled and measured. *Boogie Nights* is as baroque, recklessly self-indulgent and nervously energised as its ensemble, an extended family of cast and crew working in the porn film industry that thrives in the Valley behind Los Angeles, on the other side of the Hollywood billboard. If *Hard Eight* is an object lesson in knowing one's limits and facing life with calm realism and calculation, *Boogie Nights* is about people incapable of grasping the concept of limits, whose reality principles are impaired, who are in the dictionary under Spoiled Identity. And if *Hard Eight* is a kind of tightly constructed, discreet chamber drama of four inextricably interconnected characters, *Boogie Nights* is a sprawling, exhibitionist epic, a sensationally over-populated family saga in which damaged children manufacture 'adult entertainment' to please daddy.

Hard Eight may be a near-perfectly realised gem where *Boogie Nights* is amiably flawed and somewhat selective in the depiction of its milieu, but the latter has ambition to spare and a lot more on its mind, and ultimately it forgoes closure for troubling question marks. Though it begins in the generality of any Valley boulevard, that continuous opening shot that finally arrives at one chosen Valley youth calls across the ruptures and discontinuities of the subsequent narrative to its matching, domesticated bookend: a long steadicam shot commencing this time not with the glamour of a movie marquee but with the grunt-work reality behind it – the trusty crew unloading a truck. It proceeds into and through porn auteur Jack Horner's well-appointed ranch house, finding most of the film's now-familiar characters settled in place, come to terms, if not at peace, with themselves and what they do; this series of vignettes, each a playful travesty of familial harmony, culminates once again with Eddie, now renamed Dirk Diggler and no longer the 'innocent' of that first shot, capping this simulation of a happy ending with a payoff that surely reasserts his profound alienation, confronting his alter ego in the mirror, and proving the reality of his existence the only way he knows how.

*   *   *

Gavin Smith: One of the things that's interesting about *Boogie Nights* is its tone shifts, for instance between dramatic and comic/parodic.

Paul Thomas Anderson: There are two answers to that. First, two of my favourite movies are F. W. Murnau's *Sunrise* (1927) and Jonathan Demme's *Something Wild* (1985), what I call gearshift movies, that can change tones [snaps fingers] like that. I like to see that in movies because that's what real life is like, and it's also good storytelling. And second, this relates to how I came to this story. The first version was a film I made called *The Dirk Diggler Story*, when I was seventeen. That has some of the same textures, but it's much funnier. It's my point of view as a seventeen-year-old, and what was funny to me then was the titles. As a mass audience, we're amused and turned on by porno titles – *Ordinary Peepholes*, *The Sperminator*, *Edward Penishands* – but then this is quickly not funny. There was something in that short film that was darkly comic, but there were a lot of smartass moments. Over the course of ten years, just by getting older and slightly sick of it all, that's where more of the sadness and drama comes into it. I just sat there and lived with it and it was just not fucking funny anymore.

Gavin Smith: But isn't the coda a fantasy redemptive happy ending?

Paul Thomas Anderson: No, I tried to come up with the saddest happy ending I could come up with. It would be way too easy to punish all those characters, to have them die or whatever. That's not how I felt about them, and that's really not usually the case in real life. The bottom line is that Dirk Diggler and everyone else are preparing to go and make another porn movie. But after this whole journey, what have they learned? If that's happy and redemptive, okay.

Gavin Smith: Do you still watch porn and has your viewing changed? Do you watch it as narrative, all the way through, rather than fast-forwarding to the fuck scenes?

Paul Thomas Anderson: The porno you fast-forward to get to the action are today's films. They're movies for consumers and the makers are aware that the home viewer has a fast-forward button – that's why there is no paying attention to any kind of plot or story. The audience is at home going, 'Where are the tits? Where's the dick? How can I get to it fast?' That's why *Boogie Nights* romanticises the heyday of porno – you can't watch it at home, you're going into a theatre.

Gavin Smith: What porn films from the 1970s would you single out?

Paul Thomas Anderson: The first one I saw was *The Opening of Misty Beethoven*, directed by Henry Paris. When I first saw the John Holmes 'Johnny Wadd' series when I was about seventeen, I thought, 'This is fucking fascinating.'

Gavin Smith: Are you a fan of Paris's other films?

Paul Thomas Anderson: I don't really know enough about the rest of his work, I've only seen a couple of his other movies. It's not an auteur-driven genre, you're really focusing on the actors involved.

Gavin Smith: Artistic aspiration or self-improvement consume all of the main characters in *Boogie Nights* one way or another. But your response to porn films seems to be a camp one: you don't expect genuine artistic value.

Paul Thomas Anderson: None are successful on the terms that I would consider make a great film, even a great porno film. But there are those – like *Three A.M. at the Jade Pussycat*, *Amanda by Night* and *The Opening of Misty Beethoven* – that get A for effort and have their heart in the right place. With genuinely wonderful moments of intent, of storytelling approach or shot choice – or cinematic approach to shooting a sex scene. Then there's whether it's a successful sex scene that can turn me on. One thing I was really fascinated by was the structure in the 'Johnny Wadd' series – in *The Jade Pussycat* for instance, which combines a murder mystery with a sex film. It set up – with some bad acting, but also some good acting – a mystery plot: where is the Jade Pussycat? So in the journey to find it, there are these set pieces of sex in between solving the murder mystery. You want to see the story progress and see him find the next clue, but you're also there as the guy who sat down to watch a porno movie, wanting him to have sex with that girl he's getting the clue from.

Gavin Smith: Which is Jack Horner's ideal.

Paul Thomas Anderson: Absolutely. And I'd be a liar if I didn't say Jack's probably talking for any young romantic idiot like me who has notions of trying to make a good movie. It certainly projects my feelings onto him.

Gavin Smith: When you talk about porn as a genre stifled before it got going, what direction did you hope for?

Paul Thomas Anderson: Where I romanticise it could have gone was a place where acting, storytelling and camerawork got better. With interesting characters where you also had the luxury to show them fucking. We can't see Forrest Gump fuck Jenny Curran, to make that kid. But God, wouldn't that be a great scene? Not just because I want to get off watching Tom Hanks fuck Robin Wright, but think what can be told about Gump through watching him have sex. Here's this big long movie investigating this guy – well, what's he like in bed? What's that like for him? That's a big human question. My romantic notion is that if porno films had been allowed to breathe, and the stories eventually really did come first, then we would have been able to see an actor playing a role and then being able to try on a new way of having sex in a scene. Like trying on an accent. Which would do away with the gratuitous obligatory sex scene that every movie has to have, which is the ultimate bullshit moment.

Gavin Smith: So you see contemporary porn as a fallen form?

Paul Thomas Anderson: Pretty much, yeah. I still find it interesting to watch some of it. There's a series called *Dirty Debutantes*: when I first saw it, the mythology was that the porn star was gone, and it's amateurs now, 'real-life people'. So it was wonderful when I realised that *Dirty Debutantes* was maybe 80 per cent faked. They're not 'real people' recruited off the street: most are actresses – a version of people off the street as they haven't done too much work, they mustn't be recognisable – but they have agents, porn agents. So now watch them again – you'll see some of the best acting you've ever seen.

Gavin Smith: How close to the porn industry did you get?

Paul Thomas Anderson: The only research was growing up in the Valley and watching a ton of porno movies and blooper tapes, which really tell you what goes on behind the scenes. When I finished the draft, I thought maybe I should go verify what I think is the truth is the truth. I probably went on twenty sets over a couple of years. And I found I was pretty much spot on. But it was funnier than I thought, and sadder. It kind of got me down, watching six hours of solid fucking. You really don't have any desire to go home and kiss your girlfriend.

Gavin Smith: Most human collective endeavours tend to adopt the extended family as a guiding fiction, so as a structuring device this lends a certain realism – yet it also endorses a mythologically idealised view. Does such a mentality really apply in the porn world?

Paul Thomas Anderson: Absolutely. At the awards ceremonies there are all these tables, all these weird versions of surrogate families. It happens in so-called legitimate films, too, having to form a surrogate family during the making of them. But here's the thing: in porno, you have no other choice. You are doing something really odd that not a lot of people do. So you are forced to look for other people going through what you're going through and latch onto them. They can only find understanding with each other.

Gavin Smith: What *Boogie Nights* doesn't really acknowledge is that this industry thrives on the exploitation of people as commodities – that a lot of people working in porn are expendable and don't find a safe berth in some dysfunctional but caring community of peers.

Paul Thomas Anderson: That's true. You probably find that side with the Johnny Doe character, the guy who replaces Dirk – we just don't happen to branch off with him and watch him hang out at Jack's house, fuck around, go over here, fuck around, not really find anybody, really be a lost soul. But when Jack hugs Dirk at the end and welcomes his 'son' back, sure, it's probably only within a day or two that he's thinking of a box cover saying 'The Return of Brock Landers'. When John Holmes got out of jail, it was 'The Return of Johnny Wadd'. It was something to sell.

Gavin Smith: It's curious to me that your film inverts the porn industry paradigm in which the male stars have career longevity while the women stars come and go within three or four years: in *Boogie Nights*, the men are expendable, while Amber Waves remains a fixture.

Paul Thomas Anderson: That's true, but Amber is probably the equivalent of somebody like Seka, say, or Marilyn Chambers or Veronica Hart, actresses who were box office for a long time and still have a following. That's five out of 500. Rollergirl is more of a novelty and certainly not as big a star as Amber.

Gavin Smith: There's the scene in the limo, where they pick someone up off the street to have sex with Rollergirl on live television. Does that maybe hint at this, too?

Paul Thomas Anderson: 'On the Lookout' in *Boogie Nights* is based on *On the Prowl*, a real video where they had a real porn star in the back of a limo and went searching San Francisco for a real guy. Heather Graham watched it and she brought that stuff to it as Rollergirl. What she was doing was what the girl in the real video did: her behaviour is very unnatural, like she's almost vamping and presenting this defensive façade – to me it suggested a decline into affect from an initially natural way of acting. All I had *written* was 'HOLD ON ROLLERGIRL': I didn't know what it would be, and I wanted to get through it without ever having to talk to Heather about it and just see what would happen. She did what she did – you can't write that down for an actor, you can't explain it. There are younger girls I've talked to in the industry and you can't get a handle on them. You spend an hour grilling them – nothing. You won't get anywhere. 'What's going on with you?' 'You know.' 'Well, how do you feel?' 'Oh, you know ...' It's my theory they will one day burst the way Rollergirl bursts.

Gavin Smith: That's interesting, because what's striking about *Boogie Nights* is that none of the characters seems to know themselves or have real emotional honesty.

Paul Thomas Anderson: I think they have an emotional honesty, but there's something stripped and raw and childlike about a lot of them. And that's what I saw in that world, so it's truthful. But for instance Jack introduces himself as 'Jack Horner' – I think he's a character who probably forgets his real name. And in the course of five minutes the Mark Wahlberg character goes from being Eddie Adams to Dirk Diggler to being 'John'. There's no going back for this kid, no way back to Eddie Adams. And then there's a third identity, Brock Landers. In the documentary, he's telling Amber, 'I am Dirk Diggler, Brock Landers is a character that I play' – but he's looking in the mirror at the end of the movie and says 'That's right. I'm Brock Landers.'

Gavin Smith: This is the core of the film, everyone struggling to become some kind of alter ego and deny the reality of who they are.

Paul Thomas Anderson: Well, who wants to be the kid in Torrance being beaten up by his mother?

Gavin Smith: When Amber and Rollergirl get coked out together in the bedroom, Amber keeps saying, 'You could be anything you want.'

Paul Thomas Anderson: Oh, that's funny, that's a nice point, I hadn't thought of that. To me, that dialogue is really just true cocaine dialogue, the mentality when you get so hyped up on that stuff.

Gavin Smith: That's why I see the ending as being dreams coming true: Jessie is painting, Reed doing his magic act, Buck has his stereo store.

Paul Thomas Anderson: I don't think any of the outcomes is untruthful – I could point to real-life examples in the world of pornography that parallel each of these characters. That's not to say that I haven't taken it upon myself to give them five minutes of happiness – I felt it was important, even though we all know what's going to happen five minutes after the movie ends.

Gavin Smith: Your generosity towards the characters, and your ability to suspend the narrative and just stay on somebody for moments that are incidental, give the film much of its power, yet are also detrimental to it. Do you know what I mean?

Paul Thomas Anderson: Yes, I do. But there's a point where you have to say, Fuck it, I know I'm being slightly indulgent to this character here. I think that comes from hiring and writing parts for my friends. There is a part of me that knows what better storytelling and better momentum for the film might be, but there's also a part of me that really has an obligation to say, I've seen this actor do something that is wonderful, I was lucky enough to be there with a film camera and get it, and it's too late now, I've got $15 million, the movie's too long anyway, I am going to abuse the privilege and preserve it. If the moment happens, like Phil Hoffman who plays Scotty J, who gets in the car and calls himself a fucking idiot, it may go on too long, I don't care but, fuck it, that's what happened to Phil.

Gavin Smith: What things determined the style of the film for you?

Paul Thomas Anderson: In terms of structure and emotion, it was clear: first half/second half, 1970s/1980s. And this is probably more an afterthought, but I felt it should maybe resemble my personal experience of watching a porno film: incredibly funny one second, turns me on the next, then incredibly depressing and so on, up and down. The original script was also really trying to beat up the language: 'Come on my stomach and my tits if you can.' It could be very funny and odd to hear that in a movie within the first half hour, and I wish there could have been more of it sprinkled throughout, but some scenes were cut down and there was some MPAA classifications stuff. My plan was that by hour two the stuff was still being said, but it wasn't funny anymore, but boring and repetitive, like a porno movie.

Certainly a lot of it was driven by trying to cram so much story into a reasonable amount of time. Stylistically the influences were *Nashville*, *GoodFellas* and *The Battle of Algiers* in terms of the immediacy. And the music led the way, to tell you the truth – camera moves and stylistic stuff really came from listening to the music, which I was listening to while I was writing the screenplay.

Gavin Smith: Did you have the songs written into the script?

Paul Thomas Anderson: I wrote it in a notebook because I didn't want to be tied down – because if you go to get the publishing rights and they see that you've written it into the script, then they know you really want it.

Gavin Smith: You play with the tension between edited time, at its most extreme in the montages and in the drug sequence, and real time, where you'll do something in one long take or pause to study an actor reacting.

Paul Thomas Anderson: There are sequences where it was clear to me that we had to go in the front door and stay until we walked out. The drug-dealer scene is one and Little Bill shooting his wife is another, and there's one shot in the pool-party sequence that just kind of sticks. I'm a great believer in that rule of drama, Get in late and get out early, it applies a lot of the time, but there are moments where it's great to stop and suffer and watch something happen. To me, the moment of Little Bill walking through the house is the result of not being able to figure out when he decided to kill his wife, when he snapped. I could never really say, so I could only start with him as he walks into the party, follow him to find her and make sure I follow him all the way out. Is it when he sees them? Is it when he closes the door? Is it when Rollergirl flashes the Polaroid in his face?

Gavin Smith: As the film progresses, the style shifts from an almost dreamy poise to jittery, neurotic mannerism, particularly in terms of cutting and camera movement.

Paul Thomas Anderson: Maybe in moments, not as an overall plan. That kind of thinking I probably only applied to sequence D. We broke the film down into five sequences, and D was where everything spirals out of control after Dirk has been fired. It was sort of notorious – in shooting it, matching didn't matter, so everybody could just get freed up: 'It's sequence D, it's a fucking free for all, cocaine madness.' So the camera moves reflect that. That sequence in *GoodFellas* where Ray Liotta is running around, everybody responded to it. I got this sick-to-my-stomach feeling. I was working as a messenger in LA at the time and I would do coke all day long and run around and I swear *GoodFellas* accurately portrayed what it feels like. There's one shot in that *Boogie Nights* sequence that I really feel good about, when Heather Graham snorts a line of coke and the focus shifts from the mirror to the coke to her and it's blurry for a half a second, it's a very quick shot, then it whips over to Julianne Moore and then Heather brings her head up – that's the one shot where I can go, Yeah, that what it was like to my eye. If you've ever leaned down to do cocaine, it's a really odd moment where you feel gross about what you're doing but you're in this panic and frenzy, you're so close to something your eye is trying to adjust, it's this weird blurry moment.

Gavin Smith: There's a real feeling of the camera going out of control, those whiplash pans and shots where you change the frame rate and rush in on somebody.

Paul Thomas Anderson: My first film I probably treated as something very precious, but this time I was really rough with it. If the camera move wasn't fast enough, I'd say, 'Well, we've got to find a way to make it faster and if it's out of focus it doesn't matter. However it has to get there, get it there.' That's something you see in *Jules et Jim* – if he didn't have a close-up, he'll iris in on something or box it in or blow it up with some kind of fucked-up optical, just [*pounding fist into hand*] being rough with it and saying I've gotta get there somehow. In the party scene at Dirk's house, when Julianne says to Mark, 'Let's go walk,' there was a very fast camera move we did on the set, everybody went, 'Wow, that's so fast,' but when I saw it in the editing room it wasn't fast enough, so we skip-framed it – we gotta find it, find how it feels.

SINGING IN THE RAIN

Mark Olsen

Messy is probably the best word to describe Paul Thomas Anderson's *Magnolia*, a grandiosely sprawling, audaciously earnest concoction that yearns to find meaning and connection among an overextended roster of characters in Southern California's San Fernando Valley during the course of one extremely eventful day and night. In structure, style and content, *Magnolia* is a magnificent train wreck of a movie, an intimate epic of full-throttle emotions that threatens to go off the rails at any moment during its three-hours-plus running time. In the inevitable media build-up to the film's US release much was made of Anderson's enviably precarious position: as the whiz kid behind *Boogie Nights* (1997), this is his moment with the golden ticket and the keys to the castle.

Anderson's first feature *Hard Eight* (1996) was a neo-chamber piece of breathtakingly precise detail set among Nevada's casinos; *Boogie Nights*, his next, set in the 1970s porn industry and significantly larger in scope and scale, leaped off the screen with a vicious exuberance. Both films did moderate box office, but the truckloads of critical praise they received left the door wide open for Anderson's perennially blossoming aspirations. And, quite simply, the kid ran with it, creating in *Magnolia* a film of rare ambition and beauty.

If Quentin Tarantino faced his post–*Pulp Fiction* moment with the sublimely understated *Jackie Brown*, Anderson has demanded the spotlight be turned up, not away. *Magnolia* contains eleven main characters and a handful of smaller roles and interweaves nine distinct storylines linked through similarities of situation and emotion as well as the extensive use of music by the singer/songwriter Aimee Mann.

It doesn't really have a plot, though it incorporates a botched heist, sons searching for fathers, fathers looking for forgiveness and myriad other stock movie motivational devices. Jimmy Gator (Philip Baker Hall), a much-loved television gameshow host, attempts to reconcile with his emotionally estranged and chemically addicted daughter Claudia (wonderfully captured by Melora Walters, in a performance destined to be overlooked) before he succumbs to terminal cancer. Linda Partridge (Julianne Moore) must go about the unpleasant formalities of preparing for the impending death of her husband Earl (Jason Robards) while attempting to find something akin to healing for herself. Earl's nurse and caretaker Phil Parma (Philip Seymour Hoffman) likewise does what he can to ease the pain, tracking down Big Earl's long-lost son (Tom Cruise), who has recreated himself as Frank T. J. Mackey, promoter of an extremely successful men's sexual self-help programme. *Magnolia* wends its way across the city, recording the hours of people whose lives seemingly don't relate and finding ways that they do. The film's structure is like a skeletal spine that creates connections between characters and scenes as lines of dialogue bounce off each other, ringing and rhyming in the viewer's head long after they've ambled by.

The film opens with three short vignettes interlinked by a voiceover from *Boogie Nights* alumnus Ricky Jay pondering the nature of fate and the meaning of chance. The energy and extravagance of the pre-credits sequence – an aerial shot of a plane swooping across a lake fills the frame; the camera glides across a rooftop as a man jumps from it, stopped in mid-air so the precise geometry of his trajectory can be mapped out – are already more than most movies could contain. Then, after a few title cards and a tinkling electric piano, a blooming flower fills the screen and Mann goes full force into Harry Nilsson's 'One' ('the loneliest number') as a map of Los Angeles kaleidoscopes in the background. It is only now that the film presents its own enigmatic title, quickly moving on to introduce all the main characters and their situations, the song stopping and starting and stretching itself out to seem part of the fabric of their lives. Altogether this takes about fifteen minutes, the pace not that of a disciplined marathoner preparing strategically for the journey ahead, but of someone simply running as fast as they can, daring exhaustion to set in.

Mann's music is central to the film's structure. 'It was really important to me that the movie felt like one story,' says Anderson. 'There are nine different plots, but I wanted to make sure it didn't feel like a vignette movie. So having one voice to unify it all seemed a good idea.' Anderson had access to unreleased material by Mann (her husband Michael Penn scored his two previous features) and found particular inspiration in 'Wise Up', a song that featured on the soundtrack album to *Jerry Maguire*. Anderson commissioned Mann to write a handful of new songs specifically for his film, including the closing-title number 'Save Me'. Mann's 1970s-esque songwriting and production are neatly analogous to the ways Anderson freely appropriates from his personal pantheon of post-studio-system maverick film-makers (chiefly Altman, Demme and Scorsese) while at the same time striving to bring his own original vision to the screen.

Nowhere is this better demonstrated than in the winningly inventive sequence Anderson has created around 'Wise Up'. Some two-and-a-half hours into the movie, after countless moments of intense emotional trauma and physical pain, each of the main characters is at the end of his or her tether. It has been raining on and off, adding to the general dark-night-of-the-soul atmosphere which threatens to swallow the film whole, and a gentle piano progression aches out through the night. The camera slowly moves in on Claudia Gator as she sits alone in her apartment, and she softly begins to sing along. Cut to Jim Kurring (John C. Reilly), a lonely police officer (to be Claudia's date for the evening), who picks up the song where she left off. And on it goes from one character to the next, each in turn singing along to the mournfully wry lyrics, until the camera pulls back from the last of them, ending the sequence that formalises their bonds. One's initial reaction is to scoff, as if Anderson has finally gone too far. But the plaintive tone of the song maps the characters' connectedness in ways scene after scene of dialogue never could.

'Hopefully it unifies everything, calms everything down and feels completely natural,' says Anderson. 'Haven't you ever sung along to a song on the radio? In the simplest way, it's just that. I never thought it would be such a big deal. But I'm happy people respond to it.' It didn't strike Anderson as audacious? 'I thought it was going to be something very sweet, sentimental in the best way. I didn't consider it outlandish. And I still don't.'

If it's difficult to explain the exact course of events in Magnolia, it's equally hard to unravel the chain of relations that links the characters. Late on in the film Anderson uses the end credits of the television game show that occupies much of the second hour to complete another circuit, reveal a new piece in the puzzle of the life of the dying Earl Partridge and create a new set of implied relationships around a character who never leaves his bed. It's tempting throughout to look for the secret centre of the film, and when Ricky Jay appears briefly as a producer of the game show – a bizarre kids-versus-adults trivia challenge called *What Do Kids Know?* – for an instant you think it might be him. But he quickly fades back into the tableau and we realise that here everyone stars in their own film, if only for a while. It's this skilful withholding of information that keeps the viewer focused, just as in *Hard Eight* Anderson pulled the viewer ever deeper into his characters' lives by constantly revealing with one hand while concealing with the other.

Like Tarantino, Anderson belongs to a generation of film directors weaned on the video store for whom watching movies is part of everyday life, not a ritualised experience like going to church. This has in part created the cinema of referencing so common among younger directors, the nerdy delight in out-obscuring one another. *Boogie Nights* borrowed from a wide variety of sources, and in *Magnolia* Anderson uses Jason Robards (star of an Anderson touchstone, Jonathan Demme's *Melvin and Howard*) and, in smaller roles, iconic Altman actors Michael Murphy and Henry Gibson (the latter as a scathing velvet menace preposterously named Thurston Howell, who flippantly tosses off a bar-room cruelty reserved exclusively for strangers). Anderson claims he chose Gibson simply because, 'I really wanted to work with that guy.'

Magnolia is a film obviously in thrall to the process of movie-making, but its mournful overtones ring surprisingly loud from a film-maker barely thirty years old. By grappling with the fissure between the idealisations of the medium and the realisation of what it may lack (at one point Philip Seymour Hoffman pleads into the phone, 'This is the scene in the movie where you help me out … This is that scene'),

Anderson seems to be stumbling towards a maturity beyond the confines of a movie-made life. 'I'm a product of growing up on movies, but when the movies betray you and haven't taught you how to feel something or what to do – for instance, if someone in your life dies – it's flabbergasting because the movies haven't shown you how to deal with that. I haven't been taught what to do when I can't find my car keys and I've got to go to the funeral. That's a scene you don't see.

'I hope my film is both very movie-wise and very reality-wise. I don't think you can pretend you haven't seen a movie if you're a director – I think part of my job is to acknowledge how many movies I've seen and how much that informs our lives. Movies are a big influence on how we deal with death, with family relationships, and I wanted to show that. But they can also be a complete betrayal in terms of how to live your life.'

Keeping *Magnolia* grounded in 'reality' is largely up to the actors, who bring depth and feeling to characters who could easily skid off into caricature. Anderson usually has a specific performer in mind as he's writing each part, creating custom-fitted hot rods ready for each actor to take out for a spin. Here no one rises to the occasion better than Tom Cruise, who in the showboat role of a men's-movement snake-oil salesman obviously relishes the opportunity to put a devilish twist on his superstar charisma. If he stumbles during his climactic scenes you still admire the effort, and no one else could pull off Frank's interview-gone-awry with such electrically inviting hostility. ('What am I doing?' he coldly says to a journalist after she reveals she knows more than he wants her to. 'I'm quietly judging you.')

More than any other recent film, *Magnolia* – its disorder, confusion and discomfort such a part of the movie the very film stock seems to have been steeped in it – is acutely aware of where we're at, precisely reflecting our daily lives. And going one better than the bittersweet victories that end *Hard Eight* and *Boogie Nights*, Anderson here provides a glimmer of hope as a reward to those who have endured the emotional maelstrom. Waiting for something, anything, to lift them up, two unlikely souls come together in one moment of genuine connection: Claudia Gator, seen quite literally in a different light, smiles brightly at the arrival of Jim Kurring, and the fog of her troubles burns off, if only for an instant. As for the rest of *Magnolia*'s ragtag crew, they, like the rest of us, will continue to persevere, waiting for their frogs to fall.

Abel Ferrara

BAD LIEUTENANT
USA 1992
Director: Abel Ferrara

The Bad Lieutenant works for the NYPD. His addiction to crack, heroin and alcohol have led him into debt, from which he hopes to escape by betting on the Dodgers baseball team in the National Championship Series. When the Dodgers lose a key game, the Lieutenant is unable to settle his debts and persuades his bookie instead to double his stakes for the next game. The Lieutenant takes out his frustration by sexually harassing female members of the public and getting high with a junkie girlfriend. When a nun is beaten and raped in a local church by two young thugs who also steal holy sacraments, a reward of $50,000 offered by the Catholic Mafia lures the Lieutenant. He pursues the nun and overhears her holy confession in which she reveals that she knows the identity of her assailants. But the nun refuses to answer questions about their identity, preferring to forgive them for their crime. Incensed by her intransigence, and ravaged with despair, the Lieutenant collapses before the church's altar and is visited by a vision of Christ. Emerging from his stupor, he wakes to find an old woman returning to the church the golden chalice stolen during the rape. She leads him to a nearby housing project where he confronts the rapists; on television, the Mets/Dodgers game, on which the Lieutenant's hopes rest, begins. The Lieutenant shares a pipe of crack with his prisoners before delivering them to the downtown bus station and putting them on a coach out of town, making them swear never to return to New York. The Lieutenant drives to a rendezvous with his bookie as the game reaches a climax: Dodgers hero Strawberry is at bat, and could win the game with a home run. As the ball is played, the Lieutenant is shot dead from a passing car.

*   *   *

After the relative gloss of *The King of New York*, this terrifyingly powerful film seems at first glance to mark a return to Ferrara's early days as an underground film-maker. Like *The Driller Killer*, the style of *Bad Lieutenant* is ragged and punky: from the opening credits, consisting of harsh typeface crudely emblazoned upon a blank background with no accompanying music, Ferrara deliberately distances his latest film from the cosy conventions of the mainstream. Extensive use of a handheld camera and numerous sparsely edited sequences create a documentary-like quality reminiscent of the director's long-banned debut.

Similar, too, is the unresolved narrative which sets up wrong-doers for punishment, but then denies the audience the cathartic release of seeing them put to justice. Just as *The Driller Killer* ends with a haunting close-up on the eye of the giant bull painted by the unpunished murderer (we are left, as Martin Barker points out, 'in the eye of the storm'), so *Bad Lieutenant* frustrates the desire for closure by allowing the rapists to go free. The satisfying black satire of the rape-revenge cult hit *Ms. 45/Angel of Vengeance* (devised by and starring *Bad Lieutenant* co-writer Zoe Tamerlis, a.k.a. Lund) is entirely absent here. Instead, the audience is deliberately left disorientated and uneasy.

It is ironic therefore that, despite such an apparently disruptive format, *Bad Lieutenant* has a classical narrative more akin to Ferrara's reworking of Romeo and Juliet in *China Girl* than to any of his other less mainstream films. While the structure and style hark back to the amorality of Ferrara's earliest work, the story itself is almost biblical, an unashamed tale of the redemption, via divine intervention, of one who has fallen from grace. Throughout the film, the Lieutenant punctuates his sins (drug taking, sexual harassment, stealing, cheating, avarice) with mournful pleas for God to save his miserable soul. In one sequence, played to the hilt by Keitel in a shockingly brilliant performance, the drug-addled cop stands naked before the camera, arms outstretched in Christ-like pose, howling like a dog begging to be put down. Only when he subjugates himself before the altar is redemption finally offered, in the shape of the chalice which Jesus himself appears to deliver. Empowered by this grail, and led by the nun's example, the Lieutenant performs a single, saving act of forgiveness, made all the more worthy by the pain which this act causes him. Thus redeemed, he is swiftly removed from the horrors of earthly life, shot dead by a bullet which could itself be interpreted as divinely driven.

The extreme religious orthodoxy of such a narrative may give Ferrara fans cause for concern, for despite the on-screen depravity (it is hard to imagine a more hideous spectacle than that of the Lieutenant mouthing obscenities while frenziedly masturbating over two young female offenders), *Bad Lieutenant* is ultimately a paean to the virtues of true Catholicism. Like *The Exorcist*, the film frequently seems to revel in obscenity, but remains draped throughout in the pious clothing of the priesthood. Small wonder, then, that the BBFC have passed *Bad Lieutenant* uncut, for, although it is visually visceral, its narrative heart is palatably spiritual. Meanwhile, *The Driller Killer*, which almost ten years ago was declared obscene on video-tape by the DPP, still awaits certification.

Mark Kermode

DEALING WITH THE NOW

Gavin Smith

I have never seen Abel Ferrara sit. He is constitutionally incapable of staying put or containing himself – everything about him is vivid, dramatic, kinetic, unpredictable. He personifies the erratic, convulsive energy of his movies and their absolute commitment to going all the way; surely every Ferrara film is at some level a self-portrait, just as it is a process of thinking through questions of conscience, a restless, troubled search for meaning? If American film-makers were twinned with European counterparts, Ferrara's would be French director Maurice Pialat: *Under Satan's Sun* and *Le Garçu* could both be Ferrara films.

Ferrara is the most prolific, driven American film-maker in American cinema – who else has made seven films in seven years? *The Addiction* (1994) and *The Funeral* (1996) are already far behind him. He has completed a ten-minute segment of a Jonathan Demme–produced HBO anthology film, *Subway Stories*, called 'Love on the A Train', featuring Rosie Perez. He is now in the final stages of editing and mixing *The Blackout* in time for Cannes. He is champing at the bit to start *New Rose Hotel*, an adaptation of the William Gibson short story, projected to star Willem Dafoe and Christopher Wren.

With the exception of screenwriter Nicholas St John, most of Ferrara's extended family of regular collaborators contributed to *The Blackout*: masterful, versatile DoP Ken Kelsch (a former Vietnam Green Beret), editors Anthony Redman and Jimmy Mol, composer Joe Delia, grip John McIntyre. Stylistically, *The Blackout* goes several steps beyond the monochrome suspension of *The Addiction*: it combines intercut film and video, layered, dreamy visuals and radically fragmented editing to create a halluc-inatory, subjective style entirely opposed to the steady, unflinching observation of *The Funeral*, closer to the feel of *Dangerous Game* (1993).

In front of the camera, it's all change. Matthew Modine plays Matty, a movie star with a drug problem who comes to Miami in search of reconciliation with *femme fatale* Annie (Béatrice Dalle). He becomes embroiled in the sleazy activities of a club owner and video-maker (Dennis Hopper) who is shooting a kinky candid-camera remake of *Nana* amidst the banal nightlife decadence of Miami's beautiful people – with Annie as the star. Things spin out of control; cut to eighteen months later; Matty in New York, in rehab and therapy, and settled in domestic stability with his girlfriend (Claudia Schiffer) until trace memories of something that happened back in Miami start to resurface...

Ever since *King of New York* (1990), Ferrara's films have become progressively less bound by the imperatives and structures of genre and more and more introspective and morally claustrophobic. Their originality is that they relentlessly probe the great themes of postwar European art cinema from Rossellini on – the state of people's minds and souls and the corruption of the human condition – but in a visceral, pulp mode. Ferrara and St John are deadly serious – they mean their films. Not for nothing are Ferrara's film idols Jean-Luc Godard, Pier Paolo Pasolini and Rainer Werner Fassbinder. (Until Marcello Mastroianni's death, Ferrara was planning a video remake/sequel to *La dolce vita* set in Miami to star Benicio Del Toro as Mastroianni's son.) In *The Blackout*, the protagonist is once again submerged in self-consuming excess until reduced to a state of abjection, everything stripped away to prepare for decisive self-confrontation: it's the quintessential Ferrara experience.

* * *

Gavin Smith: What inspired your original treatment of *The Blackout* in 1994?

Abel Ferrara: This guy goes back to the house he grew up in, in Mount Vernon, Westchester. His parents haven't lived there in eight years – and he killed a couple in the bedroom. The fact that people commit murders and forget about them – until suddenly everything comes back – is fascinating. The original story was about a guy who murders a woman for leaving him, coupled with the blackout story. And I wanted to write it myself because with *Bad Lieutenant* I'd had the idea and got Zoë [Lund] to write it. I managed to get out thirty pages or something. Marla [Hanson, Ferrara's former girlfriend and associate producer on *The Addiction*] was doing most of the writing.

Gavin Smith: Was there a personal angle for you?

Abel Ferrara: I don't think there was. I was trying to get away from that after *Dangerous Game* came out. The idea was, let's do Hitchcock, a take on *Vertigo*, where a guy investigates a murder and he finds he committed it. But then it came back around with the break-up of my relationship with Nancy [Ferrara's wife] and Marla.

Gavin Smith: What's the significance in the film of the tape recording that Annie plays back to Matty when they fight in the hotel room?

Abel Ferrara: The guy has blackouts, and when he does that he flips. One time he kills somebody. One time he forces a woman to have an abortion. It's Jekyll and Hyde, he has a devil inside him. When that guy comes out, he ain't going to face up to him. He doesn't want to know him. Now, who is the other Matty? The voice on the tape recorder. The recording is a phone call he made, basically telling her, 'Get rid of the baby.'

Gavin Smith: Do you see the movie as some kind of metaphor about screwing up the best things in our lives?

Abel Ferrara: Yeah. I feel that way because he has it good with the Claudia Schiffer character, and he has it with the waitress, Annie 2. It's not that he thinks the waitress is Annie, it's that he knows Annie 2 is somebody he actually might have an opportunity of having a decent relationship with. So he kills her [*laughs*]! It's that devil inside him.

Gavin Smith: You still believe in God?

Abel Ferrara: Yes.

Gavin Smith: So you believe in devils?

Abel Ferrara: [*Pause*] Yeah.

Gavin Smith: How do you relate the ending of the new film to the ending of *The Funeral*?

Abel Ferrara: Yeah, I know, I can't take the fact that they're all suicide endings. It wasn't meant to be that way. It's a funny thing because on the one hand it's a cop out, but on the other it's a righteous act. In *The Blackout*, Matty is judge, jury and executioner of a murder, and he gives himself the death penalty. Chez in *The Funeral* kills himself and that prevents Gaspare's brother from coming over there and blowing his brains out. I don't think they're about despair. There are very complex reasons.

Gavin Smith: By killing himself and his surviving brother, isn't Chez putting an end to his family and its heritage of violence?

Abel Ferrara: You want me to top that? I agree with you, and I don't mean that facetiously.

Gavin Smith: How does the style of *The Blackout* differ from *The Addiction* and *The Funeral*?

Abel Ferrara: Visually we try not to be heavy handed. We tried to see Miami as it really is. It's an amazing place to film: the sunsets, the shadows, the light. We're trying to understand the light and the architecture just like we're trying to understand the character. It's about sunlight at midday, which we usually run like the wind from; you don't see a sunny day in the last ten movies. Now we went to the other side to try to use sun, to try to find the beauty. And it's also dealing with the element of the sky, which you never see in New York.

Gavin Smith: You were intercutting film and video before *Natural Born Killers* triggered that trend – on *Dangerous Game*, and also in this film. What's your thinking on that?

Abel Ferrara: Video is a great image tool. As much as we talk about it, we don't even pay lip service to the immediacy of the video camera – you just pick it up and shoot. There's so much involved in controlling the look of film – the camera, the processing, the duping, the negative – and so many people making sure that it's exactly the way you want it to be that sometimes that gets to be a burden. Sometimes you just want to wing it, and video is that. I want to shoot a film on video.

The real breakthrough is the AVID digital editing programme and the way you can use it to layer shots, putting shots on top of shots. It's right for *The Blackout* because what you want is a dream, that's what we're trying to get at. The problem we always had using opticals and dissolves before was that you don't do them yourself, just like the whole reason we don't use Steadicam – because we don't control it. Now on the AVID we can control opticals.

It's a funny deal making movies in this day and age, where so many people end up seeing them on video. Video technology has been great in terms of getting our work out there, but when you're watching the big screen, all of a sudden you realise why you have to worry about every detail in a shot. The problem with video is that you can't see into the actor's eyes, so you're not even watching. Second of all, when you're watching a movie going through a projector, it's twenty-four frames per second, stop and go, stop and go – you put together all those stops, and I know it sounds stupid, but the audience is sitting in the dark for maybe eight, ten minutes. And *that's* when your imagination is in there. When you're watching video, which is rolling constantly, you're being led along by your nose.

Gavin Smith: When you did *Body Snatchers*, you used widescreen Panavision.

Abel Ferrara: It was an experiment in the use of space, the width of 'Scope. That's the norm – your vision is like that, you don't walk around seeing everything like a television set.

Gavin Smith: How did you react when Nicky St John gave you the screenplay for *The Funeral*?

Abel Ferrara: When I read his stuff, it's mind-blowing, I get very jealous. I went to the same high school as him and I got better grades than him. I didn't know he was doing it until he sent it to me.

Gavin Smith: At what point do you arrive at some idea about what a movie is about?

Abel Ferrara: The process of making the movie is trying to understand it, and it constantly changes – the script changes, the actors change it. As Kubrick says, a film is not an inverted pyramid based on one idea. In *The Funeral*, I liked the idea that Ray was going to avenge his brother Johnny's death. Somebody's going to get hurt tonight and I don't give a fuck who it is. There's people like that.

Gavin Smith: In *The Funeral*, Johnny says, 'I would say life is pretty pointless – without the movies.' What does that line mean to you?

Abel Ferrara: From Johnny's point of view, he's a young kid from a family that thinks the movies are a major waste of time. You don't go to the movies when you could be getting laid. The only thing you can do at the movies is put your hand down the pants of the chick next to you. From a moron Italian background, movies are about jerks play-acting for other jerks. To go and see *The Petrified Forest* in the middle of the afternoon – it's what a certain kind of young intellectual would do, and he prides himself on it.

Gavin Smith: *The Funeral* is also about how love and family can be the source of incredible violence.

Abel Ferrara: Because they didn't understand each other. Did they really love each other? Sure, Ray [Christopher Walken] would kill for his brother, but he wouldn't listen to him. He had no idea where the kid was coming from. The other brother, Chez [Chris Penn], can't even talk to them. I don't have any brothers, but I love my sisters. But at times we don't even have a chance to communicate.

Those guys had to communicate. Their father is teaching them togetherness, he brings them together for that murder. So why are they strangers? It's not for lack of love. They're at the bar together and Johnny [Vincent Gallo] is telling Walken something and Walken ain't even hearing him, he can't imagine his young brother being a communist. At the same time, Gallo could not talk to him. And that was because he loved him. So that's a very odd thing. The young brother doesn't give fuck about money because he's a communist. For a Sicilian to be a communist is a contradiction in terms. Where I come from, Salerno, near Naples, there's an expression my father always used: 'The only friend you got is the money in your pocket.' That's a really ugly thing, especially to tell a kid on his way to Woodstock. I had hair down to my waist and a stack of Bob Dylan records. That's the contradiction between Walken and Gallo in the bar. Walken thinks it's a joke. 'We're guineas, right? We exploit situations. We don't believe.' But Gallo does. You got to get outside yourself, you can't just walk round thinking, 'The only thing that counts is me.' You got to think about something other than yourself.

Gavin Smith: Is that the same problem Lili Taylor's vampire character has in *The Addiction*? That she's too wrapped up in her own mind and philosophical pontificating.

Abel Ferrara: Yeah, because you can't get there from the body or the mind – you gotta have it from the spirit. She goes down into it: 'Say it like you mean it,' believe it, in other words. You've got to have belief. It's like holding a crucifix up – it's a piece of wood unless you've got faith.

Gavin Smith: How does she find redemption at the end?

Abel Ferrara: She wants it. She wants to believe. She knows it. She's not a stranger to Christ.

Gavin Smith: You're the only film-maker in the United States regularly dealing with questions of the soul, with spiritual or religious questions.

Abel Ferrara: I don't believe that for a minute. What about Spike Lee, *Get on the Bus* and *Girl 6*? Theresa Randle [in *Girl 6*] is coming to terms with who she is. If we make films that are spiritual or intellectual, in our films we're gonna maximise every ounce we've got, we're not gonna reduce ourselves or try and address the lowest common denominator.

Gavin Smith: So you're using film to wrestle with questions of redemption?

Abel Ferrara: Of course. It's not my films, it's my life. A film is not a ninety-minute thing. A film is everything that I am. We keep coming back to the point of, 'Who are we? Where do we come from? What's our future?' We do plenty of dealing with the now. But I don't know how you can fucking live and not question where you're from. When you're brought up in a Catholic school, they tell you, 'Don't ask those questions, they'll make you crazy.'

Gavin Smith: What's your idea of redemption?

Abel Ferrara: I just don't wanna walk out of here having fucked somebody around, or have someone suffer for the fact I was on this Earth. I might try, but I'm not gonna count on being some big positive force in the world.

Gavin Smith: *The Addiction* and *Dangerous Game* both present a world in which people are either predators or prey, where everybody is trying to exploit everyone else. Is that your view of the world?

Abel Ferrara: Yeah, definitely. Once you're a predator, you better take it all the way – but Taylor in *The Addiction* has a way out: *Our Father who art in Heaven*. That's about the hardcore reality of Jesus Christ as the Son of God. With Nicky St John there ain't no search for nothing. It's right in front of you if you get out of your own ego and your own bullshit. He's there, waiting for you.

Gavin Smith: But you're interpreting Nicky's ideas.

Abel Ferrara: Well, considering the fact that he's on the set every day and in the editing room and wrote the script… The bottom line is, he's a believer and it's a simple thing on the one hand, the hardest thing in the world on the other. I'm a believer, but am I a follower?

Gavin Smith: Is that the difference between you and Nicky?

Abel Ferrara: It starts there.

Gavin Smith: Tell me about *New Rose Hotel*. How do you turn a ten-page story into a ninety-minute film?

Abel Ferrara: It's *Notorious* meets *Death of a Salesman*. First of all, I'm not gonna use the structure of the story. The key is Sandii, the girl – she's a hooker, a sleazy, tattooed, acne-faced freak. She's gotta be a baby, not a knowing freak. In Gibson's mind, she was fourteen years old. She's gonna have short black Louise Brooks hair, shades, chewing bubble gum – think Betty Boop.

Dafoe is our guy. Fox is Walken, the last hustler, this guy who's gonna make the ultimate score. The pair are set to kidnap Hiroshi from Maas in Vienna [for Hosaka, a rival corporation]. How? Hiroshi's not some little nerd, he's a classy guy and they know it. He's got all this security around him. You don't kidnap him, you get him to leave. So the first half we're making a James Bond movie or *The Day of the Jackal*. But they gotta know in their hearts they'll lose. But Fox has got to do it, it's *Death of a Salesman*, he can't help himself.

And now it's *Notorious*. They start training this chick: 'The rain in Spain falls mainly on the plain.' Our guy [Dafoe] has to teach Sandii how to make another man fall in love with her himself, but can't show it. We're in real time, we've never seen the New Rose Hotel.

The big moment is snatching Hiroshi. But Maas [for their own nefarious reasons] are just letting him go. No one knows if the girl was always working for Maas, or if they turned her. Fox says they turned her – he doesn't want to believe he's been duped by a *fourteen-year-old*. The student outsmarts the professor. Who knows if she loves our guy – that's what he's thinking at the New Rose Hotel. He's gotta think back to every event – and now we go right to the short story and start from the beginning. It's *Rashomon*, we play the scenes over again. I can't wait till we show the same scene exactly the same way, only knowing she's not a little baby. What is he gonna be thinking, lying there waiting to die? It's all about despair, like *The Blackout*.

Gavin Smith: So you've cracked the problem of how to make this into a film.

Abel Ferrara: There are no special effects. Guys, get with the programme, it's *Alphaville* and *Notorious*. We've got to get the audience thinking they're watching a James Bond movie and then an hour in, boom, our guy's in the New Rose Hotel, a room three metres by three metres.

THE BLACKOUT
USA/France 1997
Director: Abel Ferrara

Matty, a Hollywood actor with a drink and drugs problem, returns to his Miami home, intent on proposing to his pregnant girlfriend, Annie. Matty and Annie spend an evening at a club run by Mickey, a guru figure who is shooting a *vérité* version of Emile Zola's novel *Nana*, using his friends as actors. Annie may star in it. Though she at first accepts Matty's proposal, Annie eventually tells him that, as per his stoned and abusive advice, she's had an abortion. She leaves him, and Matty continues on a drug binge, partying with Mickey and two local girls. Matty blacks out and comes to in a diner, where he is struck by a young waitress, also called Annie. Later, he introduces Annie 2 to Mickey, who kits her out in a wig to resemble Annie 1 and encourages her to play a scene with Matty for his camera. Matty blacks out.

Eighteen months later, Matty is sober and living in New York with a new girlfriend, Susan. However, Matty is tormented by dreams of Annie 1. When Susan has to go out of town, Matty is compelled to go down to Miami, where he tries to stimulate his memory with drink and drugs and seems to recall strangling Annie 1 while Mickey videotaped the scene. Mickey brings Annie 1 alive to his room; she is disgusted by his state. Later, Mickey shows Matty a tape of what happened during Matty's blackout: Matty actually killed Annie 2. Mickey verbally abuses Matty and, though Susan turns up to try and save him, Matty commits suicide by swimming out to sea, encountering the dead girl in an afterlife.

*   *   *

It is a sign of just how despairing this latest Abel Ferrara movie is that the city of New York, previously his semi-private inferno of bad faith and psychotic violence, represents a perhaps illusory oasis of calm and reason where the protagonist can temporarily get his head back together. Using a lead character associated with Hollywood, an insistent interplay between the staged and the actual filtered through the omnipresent camera, and even a blonde (Claudia Schiffer) in a lead part no one could possibly take seriously as an actress, *The Blackout* recalls Ferrara's film-within-a-film, the Madonna-starring *Snake Eyes* (a.k.a. *Dangerous Game*). The latter was the least satisfactory of his mature works, so maybe *The Blackout* is trying to get right what was fudged at the first attempt. If that was the intention, then the spell of the original, as with Annie 1's shadow over Annie 2, proves hard to shake off, for this lacks, as did the earlier film, a precision in its insanity that marks the best of Ferrara. However, its singular focus on protagonist Matty and the relegation of the director figure to the role of nemesis/conscience/monster at least gives it a more direct, cogent feel.

In all of Ferrara's works, stretching back to *The Driller Killer* (1979), the central character is out of control and on a course for self-willed death – here, in a weird variant on *A Star Is Born*, complete with a post-mortem communion with the martyred Annie 2 ('Did you miss me?') – and the director deliberately blurs distinctions between character, performer and creator. In his first film, Ferrara actually stepped centre-screen and played the psychotic artist with the power drill, while in *Snake Eyes* he used Harvey Keitel to play a film-maker obviously modelled on himself. Here, he distances himself a little from Matty, allowing Matthew Modine to invest the collapsing actor with a battered little-boy charm that is perhaps more seductive than that of the typical male Ferrara psychopath.

As in *Ms.45* (a.k.a. *Angel of Vengeance*), *Bad Lieutenant* and *The Addiction*, a descent into violence is as much a process of self-discovery as dissolution. (And a theme from *The Addiction* is subtly carried over when two party girls crawl over the stoned Matty, prompting him to muse, 'It's like I'm in a vampire movie.') The film's most disturbing sequence finds the sober Matty alone in the hotel room where he once argued with Annie, calculatedly draining vodka miniatures from the minibar and hooking up with his old drug connection, not to get high, but to get in touch with his memory of what happened during the eponymous blackout. It is perhaps inevitable that, embodied by Claudia Schiffer, sanity is a somewhat less appealing prospect than madness. Represented by smooching to classical guitar, psychobabble at an AA group and a psychiatrist, the clean life in New York is far less involving or intriguing than the admittedly nightmare world of Miami. There, Béatrice Dalle smoulders with a huge tattoo on her shoulder while Dennis Hopper reinvents Emile Zola's novel *Nana* in a style somewhere between *Showgirls* and a snuff movie.

Hopper seems here let off the leash for the first time since *Blue Velvet*, playing Mickey – presumably at least in part the Ferrara substitute – as mercurial, abusive, Mephistophelean and finally sane. Hopper brings along forty years of movie baggage as he embarks on what could be seen either as a caricature of the Ferrara method, or a self-aware critique of the dangers of stepping half into a sea of madness in order to capture on film the thrashing of the poor souls who can't make it back to the shore. The script comes perilously close to editorialising in Mickey's final abusive speech as he drives Matty to suicide by exposing his worthlessness, but Hopper plays it with a manic edge that suggests his own character's complicity in what Matty has done. Indeed, it also suggests Ferrara's own complicity in its condemnation of a character he has himself created and shaped.

At this stage in his career, a Ferrara movie commands respect and demands multiple viewings. If *The Blackout* seems not quite up to the level of his most recent masterpieces – *King of New York*, *Bad Lieutenant* and (especially) *The Addiction* – it might be that it misses the input of his usual screenwriter Nicholas St John and denies itself the now-familiar milieux of New York and Catholicism. Nevertheless, no one in US cinema is willing or capable to go as far as this, and Ferrara must be classed as one of the greatest directors currently working at the top of his form.

Kim Newman

Spike Jonze

HOW TO GET A HEAD IN MOVIES

John Mount

Watching *Being John Malkovich* was one of the most restorative experiences I've had for a long time. Not only is it a more audacious and genuinely unpredictable commercial American film than one could possibly hope for, but it was also made by self-effacing young pop-promo director Spike Jonze and debut scriptwriter Charlie Kaufman, who, so it would seem, have discovered the alchemy of Buñuel's late films with Jean-Claude Carrière and updated it to appeal to their contemporaries: the mass audience of Generation X and Y cinemagoers. The result is a dark, surreal comedy with Borgesian plot twists that get more and more confounding. Film critics love it, obviously, and so do audiences.

Jonze chose for his feature-film debut a script which almost every executive who read it admired, but couldn't imagine being made, with the exception of Michael Stipe of REM who acquired the rights for his production company. New York scriptwriter Kaufman had written for a number of short-lived but cultish television comedy series, including *Get a Life* and *Ned and Stacey* (he'd also spent a lot of time working in warehouses and answering the phone for a living), but his script made no concessions to commerciality and was totally reliant on John Malkovich agreeing to play a less than flattering version of himself.

What the film is about is hard to define. John Cusack plays Craig, a failed puppeteer who on discovering a portal into the brain of actor John Malkovich turns it into a consumer attraction (with the sales pitch: 'Have you ever wanted to be someone else?'). Eventually Craig becomes Malkovich's ruthless puppet master in order to defeat his dowdy wife, Lotte (Cameron Diaz), in an obsessive love wrangle for his beautiful business partner (Catherine Keener). What begins as a Warholian parable on the nature of celebrity, obsessive fandom and artistic failure mutates into a fantasy about immortality and body snatching. The film opens up, in Craig's words, a 'metaphysical can of worms'. Jonze shrewdly eschews the opportunity to add any MTV-inspired mayhem to the mix (and herein lies the film's success) and opts for restrained, conventional direction and casting against type. Nevertheless, he couldn't resist including a flashback from the point of view of a chimpanzee and a parallel universe in which everyone looks like John Malkovich, be they midgets or lounge singers in drag.

Jonze, who was born Adam Spiegel in St Louis in 1970, started his career making videos about skateboarding (an abiding passion). The rock band Sonic Youth saw one, asked him to direct their next promo and his reputation grew. Before *Being John Malkovich*, he had directed some of the most innovative, left-of-field music videos of the 1990s including Björk's 'It's Oh So Quiet', Fatboy Slim's 'Praise You' and REM's 'Crush with Eyeliner', as well as numerous commercials for Lee Jeans, Nike and Coca-Cola. In addition to directing, he acted bit parts in such films as Allison Anders's *My Crazy Life* (*Mi vida loca*, 1993) and had his photography widely published. The success of *Being John Malkovich* puts him inadvertently at the crest of the next new wave of pop-promo directors turned film-makers, including Michel Gondry, Chris Cunningham (mooted to direct William Gibson's *Neuromancer*) and the Swedish collective Tractor. But any attempts to draw some mission or shared aesthetic from these auteurs would be false.

Last November, Jonze and Kaufman visited the London Film Festival to promote their film – a task that came easily to neither of them. Jonze is shy and superficially inarticulate, Kaufman nervy and defensive. John Malkovich – who committed to the film after some understandable hesitation – joked in interviews that Jonze has only five or six phrases in his vocabulary, yet there is a sharp creative mind operating behind the floppy fringe and retiring manner. Malkovich was advised by Jonze's father-in-law Francis Ford Coppola: 'In ten years' time, we'll all be working for this guy.'

* * *

John Mount: How did the film get into production?

Charlie Kaufman: I wrote the script five years ago and it took me about six months to finish the first draft. I don't know where I got the idea from, but I allowed the story to evolve as I was writing the draft and then refined it. The script made the rounds, but it was always, 'This is very funny, but no one will ever make this movie.' Then two and a half years later, Spike expressed interest in directing it at the same time as Michael Stipe's production company Single Cell Pictures optioned it. I met with Spike and saw his video work, and that was it.

John Mount: What involvement did Stipe have?

Spike Jonze: Michael pretty much let us do what we wanted. He helped with getting investors – it took a long time, but he and his business partner Sandy Stern kept trying. He didn't interfere and he really believed in the film.

John Mount: Did you make any changes to the script?

Charlie Kaufman: We spent a week going through it line by line and Spike would say, 'What does the character mean here?' and I'd clarify it. It was an important process.

John Mount: How easy was it to cast?

Spike Jonze: John Cusack had read the script years ago and wanted to do it. Then when John Malkovich came on board it became much easier.

John Mount: Did Malkovich bring anything to the film that hadn't been there before?

Charlie Kaufman: He didn't and he didn't want to. He was more interested in depicting the public's perception of him than in showing who he actually is.

Spike Jonze: If anything he wanted to push the character further. He said we should make things impossible for him, be mean to Malkovich, the meaner the better.

John Mount: Did you know in advance exactly how you wanted each line read or did you respond to the actors' interpretations?

Spike Jonze: There were some things I knew were very important and I was very strict. But at other times I let the actors try things out and then made my suggestions.

John Mount: What were you trying to explore in the twisted love triangle and the satire on celebrity?

Charlie Kaufman: I don't know if I was consciously trying to do anything but decide what would happen to these individuals – say, what would happen if Lotte went through the portal and liked the idea of being a man. A lot of people say there are a lot of surprising things in the script and I think that's because I was surprising myself. If I'd had a single idea I was trying to get to then the writing wouldn't have worked so well and people would have been better able to anticipate what's coming next.

John Mount: How did you decide on a style for the film?

Spike Jonze: Before we even got close to shooting we were trying to figure out how much we pushed different things like jokes. And we decided the key to the story was the characters, so we had to make them believable and keep it as naturalistic as possible.

John Mount: Why did you choose a conventional orchestrated score rather than a pop soundtrack?

Spike Jonze: We used Carter Burwell, who writes the music for all the Coen brothers' movies, though there is some Björk in there. Like I said, we wanted to play it naturalistically. The music was designed to illustrate the emotions of the characters and the mood of each scene. When I'm making videos I try to think how the songs might be used in another context – in a movie or in a gymnastic routine. So it was a totally different experience putting music to the images to draw out what's going on with the characters and the story.

John Mount: Film critics have made many highbrow references – Borges, Buñuel, Svankmajer. Did you have any sense of those influences?

Charlie Kaufman: I don't think we tried to make the film look like anyone else. It was fun coming up with ideas of our own. I don't mind hearing the comparisons, it's very flattering. Sometimes I get mad at myself because I'm not enjoying it all like I'm supposed to. But if I force myself to consider what the alternative would have been, I know I'm really glad it's not that.

John Mount: Are you going to work together again?

Spike Jonze: Right now we're working on something that Charlie wrote and that Michel Gondry is directing. The script is called *Human Nature* and it's about a woman whose hair just keeps growing.

Charlie Kaufman: I hope it's about little people with little problems. I don't think it has the same kind of surreal elements. I don't want to get tagged as the guy who does the weird stuff.

BEING JOHN MALKOVICH
USA 1999
Director: Spike Jonze

Manhattan, the present. Under pressure from his wife, Lotte, street-puppeteer Craig Schwartz takes a job as a clerk with LesterCorp., run by Doctor Lester, a company located on the low-ceilinged seventh-and-a-half floor of an office tower. He falls in love with his co-worker Maxine. Craig discovers a hidden door leading to a passage which sucks him into the head of actor John Malkovich, whose life he experiences for fifteen minutes before being ejected on to the side of the New Jersey Turnpike. Craig introduces Lotte to being John Malkovich, and while she is inside him, she/Malkovich makes love to Maxine; the two women fall in love, but can only enjoy each other physically when Lotte is in Malkovich.

Craig and Maxine start a business charging people to be Malkovich. Eventually Malkovich rumbles their scam and enters his portal himself, discovering a world where everyone is him. Craig and Lotte struggle for possession of Maxine. Eventually, Craig uses his puppeteering skills to enter Malkovich permanently and turns Malkovich into a world-famous puppeteer; Maxine becomes his lover. Lester explains to Lotte that Malkovich is the latest in a line of conduits used by a secret society to enjoy eternal life in new bodies. Craig is forced out of Malkovich. Years later, Malkovich has joined the channellers; Lotte and Maxine are a happy couple with a daughter; Craig is inside their daughter, still in love with Maxine, now his mother.

* * *

There's a current running joke about *Being John Malkovich* that speculates on what the film might have been if its star and ostensible subject hadn't agreed to play along: what, in other words, if Spike Jonze had to settle for *Being Jeremy Irons? Charles Dance? Julian Sands?* You can only imagine that Malkovich agreed out of a sort of inverse vanity: 'Be mean to Malkovich,' he apparently urged the film-makers. It's not unusual for actors to dismantle their own image on screen, but, in most cases, they have the safety net of fiction. What's remarkable here is that Malkovich agreed to supply his name, face and presence, and then to have all three subverted in a manner that is anything but gently well meaning. The film makes rich capital out of Malkovich's peculiar public image, yet this is just the tip of the iceberg. The most eccentric US debut feature in recent memory – for both Jonze and screenwriter Charlie Kaufman – is at once a Dada screwball comedy; an inquiry into the nature of personality; a metaphysical conspiracy story; and a comment on the way we invest our own desires into public figures, hollowing them out into blank receptacles.

The film's jibing at Malkovich is certainly its most approachable aspect. In recent years, his career choices have been far stranger than anything the film imagines, from high-art foreign-language roles for Raúl Ruiz and Manoel de Oliveira, to the barmy and often lazy overplaying in commercial fare such as *Rounders*. But here Malkovich may have found his greatest role, playing himself, or a vain, lasciviously suave caricature of himself, lounging in his penthouse with a copy of Chekhov, or attempting to lure a lover with a murmured, 'Shall we to the boudoir?', Malkovich's air of narcissism is such that it comes as no surprise when, as the film puts it, he goes 'up his own portal' – into a screen actor's poetic-justice nightmare world in which everyone has the face of Malkovich.

The film is partly about the empty nature of modern fame: people know your face and name, but not what you've done. No one can think of a Malkovich film, except the one in which he played a jewel thief (but there's no such film, he protests). He becomes literally a locus for other people's dreams. People inhabit him for a while: one man learns what it is like to be Malkovich ordering towels by phone. Lotte and Maxine use him as a sort of prosthetic love attachment, an animated trysting place; Craig sees him as 'a really expensive suit that I enjoy wearing'. In this sense, the film is an extended joke about the contemporary dreams of vicariousness and virtuality: the actor's body becomes a living version of the *eXistenZ* computer game devised by David Cronenberg. (Alternatively, you could see the film as a rewrite of the sci-fi topos of dimension travel: a celebrity-culture Stargate.) But the process works both ways: Craig gets to inhabit the actor and achieve his dreams, by making Malkovich the star puppeteer he could never be. They're made for each other, the actor's pretensions easily matched by Craig's delusions of profundity. But it's Malkovich who reaps the rewards of fame and a new existence, while Craig remains anonymous and in the cold.

But the film constantly shifts too much for us to pin it down: it can't easily be tagged as screwball or surreal, as a paranoid fantasy or a media satire. It's forever slipping into sideshows and diversions, from a lunatic corporate video to a hallucinatory sequence inside a chimp's memory. Nor is it in any way a typical video-maker's movie (Jonze won his spurs directing for the Beastie Boys and Björk et al.), but a visually low-key, formally sober film that above all values shifts of tone and a very concrete sense of space, playing claustrophobia against spatial fluidity (the film begins in the enclosure of a puppet theatre and ends underwater, in a swimming pool). There's extraordinary use of sound, too, as if the world turns inside out when we're in Malkovich's head: we actually hear a hand brushing roughly across his scalp.

Finally, the film is a triumph of casting in which no one is what we expect them to be. John Cusack's face is barely visible behind the shaggy hair, Cameron Diaz barely recognisable under baggy tracksuits, fluffy wig and a scowl of discontent. The biggest revelation is Catherine Keener, usually cast as an ingenue doofus. Here she's a sleek, impeccably cruel vamp who sets the film's initial sexual certainties spinning wildly out of control, seducing both Malkovich himself and Lotte, who hides out inside the actor's body. *Being John Malkovich* is an incredibly rich and entertaining (not to say, laudably malevolent) film that far transcends its already way-out title premise: not just a Larry Sanders self-reflexive swipe at stardom, but, as Craig puts it, 'a metaphysical can of worms'.

Jonathan Romney

Harmony Korine

MOONSHINE MAVERICK

Geoffrey Macnab

In *Hearts of Darkness*, Fax Bahr and George Hickenlooper's 1991 documentary about the making of *Apocalypse Now*, Francis Ford Coppola came up with an unlikely prediction. Exhausted by the stress of making a multi-million dollar folie du grandeur deep in the jungles of the Philippines, he speculated about where cinema could go. The future, he suggested half-ironically, would probably lie with a teenage girl in the Midwest making home movies with a camcorder.

Twenty-three-year-old Harmony Korine may not quite fit Coppola's description, but his debut feature *Gummo*, shot on location in Nashville with a mainly non-professional cast, has a humour and originality that mainsteam Hollywood cinema misses by a mile. On the surface, Korine's subject matter seems familiar enough. From *Back to the Future* to *American Graffiti*, from *The Last Picture Show* to *Pretty in Pink*, countless other film-makers have attempted to capture the agonies and ecstasies of small-town American adolescence. Korine's characters, however, are a long way removed from the prom queens, leather-clad rebels and high-school football jocks we are used to seeing. His inspiration comes as much from Buñuel's *Los Olvidados* and Hector Babenco's *Pixote* as from Hollywood teen pics. There is something picaresque and cruel about the two scrawny protagonists Solomon (Jacob Reynolds) and Tummler (Nick Sutton), who ride around town on their bikes killing stray cats. It is easy enough to see them as victims of poverty and broken homes, but in their own irrepressible way, they might equally be described as 1990s counterparts to Tom Sawyer and Huckleberry Finn. (With his curly hair and oversized head, Reynolds even looks as if he might have stumbled out of a Victorian children's fantasy.) Korine insists he has no polemical axe to grind. Despite all the *vérité*-style camerawork, he is not making a neo-realist drama-documentary about the plight of the urban poor in the Midwest. The title itself suggests that the writer-director is not entirely in earnest: Gummo was the little-known Marx brother.

Korine dispenses with the niceties of plot (a word he loathes) and instead offers a series of snapshots of young adolescents running amok in a small Ohio town. Imagery ranges from the sublimely poetic – a kid with enormous pink rabbit ears walking across a grey, rain-strewn cityscape – to the bizarre: Solomon and Tummler with airguns firing off pellet after pellet at the carcass of a dead cat. Certain sequences – for instance, the drunken arm-wrestling contest between a disabled dwarf and a beer-swilling redneck – seem like blue-collar realism given a surreal twist. Others – the ritual shooting of Bunny Boy by two eight-year-old cowboys – could be straight out of Lewis Carroll.

At times, the film has the directness and naïvety of a home movie. Whether Dot (Chloë Sevigny) and Helen (Carisa Glucksman) putting masking tape over their nipples or the two skinhead brothers beating lumps out of each other in the family kitchen, the camera captures moments that seem private and spontaneous. *Gummo* is also often highly stylised. Korine wrote the film as a series of self-contained scenes: 'a mother washes her son's hair, twisting it into a fluffy shampoo peak on top of his head'; 'a boy and two girls goof off in an above-ground swimming pool during a summer storm. Raindrops bounce off the surface of the water as they splash around, kissing and playing.' The cinematography has a studied informality about it, as if director of photography Jean-Yves Escoffier was under instruction to make everything look as if it was shot on the hoof, even as he went to elaborate lengths to stage and light each sequence.

Like *kids*, which Korine wrote for director Larry Clark when he was eighteen, *Gummo* has been given a rough ride by the censors. And US critics have already labelled the film 'one of the most repellent cinematic efforts in recent history' and 'the worst film of the year'. The *Hollywood Reporter* suggested that, 'whatever small audiences *Gummo* attracts – and they will be drawn mostly by the prospect of watching something "shocking" – will wind up leaving the theatre in a state of disgust.' As usual, the negative hype seems wildly misplaced. The inhabitants of Korine's world may all be oddballs, but he treats them with tenderness and humour. Just as critics and audiences in 1932 were so repelled by Tod Browning's *Freaks* that they failed to realise what a humane film it was, many of *Gummo*'s detractors seem blind to the warmth and humour in Korine's small-town fable.

Korine knows his cinema. His conversation is liberally laced with references to Bresson, Fassbinder, Godard and Cassavetes. He is tiny, politely spoken and highly articulate. *Gummo* is his third script, after *kids* and *Ken Park*, also written for Clark, but shelved after bickering between the director and his collaborators. 'I was fed up with the whole thing,' Korine says now of the aborted project. 'I wanted to make another film, but I didn't want to write for other people. *kids* was a success, so I knew it was my time.'

At the press conference for *kids* in Cannes in 1995, Korine loftily proclaimed that he was 'going to make movies like nobody has ever seen before'. With *Gummo*, he has been as good as his word.

* * *

Geoffrey Macnab: Tell me about the gestation of *Gummo*.

Harmony Korine: I wrote *Gummo* in two or three months. I didn't write straight through – it was more like I was thinking of the film as individual scenes, almost like photographs, things I wanted to see. Then after I'd written about 200 scenes I started to play with the order, trying to find, if not a narrative, a story that went through the film. Then Fine Line gave me the money and I went away to where I grew up – Tennessee – and made the film with the people I grew up with.

Geoffrey Macnab: There are only four or five professional actors in the film.

Harmony Korine: I have almost no interest in actors. If I write a script about someone who fights alligators, I'd rather find the person who would fight the alligators for real than ask Tom Hanks to play the part.

Geoffrey Macnab: What was your approach to filming?

Harmony Korine: I was mostly concerned with setting up a chaotic environment, giving my sister a camera, handing everyone Polaroids, 16mm and 35mm cameras, whatever was to hand, letting situations happen and not concerning myself with story or anything like that. I wanted to set up situations so I could turn my camera one way and film and then turn it the other way and there would be something going on. Then from the chaos I would work out everything at the editing stage. As long as what I was filming was compelling and what I wanted to see, then I knew it would make perfect sense. I think film ought to be like collage.

Geoffrey Macnab: You use a lot of videotape.

Harmony Korine: I think video is beginning to change the way people make films and watch cinema. Hopefully it will change cinema not only aesthetically, but will make it a less elitist art form.

Geoffrey Macnab: Were you ever worried about patronising your characters or about falling into the trap of 'white trash chic'?

Harmony Korine: No. I don't patronise anyone. I spent months before the production just photographing these people, going inside their homes and spending time with them. I knew almost everyone who appeared in the film from hanging out with them beforehand. For me as a film-maker or an artist, to go in and make fun of someone – I don't even understand the concept. As long as I'm not forcing anyone to do what they don't want to do, I don't see how there could be any question of exploitation.

Geoffrey Macnab: How would you place *Gummo* alongside other teen movies?

Harmony Korine: I think I've seen every youth picture ever made. But I don't think *Gummo* is a teen film. It goes beyond that.

Geoffrey Macnab: I was intrigued by the casting of Linda Manz. She seemed to have disappeared after *Out of the Blue*.

Harmony Korine: I'd always been a fan of her work, so I tracked her down. It turned out she had married an orchard-picker in northern California. He was the guy who threw a wet rag over Michael Jackson's head when his hair caught fire during that Pepsi commercial. Linda was working at a hospital at the time, so when Michael was rushed into hospital Linda must have fallen in love with the guy who saved him.

Geoffrey Macnab: I heard you had difficulty getting the film past the censors.

Harmony Korine: What is really hard in the States is the ratings board. They were kicking me with an NC-17, and my only requirement was that I had to turn in an R film. They were giving me an NC-17 for 'nihilism' – how absurd can you get? I had to recut the film seven times. They really tried to destroy the movie. You can't hold them to any kind of rules – there are no guidelines to follow and everything is subjective. They were offended by the film in a hundred different ways. They'd tell me to cut fifteen seconds. I'd cut the fifteen seconds begrudgingly and then they'd say it wasn't enough. At one stage I wanted to scrap the whole fucking movie.

Geoffrey Macnab: Which scenes caused problems?

Harmony Korine: The scenes that bothered them most were the ones that dealt with little kids using drugs. Remember the scene where the little boy moves the picture and the bugs run out across the wall? The camera shows the kids sitting on the couch, huffing aerosol cans. (When I was little, that's what we used to do – take socks and put them over aerosol cans to breathe in the fumes.) The little boy was sitting on his sister's lap. The camera pans up, showing all the bug bites on his legs. There's a Bach cello piece playing in the background. Anyway, without any direction from me, the kid grabbed the can out of his sister's hand. He was a four-year-old kid and it looked as if he was getting high. In fact, the cans were empty. But it became something almost holy to see this kid, who looked like he was a baby nursing a bottle. To me, that meant everything. It was the whole film. It showed the repeating process, the dysfunction. But the ratings board flipped when they saw that. They said it was the most disgusting thing they'd ever seen. I didn't give a fuck what they thought – it's just that they have the power to say that if I don't cut that shot out, nobody would see my film.

Geoffrey Macnab: Roaming around town, Solomon and Tummler remind me of Huckleberry Finn and Tom Sawyer. Would you agree there's an innocence there, despite the mischief?

Harmony Korine: Definitely. Even when they murder the grandmother, when they kill the cat, I don't think any of it is done out of any kind of evil. I know from growing up, the way I lived, the things I've seen, that all that kind of dysfunction and messed-up living comes out of boredom. When you have nothing, and nothing to do, you make do by experimenting.

Geoffrey Macnab: What was your budget? And did you have final cut?

Harmony Korine: The budget was around $1.3 million. I would never make movies if I didn't have final cut. If anybody told me what to do, I would quit. I can't understand people who collaborate like that. If there comes a point in my life where I have to listen to studio people, if there is a chance someone can take the film away from me, I won't make the film. The movie should be one person's vision, and that's it. The reason most movies are the way they are is that there are too many voices. I wouldn't allow that. Anyway, *Gummo* is the kind of film that baffles studios, and that's fine by me. I liked the idea of them just giving me the money and leaving me alone.

Geoffrey Macnab: I heard it said that Alan Clarke was a major influence on *Gummo*. Is that true?

Harmony Korine: Alan Clarke is maybe my favourite film-maker, the best of the British New Wave. *Christine* is a masterpiece and I like *The Firm* and *Made in Britain*. What I like is that he approaches drama in a different way. There is never a beginning, middle and end – the films just exist, the drama just seems to happen.

Geoffrey Macnab: How did you come to see his films?

Harmony Korine: A few years ago, they screened about twenty of his films at MoMA. That's when I saw them all. I've seen so many movies. There was a time from when I was about seventeen until I was twenty when my life seemed to consist mainly of seeing movies. I had difficulty sleeping so I would see about four or five a day. I rapidly ate up movies. I thought I'd already found all the masters – and then I saw Alan Clarke. I couldn't believe that here was somebody who made movies in this way and I'd never heard of him.

Geoffrey Macnab: What is it about his films that you like?

Harmony Korine: He was doing something dramatically that I'd never seen before. And his films are so honest – the way the characters speak, as if they just exist, as if they're organic. Plus, of course, his use of violence is very interesting to me. It's more than real. And there's such an energy to his camera, such a fluidity to his movies. The steadicam shots can last for five minutes at a time.

Clarke had a real style. And there is no one less pretentious. With a lot of British film-makers, politics tends to get in the way of the storytelling, but Clarke seemed to be more interested in telling stories than in solving problems. There are shots in *Gummo* that I took straight from his work, like the scene where the two girls are walking and talking right after they've watched the boy playing the tennis match. The use of the steadicam shot there is pure Alan Clarke – stylistically at least.

Geoffrey Macnab: Could you say something about your family background?

Harmony Korine: My father was a documentary film-maker. I didn't go to school much because I was following him around where he was working. He was very much into circus clowns and children who rode bulls. He had these obsessions which would require the family to follow him. At one stage he tried to do a movie about the last great moonshiners. So I spent a lot of time in rural communities when I was growing up. I started to drink moonshine when I was young. That was a big influence on me, both aesthetically and otherwise. Then, at a certain point, he became a Trotskyite. He really got into Marxist propaganda and started fire-bombing empty houses across the South. That was when I broke away from him.

When I was growing up he didn't speak to me so much. He'd throw shoes at me or hit me, but he did it out of a sense of love. One way he communicated with me was through film. We would watch a lot of movies together. When I went back to Nashville, where he had a house, there was a theatre near the university that would play double features every day. That was where I saw a lot of the films that influenced me early on – *Night of the Hunter*, Dreyer's work, early Bresson.

Geoffrey Macnab: You were chucked out of high school when you were a kid for assaulting a librarian.

Harmony Korine: No. What happened was that when I was about thirteen, I was reading a book which quoted Kierkegaard so I went to the library, found a book by Kierkegaard and tried to check it out. I looked young for my age – I was thirteen, but I probably seemed about eight. The librarian verbally assaulted me and told me I wasn't old enough to check the book out. And the same thing happened when I tried to check out Walter Benjamin's *Illuminations*. I wanted her to die and I said so to her face. 'Die, bitch!' I told her. I threw a chair at her. I was thrown out of school. One week later, she went skydiving. Her parachute didn't open and she died. I went to the funeral and I tried to dance on her grave. Then the police came. It was a fucked-up situation.

Geoffrey Macnab: The film's little corner of small-town America is very distinct. Are you going to be tackling the same sort of locale and subjects in your future films?

Harmony Korine: Well, Middle America is where I came from. To me, it's the most interesting and left-out part of the US. America is not New York and Los Angeles.

Geoffrey Macnab: Do you see yourself as following in any sort of tradition?

Harmony Korine: There's no tradition of an American New Wave, but there is a tradition of American mavericks. There were certain directors – Peckinpah or Cassavetes, for instance – who told stories that dealt with sections of America that for the most part have been ignored.

In my next movie, I want to go even further with the kind of fracture I was exploring in *Gummo*. I want it to be completely random. I'm aiming for completely objective film-making, where it's all about the images – about something you can't verbalise.

THE BEAT-UP KID

Danny Leigh

Whether *Fight*, his on-off paean to the art of getting beaten senseless, ever sees cinematic action, this much is clear: no one takes a kicking like the young director Harmony Korine. Look closely and you can probably still see the bruises left by the critical reaction to *Gummo*, his 1997 directorial debut – and for this writer perhaps the most inspiringly singular American film of recent memory. For the vast majority of reviewers, however, all *Gummo* represented was a celluloid red rag for a series of outbursts so splenetic they seemed the prelude to some kind of mass journalistic aneurysm. Janet Maslin, the *New York Times*'s famously delicate former critic, captured the mood by calling it 'the worst film of the year' in her opening sentence.

Now he's back for more. *Julien Donkey-Boy*, Korine's second feature, finds its director armed with the Dogme 95 vows of chastity to detail the story of nascent schizophrenic Julien (Ewen Bremner) and his splintered, dysfunctional family (including Chloë Sevigny as sister Pearl and an admirably demented Werner Herzog as their unnamed father). Following a hazy but probably lethal confrontation between Julien and a small boy on a bleak New York riverbank, we track Korine's troubled protagonist as his condition deteriorates (the intention being to portray a character 'right on the cusp' of the illness). With his mother dead, Julien's relationship with his mono-maniacal father is coloured by the latter's frenzies of bullying, typified by his reaction to a chaotic ramble delivered by his son over dinner ('It's so artsy-fartsy ... I think I hate his poem'). His bond with his sister, however, remains strong and – as the film later reveals – more than fraternal. Julien's younger brother Chris (Evan Neuman), meanwhile, obsessively practises his wrestling, another victim of their father's crazed determination to spawn 'winners'.

Like *Gummo*, *Julien* is a flawed but frequently exhilarating piece of film-making. Sadly, like *Gummo*, it's also an invitation for Korine's deskbound nemeses to sharpen their claws. The webzine Salon describes the film as 'at once repulsive and clichéd ... its lessons and themes are merely scattershot afterthoughts to the project of making a movie this bad.' Harsh words for a work whose use of DV's bold intimacy, with its scan lines replacing the warm grain of conventional film stock, may be disorienting but is hardly clichéd. Or one whose unflinching eye for the extremities of human behaviour could repulse only those smitten by the homogeneity of the Hollywood value system.

What soon becomes clear is less the impulse to critique the film itself than to express personal odium towards Korine and his audience. To find anything of worth in Korine's work is, it seems, a tacit admission of – to borrow a pair of Maslin's choicer epithets – your own cynicism and pretension. 'Even today,' Salon continues, 'the Net (and the Lower East Side of New York) is littered with those who argue that the squares who don't like Korine's work just lack the intellectual strength to understand it ... If there's one thing to admire about Korine, it's his skill for exposing the open sore of hipster insecurity.' And the strange thing here is that Salon is right. While faintly leftist cultural commentators and reactionary curmudgeons unite in their antipathy, Korine's backing from at least one sector of the media – the cheerleaders of the fashion/style press – has rarely been other than feverish.

With his heavily documented wunderkind status (even at the ripe old age of twenty-six) and his relationship with starlet Sevigny, Korine has provided the ad-heavy glossies with everything they could hope for in a bright young film-making thing. A recent issue of the *Face* devoted eight pages of breathless prose to 'Chlo'n'Harm' (even if its underlying priorities could be glimpsed in its cover image, wherein a pouting Sevigny held up a small Polaroid of her boyfriend). Unfortunately for Korine, it appears the baggage of his celebrity has largely overshadowed any real discussion of his film-making talents. Adopted by the style media as a cinematic totem alongside their parade of models and obscure haberdashers, he has been positioned by the vapid approbation of the *Face* et al. as a cipher for all that is fraudulent and transitory. Whether by acolyte or adversary, his age, dissipated aura and itinerant upbringing have all been used to transform a promising director heading for his late twenties into the slack-jawed brat of popular imagination.

Of course, Korine is hardly the first individual to have found their art buried under a mound of obsequity and reactive venom or to witness their artistic persona boiled down to a reductive, user-friendly 'personality'. One need only look at Nan Goldin, whose photographs of early 1980s East Village bohemia (most notably in her slide show *The Ballad of Sexual Dependency*) were later seized upon by friend and foe alike as the ground zero of heroin chic. Despite the maturity of her later work, and notwithstanding her having photographed only two fashion sessions in her life, Goldin would forever be cast as the woman who made junkies cool. Similarly Larry Clark – whose 1971 overview of speed-freak culture *Tulsa* was cited as an influence by Goldin before his venture into features with the Korine-scripted *kids* – has monoto-nously been portrayed as an ageing and possibly dangerous ex-con with an unhealthy predilection for adolescent flesh, even when such ideas are irrelevant to the project at hand (for instance, the prosaic 1998 feature *Another Day in Paradise*). And then there's Tracey Emin, Margate's own (initially) self-styled 'slag with big tits', which image the media used to belittle the wit and power of her installations.

Korine, Goldin, Clark and Emin: connected by a daisy chain of aesthetic sensibilities, their collective gaze routinely falling on the disenfranchised and the detritus of lives (frequently their own) going awry. Each has built a reputation on an often semi-voyeuristic commitment to the dark side of urban existence, on portraits of low ebbs and getting high, of black eyes and bad company. The role of all four has been to document the grimy, disturbing and occasionally uplifting minutiae of modern day-to-day life, to provide a mirror (literally for Goldin and Korine, both of whom have frequently used looking glasses in their work) to reflect what would otherwise remain unseen. And with that commitment has come a certain kind of celebrity through which each has been diminished.

That said, only the naive would portray Korine as an innocent in his own commodification. Whether from genuine exuberance or a more artful desire to manipulate the press (having heard him talk for five hours straight on everything from Baader-Meinhof to Houdini, I'd hesitantly say the former), he certainly gives the media what they want. (Which, in the short term, could be prudent: after all, how much exposure can any other director of his non-existent commercial profile call upon?) In a culture obsessed with the real, and in which the real is in increasingly short supply, Korine provides the media with a priceless frisson of *vérité*. No ostensible commentary on his films is deemed complete without a tangential foray into their director's sex life, drug use or fragile state of mind; the scent of autobiography, the gamier the better, remains as powerful to Korine's chroniclers as it once did when Goldin referred to *The Ballad of Sexual Dependency* as 'the diary I let people read'. Again, the parallels among his antecedents are legion: the perception of Clark as uncontrolled reprobate was only fuelled by his inclusion of self-portraits in 1983's *Teenage Lust*, while Emin's finest – and most talked about – hour came with her *Everyone I Have Ever Slept with 1963–1995*. Though Emin's and Goldin's careers have been more nakedly autobiographical than Korine's thus far (autobiography doesn't come much more naked than Emin's soiled bed covered in empty bottles or Goldin's self-portrait after being beaten by her boyfriend), he, too, has let the autarkic urge seep into his work. There it is in his appearance in *Gummo* (making sexual overtures, lest we forget, to an encephalitic dwarf); there it is again in his admission that much of *Julien* is based on the mental illness of his Uncle Eddie.

While drawing on life as lived lends the films a rare potency, it also encourages those who would wish to render their maker as a clown savant, unable to produce anything but a simple-minded regurgitation of his own experience. And the oft-discussed subject of age brings with it a further whiff of the supercilious. Scriptwriter at twenty, director at twenty-three, author (of the eccentric *A Crack up at the Race Riots*) a year later, Korine was always going to find his youth piqued the interest of observers. What this fascination has led to, however, is its employment from all sides to imply untutored genius or charlatan imposture. Scrutinise either the hostility of the critics or the clammy hagiographies of the style press, and it's hard to avoid the dynamic at hand: the middle-class, over-educated media professional engaging with Korine's ill-bred young autodidact.

None of which would matter were his second feature not so extraordinary. Certainly, within its loosely bound structure of semi-improvised vignettes, Korine's touch falters, a number of scenes descending into an addled murk of inarticulacy. Equally, at times, the electrifying audacity that characterised *Gummo* appears a one-time deal, leaving its successor looking drab by comparison. But compensation comes in the form of proof of a growing maturity. While his screenplay for *kids* revolved around teenage mores, a preoccupation further explored through *Gummo*'s leading boys, *Julien* is, at heart, an abstract, ruined coming-of-age story. For Korine, you sense *Julien* is the marker for a similar transition from *enfant terrible* to cinematic force.

Visually pushing at the boundaries of DV's possibilities, his free-ranging imagination now includes a cogent sense of cinematic grammar: a sequence in which Julien helps out at a home for the blind dazzles with its interplay between film and still photography, while the understated punctuation of Bremner walking towards camera soundtracked by a sombre, two-note guitar refrain lingers in the mind for longer than much of *Gummo*'s raw iconoclasm. The three silent, monochromatic shots that end the movie are genuinely moving; a salutary lesson for those who view Korine as merely a glorified fashion hack ('the difference between art and fashion,' Nan Goldin once remarked, 'is when has a fashion photograph ever made you cry?').

Moreover, after the pointedly random trajectory of his debut, *Julien*'s focus on its central family – first seen atomised in their respective bedrooms – represents a real advance from the one-dimensional character sketches of his previous work. The progression is bolstered by the authority of the cast – whereas *Gummo* relied on the unvarnished energy of non-professionals, *Julien* thrives on the disciplined vigour the right actor can deliver. And deliver Bremner does, bringing a ferocious conviction to scenes as potentially insipid as a telephone conversation with his dead mother (with Sevigny play-acting mom). Add in the Dadaist bravura of Herzog, loitering in his gas mask and muttering 'give me some Everest' at a bottle of health tonic, and Korine's capacity to shift gear between deadpan absurdity, nerveless brutality and an almost unbearable poignancy becomes entirely persuasive.

Yes, *Julien* is an imperfect, frustrating, transitional project. But in its appreciation of those marginalised, stutteringly incoherent people existing without the benefits of a scriptwriter's cosy narrative arc – playing out their lives in the typically unseen spaces of bedrooms, bathrooms and kitchens (territory previously associated with Goldin et al.) – we should be reminded how fascinating the results of that transition might be. You can only hope that between the fickle plaudits and the destructive bile, between his acclaim as multiplex-trashing insurrectionary and scorn as empty-headed mannequin, Harmony Korine continues to get the chance to prove his worth.

David Lynch

TWIN PEAKS: FIRE WALK WITH ME
USA 1992
Director: David Lynch

When Teresa Banks, a waitress, is found dead in Washington State, FBI chief Gordon Cole sends Special Agent Chester Desmond with his younger associate Sam Stanley to investigate. Despite the hostile local sheriff, Desmond unearths significant clues before he mysteriously disappears. Agent Dale Cooper, who suffers from precognitive dreams, is distracted by the brief spectral reappearance of Phillip Jeffries, another vanished agent, but concludes that the killer will strike again.

Later, in Twin Peaks, Oregon, high-school princess Laura Palmer is torn between Bobby Briggs, her cocaine connection, and James Hurley, a sensitive biker. Increasingly indulging her drug habit, she confides in best friend Donna Hayward that she has regularly been molested in her home by Bob, a demonic figure. Leland Palmer, Laura's father, is in fact Bob, having either been possessed by an extra-dimensional entity or driven mad by incestuous urges. As Cooper has further dreams, in which he sees Bob in a curtained netherworld called the Lodge, Laura gradually realises that Bob and her father are the same being.

Donna insists on coming along on one of Laura's nocturnal excursions, where she earns money for drugs through prostitution – in which enterprise she was connected with Teresa Banks – in a hellish club run by Jacques Renault on the Canadian border. Although she surrenders to the advances of a loutish man, Laura is shocked to see a drugged Donna similarly degraded, and rescues her friend. Laura accompanies Bobby when he goes to make a drugs connection, and witnesses his impulsive shooting of a corrupt deputy – who had tried to obstruct Chester Desmond – delivering cocaine.

An angel in a picture on Laura's bedroom wall vanishes, and she is visited by Annie, a bloodied vision from the future. She tells Laura that Dale is trapped in the Lodge, referring to Agent Cooper's future possession, after Leland's death, by Bob. Laura confides in James, who refuses to believe in her secret life, and then joins Jacques, hooker Ronette Pulaski and local thug Leo Johnson in an orgy. Left tied up by Jacques and Leo, Laura is found by Leland/Bob and, along with Ronette, dragged to a disused railroad car, where she is further abused and killed. After death, Laura is transported to the Lodge, where she has a vision of an angel, and smiles.

*   *   *

Given that *Twin Peaks*, the television series, represents a bizarre fusion of the values of prime-time soap-mystery with the sado-delirium of David Lynch's evolving vision, it is at once surprising and horrifyingly inevitable that this feature spin-off should pare away all the elements that made the show bearable and cultishly appealing, coming up with what may well be the director's cruellest film since *Eraserhead*. Refusing to satisfy the series' fans' wish to know what happens next by not picking up from the show's cliff-hanger ending – which is referred to obliquely by the momentary appearance of the inexplicable Annie, who refers to a future when Bob has (temporarily?) prevailed over Agent Cooper – the film instead returns to the backstory of Laura Palmer.

Furthermore, in pruning the catchphrases, comic sub-plots, big-business soap, eccentric flourishes, playful eroticism, and detective story elements, not to mention many popular characters/actors, from the original series, the film deliberately chooses to alienate a large segment of the audience who found the show likeable – as witness the extremely hostile reaction to its screening at Cannes – and to concentrate on a genuinely disturbing, genuinely frightening descent into Hell. Indeed, Lynch opens with a prologue designed to disorient the viewer familiar with the show by dramatising the Teresa Banks case as a capsule re-run (pre-run?) of the whole plot – another evocative theme tune, another dead girl, another FBI agent, another sheriff, another diner, another forensics man, another clutch of eccentrics.

The difference is that this presents a joyless, glum and senile community bereft of the pretty girls, natural beauty, ensemble acting camaraderie and skewed charm which make up much of the appeal of *Twin Peaks*. The only familiar element is Lynch himself, cast in the role of the hard-of-hearing Cole, who introduces Agent Desmond to his dancing mime cousin. Her peculiar act delivers a complex message which Desmond then decodes for his sidekick, Kiefer Sutherland, in a parody both of the process of intuitive deduction from minimal clues upon which Cooper's investigations depend, and the way Lynch's own works tend to be combed for multi-level symbols and signifiers that, in the end, may be no more than atmospheric set-dressing, multiple McGuffins.

Although the first half of the series was mainly concerned with raking over the ashes of the past shown here, *Twin Peaks*, the television show, abjured almost completely the use of flashbacks, preferring to present possible versions of the past as various characters were drawn down the same path as Laura Palmer. The most powerful moment, in a Lynch-directed episode, was Leland/Bob's murder of Laura's lookalike cousin, named Madeleine Ferguson in a nod/reference/homage to Vertigo, and also played by Sheryl Lee. This renders redundant in narrative terms anything in the current film, an aspect made even more bizarre by the inevitable process of time, whereby all the actors who return from the show are now older, even though the film takes place before everything we have seen. The only replacement cast member – Moira Kelly taking over from Lara Flynn Boyle – is actually more convincing as a younger version of her character than any of the others, who are taking up not from where they left off, but from a point prior to where they started in the first place.

The conventional way of providing a film to cap the cancelled series would have been to take up all the unresolved plot-lines and tie them in a neat knot, preferably allowing Cooper a victory over Bob and revealing which characters survived or were killed in the explosion that untidily scrambled a whole bunch of storylines in the final episode. This prequel, however, is actually more in line with the general drive of *Twin Peaks* which, with all its time-hopping, was as concerned with delving into the hidden past as progressing into the narrative future.

After the prologue, there is a flurry of re-establishing touches – micro-cameos from series regulars such as Mädchen Amick and Eric DaRe, capsule scenes to re-create plot elements – before the film plunges into Laura Palmer's degradation. In the monster father figure of Leland/Bob, Lynch has a bogeyman who puts Craven's Freddie Krueger to shame by bringing into the open the incest, abuse and brutality which the *Elm Street* movies conceal behind MTV surrealism and flip wisecracks. When Donna is slipped a hallucinogen at the Renault roadhouse, the images (and, as usual with Lynch, the multi-layered and terrifying soundtracks) couldn't be any more disturbing.

The film's many moments of horror – an excursion into a drab room in a picture given Laura by a spectral old woman and which turns out to be one of the entrances to the Lodge; Laura's hysterical and numbed laughter as Bobby is shocked by the murder he has committed; the alternations of the glowering Leland with the insanely evil Bob – demonstrate just how tidy, conventional and domesticated the generic horror movie of the 1980s and 1990s has become. The angel that finally adds a touch of hope in Laura's afterlife, and which could have strayed in from Lynch's *Wild at Heart* where she was played by Sheryl Lee, is the single up-beat element in a movie relentlessly concerned with nightmare. While not exactly comfortable or pleasurable viewing, *Fire Walk with Me* succeeds in showing the sour heart that has always lurked beneath the onion leaves of the show.

Kim Newman

DAVID LYNCH: MR CONTRADICTION

Chris Rodley

LA, 15 February 1996. A day like any other, with a score of film and television crews shooting on location all over the city: Los Angeleans driving home from work tire of traffic diversions, while the city's Permit Office rings its cash registers. Around the All Star Bowl in Eagle Rock, thick black cables snake the sidewalks, spreading out from throbbing generators to engulf this 1950s-style Ten-Pin bowling alley. Catering trucks clatter. Enough equipment to lay siege to a small fortress is unloaded and assembled. Everyone moves purposefully and efficiently to some complex plan. In this particular ant colony, in the absence of more highly developed forms of communication, it's necessary to use walkie-talkies. The First Assistant Director, pushy but pleasant, understanding but firm, elects to use his lungs.

But this is no ordinary Hollywood shoot – the All Star Bowl is fast becoming another dark and dusty corner of that neighbourhood best described as 'Lynchland'. Which could be your neighbourhood. Look under any rock, peek behind any curtain, hide in any closet: should you glimpse the possible key to a disturbing, dangerous yet delicious mystery, lurking just beneath the shiny normality, you'll feel at home. In an *unheimlich* sort of way.

At the quiet centre of all this activity is David Lynch, once affectionately described by Mel Brooks as 'Jimmy Stewart from Mars'. The movie being shot is *Lost Highway*, his first in four years. Despite the fact that the crew is working a night shift (wrapping at around 3 a.m.) and that these are the last days of a 54-day shoot, spirits are more than high. Lynch seems happiest of all: he constantly and enthusiastically praises the work of technicians, joshes with actors or finds the time to listen to a piece of music brought in by a member of the cast, as well as paying strict attention to the smallest detail of what's about to happen. As the first take of the night is prepared for, he offers $10 to anyone who gets a strike during filming. Take one costs him $20, with several more to go. His euphoria at being back in the movies seems highly contagious: euphoria is an important sensation to Lynch.

This is just a neighbourhood bowling alley, but it won't look or sound it on-screen once Lynch and his crew are done. Cinematographer Peter Deming isn't shooting at twenty-four frames per second. And 'Gave Up', a corrosive song by Nine Inch Nails, is blasting through speakers: 'Smashed up my everything. Smashed up what was true. Gonna smash myself to pieces. I don't know what else to do.' Prior to a take, Lynch reminds Balthazar Getty (as mechanic Pete Dayton) that he's 'still a bit in never-never land'. By now Getty, sporting a prosthetic haematoma on his forehead, must be accustomed to Lynch's mastery of the understatement.

At this point in *Lost Highway*, Dayton is recovering from a major trauma. Dazed and confused, he turned up inexplicably on Death Row in the cell of jazz musician Fred Madison (Bill Pullman) with a head wound and swollen, bloodshot eyes. Pete has no memory of how he came to be there, and Fred has gone missing. Pete is released – after all, you can't send the wrong guy to the chair – but the garage where he works offers no refuge from his unease. Regular customer Mr Eddy, a mysterious and powerful local 'businessman', now has a woman called Alice (Patricia Arquette) in tow, who strikingly resembles Madison's murdered wife, Renee. Pete, trying to make sense of why his own life has become so strangely unfamiliar, only feels that he *seems* to know her. However, he's severely disoriented, stumbling through what seems to be a nightmare of someone else's making. It's just possible (in Lynchland) that he is actually part of a highly organised hallucination: Madison's mental creation. But more of this weirdness later.

If the atmosphere and setting of tonight's shoot seem as playfully ordinary as *American Graffiti*, *Lost Highway* is nonetheless a very disturbing affair. The script, an original creation of Lynch and co-writer Barry Gifford, is compulsive yet baffling. The reader is quickly drawn into a dark mystery which may involve a wife-killing, though it refuses to yield its many secrets readily. It dares to be the script of a film, but at best only indicates what we will eventually see, hear and even feel when all is complete. What is actually going on is far from 'legible' on the page – normally an absolute requirement in this age of committee-system movie-making.

It's the kind of script that worries 'the money'. However, as each scene unfolds before the camera, it's clear that Lynch knows *exactly* what's happening; he just doesn't like to talk about it too much. He puts his trust in images and sounds as opposed to words, knowing that all will be clearer when *Lost Highway* is experienced, not read. For us and for him.

But while shooting on location, actors – stereotypically anxious about 'motivation' and meaning – have to put a lot of trust in Lynch. *Lost Highway* obviously presents its stars with serious conundrums. But Natasha Gregson Wagner, an actor relatively new to movies, seems to welcome this. The daughter of Richard Gregson and Natalie Wood (and a ringer for her mum), she plays Pete's girlfriend, Sheila. Tonight she must tell him that he's recently been behaving like 'a different person' (understatement again), particularly since a certain very significant night. One which the audience will never see, and which the characters only allude to, ominously.

Between takes, Wagner confesses: 'I wouldn't say that I understand the script completely, but I like that. I know that when I see the movie I'm going to be surprised by how it all fits together. We all have our own fantasies about what the secret of *Lost Highway* is. At times, in David's direction, he'll give you an idea and you'll think you're on to something. Then the next day it will be completely the opposite.' So what does Wagner think happened *that* night? 'I think it's up to everyone's own imagination: the audience's, and that of the actors playing the roles. If you want to be incredibly literal you could be, but I don't think this is the place to be incredibly literal. I filed my literal side away. For another movie.' And of her director, a man responsible for perpetrating some truly disturbed and disturbing cinematic experiences? 'He's such a dignified, handsome, nice man. Such a great contradiction.'

During each take, Mr Contradiction watches and listens intently. Between takes he often goes onto the floor, scrumming down briefly with Getty and Wagner, talking in hushed tones, and strictly on a 'need to know' basis. The dialogue in *Lost Highway* is sparse and enigmatic, and Lynch has a very precise delivery in mind. He doesn't give line readings – but gives indications of mental states. Then it's up to the performers. Occasionally, he might simply bellow through a megaphone from behind the video assist. Then he sounds like Jimmy Stewart from Mars. Such moments seem to contain their own sense of performance. That voice; that hair. They serve to remind that on a Lynch film, the real star is perhaps Lynch.

But this star is interview-shy. He seems to view them much as he does test screenings of his movies: 'They're like facing the firing squad. Except you don't die.' But it's 11.00 p.m.; 'lunch' break. Time to light a cigarette, put on the blindfold, and wish he was back in Pete's (or should that be Fred's) head.

Lynch is wearing exactly what he wore in November 1995, when we last met; shirt (black, buttoned up), jacket (black), shoes (black) and trousers (khaki). Theory: like Seth Brundle in Cronenberg's *The Fly*, he has several such outfits; one less decision to make on this film. Then there's how to describe it. The opening page of the script of *Lost Highway* announces: 'A 21st-century noir horror film. A graphic investigation into parallel identity crises. A world where time is dangerously out of control. A terrifying ride down the lost highway.'

Lynch laughs. 'Yeah, that's sort of baloney. You know what I mean?' Just checking. 'It's a dangerous thing to say what a picture is. If things get too specific, the dream stops. There are things that happen sometimes that open a door that lets you soar out and feel a bigger thing. Like when the mind gets involved in a mystery. It's a thrilling feeling. When you talk about things, unless you're a poet, big thing becomes smaller.' So what kind of thing is *Lost Highway*? 'I don't like pictures that are one genre only, so this is a combination of things. Horror. Thriller. But basically it's a mystery.

'Actors ask a lot of questions. But they're strange, because they seem to understand things – abstract things – pretty easily. They can buy into an abstraction without too much trouble. In the beginning we rehearsed certain scenes because somehow those scenes – in our minds – defined the characters in some way. Once they got those scenes, the rest fell into place. But then there's always some scene that needs more explaining than others.'

Lunch is over; back to work, out of the bowling alley and into the small adjoining bar and dance floor. What is so striking about watching Lynch at work is that every shot is considered not only in terms of how it can be made visually and conceptually arresting, but also how to encode it with some sense of the whole. This involves attention to colour, texture, sound, mood and meaning (not talked about), as well as performance. At one point, he insists that some inconsequential dialogue be recorded later so that a track by The Pixies can be played through a scene. 'I *must* have this music. *Please!*' This is as tyrannical as it gets with Lynch. The First AD concedes.

Lynch is constantly seeking the right feel, and he wants that mood to be felt on set or on location as far as possible. It helps the performers, and also helps him sense if the scene is working as it unfolds before the camera. This affords the opportunity to play with what is actually happening on a moment-to-moment basis. And few directors are as prepared as he is to go with an unforeseen opportunity. A delicate balancing act of intuition and absolute control, and difficult to talk about. Hence Lynch's reputation for being an interviewer's nightmare when it comes to 'explaining'. But the results speak for themselves. When Frank Silva – a member of the props department on the pilot episode of *Twin Peaks* – was 'accidentally' reflected in a mirror during a take, he instantly became Killer Bob, an idea not till then considered for the series by either Lynch or his (then) collaborator Mark Frost. The rest is history.

Wednesday 21 February. Tonight in a large furniture warehouse in downtown LA, a *Lost Highway* crew shoots insert work. The cold, cavernous space boasts a very convincing five-foot-square facsimile of the Mojave Desert. Actor Michael Massee, drenched in blood, awaits an appointment with a glass-topped coffee table.

Star Patricia Arquette is back for the day. She stands, restrained by various contraptions, her body draped in black velvet. On the video assist, her head appears to float in a dark void, resembling the figures often glimpsed stranded in Lynch's own near-black paintings. Peter Deming runs the camera at forty frames per second. A (warm desert?) breeze plays across Arquette's hair and face, just before the electricity hits: that special Lynch electricity that flashes like lightning, those surges of energy that so often signified trouble or revelation in *Twin Peaks*. It also accompanied not only Laura Palmer's horrendous murder in the movie prequel *Twin Peaks: Fire Walk with Me*, but also, in its closing scene, her finally meeting her Angel.

Lynch is ecstatic, and everyone knows it. That voice again, ricocheting around the showroom: 'That's *beautiful*, Gary.' Special Effects Co-ordinator Gary D'Amico might well be pleased. It does look beautiful. And it's achieved in camera. None of that 'we'll sort it out in post production' nonsense. It's happening right now. It's a painting. A moving painting.

For Arquette, *Lost Highway* is a real challenge. She plays not one woman but two. Or does she? We'll first see her as Renee, wife of Fred Madison. She's then horribly murdered, probably by her husband, probably for infidelity. But when Fred is imprisoned, he inexplicably mutates on Death Row into the younger, virile Pete. When Pete is released, Arquette appears in his life as Alice, girlfriend of the sinister Mr Eddy. Her carnivorous sexuality leads the bemused auto mechanic into a world of shady characters, pornography and (inevitably) murder again.

Arquette has thought carefully about her role(s): 'This movie is just about an obsessive love affair. It doesn't have to make sense to anybody else. It's like stepping into the mind of someone who's obsessed. Usually I'm cast as a character of hope, or love. But this is about the darkness of woman. The destructive element of woman. It's a man's concept, but I've never played that before. And I've never done a lot of nudity, so that was a whole other confusing problem. Not just in film, but in my own life. So I thought that maybe I should go through the gates of hell and face up to all my fears.'

So what about Renee and Alice? 'My first concept was that they were two different people. But then David said, "No, no, no. They're the same person." So then you have to cross over a reality border, because they can't be the same person and one of them *die*. I was adrift there for a while. So maybe one of them is an hallucination.' At the risk of making a bigger thing smaller, Arquette has arrived at her own solution to the mysteries of *Lost Highway*, by buying into an abstraction. 'I play two different interpretations of the same woman. I think it's about a man trying to re-create a relationship with the woman he loves so that it ends up better. Fred re-creates himself as Pete, but the element of distrust in him is so strong that even his fantasy turns into a nightmare.'

Whatever the answer, there's no doubt Lynch is back, creating serious mischief. The last four years have seen him working largely in television. But why has it been so long since the critical and box-office failure of (the underrated and misunderstood) *Twin Peaks: Fire Walk with Me?* 'I tried to get some things going, but for one reason or another, nothing ever happened. It's a matter of finding something that you're in love with. You fall in love with the material and you're excited about it. Otherwise you'd never be able to sustain the trip. To make a movie for money, or for any other reason is wrong.'

Back at Asymmetrical Productions, Mary Sweeney – Producer, Editor, Lynch's partner – sits in a semi-circle of four Steenbecks, looking at a previous day's rushes. What appears on the screen is as unexpected to her as it is to anyone else. An ordinary scene of four characters in a car, driving to the All Star Bowling Alley, has been transformed into a mini-nightmare. With the use of a simple but ingenious device on the camera, it looks and feels like being inside someone else's migraine. One suspects that few editors get to be so constantly surprised and delighted on a day-to-day basis: 'Lost Highway is a very interesting synthesis of different films he's made. David's developing his art and his language. With each film I've worked on with him, his demands on the camera have become more sophisticated and dynamic. He really thinks hard about how he can make the simplest scene interesting, both visually and emotionally.'

Sweeney puts up another sequence, a single shot lasting three-and-a-half minutes. It's night. A cabin in the desert is burning ferociously. But something isn't quite right. The spare, painfully melancholic strains of This Mortal Coil's version of Tim Buckley's 'Song to a Siren' accompanies the conflagration. It could have been composed for the sequence. But now it's clear that the flames are retreating. The sequence has been shot in reverse, and the song is ending. The delicate voice of Elisabeth Fraser almost whispers its closing promise: 'Here I am. Here I am. Waiting to hold you.' The cabin now stands, completely intact, alone in the dark desert. A small light above the door glimmers like a distant beacon. There's a sudden chill in the editing room. Goose pimples and hairs rise to give their standing ovation.

This is your Neighbourhood Watch calling. You are entering Lynchland. Doesn't it feel good to be back home? In an *unheimlich* sort of way?

LOST HIGHWAY
USA 1996
Director: David Lynch

Los Angeles. Saxophonist Fred Madison discovers on his doorstep a videocassette of his house, shot from the outside. The next day, another videocassette includes footage of a track through his home, showing Fred asleep with his brunette wife, Renee. The Madisons call the police, who have no explanation. Renee takes Fred to a party thrown by Andy, a shady character, and Fred is accosted by a mystery man, whose face he has glimpsed in the shadows. The mystery man claims to have met Fred at his house, and that he is there right now. He produces a mobile phone so that Fred can confirm this, by phoning home and talking to him. The next videotape shows Fred with the dismembered corpse of Renee. Convicted of his wife's murder, Fred suffers strange headaches and in prison transforms into another person entirely – a young mechanic named Pete Dayton.

The authorities return Pete to the charge of his parents, and Pete picks up his life, doing work for his gangster patron, Mr Eddy. Mr Eddy's mistress, Alice Wakefield – a blonde incarnation of Renee – begins an affair with Pete. Alice talks him into robbing Andy, an associate of Mr Eddy's who lured her into prostitution and working in pornographic films. During the robbery, Andy is killed and Pete notices a photograph of Andy and Mr Eddy with Alice and Renee. Pete drives into the desert, where Alice has arranged to meet a fence. She disappears into a shack – and, as it turns out, from the photograph at Andy's – and Pete transforms back into Fred. Mr Eddy appears on the scene, and is executed by the mystery man. Fred returns to the city to deliver a message to his own home that Mr Eddy, also known as Dick Laurent, is dead, and drives again into the desert, with the police in hot pursuit.

* * *

The legend of Luis Buñuel's collaboration with Salvador Dali is that if either included an image or incident open to rational explanation or interpretation, it would be dropped. Yet *Un chien andalou* and *L'Age d'or* afford many meaningful readings. It may well be that with *Lost Highway*, director David Lynch and co-screenwriter Barry Gifford – author of the novel *Wild at Heart* – have succeeded where Buñuel and Dali failed, creating an almost entirely meaningless, or perhaps senseless, film.

A synopsis can only be tentative, since the film delights in contradictory or unexplained events, fracturing narrative logic at every turn. At a party, the film's first protagonist Fred asks the host who the mystery man is. Fred is told that he is a friend of the recently deceased Dick Laurent. But later it emerges that the gangster Mr Eddy is also called Dick Laurent – and when Eddy dies in the course of the film, Fred drives to deliver the news of his death, apparently to his own house. While in Lynch's *Blue Velvet* and *Twin Peaks*, the noir plots are surprisingly worked through and explained, *Lost Highway* goes out of its way to be inexplicable. The twinning of Fred's wife, Renee, and Mr Eddy's moll, Alice, is impossible to rationalise as a *Vertigo* (1958) imposture, a *High Plains Drifter* (1972) resurrection or a *Mirror Images* twin-sister exchange. As a photograph at one point demonstrates, Renee and Alice are sometimes separate and sometimes one. If this bothers you, then there is no way into or out of *Lost Highway* for you.

The opening 'Fred Madison' section of the film, climaxing with Fred's transformation, is so powerful that the 'Pete Dayton' sequence inevitably disappoints. Fred and Renee receive the videocassettes, each showing more as the camera gets closer to them. Then Fred encounters the mystery man – Robert Blake in Bela Lugosi make-up, delivering arguably the most frightening performance in 1990s cinema – and by this point Lynch fulfils his declared intention to fashion 'a 21st-century noir horror film'. He invests the Madisons' house with shadows that, in Raymond Chandler's phrase, betoken 'something more than the night'. Lynch has always excelled at sidesteps into pocket-sized universes – behind the radiator in *Eraserhead*, within the Black Lodge in *Twin Peaks* – but here he makes the simple shadowed corner into which Fred fades the most dreadful place his cinema has ever taken us.

Although the film slackens off when Balthazar Getty takes over the lead, Bill Pullman, an older version of the characters previously played by Kyle MacLachlan, represents Lynchian Man at his most susceptible to the forces of darkness, as demonstrated in the astonishing first encounter with the mystery man. More significant, perhaps, is Fred's explanation to the cops that he hates video cameras because 'I like to remember things my own way ... how I remember them, not necessarily the way they happened'. This whole film is not necessarily the way things happened. The Fred/Pete transformation just about makes emotional sense in terms of the entrapment of the noir hero within the narrative and the wiles of an eternally reborn *femme fatale*; while the twinning and melding of Alice and Renee play perfectly, thanks to Patricia Arquette's mastery of the art of holding back. But the 'Pete Dayton' section of *Lost Highway* founders a little on its lack of specificity. Have Fred and Pete exchanged bodies, with Pete coming out of some limbo to usurp Fred's place in the world (as Bob did with Agent Cooper in the last episode of *Twin Peaks*)? Or has Fred transformed only into a *physical* likeness of Pete, retaining his own memories and personality? On the one hand, Pete has his own skills at intuitive engine tuning – 'The best goddamn ears in town', Mr Eddy comments patting the film on the back for its consistently superb soundtrack, designed by Lynch himself – but on the other, he seems disturbed by Alice's resemblance to Renee.

Fred Madison lives in a horror story where an ordinary life can be pulled apart because of a stray thought and none of the trappings of American success can offer more than illusory comfort. But Pete Dayton's world is culled from the noirs Gifford extemporises on in his distinctive book of movie reviews, *The Devil Thumbs a Ride and Other Unforgettable Films*. Robert Loggia's Mr Eddy, like Frank of *Blue Velvet* and Bobby Peru of *Wild at Heart*, is a parody crime boss, brutally pistol-whipping an obnoxious motorist who has tailgated him, forcing him to promise to learn his highway code, and repeatedly emphasising the punishment he would inflict on anyone who slept with his mistress.

The Pete scenes trot out noir motifs – fleeing lovers, double crosses, a fall-guy protagonist – as landmarks rather than events, but the potency of the Fred scenes is never entirely dissipated. Among the most disturbing moments in the film are a terrifying phonecall from Mr Eddy and the mystery man (lying together in suggestive darkness) to Pete, and later Alice's reminiscence of being forced at gunpoint to strip for Mr Eddy (with Marilyn Manson proving against the odds that it is possible to outdo Screamin' Jay Hawkins with a more demented rendition of 'I Put a Spell on You'). Fred returns at a desert site where time has run backwards, so that the mystery man's shack is first seen in flames, and then de-explodes to wholeness. The last section of the film, which jumbles elements from all that has gone before, is all momentum where most movies would be all explanation, fading out with the lost highway of the title (a stray phrase from Gifford's novel *Night People*, not a reference to Hank Williams) and a high-speed car chase into a desert darkness.

As always with Lynch, it is hard to distinguish between a fictional universe created to force a reassessment of your relationship with the real one, and a personal world that suggests an unsympathetic interpretation of its creator's feelings. The abused and murdered women of *Blue Velvet* and *Twin Peaks* are again featured, though there is more eroticising here of living bodies than of dead ones. However, when it comes to genuine film fear – as opposed to Wes Craven's rollercoaster scariness with pop-culture footnotes – Lynch's is the only game in town. This is post-genre horror: playing down explicit shock (even Andy's head-impaling on the corner of a glass table is not given set-piece treatment), it works on the evocation of unease through subtle sounds and blaring doom metal, offering blurred moments that resolve briefly into dreadful clarity. After 100 years of cinema, it is still possible to make a truly terrifying picture.

Kim Newman

John Sayles

CITY OF HOPE
USA 1991
Director: John Sayles

Hudson City, New Jersey. Nick, son of Italian building contractor Joe Rinaldi, walks out on a construction job in a gesture of independence. He is approached by Bobby and Zip, musicians-turned-crooks, to be getaway driver for the burglary of Mad Anthony's electronics store, which has been arranged by Carl, a garage owner/hoodlum crippled in a car crash caused by Nick's elder brother Tony, who died in Vietnam. Joe owns L Street, a decaying slum that has been targeted for demolition to make room for a high-profit business project. He refuses to evict the no-hope tenants, despite pressure from Mayor Baci. Baci needs to push through the redevelopment because Assistant District Attorney Zimmer, who is involved in the deal, has threatened to expose the mayor's administration for feather-bedding and nepotism.

Moderate black councilman Wynn has just got his brother-in-law Franklin a job as night security guard with Mad Anthony. At a gig where Bobby and Zip are performing, Nick meets Angela, a girl he knew in high school, who was once married to Rizzo, an unstable local cop. The robbery is bungled and Franklin apprehends Bobby and Zip, but Nick gets away. Desmond and Tito, black kids from L Street, are harassed by beat cops, and in the park on the way home, Tito expresses his frustration by mugging Les, a professor who works with Reesha, Wynn's wife.

Bobby and Zip are arrested, but refuse to name Nick as the third man. However, O'Brien, a politically ambitious detective, manages to get Carl to inform. He then turns Nick over to Baci's faction, so that Joe will have to agree to demolish L Street in return for getting Nick off. Desmond and Tito, who have also been arrested, allege that Les propositioned them, and hard-line radicals Levonne and Malik pressurise Wynn to stand up for the kids. Rizzo, who has seen Nick and Angela together, jealously attacks Nick in the street and, learning that he is a wanted man, swears to bring him in.

Joe is ordered by retired Irish godfather Kerrigan to co-operate with Baci, and employs Carl to arrange the arson of L Street, which results in the deaths of the girlfriend and child of Ramirez, a drug-dealing L Street squatter. Wynn consults Errol, the black ex-mayor, and is told to respect the wishes of his community. He persuades Les to drop charges against Desmond and Tito, and turns up at a meeting in support of the kids. He turns the subject around to the suspicious fire on L Street and leads a march on a mayoral dinner, where he questions Baci about the deal. Rizzo bumps into Nick on the street and, following an argument, shoots him. Nick finds Joe at the construction site where he used to work, and they talk about their shared guilt over the L Street fire. Joe realises that Nick is badly wounded but his son won't let him leave. His cries for help are heard only by the deranged vagrant Asteroid.

* * *

Inevitably inviting comparison with the sprawling, multi-character 1970s films of Robert Altman, John Sayles's *City of Hope* is quite different in intent and effect. Whereas Altman approached politics obliquely through generic conventions, Sayles explicitly uses political issues to explore private ones. Caught in a complex web of corruption in which elected officials, ex-office holders, ward-heelers and constituents interact in a creaky political machine that extends from golf course to police cell, his characters are haunted by their failed relationships, by the past and by family ties.

City of Hope, following *The Brother from Another Planet*, *Eight Men Out* and *Matewan*, depicts a system mired in dishonesty for generations, with the Italians taking over from the Irish as the hidden rulers of the city and the blacks hustling to take their place. But the most corrupt of Sayles's politicians have some noble motives, while the most apparently honest are potentially crooked. Wynn's crucial conversation with Errol, a black mayor who resigned rather than face the kind of corruption charges Zimmer is holding over Baci, reveals that even the well-intentioned Wynn was implicated in the featherbedding of Errol's twelve-year regime. Wynn's subsequent 'heroic' confrontation with Mayor Baci, which is cut away from before the mayor can answer the councilman's pointed accusations, is overshadowed by his earlier acts of nepotism.

The interconnectedness of all the film's characters is reminiscent of the gritty soap of *Hill Street Blues* (evoked by the presence of *Hill Street* semi-regular and all-purpose genre icon Lawrence Tierney). The storyline progresses like a chain of knocked-over dominoes, with each event depending on other events and each character linked with all the others. The pattern is reinforced by camera movements which follow one character then switch to another just as the new character takes centre screen, binding together the vast *dramatis personae*. Sayles throws in a handful of scenes whose only purpose is to make links between characters more apparent, as in the meeting between Nick and Franklin, when they fool around with a basketball and discuss Nick's dead brother Tony. Tony's transformation from high-school hero through drunk driver to Vietnam casualty is the trigger for the story.

As usual, Sayles enlivens the conventions through his sure touch with characterisation, both in the non-stereotyped scripting and his confident direction of the large cast, several of whom are on the point of cementing their Sayles-bred screen images. Among the Sayles trademarks are his own appearance in a carefully selected role, small but vital and peppered with laugh lines, and a habit of playing tricks on the audience – as when the cop Rizzo hassles Nick with accusations we take to be about his activities as a getaway driver, but which turn out to refer to the affair Rizzo assumes Nick is having with his ex-wife Angela.

Slightly too arch, perhaps, in the pointedly ambiguous resolutions of Nick and Wynn's stories, *City of Hope* is nevertheless a major film, suggesting that Sayles might become as significant a film-maker for the 1990s as Altman was for the 1970s.

Kim Newman

SAYLES TALK

Trevor Johnston

As the latest young turks fight to see who can make the cheapest 'guerrilla' feature, John Sayles's position as the doyen of American independent film-making seems more than ever assured. Having started his career as a novelist and learned his screenwriting craft at the Roger Corman school of exploitation graft, Sayles's 1980 feature debut as writer-director with the seminal 'reunion' picture *Return of the Secaucus Seven* proved it was possible to finance your own movie, get it released and capture the attention of the Hollywood majors into the bargain. The $60,000 price tag gained as much notice as anything else, but in its ensemble structure, broadly liberal sympathies, tart dialogue and willingness to focus on the concerns of the over thirties, the film now stands as a fair record of the forms and questions its maker would continue to address. His subsequent output remains poised in both creative and budgetary terms between the mainstream's dollar-intensive factory product and the indie sector's modestly resourced pioneer activity.

Sayles's latest offering, *Passion Fish*, marks an effective honing down of his concerns to date. The film is founded on a wry, clearly delineated script and close attention to the performance of Mary McDonnell as an injured television soap star coming to terms with her newfound physical handicap under the care of Alfre Woodard's equally trouble nurse.

Where Sayles's earlier union conflict chronicle *Matewan*, baseball corruption story *Eight Men Out* and contemporary urban survey *City of Hope* pored over wider social and historical frescoes to pick away at the land of the free's obfuscatory ideological myth-making, the new film is scaled down in approach. Yet, as a wise spin on the problem pic, it still cloaks itself, like many of its predecessors, in approachable generic garb. From his earliest commissioned screenplays, Sayles has been nothing if not resourceful in his mastery of sundry genre formulae. His own films have injected familiar stylistic routines with a greater sense of thematic commitment – as in the science-fiction *The Brother from Another Planet* and the sports picture *Eight Men Out*.

In this light, it is easy to read Sayles's films as issue-led, each presenting the particular challenge of finding the right package in which to box a relevant social ill or question. While *Return of the Secaucus Seven* mines the insecurity of the 1960s angry generation, *The Brother from Another Planet* tackles racial problems. Even Sayles's horror scripts for *Piranha* and *Alligator* are imbued with a whiff of eco-conscience, while the films where the genre element is less pronounced (*Lianna*'s lesbian coming out, *City of Hope*'s state-of-the-nation address) tend to leave the mechanisms of their ideological apparatus more vulnerably exposed.

To his detractors, Sayles's too-perfect liberal conscience can feel like over-earnest PC point-scoring, yet, with *Passion Fish*, his human and societal insights are earned by the progress of the drama rather than willed into it from above. What's more, Sayles's unpredictability from project to project – who'd have guessed his next movie might be an Irish-set kids 'n' animals adventure – while still managing to retain an identifiable signature stands firmly in his favour.

* * *

Trevor Johnston: After *Eight Men Out* and *City of Hope*, were you intentionally looking to do a more intimate piece such as *Passion Fish*?

John Sayles: I never make the movies in the order that I write them or think of them, and *Passion Fish* harks back to when I worked in hospitals twenty years ago. People had seen *Persona* by that time and would go on about the symbolism. I thought it was about a nurse and a patient, and I always reckoned it would be a good idea to do a comedy American version. What influenced me more was not going from the social to the personal, but the fact that I'd done three 'guy' movies in a row, which is basically what politics still consists of. Maggie Renzi, my producer, asked me if I had any stories for women, so I thought we'd do the hospital one next. A lot of things clicked together: we were travelling down South and hooked up with a friend who plays in a zydeco band, we stayed in his parents' house and both the band and house ended up in the movie.

Trevor Johnston: As in previous films you seem to be dealing with an area of American experience – the Cajun culture – that could be seen as peripheral.

John Sayles: There are specific reasons why I chose that place. I wanted it to be very much somewhere that wasn't New York, so that it was evident that May-Alice, the Mary McDonnell character, had to change herself to make it in the city. And there aren't that many places left in the US that are different from McDonald's shopping-mall America. In that part of the South, people still speak French on the radio, they have their own food, their own music.

I also needed a place where, if you came back as an unmarried woman of thirty, people would know about it and you would know they knew. I needed a place that was sensual in nature: here are two women denying their senses or closing them down – Alfre Woodard's Chantelle has decided to become a nun and keep herself away from temptation, May-Alice is drowning her senses in alcohol and soap operas. It needed to be fleshy and sensuous, so there are more dissolves in that movie than I've ever had before.

Trevor Johnston: Your films seem to run counter to McDonald's shopping-mall America in their examination of social, cultural or political specifics.

John Sayles: A lot of my movies are about community. Their culture is an attempt at community culture rather than mass culture. May-Alice is an exile from the mass culture of the soaps, but it's still coming at her through her TV. It's only when she turns that off that she's able to appreciate what's around her.

I'm aware of mass culture, and I'm aware that I'm part of it. The stuff I do goes into theatres, it's advertised, I do interviews. But I want my work to be about it, but not necessarily of it. What I do in film is not just another meal at McDonald's, it's more a case of opening a funky little restaurant that becomes a cool hang-out. One week you do Cajun food and the next you do something else, on the understanding that most people aren't going to eat there. The bottom line is that they don't like that kind of food: it's too spicy, it's too foreign, they can't find the address. Most people don't see our movies in a theatre because they can't get to them. We don't get played in the chains.

Trevor Johnston: The film could be summed up in a soap opera way – alcoholic wheelchair-bound ex-soap star recovers with the help of ex-junkie nurse – but one of its aims seems to be to bring out the difference between the clichéd soap opera treatment of these issues and your own more sensitive approach.

John Sayles: One of the things the movie is trying to be aware of is people's desire to have an easy answer and not slug through things. To be able to place someone right away, to resolve a conflict that's not resolvable in a half-hour television slot. Even though they have the time, soap operas don't have the patience to have characters who develop in an organic way – instead, it's forget about the fact that you're only sixteen, the ratings are dropping so you've got to have a long-lost son.

So much American culture is market-driven. Demographics and research are getting everywhere. I can make my movie and sell it to Miramax, telling them that this is the final cut and if you don't like it, don't buy it. But they still bring in their marketing people, who say this is what people have said and this is why we want to cut this, and this, and this. What I'm hoping is to use that system to carry what I want to carry, but not to get eaten up by it. It's like surfing – the wave could kill you, but it could also give you a great ride.

Trevor Johnston: Do you find it frustrating that people don't see your movies in cinemas?

John Sayles: I wish they could. Usually the cinema is a fuller experience, though the television screen is an experience too – it may not be like going to a rock concert, but I still like records. It's certainly much better than there being no video, the movie playing in fifteen cities for two weeks and then hardly existing. Most of the places I've lived, like Jersey City, have never played one of my movies. People there have seen them because of video, and both *City of Hope* and *Passion Fish* were financed by home video pre-sales. That money has been vital for the independent American film movement.

Trevor Johnston: Has that situation given you a greater feeling of security for the continuance of your film-making career?

John Sayles: I would say that the continuance of my movie-making career rests on whether I can write enough screenplays and make enough money to finance or be a major investor in my next film – which will still have to be made for very little money. Right now I'm broke – the last couple of movies haven't done very well. Who knows whether I'll make back the money I put into *The Secret of Roan Inish*, the one I just shot? I've made eight or nine movies, but none of them has gone platinum. What I have is a track record that's very good in some ways, in that I attract good technicians and actors because they think my stuff is good and interesting to do. And then I shoot fast, so it's only five or six weeks out of their lucrative schedules, which means that sometimes their agents will even allow them to work with me.

But as far as financiers are concerned, it's problematic; they see me as a guy who's had nine chances at bat and lightning still hasn't struck. I've kept being a director because I always had money to put back on the table. Right now I don't have any money left, so I'm looking for work as a screenwriter. Maybe my next picture will be shot on 16mm for $500,000. When we finish one movie, we almost never know if we'll be able to do another.

Trevor Johnston: Do you rule out writing the kind of pieces that might require studio backing?

John Sayles: I write things because they're fun to write, because I want to tell the story. Then I look at them and think, 'How the fuck am I ever going to get to make this?' So rather than writing studio movies, I do movies of a certain ambition. It's a mutual thing: they're not all too interested in what I want to do and I'm not too interested in what they want to do. Every once in a while there's something close, I run it by them and the answer is 'Gee, I wish we could make movies like this! I really wanna see this movie! – but I'm not gonna give you the money to do it.' That's fine, that's a legitimate answer. As far as being a director-for-hire, I don't get many offers. I usually get asked to do things I'm writing, television movies or cable movies mainly. After *Secaucus Seven*, Roger Corman offered me *Mutiny on the Bounty in Space...* I sometimes wish I'd written that one!

Trevor Johnston: In terms of writing, what gives you the confidence to connect with individuals whose experience is completely alien to your own? That's a common thread in many of your screenplays.

John Sayles: First of all, I'm not afraid of failure. I don't get upset if people don't like it: I'm doing it because I'm interested. Second, you build up your confidence by doing your legwork. You spend time with people, you read more than one source and you always remain suspicious about anything anyone else has written. When I wrote *Los Gusanos* I had to learn Spanish to get to the books I needed that weren't translated and to get to the people I needed to talk to.

It's like being a reporter in some ways: I'm a conduit for people's voices. Like the disclaimers the networks put on some of their documentary programming, the views expressed in the movies may not necessarily be mine. Often some of my wackiest dialogue is verbatim – for instance, most of the dialogue in the car shop in *City of Hope* is just the flavour of the garage in Jersey City where I go to get my car not fixed – including my favourite line: 'Benny, you fat fucken haemorrhoid, get in here!'

Trevor Johnston: For me, *Passion Fish* is successful because of a combination of that kind of authenticity, and the fact that it is extremely well constructed. Do you think the early part of your career – whether it was writing novels, theatre or exploitation pictures – was a good school for learning your craft?

John Sayles: It all contributes. Certainly acting helps, in that it forces you to think about point of view, so when you write different characters they don't talk in the same way or want the same things. Novel-writing helps in a lot of ways too, because it makes you think about rhythm, though instead of it being a matter of words on the page, in film you establish rhythm in lots of different ways: there's camera movement, the way characters speak, cutting, music, the variation in framing and so on.

I learned a lot from the directors who made the Roger Corman movies, because they'd be straight on the phone to me, screaming for help: 'I've got $800,000 to shoot this epic you've written. It's set in 1933, we've got sixty-eight speaking parts and we start filming in two weeks. Do you know anything about the movie business? You're killing me!' Then I'd do a freebie rewrite so the movie could be better, rather than them just tearing out pages of the script at will. That way you learned what was capital intensive and what was labour intensive: what you had to throw money at and what you could overcome by ingenuity.

Trevor Johnston: Do you have work that you're more proud of as a director than as a writer?

John Sayles: It's not that interesting to me. You just try to tell the story as best you can, using all the weapons you have at your disposal. For each movie you have a different team, different demands, different logistical problems. At every point I try to zero in on the most important thing in the scene – sometimes it's the camera, sometimes it's the actors. When it's the acting I tend to keep things simple and I don't cut very much. I don't make movies because of some technique I want to try; I try a technique because there's a story I want to tell and that seems the way to do it.

Trevor Johnston: When you started out as a novelist, what kinds of movies led you to want to write screenplays and eventually direct?

John Sayles: I have wide taste. I like everything from *Cries and Whispers* to *Enter the Dragon*. I like different things in those movies, obviously – the acting in *Enter the Dragon* isn't my favourite thing about it, and the karate in *Cries and Whispers* is like nothing, whereas the storytelling grabbed me. Whenever a movie could get me into the story so I'd stop thinking about how it was made, that interested me.

Trevor Johnston: Has your career turned out the way you imagined?

John Sayles: I didn't know anyone in the movie business and I didn't know anyone who was a writer, so I had no role models. When I first went to Hollywood, I did think it through: I want to write movies and I want to direct the movies I write. How do I get to do this? They're not hiring theatre directors, they're hiring producers' sons, stars, people who work their way up through TV, and writers. Hey, I'm a writer, I can write my way to it. I'll do original scripts and assignments and if any of them make any money maybe I can suggest that I direct the next one. It was clear after writing three movies for Roger Corman that those were not the kind of movies that got any attention, so I went the Stanley Kubrick route and made my own fucking movie with *Secaucus Seven*. That was the start, because even if I hadn't got it released, at least I'd made a movie I wanted to make.

LONE STAR

USA 1995
Director: John Sayles

In Rio County, Texas, near the border town of Frontera, two soldiers unearth a human skeleton. A corroded sheriff's badge lies nearby. The sheriff, Sam Deeds, is summoned, and realises the body is probably that of his predecessor but one, Charlie Wade, who vanished in 1957. At the town restaurant run by Mercedes Cruz he questions Mayor Hollis Pogue, who used to be Wade's deputy – as did Sam's father, Buddy Deeds. Hollis recalls how Buddy defied Wade, refusing to participate in his protection rackets, and vowed to have him impeached. Soon afterwards Wade disappeared along with $10,000 of public funds. Buddy took over as sheriff, becoming a hero to all sides of the community. Sam, who returned to the town to succeed him, lives in his dead father's shadow.

At a parent–teacher meeting at the local school, Anglo parents argue furiously that the teaching of history has become too Hispanicised. The history teacher, Mercedes' daughter Pilar, is defending her position when news comes that her teenage son, Amado, has been arrested. She rushed to the jail where Sam, once her high-school sweetheart, has the boy released. Meanwhile at the black community's roadhouse run by 'Big O' Otis Payne, an off-duty soldier from the local army base is shot by a jealous rival in love. Otis receives a visit from the newly appointed base commander – his estranged son, Col. Delmore Payne. Stiffly formal, Delmore threatens to declare the roadhouse off-limits.

Convinced that his father was involved in Wade's death, Sam visits Big O's and hears how Otis, when he first came to work at the roadhouse, was publicly beaten and humiliated by Wade. At a civic ceremony, a plaque outside the courthouse is dedicated to Buddy's memory. Sam reluctantly takes part, now suspecting that Buddy may have taken bribes and conducted a long-running adulterous affair. Crossing into Mexico, Sam visits Chucho Montoya who tells him how Wade cold-bloodedly murdered Eladio Cruz, Mercedes' husband, in front of the appalled Hollis. Heading back, Sam stops off at a disused drive-in cinema and recalls how Buddy found him and Pilar there and furiously tore them apart. He seeks out Pilar, now widowed, and they renew their affair.

Urged by his son Chet, Delmore returns to Big O's to see his father and realises that Otis has followed his military career with pride. One of Mercedes' employees, Enrique, appeals to her for help; he has smuggled his fiancée across the Rio Grande and the girl has broken her leg. Usually hostile to illegal immigrants, Mercedes relents when she recalls how she herself was an illegal, helped across by Eladio.

From old letters Sam learns that his father's mistress was Mercedes. At Big O's he confronts Otis and Hollis, accusing them of having seen Buddy shoot Charlie Wade. They tell him what happened: Wade, finding Otis running a card school without cutting him in, was about to gun him down when Hollis shot the sheriff. With Buddy's help they buried Wade in the desert and Buddy gave Mercedes the $10,000 as compensation for Eladio's death. Meeting Pilar at the drive-in, Sam reveals that Buddy was her father. She responds that, since she can't have any more children, they shouldn't let the past stand in their way.

* * *

The final words of *Lone Star* are 'Forget the Alamo'. In a border region which, as the protagonist Sam Deeds remarks with laconic understatement, 'has seen a good number of disagreements over the years', the past weighs heavy, constraining and distorting relationships not only between individuals but between generations and whole communities. Pilar Cruz's words – 'All that stuff, that history – the hell with it, right?' – are a bid to break free from the trap of past guilts and enmities, and start from scratch. The film, the director John Sayles has said, is 'about history and what we do with it. Do we use it to hit each other? Is it something that drags us down?... At what point do you say about your parents, "That was them, this is me."?'

At the same time, that 'Forget the Alamo' – which Sayles at one point considered as a title for the film – shouldn't be taken too literally. Neither Pilar (a history teacher, after all) nor Sayles is suggesting anything so crude as simply junking the past, even if any of us could. Sayles's latest film develops the theme that has underpinned all his work to date: the sense of character as a product of accumulated social and cultural influences, the way people are moulded by their backgrounds and their pasts but can surmount that conditioning if they try hard enough. 'Blood only means what you let it,' Otis Payne tells his grandson, even while teaching him to be proud of his mixed Afro-Seminole ancestry. 'Most people,' says Cody, the redneck barman, 'don't want their salt and sugar in the same jar,' but under his morose gaze two army sergeants, one black and one white, are showing up the inadequacy of his metaphor as they plan their future life together.

After two relatively intimate chamber works – *Passion Fish* and *The Secret of Roan Inish* – *Lone Star* sees Sayles returning to the broad-canvas, multiple-character mode of *Matewan* and *City of Hope*. The new film, indeed, comes on very much as a companion piece to *City of Hope* – one northern and urban, the other southern and smalltown-rural, but both intent on tracing lines of tension and interconnection among a wide spread of individuals, showing how they impinge on each other no matter how much they try to hold themselves separate. Several characters in *Lone Star* strive to keep aloof: Mercedes Cruz, proud of her American citizenship, rejecting her own Hispanic background; Delmore Payne taking refuge in the rigid disciplines of army life; the Anglo parents at the school, resentful at finding themselves a minority in 'their' community. For *Lone Star* is both a film about connections and, in Sayles's words, 'a film about borders' – which, however artificial, are there and have to be acknowledged, but can still be crossed. In the final scene, Sam and Pilar deliberately decide to cross one of the most fundamental borders of all, the incest taboo, since it matters less than their own happiness.

In its visual style, too, the film elides borders. Flashbacks are presented, not by cuts or dissolves, but by the camera simply panning left or right, up or down into a different time-zone that nonetheless occupies part of the same space. The past, Sayles is indicating, isn't another country; it's still here and people like Sam are living in it, carrying it with them. And as the flashbacks accumulate, the line between moral absolutes also starts to blur. To begin with Charlie Wade and Buddy Deeds are seen as polar opposites: bad guy and good guy, 'your ol' time bribe and bullets sheriff' (in Mayor Hollis Pogue's phrase) versus the paragon of civic integrity. (The name carries its resonance; the principled hero of Frank Capra's *Mr Deeds Goes to Town* was played by that iconic figure of the Old West, Gary Cooper.) But as Sam digs away around the feet of the idol, determined to expose the clay, a less clear-cut, more human figure emerges: a man less bad than Sam wants him to be, but less perfect than the legend paints him. 'It's not like there's a borderline between the good people and the bad people,' Otis observes.

As that line indicates, *Lone Star* now and then tends to the overly didactic, and some of the plotting (such as the revelation that Mercedes Cruz was an illegal) comes a little too pat to carry conviction. In aspiring to a near-novelistic complexity of texture, Sayles over-eggs his pudding: there are half a dozen more minor plot strands than the above synopsis indicates, and some of them could be axed without doing the film much damage. But *Lone Star*, while breaking new ground in Sayles's ongoing exploration of the American myth, retains all his qualities of intelligence, political acuteness and narrative lucidity, and its widescreen photography (by Stuart Dryburgh, who photographed *The Piano*) develops the strain of visual lyricism that's enriched his films since *Matewan*. As ever, he draws nuanced performances from his cast, blending rep company regulars such as Chris Cooper (*Matewan, City of Hope*) with newcomers such as Frances McDormand (a cameo of knife-edge hysteria as Sam's estranged wife), and gives Kris Kristofferson his first worthwhile role for a decade.

John Sayles has always taken a fruitfully oblique angle on genre, and *Lone Star* turns the conventions and vocabulary of the Western to its own ends. The central strand of a man gradually stripping the legend away from an admired father figure carries echoes of Bertolucci's *The Spider's Stratagem* (to say nothing of *Citizen Kane*). But, although Sayles has often said he wants his films to make people think about their own lives, not about other films, *Lone Star*'s final revelation comes so close to the denouement of *The Man Who Shot Liberty Valance* that it can only be intentional. The whole film, in fact, could be read as a covert critique of John Ford's film, and even provides its own ironic version of Valance's most famous line when Hollis protests that suppressing the truth will leave people thinking Buddy killed Wade: 'Buddy's a goddamn legend – he can handle it.' It says a lot for Sayles's achievement that his film isn't in the least diminished by the comparison.

Philip Kemp

LIMBO
USA/Germany 1999
Director: John Sayles

Port Henry, Alaska, the present. Joe Gastineau works as a handyman at a guest lodge run by Frankie and Lou. An ex-fisherman, Joe quit twenty-five years ago when his boat sank, drowning two of his friends. At a party, he meets singer Donna De Angelo, and helps her move into a flat at the Golden Nugget saloon, her new place of work.

When Frankie and Lou persuade Joe to go out fishing, he rediscovers his joy in the job. He and Donna become lovers, arousing her teenage daughter Noelle's jealousy. Joe's half-brother Bobby, who runs a charter business, asks Joe to help him crew a boat up the coast to meet clients. Joe invites Donna and Noelle along for the ride.

En route, Bobby confesses his clients are drug dealers. They show up and shoot Bobby; Joe, Donna and Noelle escape to a nearby island. They take refuge in a hut. Noelle finds a diary left by a previous owner and starts reading from it; as the narrative grows more doom-laden, Donna realises Noelle, now feverish, is making it up. Jack Johansson, a pilot from Port Henry, arrives in a small seaplane. He admits he's working for the drug dealers, but promises to fetch help. Soon, a larger plane approaches. The three await rescue or death.

* * *

John Sayles is one of the most politically tuned-in of American independents. But the downside to his social awareness can be a tendency to didacticism, where the narrative moves predictably towards closure. Not this time, though. *Limbo* is Sayles's most unexpected film to date: not so much in its themes, which connect with his previous work, as in the shape of the story and the way it's resolved – or rather, in the way it isn't resolved. *Limbo*, as Sayles defines it, is 'a condition of unknowable outcome', and this is exactly the point he leads us to.

Locations are crucial to Sayles's work, and he has always explored cultural territory far from his own New Jersey roots. With *Limbo*, he veers northwards to Alaska, which he presents as frontier territory. Not a frontier in the adventurous, uncharted sense of the Old West, but a last-resort frontier for washed-up characters who have wearily arrived here with their disillusionments in tow. Most of them take a perverse pride in living in such a God-awful place. A running gag involves the regulars of the local saloon swapping ghoulish tales of drownings and fatal freezings.

For the first half of the film we're in familiar Sayles terrain. As in *City of Hope* or *Lone Star*, he evokes a community with its feuds and social crosscurrents, often via his signature shot: a long unbroken take meandering from group to group, picking up phrases and showing how all these people connect up. But midway, Sayles works a switch on us, lifting his three main characters out of this busy environment and dropping them into isolated jeopardy to play out a tight psychological drama.

Each of the trio carries weighty emotional baggage. Ex-fisherman Joe Gastineau is haunted by an accident where he caused the death of two friends; torch singer Donna De Angelo is the survivor of a string of transient relationships; her teenage daughter Noelle has taken to self-mutilation in response to her insecure lifestyle. Trapped on an island, and with the Alaskan winter closing in, the three are forced into close interdependence, exacerbating the fears and tensions between them. It's still a community, but shrunk down, distilled and intensified, all its edges sharpened.

They're joined by a ghost: the diary of a young girl who once lived on the island with her parents. Noelle finds the diary, reads aloud from it and starts using it as a weapon, rewriting it as she goes to mirror her own situation and get back at her mother. This set-up recalls Sayles's 1994 film *The Secret of Roan Inish*, where a family also wind up on an offshore island haunted by past presences. But that was far lighter in tone; *Limbo* introduces a harsh, unsettling note that's new in his work. Though the three confront their demons, we're left with no assurance that they'll find redemption.

As ever, Sayles gives his actors plenty to chew on. David Strathairn hits the exact note of wary gentleness, and Mary Elizabeth Mastrantonio's taut, ravaged beauty has never been better used. Haskell Wexler makes the Alaskan wilderness look at once alluring and forbidding; a shot of icy mist drifting over wooded hills has a Japanese delicacy. Over two hours long, the pace occasionally drags. Certain characters and elements – such as Noelle's crush on Joe – feel underdeveloped, almost as if the film had been boiled down from a longish novel. But when, as here, a film-maker strikes out on a daring new track, the odd minor imperfection goes with the territory.

Philip Kemp

The Limey (Steven Soderbergh, 1999)

Section 6: Generics

HENRY: PORTRAIT OF A SERIAL KILLER
USA 1986
Director: John McNaughton

Chicago. Henry, who has served out a prison sentence for murdering his prostitute mother when he was fourteen, works fitfully as an exterminator, and murders strangers, mostly women. Becky, who escaped from her abusive father by marrying an abusive husband, comes to Chicago to escape her marriage, and moves in with her brother Otis, an ex-convict who deals drugs and shares an apartment with his former prison friend Henry. Becky and Henry share their respective traumas, but Henry forms a closer tie with Otis, whom he initiates into the pleasures of murder by taking him along on a spree that ends with the killing of two prostitutes.

Henry explains his methods for remaining at large to Otis – he varies his modus operandi and always keeps on the move – and Otis becomes more enthusiastic about serial killing. He casually murders a passer-by to ease his frustration after one of his high-school drug clients has violently rejected his sexual come-on, and participates in the murder of a fence, from whom the pair then steal a camcorder. Henry and Otis watch a video they have made of their murder of a middle-class couple and their son, during which Henry is disgusted when Otis tries to molest the dead woman. Later, the pair argues over an accident which smashes up the camcorder.

Becky, who is unaware of the pair's crimes, tells Henry that she plans to return to her child – her husband being in jail on a murder charge with a million-dollar bail – and asks him to come with her, initiating a sexual encounter that is cut short by Otis's return home. Henry goes out for cigarettes and returns to find Otis raping his sister, whereupon he attacks him. Becky saves Henry from Otis's murder attempt by stabbing him in the eye with a comb, and Henry kills Otis, dismembering his body for easy disposal. Henry and Becky leave the city, and check into a motel. But the next morning, Henry leaves alone, depositing a bleeding suitcase by the roadside ...

* * *

Exceptionally well acted and shot for a zero-budget movie, and resolutely unexploitative in its approach, *Henry: Portrait of a Serial Killer* marked a distinctive debut for John McNaughton, who has subsequently made the still-shelved s-f horror picture *The Borrower* and is working under the supervision of producer Martin Scorsese on a Robert De Niro gangster saga. The four-year delay between the 1985 conception of *Henry* and its American release, with a further two years between that and its appearance in Britain, means that the movie has run the risk of coming out long after the *cognoscenti* have elevated it to cult status and the creative personnel have joined, albeit ambiguously, the mainstream. Even lead actor Michael Rooker, taking his first major role as Henry, has in the years since this performance become a familiar face with villainous roles in *Eight Men Out*, *Mississippi Burning* and *Sea of Love*.

Henry is loosely based on real-life convicted mass murderer Henry Lee Lucas who has, as is admitted in a recently added pre-credits caption, recanted many of the confessions that served as the basis of the film, and also criticised from prison the whole enterprise of making a movie about his alleged crimes. This is an unflinching portrait not only of its eponymous killer, but also of the world that at once turns him into what he is and allows him to get away with it. The product of an unspecified childhood trauma whose details change each time he recalls it, Henry, whose behaviour has not been modified by unsuccessful institutionalisation, drifts from job to job, murdering women whenever the mood takes him. In the powerful opening sequence (only slightly blunted by minimal BBFC cuts), the camera pans across the bodies of Henry's latest victims while their torture murders are heard on the soundtrack.

The minimal plot unnervingly bears out Elliott Leyton's musing in *Hunting Humans*, the definitive anthropological study of the phenomenon of serial killers, that the stresses which produce such aberrant behaviour are so widespread that it is surprising so few serial killers stalk America's streets. Henry is compared constantly with Otis, whose increasing delight in all-round depravity shocks and disturbs even Henry, perhaps because his verminous presence gives the lie to Henry's neutral sham decency, forcing the killer to recognise his own monstrousness.

Even the subtitle – which deliberately excludes Otis from consideration, unlike the co-murderers of *The Honeymoon Killers* or *The Case of the Hillside Stranglers* – suggests that Henry counts for more than Otis. The latter's sexual degeneracy, expressed through rape, incest and necrophilia, conflicts with Henry's almost respectful, joyless re-creations of the murder of his mother, who has made the whole notion of sexual congress beyond consideration for him by performing in front of his younger self with her clients.

The most deeply disturbing moments are perhaps the quieter sequences that bracket the killings, as when Henry pulls Otis out of the shock that follows their first, swift murders by offering him coffee and fries and bringing him back to a resolutely ordinary life. However, the film's strongest, hardest-to-sit-through sequence is the videotaped home invasion which, when the image becomes static because Henry has dropped the camera on its side so he can kill the interloping son, strongly recalls *A Clockwork Orange* and the torture, murder and sexual abuse as seen by the Patrick Magee character.

The impact of this scene depends on an audience's instinctive wish to turn away from the material Henry and Otis blankly watch on their television. The most horrific moment is Otis's line: 'I want to watch it again', which leads him to reshow on frame-advance the sequence of images an audience must be relieved to think is over. McNaughton's camera homes in threateningly on the television image, holding it for a horrifying few seconds before the tactful fade to the film's one calming-down scene, Becky talking to her child on the telephone.

Henry – who develops genuine if peculiar relationships – seems to be the most normal, well-balanced person in the film, but he is made even more chilling by his matter-of-fact explanations of his lifestyle. After the horrors of the home invasion and Otis's killings, McNaughton is even able to pull off an ambiguous but shattering finale. Henry literally dumps the girl who might have been his only chance for normality by the roadside, and disappears into the American vacuum from which he emerged in the beginning, to kill and kill again without hindrance. What makes this seem so inevitable is that – unlike the Thomas Harris–derived films and other entries in the serial-killer cycle – *Henry* has no interest whatsoever in the cocktail of issues that surround the killings. It never cuts away to the police, the media or the politicians, suggesting that Henry has gone undetected for years because of his evasive actions.

This narrowing of focus to the unbearable means that the film is far more likely to be targeted for adverse criticism or censorious pressure (it was initially given the prohibitive 'X' rating in the United States for 'general tone') than the *Silence of the Lambs*, which for all its qualities is a conventional 'entertainment'. Henry consciously incorporates into its own strategy the viewer's inevitable reactions against what is on-screen. This renders it a far more challenging, uncomfortable and honourable approach to real-life horrors than any attempt to dress up its psychological or sociological subject matter with thriller or horror-movie trappings might have been.

Kim Newman

ONE FALSE MOVE
USA 1992
Director: Carl Franklin

South Central LA. A young black man is shooting a video at his birthday party when a friend, Fantasia, lets in her white boyfriend, Ray, and his black partner, Pluto, who beat up the guests to discover the whereabouts of Marco, a local drug dealer. Ray and Fantasia then visit Marco and get him to reveal his stash of cocaine and money; while Ray strangles the witnesses, Pluto stabs the partygoers. Ray asks Fantasia to look for Marco's child; she finds him, but decides to say nothing. Detectives Cole and McFeely identify the gang and get a possible destination from Fantasia's voice on the party video – Star City, Alabama, where Ray has an uncle. Local police chief Dale Hawkins is contacted, and he confirms that the uncle's house is a likely hideout. Cole and McFeely fly down south and accompany Hawkins as he visits Ray's uncle. That night Hawkins's wife tells Cole how excited Dale is to be in on a big case.

Pluto insists that the gang head for Huston to sell to his drug connection, Billy. He sees his and Ray's pictures in a newspaper and they switch cars. In a roadside store, Ray and Fantasia meet a suspicious traffic cop who follows their car and pulls them over, but Fantasia shoots him.

Hawkins overhears Cole and McFeely mocking his ambitions, but stifles his pride to tell them about the shooting. When a picture taken from a store video camera arrives, he recognises Fantasia as local girl Lila Walker. They visit Lila's mother, brother and five-year-old son. McFeely suspects that there was once something between Hawkins and Lila.

In Huston, the gang have to wait a day for Billy. Lila suggests that she go ahead to Arkansas. Her brother meets her outside town to warn her off, but she insists on seeing her child. They arrange to meet later at an empty house. When Billy returns to Huston, he tries to back out of the deal, and Ray and Pluto shoot him and his cohorts. Pluto wants to split the money but Ray discovers that Lila has taken most of it. Lila's brother sneaks her son out to the car at night, but Hawkins follows. The following morning, Hawkins confronts Lila; it turns out that he is the father of her child. Cole and McFeely visit the Walkers and ask the child to retrace the route to his mother. As Ray and Pluto arrive at Lila's hideout, she waves them in to where Hawkins is waiting. He wounds Ray, is stabbed by and shoots Pluto, and is himself wounded outside. Ray shoots Lila through the head and Hawkins guns Ray down. The detectives arrive with the boy and, as Hawkins lies bleeding, he talks to his son for the first time.

*　*　*

The route from LA to the dusty roads of Arkansas reverses the direction of the great black migration from the rural South to the industrial cities of the North and West. In the Afro-American imagination, this journey is still a metaphor for going home. Whether or not this metaphor was pertinent to scriptwriters Billy Bob Thornton and Tom Epperson, in black director Carl Franklin's hands, *One False Move* is set on tracing American race conflict back to its seed bed in the South.

A hybrid of a road movie and a *High Noon*–style portrait of a fragile would-be hero, the film transcends the usual low-budget thriller concerns via an intricate script which emphasises the racial theme through a number of black/white relationships: the mixed-race Fantasia/Lila and her two white lovers, Ray and Dale, Ray's partnership in crime with Pluto, and the LA cop team of Cole and McFeely.

It's unusual enough to find these concerns in a genre thriller, but their use in one modelled on the hard-boiled fiction of writers such as Jim Thompson and Charles Williams borders on the audacious. Recent films in the genre by Dennis Hopper (*The Hot Spot*) and James Foley (*After Dark My Sweet*) emphasised sickly humour at the expense of the fiction's characteristically overheated psychodrama. Truer to the genre's icy characterisations, the cocaine paranoid Ray and the impassive Pluto, with his IQ of 180 and his pleasure in using a knife, make a suitably Thompsonian pair. Franklin's interest in the road movie element lies more in teasing out the tensions that a plausible inter-racial gang would signify than in playing his heavies for grim laughs.

While Ray and Pluto argue about what to do, Fantasia is the film's quiet agent of change and discovery – not for herself (it is she who is literally returning to an identity she cannot escape), but for her son and his white father. Her adopted name, coupled with her apparent passivity, might lead one to suspect she is merely a projection of white male fantasy, but her actions belie this. She saves the dealer's child, shoots the traffic cop, and steals the money for her son – virtually all the decisive moves undertaken on the road. Nevertheless, her dreamy, listless persona and her active duplicity still fit her for the role of *femme fatale*, and it is on her image that the whole film turns. What distinguishes her from a noir archetype is that she is given psychological cause for her enigmatic behaviour.

Before the arrival of Fantasia's photo – the moment when she 'becomes' Lila – Dale Hawkins is an excitable childlike good ol' boy in awe of the big city cops. As his wife tartly says while apologising to Cole for his use of the word 'nigger' in front of black cop McFeely, 'Dale watches TV, I read non-fiction.' His bravado is just part of his Southern cowboy charm, as casually employed as it presumably was in bedding Lila.

But on seeing her picture straight after suffering his colleagues' ridicule, the reality of a personal connection arrives with too abrupt a force. The transformation from buffoon to tragic figure (from adolescent to man) is more than actor Bill Paxton can handle, and it surely should have been managed by degrees.

In turning the film so radically on one moment, Franklin may have robbed himself of a plausible psychology for Hawkins, but he has an alternative protagonist, beautifully played by Cynda Williams (*Mo' Better Blues*), and all along he invests more in Fantasia/Lila's subtextual sacrificial journey than the one Hawkins makes from his daughter's cradle to his son's side.

Nick James

AT HOME ON THE RANGE

B. Ruby Rich

Think of spring. Spring 1993, to be exact. Visiting my friend Holly's painting studio, I discovered a wall of toy guns and holsters from the 1950s, testimony to her childhood passion. And not just hers. When my friend Judith comes to New York, she insists on eating at the Cowgirl Hall of Fame, a restaurant in the Village that serves perfectly passable food, but is really frequented by grown women with cowgirls on the brain who deem digestion more pleasurable when surrounded by the cowgirl kitsch of some half-dozen decades. Even my friend Kate, who grew up in Amarillo and used to answer to the name of Tex, returned to her roots (sort of) to make a little videotape titled *Queers on Steers*. Now, Holly's six-gun wall has been around for ages, Kate shot that footage a while back, and even the Cowgirl Hall of Fame wasn't nearly new – but suddenly Holly and Judith and Kate's tastes were hip and fresh instead of outré. Dear reader, you're uh, forgiven if you think you know why.

Yes, Clint swept the Oscars and, going one step forward, cowgirls were now a good idea. The wonder, I suppose, is why it took so long, given the prevalence of cowgirl myths in girlhood fantasy, for the subject to dawn on LA. No matter; suddenly the name of the very upmarket Rodeo Drive took on new meaning and, if the trades were to be believed, LA overnight turned downright cowgirlesque. *Variety* didn't give a damn if generations of American girls had been busy dreaming up cowgirls of their own. There were deals to be made.

Maggie Greenwald and Gus Van Sant were ahead of the pack. She had just finished directing Suzy Amis in *The Ballad of Little Jo* and he already had directed and edited Uma Thurman and company in *Even Cowgirls Get the Blues*. But rumours and trade stories about new female Westerns appeared in the press nearly every week in early summer. Tim Hunter was set to do one called (really) *Guns'n'Roses* with various rumoured actresses, at one point including (really) Sharon Stone. Producer Denise Di Novi had teamed up with John Duigan to do *Outlaws* for Columbia. Tamra Davis was hired to direct *Bad Girls*, a five-prostitute Western for which she picked actresses such as *One False Move*'s Cynda Williams and *Guncrazy* star Drew Barrymore.

By September, the hot weather was over and so was the hot trend. Tim Hunter's project was a no-go, *Outlaws* was put on hold, and Tamra Davis was fired from *Bad Girls* along with cinematographer Lisa Rinzler and actress Cynda Williams. What was left? The two independent productions. *The Ballad of Little Jo* had an okay run, while *Even Cowgirls Get the Blues* caused early consternation on the festival circuit. Meanwhile, for this writer, as for others before me, the air began to swirl with new tumbleweeds: ideas about female Westerns, what they are, the genre to which they claim to belong, and the reasons why the road to putting cowgirls on the screen leads to such a rough ride.

Renegade Westerns

'The Western hero, who seems to ride in and out of nowhere, in fact comes riding in out of the nineteenth century... Every word he doesn't say, every creed in which he doesn't believe is absent for a reason... The point-for-point contrast between a major popular form of the twentieth century and the major popular form of the nineteenth is not accidental. The Western answers the domestic novel. It is the antithesis of the cult of domesticity that dominated American Victorian culture.'

Jane Tompkins took a beating for her film analysis in last year's *West of Everything: The Inner Life of Westerns*, yet her assessment of the genre's overarching significance in literary as well as cinematic form is right on target. If civilisation and language had become female spheres, Tompkins argued, then the Western represented an attempt by men to get back their own, by creating a separate sphere where language was fundamentally a mark of weakness and where technology, religion, cultures and the female sex were marginalised, or devalued, or absent entirely. If the Western, then, is the male half of a universe bifurcated by gender, then no wonder that the female Western is having so much trouble being reborn.

Tompkins goes so far as to assert that the 'Western doesn't have anything to do with the West as such'. She rejects all the arguments regarding Western metaphors, the tropes of civilisation and frontier, and argues that the Western is more truly 'about men's fear of losing their mastery'. The ritual nature of Westerns, then, might well be linked to male insecurities about that mastery and the need to have the certainty of their power reaffirmed through an eternal cycle of repetition – in other words, through the elaboration of a genre. (Don't forget, here, the equivalences that the critic Linda Williams traced between Westerns and pornographic films: the link to pornography could prove as important to thinking anew about the Western as the examination of the Western was for her rethinking of porn.) Tompkins and Williams both have their focus upon the Westerns of the past; I have mine upon the present. Once the cracks in the hegemonic façade of Wild West mythology began to crack, it seemed only a matter of time before transgressive forms of the genre would start to show themselves. Once the Smithsonian could mount a show decolonising Western mythology and Mario Van Peebles could use star-power to put black posses on the screen, then the No Trespassing signs could start to come down along lots of the borders governing access to the genre. Was it, then, only a matter of time before the gender-bending fashion so prevalent in most other spheres of US culture in the post–*Crying Game* era would bring gender trespassing to the Western? Think again. It's just as possible that *Posse* could work precisely because the in-the-hood genre it transplanted to the frontier was just as committed to a violent all-male universe as the Western ever was.

Also, keep in mind that cowgirls mean different things to different people. This summer, when cowgirls were still enjoying their green-light momentum, *Harper's Bazaar's* Joseph Hooper wrote an article on the male fantasy of the cowgirl that's the very embodiment of wet-dream projection, straining to define the cowgirl mystique in boy-consumption terms and foolishly concluding that the cowgirl aura persists because she is profoundly 'reassuring' to men. She proves that nature and sex are good – and on his side.

Take Hooper as representative of the normative, red-blooded American male's sense of cowgirls: tight jeans, rolls in the hay, spunky but ultimately less mannish than stand-by-your-mannish. You would never know, from reading Hooper or watching Greenwald's film or reading the original Tom Robbins novel from which Van Sant adapted his film, that the cowgirl myth is a centrepiece of lesbian culture, too, nor that the history of cross-dressed 'passing women' on the frontier has been found in lesbian archives, rather than Western museums. You'd never know that the figure of the cowgirl has been a source of power to heterosexual women, too, embodying strength and freedom as forcefully as the male counterpart sparks fantasies of escape in the menfolk, at least in the United States. Indeed, in the 1990s, such male claims to cowgirl fantasies sound an awful lot like compensatory and proprietary gestures towards an out-of-control object.

For all Hooper's certainty, the history of the Western periodically reveals renegade attempts to shift the ground. Given any genre's always-voracious need to reinvent itself in order to stay the same, even female characters occasionally rise to different positions in defiance of genre codes. Such shifts are particularly pronounced in the Westerns made in the 1950s, when Marlene Dietrich starred in *Rancho Notorious* (1952) and Barbara Stanwyck in *Forty Guns* (1957), and when Joan Crawford and Mercedes McCambridge tangled in the great lesbian-cult-Western, *Johnny Guitar* (1954). The genre rules get bent again in the 1970s, with feminist critics of the Western pointing to films such as *The Hired Hand* (1971), *Hannie Caulder* (1971) and *Comes a Horseman* (1978) as similar openings for women in search of the kind of power Tompkins says the Western is specifically constructed to deny.

Tamra Davies, researching past Westerns for clues to her future one, went for *My Darling Clementine* (1946) and *Once Upon a Time in the West* (1968). But she, and we, would do well to heed the opinions of Jacqueline Levitin, who in her early 1980s reappraisal of the Western contends that only Mae West is able to triumph over the obstacles of the form. *Klondike Annie* (1936) and *My Little Chickadee* (1940), both half a century old, are still in the vanguard. Levitin argued that they are the only American-made Westerns that 'bear the stamp of a woman's point of view, and the only ones that deal with the West from the perspective of women's power'. But what about today? Fifties. Seventies. If the urge strikes every other decade, then female Westerns should be on the schedule again.

Enter Maggie Greenwald. Greenwald says she has wanted to make a Western ever since she was a child. Indeed, there's something childishly fairytale-like about *The*

Ballad of Little Jo, not at all what you'd expect from the butched-up descriptions of the rugged cross-dressing Western the press kit describes. Suzy Amis plays an Eastern society woman who slips up and gets herself pregnant. In short order, she's exiled from her family and community (i.e. the East) to the horrors of poverty, vulnerability, attempted rape and betrayal (i.e. the West). Traversing the frontier on her own, without protection, she realises that there's only one way a woman can survive the West: to disappear into manhood. So she cuts off her hair, cuts a scar in her face, changes her clothes and, presto, Josephine is Jo, without even the benefit of now-fashionable surgical assistance. Little Jo finds the town of Ruby City, where 'he' passes, becomes a miner and then sheepherder, and finally settled rancher; Jo fights the cattle interests and becomes just one of the guys all the way until death reveals her secret. Greenwald chooses a journey-of-the-innocent structure and, whenever the going gets rough, hey-donny-donny music surges on to the soundtrack and a montage of images tries to move the narrative along to its next high-point. I guess that's the 'ballad' part of the title.

It's obvious early on that *Ballad* is not a film 'about' cross-dressing or sexual transgression, nor about Little Jo's psychology or inner life. Rather, what Greenwald offers is a view of the West from the perspective of a changeling, a creature whose alteration of herself alters, as well as her (and our) experience of the frontier and the kinds of life it dictates to its inhabitants. Greenwald's view of Little Jo's transformation as lack rather than gain is certainly disappointing to viewers in search of lesbian prehistory or convincing butch behaviour (especially so because the film is based on an actual woman, Jo Monaghan, whose true gender was only discovered after her death). The film does better on what must have been more comfortable ground for its director: the ever-presence of male violence – against other men and, in its sexual form, against women – and the absence of female options.

Greenwald wants to immerse us in the brutality of the 'real' old West, but along the way she stumbles on to something much more interesting and unexpected: the interplay of race and gender. David Chung plays Tinman, an ailing Chinese worker whom Jo rescues from lynching and takes on as a hired hand. A fellow outsider to the white male West, he immediately detects Jo's true gender and they become secret lovers. While Greenwald seems pretty unconscious of the stereotypes of feminised Asian masculinity that she finds it convenient to deploy here, the scenes of Amis and Chung making love are truly hot, with his long hair and her Nautilised body played for counterpoint. They're also *Ballad*'s most transgressive scenes, suggesting as they do the exchange of roles and the interplay of dominance and submission that Greenwald is so loath to explore in any same-sex pairings.

Actually, Greenwald comes close to doing just that – but the scenes involve Jo and a man, not a woman. Ian McKellen is cast in a minor role as Percy, a woman-hater whose intimate affection for the male Jo turns to rage when he discovers the truth. I don't know whether Greenwald's casting of McKellen here is ironic, iconic or subtextual red herring, but it's an interesting spin. Jo, though, is ultimately more rancher than cowpoke. For the ever-elusive figure of the cowgirl, look elsewhere.

Cowgirls' revenge

'Ha!' said Jelly with dramatic disdain. 'Movies. There hasn't been a cowgirl in Hollywood since the days of the musical Westerns. The last movie cowgirl disappeared when Roy and Gene got fat and fifty. And there's never been a movie about cowgirls... Cowgirls exist as an image. The idea of cowgirls prevails in our culture. There, it seems to me, the fact of cowgirls should prevail ... I'm a cowgirl. I've always been a cowgirl. Caught a silver bullet when I was twelve. Now I'm in a position where I can help others become cowgirls, too. If a girl wants to grow up to be cowgirl, she ought to be able to do it, or else this world ain't worth living in.'

Enter Gus Van Sant. The infamous Bonanza Jellybean (henceforth Rain Phoenix) delivers this speech in the original Tom Robbins novel, and most of it has made it into the film as well. But perhaps I'm getting ahead of the story. For everyone who post-dates the 1970s, know that *Even Cowgirls Get the Blues* concerns the adventures of one Sissy Hankshaw (that's Uma Thurman to you), born with giant thumbs and a consequent talent for hitchhiking. Sissy, star model for the Yoni Yum line of female-hygiene products, is dispatched by her employer, the arch-decadent Countess (John Hurt), to his Rubber Rose dude-ranch-cum-health-spa, where he has similarly dispatched a team of German admen to shoot a commercial of Sissy's cavorting in nature, in this case, in a pas de deux with a flock of whooping cranes.

Alas, the Rubber Rose manager Miss Adrian (Angie Dickinson) has her hands full, battling a crew of ornery cowgirls who aim to overthrow the patriarchy and restore the ranch, its clients and herds to the natural state of equilibrium of cowgirls and nature. Oh, and overlooking all the action from his mountain home is the Chink, a Japanese-American escapee from a World War II internment camp misnamed by a renegade group of Native Americans called the Clock People who rescued him from a snowbank. Add to that a serious side-plot concerning the whooping cranes, peyote, the FBI and a certain Delores Del Ruby (Lorraine Bracco) and you can begin to imagine what Van Sant has taken on.

Or can you? The film has already managed to divide critics by both gender and generation, and only the goddess knows what a mass audience will make of it. My guess is that it's an instant, serious and lasting cult film. For sure, it's the craziest, most gender-bending, transgressing Western that's ever made it to the screen. But remember that this is a film based on a novel that originally appeared in 1976 in serial form in a magazine called *High Times* – and it bears all the marks of its time of origin. For all the buzz, two decades long, regarding *Cowgirls* as a classic feminist text, on closer examination it's no such thing. Robbins would be quite comfortable with Hooper, both of them happy to provide sexual services to any cowgirl that might cross their path.

The Robbins novel surprises the faulty memory with its determined hetero-sexuality and male-centred narrative: the narrator is constantly inserting himself into the action and finally even awards himself a central role in the plot. This was great literary fun, but rather undermines the conception of the novel as a dyke playground. Instead, it's true to its time, offering a reminder of what sexual liberation, heterosexual-style, was like. Robbins even has Bonanza Jellybean explain all the girl–girl sex to Sissy as just a man-shortage thing. The cowgirls on the Rubber Rose Ranch? 'There's not a queer among 'em,' declares Bonanza.

Gus Van Sant, bless his soul, has changed things a bit. In fact, he's taken almost every bit of heterosexuality out of the movie (except the Chink, but that's another story) and queered things up. Bonanza and Sissy fall so sweetly in love that it nearly gave me an acid flashback to the earliest days of innocence of lesbian feminism. The cowgirls' debates over group action and gender-appropriate strategies made me remember the worst nightmares of consciousness-raising groups and collective decision-making. My favourite line? 'This furniture's too masculine!' The showdowns between Miss Adrian and Delores are hysterical reminders of how the women's movement divided women, with femininity pitted against revolution as either/or decisions. The whole plot of the whooping cranes is probably as good a fantasy as any regarding the origins of eco-feminism.

As this article goes to press, *Cowgirls* has not yet been released, not even in the United States (where it's scheduled for the autumn), so it's too early to say how the general public will react to its hip mix of history, humour and whacky intelligence. The cameos alone should be a tip-off that this is no normative biopic: Roseanne Arnold as a palm-reading psychic who angers little Sissy's mother by predicting 'lots and lots and lots of women' in her child's future; River Phoenix as a guru-seeking hippy who tells Uma how 'bummed out' he and his pals were by the Chink's shaking his wanger at them; William Burroughs as a random pedestrian worried about how gloomy the sky looks.

So far, *Cowgirls* has had two festival debuts. Word from Venice was mixed. At the Toronto Film Festival, the critical reception was chilly if not hostile. Keep in mind, though, that today's film press corps is a markedly male fraternity. Many of my beloved colleagues are just too square, too old, too young, or too heterosexual to enjoy the hallucinatory irony that this time-machine movie provides – though the notably hip editors of publications such as *Vibe*, *OUT* and the *Village Voice* are on my side in believing that the movie has a great constituency in store, both today and in the years to come.

It may, though, be ahead of its time. Or maybe Gus stumbled on his way to the 1970s revival and landed, not in a Robbins-replay commercial dream, but rather in a genuine lesbian-feminist movie. If so, while popular Richard Linklater picks up accolades for *Dazed and Confused*, his bland-revival party movie, Van Sant may suffer the critical scorn usually reserved for women directors. No matter; *Cowgirls* is irresistible fun. But is it a Western? Only a fraction of the film actually takes place at the Rubber Rose ranch: the rest of it transpires in the sites of Sissy's childhood, or in the New York apartments of the Countess or Sissy's erstwhile suitor Julian and his Beautiful People friends, or in one of the mysterious Clockworks, or on the road, à la *My Own Private Idaho*.

Ah, but the Rubber Rose scenes that are there allow us to begin to imagine what a female Western might look like, if one could ever really be made. If, say, *Johnny Guitar* could borrow Susan Sarandon and Geena Davis from *Thelma & Louise* (the closest thing to a female Western so far) and imagine them shooting not at each other, but at the good ole boys just outside the circle of firelight. You see, I suspect that the only way a female Western could ever be devised, one that could take advantage of the formulas and retain the magic of the genre, would be to replace race (cowboys versus Indians) with gender (cowgirls versus varmints).

Whatever solution anyone decides to try, if any other female Westerns make it into celluloid this decade, it would be wise to heed Jane Tompkins once again, who warns that 'Westerns pay practically no attention to women's experience' in part because 'when women wrote about the West, the stories they told did not look anything like what we know as the Western' since 'women's experience as well as their dreams had another shape entirely'. Offering no genre solution, she points instead to the work of feminist historians and literary critics who work on such material.

But what about the movies? It's clear that the Western genre is still strong, and that it remains pretty resistant to attempts by anyone not empowered by the original formulas to find a way in, be they women or Native Americans or Asian-Americans. In film, where metaphor is so much more literal and images more condensed than in literature or history, the basic dilemma facing anyone intent on fashioning a main-stream version of a female Western is obvious: how to find a way to give women as much power as men without making them lesbians, how to avoid pitfalls of butch and femme while retaining credible female characters, how to fashion any truce at all between sexuality and exploitation. I like to imagine Julie Christie, retrieved from the archaic world of *McCabe and Mrs Miller*, set into a newfangled Western where she could kick her opium habit and get on with the next chapter. Hey, no one said it would be easy.

Epilogue

Winter approaches. A new print of *Johnny Guitar* has just played to packed houses at New York's Public Theatre. k.d. lang is about to release her soundtrack CD to *Even Cowgirls Get the Blues*. Word has it that Di Novi and Duigan are starting work on a production of *Little Women* instead of *Outlaws*, a move from the frontier to the sitting room that could make Tompkins look like a prophet. Jonathan Kaplan is directing *Bad Girls*, the Western that promised to be a transgressive Tamra Davis film, with a budget more than double the size she was given. Kelly Frost, an actual cowgirl and cowpoke-consultant-to-the-stars, is awaiting the release of *Lane Frost*, a biopic on her late husband.

Maybe *Bad Girls* or *Lane Frost* or something else in the works will mess with the formulas, prove me wrong, get things right. I'm not holding my breath. I suspect that Jon Tuska was right when he said he very much doubted that 'a Western film that is not a mandate to go forward proudly, a Western film that reveals the crimes and follies of the past rather than pretending only to find triumphs and righteousness regarded, a Western film in which everyone is consumed by some form of materialism' could ever be 'commercially feasible'.

So I'm waiting instead to see *Even Cowgirls Get the Blues* again. I'm listening to a lot of country and western music. There's a Jimmie Dale Gilmore concert coming up. But life has a funny way of playing tricks. Here's what has shown up in top-40 country-radio rotation, autumn 1993, just as this article heads for your hands. Credit goes to singer/songwriter Toby Keith for his tune, 'Should've Been a Cowboy'.

'I'll bet you never heard old Marshall Dillon say,/"Miss Kitty, have you ever thought of running away, settling down? Would you marry me?/If I asked you twice and begged you pretty please?"/She'd have said yes in a New York minute./They never tied the knot, his heart wasn't in it./He just stole a kiss as he rode away./He never hung his hat up at Kitty's place/I should've been a cowboy.'

Domesticity and the frontier. Sex and marriage. Settlement and escape. Men and women. Civilisation and its discontents. Sound familiar? Feel free to hum along.

QUENTIN TARANTINO ON *PULP FICTION*

Manohla Dargis

'I'm going to do a Monte Hellman, do two films back to back, do two $3 or $4 million movies. Shoot one for five weeks, take a week off, and then start the next one, just keep the crew. Then give one to my editor and I'll edit the other one.

'After *Pulp Fiction*, I was going to do a small film and then I was going to try and do a big movie. I didn't know what genre, just a big kick-ass movie. That was the game plan for my first four movies, but *Pulp Fiction* was such an undertaking it seemed a waste of time to do just one small movie next. I had a lot of fun floating back and forth between the different stories, and felt I could handle more.

'I've always been romanced by the idea of Roger Corman going out there and shooting two movies on location, or Monte just pulling it off, as well as anyone has ever done in the history of cinema, with *The Shooting* and *Ride in the Whirlwind*. When I finished *Pulp*, I felt my crew and I were so together we could have made another movie if we'd had one ready to go, we were in such a groove.

'*Pulp Fiction* was going to be my goodbye to the crime genre, at least for a while. It's a get-it-out-of-your-system movie, three movies for the price of one. What I wanted to do afterwards is work in other genres, all kinds. I would like to do a musical some time, I'm thinking about doing a movie that would be very personal, about something that happened to me, but again I'd break it down to genre, like a *La Règle du jeu – Shampoo* kind of thing. And that's not *The Player* kind of talk, that's just me.

'I was going to do other sorts of movies, then revisit the crime genre from time to time. I don't want to be the gun guy. I think I would become really boring if I was just known as the guy who did gangster movies. At the same time, fuck it, if it's what you really want to do... It's a little debate I'm having with myself because *Pulp* was designed to be the goodbye.

'To me, John Cassavetes' movies are a genre, he's a genre in and of himself. Merchant-Ivory are as strict a genre as you're ever going to find, they're stricter than a women-in-prison movie. I love the idea of going into a genre and taking all the familiars we like and giving them back to you in new ways. Say *The Guns of Navarone* had never been made and I read Alistair Maclean's book and wanted to do it. I'd want to deliver all the thrills and the spills, the pleasure and the fun, except that those guys would talk like my guys. They wouldn't be stock characters, they would be human beings with a heartbeat who would talk about things other than just blowing up the cannons. I want to set up a situation you've seen a zillion times before and then throw in real-life kicking and screaming so that it fucks up everybody's plans. Not just come up with a higher mountain these guys have to climb, or throw in a rainstorm or a troop of Nazis, but real-life holes they can fall into.'

A The set-up

Everything in Los Angeles revolves around restaurants. You get together with your friends at restaurants, you have dates at restaurants, business meetings at restaurants. In many other cities, you have to be of a certain wealth to go to restaurants, but in Los

Angeles we have coffee shops that are open all night long. So you can not have a pot to piss in and still afford to go to a coffee shop and hang out. My friends and I would go to coffee shops late at night and be  there for hours, like our version of hanging out in a Parisian café and discussing existentialism, except we were talking about New World Pictures and whether we were ever going to be with a woman.

B Costume

When Jean-Pierre Melville was making his crime films, he talked about how it was very important that his characters have a suit of armour. His was the sharp-brim fedora and Bogart-like trench coat. Leone had the dusters, Eastwood the poncho. I've always said the mark of any good action film is that when you get through seeing it,

you want to dress like the character. That's totally the case, for instance, with Chow Yun-Fat's wardrobe in the *A Better Tomorrow* movies. The black suits in *Pulp Fiction*, that's my suit of armour. Guys look cool in black suits, but what's interesting is how they get reconstructed during the course of the movie. When you first see Vincent and Jules, their suits are cut and crisp, they look like real bad-asses. But as the movie goes on, their suits get more and  more fucked up until they're stripped off and the two are dressed in the exact antithesis – volleyball wear, which is not cool. As to Sam Jackson's jheri-curls, that happened by mistake. I've always liked Afros – if I were black, I'd wear an Afro. I talked to Sam about wearing an Afro and he was up for that. The make-up woman went out to get some Afro wigs, but because she didn't know the difference she also showed up with the jheri-curl wig. Sam put it on, and it was great, it was Jules.

C Jackrabbit Slim's

Every big city has a couple of them, these 1950s retro restaurants. I don't like them that much, to me they are always trying too hard. In fact, the script even says, 'Either the best or the worst of these places, depending on your point of view.' This one is a cross between the 1950s restaurants that exist, the nightclub where Elvis Presley and the car racers hang out in *Speedway*, and the bar where all the racecar drivers hang out in

Howard Hawks's *Red Line 7000*. The thing that makes it work is the racing-car motif. The dance floor is done like a speedometer, and I threw in little things, as if I were running a restaurant. Most of the

posters are not just from any old 1950s movies, they're directed by Roger Corman. And if I were going to have 1950s icons on the menu, there would be a Douglas Sirk Steak. I wouldn't let them rent out a real 1950s restaurant, I wanted to do it from scratch. But when you have a set that great, you're almost intimidated by it. Oh, my God, how do I make it live? What I tried to do is introduce it through Vincent's eyes as he walks through. But the scene ain't about the restaurant, so after I get through taking it all in, just forget it. Show it off and then, fuck it.

D Dancing

I always love the musical sequences in movies, and I particularly love them when the movies aren't musicals. My favourite musical sequences have always been in Godard, because they just come out of nowhere. It's so infectious, so friendly. And the fact that

it's not a musical, but he's stopping the movie to have a musical sequence, makes it all the more sweet. The last movie I saw that did something like that was Christopher Münch's *The Hours and Times*, where all of a sudden Lennon puts on the Little Richard 45 and starts dancing. Whenever I'd see those scenes in a Godard movie, it made me wish I had a rewind facility in the camera. Sometimes they almost ruin the movie, because you love them so much, you want to go over it again and again. In *Le Petit Soldat*, when she's doing the interview, taking her pictures, and all of a sudden she puts on some classical music and dances around the room. When she takes the music off, you're like, 'Oh, it's over.' I learned that for this film, don't let it linger.

E The gold watch

In Roger Avary's original story, the fact that Butch had a gold watch came out of nowhere. Roger spent all this time trying to sell us on why Butch had to go back into danger, and he did a really good job, but he didn't quite sell it. I thought, well, it's a contrivance, and what you do with a plot contrivance is feature it. At that point in the movie, you're disoriented because the first

story has ended. And then you have Christopher Walken doing this whole long thing about the watch, and then there's the title card, 'The Gold Watch', and then there's this boxer, and you're wondering, 'What the fuck did that have to do with anything?' And then you get in that motel room and you're there forever. You've forgotten that gold watch and Walken. And then Butch says, 'Where's my gold watch?' You can write a three-page monologue and good luck on having someone deliver it perfectly. Chris Walken is one of those actors who can and rarely gets the opportunity to do so. I called him up and said, 'Chris, I have a three-page monologue for you and I promise I won't cut a word.' We planned to do it on the last day of shooting: when he came in I told him he had all day, we're not going to leave until we get it right. And we did.

F Drugs

Lance is totally LA type, he's your friendly drug dealer. Margaret Cho did a hysterical stand-up routine about the problem with going out and buying drugs: you have to feign a relationship with your drug dealer, like you're not going over to buy pot, you're going on a social visit and drugs are incidental. You have to sit down and talk about things, as opposed to here's the money, give me my shit, let me get out of here. Mia doesn't do too well by drugs. One journalist told me I could show that whole first scene of her overdose to schoolkids as an anti-drug movie. People ask me where I came up with the story about the overdose; the bottom line is that every junkie, or person who has experimented seriously with heroin, has a version of that story – they almost died,

someone else almost died and they brought them back with salt water, or put them in a tub, or jumped them with a car battery. What's interesting is that the scene is very harrowing and very funny at the same time, and that the harrowing aspect and the funny aspect are both coming from the same place, it's the reality of it that is both totally freaky and totally funny.

G Lighting

I'm really anal when it comes to the framing, but my cinematographer Andrzej Sekula handles the lighting, that's where he gets to paint. We shoot on 50 ASA film stock, which is the slowest stock they make. The reason we use it is that it creates an almost no-grain image, it's lustrous. It's the closest thing we have to 1950s Technicolor. When I first met Andrzej on *Reservoir Dogs*, I only knew that I wanted it to pop, I wanted the reds to be red and the blacks to be black. It looks great, but it's a pain in the ass to shoot with, you need light coming in from everywhere just to get an image. But because of the way I write my scenes, once you get somewhere, you're there for a while. So we

bathe the place in light, create a lot of texture and play around with the depth of field, which is something you normally don't have, particularly when you're shooting with anamorphic lenses. We carry people in the background and foreground as much as I've ever seen in a film with anamorphic lenses. When we looked at dailies I felt we were pushing the envelope.

H Gore

Every time you try to show gore realistically, it looks absurd, operatic. People go on about Tim Roth bleeding to death in *Reservoir Dogs*, but that's the reality. If someone is shot in the stomach, that's how they die. Put them in one spot in a room and they're going to have a pool growing around them. That might look crazy, but it's the truth and it's because you're not used to seeing the truth that it looks pushed. There was a line in *Pulp Fiction* with Jules and Jimmie talking that we didn't shoot. Jimmie asks

what the fuck happened to the car, and Jules answers, 'Jimmie, if you were inside of a car, and you were to shoot a watermelon at point-blank range with a nine millimetre, do you know what would happen?' 'No, what?' 'You'd get watermelon all over!' To me, even though it's got a foot in real life, it also has a foot in Monty Python. It's funny. It's about appearance; we've got to clean up the car, we've got to clean us up, we've got to get the shit out of his house so Jimmie doesn't appear to be a criminal when his wife comes home. The idea is to take genre characters and put them in real-life situations and make them live by real-life rules. In normal movies, they're too busy telling the plot to have guns go off accidentally and kill someone we don't give a damn about. But it happens, so we go down that track. And it's not just some clean little hole in the chest, it's a messy wound they've got to deal with, and it's a big problem. The humour to me comes from this realistic situation, and then in waltzes this complete movie creation, the Wolf – Harvey Keitel. This movie star walks in, sprinkles some movie dust, and solves the problem.

THE USUAL SUSPECTS
USA 1995
Director: Bryan Singer

In San Pedro harbour, California, a cargo ship explodes, leaving twenty-seven dead. There are two survivors: a Hungarian named Arkosh Kovash, lying badly burnt in a hospital bed, and a crippled New York con-man, 'Verbal' Kint. Granted immunity from prosecution in return for his testimony, Kint is questioned by US Customs Agent Dave Kujan. Kujan is convinced that Dean Keaton, a crooked ex-cop, masterminded the raid and survived. Meanwhile, Federal agent Jack Baer questions Kovash via an interpreter.

Kint recalls how he met Keaton six weeks earlier when they were pulled in on a police line-up, suspected of a truck hijack. Also in the line-up were entry-man Michael McManus, his partner Fred Fenster, and explosives expert Todd Hockney. During their night in the holding cell, McManus outlines a plan for holding up a 'taxi service' run for crooks by corrupt New York cops. Keaton, who is trying to go straight to please his girlfriend, attorney Edie Finneran, at first refuses to take part, but is persuaded by Kint.

The heist works perfectly, bringing down scandal on the NYPD, and McManus suggests they launder the loot through his regular LA fence, Redfoot. Mistrusting McManus, the others accompany him to California where Redfoot offers them another job robbing a Texan jeweller, Saul Berg. Berg, who proves to be a drug dealer, is killed in the shoot-out. The gang is later contacted by a lawyer, Kobayashi, claiming to represent the man who wanted Berg killed, the mysterious master criminal Keyzer Soze – a name also mentioned by the terrified Kovash.

Kobayashi explains that Soze engineered the original police line-up, because all five men have unwittingly trespassed on his territory. To make amends, they must now raid a drug-smuggling ship in San Pedro harbour run by Soze's rivals, an Argentinian gang. Initially the gang refuse and Fenster takes off, but he is traced and killed by Soze's men. Keaton plans to kill Kobayashi until he learns the lawyer has Edie in his power. The four raid the ship – though Keaton leaves Kint on the pier to contact Edie if things go wrong – and find no drugs, but an Argentinian, Marquez, who can identify Soze. While Kint watches from onshore, Hockney, McManus and Keaton are shot by Soze, who then blows up the ship.

Kujan furiously accuses Kint of lying, insisting that Keaton was really Soze and has faked his own death. But Kint sticks to his story and Kujan is obliged to let him go. Meanwhile Baer has had a police artist draw a picture of Soze from Kovash's description and faxes it through. As it arrives, Kujan realises Soze's true identity.

*   *   *

When, in 1950, Hitchcock included a misleading flashback in *Stage Fright*, it aroused great indignation: the director 'hadn't played fair' with his audience. It's perhaps symptomatic of a more cynical age, when the deconstructionist concept of the unreliable narrator has become a creative commonplace, that *The Usual Suspects* can be built around a long flashback narration that's a lie from start to finish. The final-reel revelation – that virtually nothing in the preceding 100 minutes can be taken as true – also, by way of bonus, neatly sidesteps any critical objections to the massive holes in the plot. Implausible! Inconsistent! Well, of course it is.

Misdirecting the audience, in any case, is the stock-in-trade of any good thriller; *The Usual Suspects* just takes it a stage further. Even when not luring us into its maze of flashbacks the film deftly sets up tensions between perception and reality, playing off what's said about a given individual with the way that person seems to be: Kint's account of Keaton against Kujan's view against the Keaton that's shown to us. (The film's rich in K-names, maybe in homage to the great Czech maze-maker himself.) Singer draws from his cast (cops no less than crooks) edgy, side-long performances that constantly hint at hidden motivations and past histories teetering on the brink of fantasy – a challenge to which his actors rise superbly. Pete Postlethwaite, faced with playing a non-Japanese lawyer with a Japanese name, displays admirable unfazability; making no attempt at a Mr Moto-style accent, he gives his performance a remote, fastidious spin with the faintest dash of oriental melancholy, like Gielgud playing Chang the Deputy Lama in *Lost Horizon*.

The Usual Suspects is Singer and McQuarrie's second film; their first, *Public Access* (which showed at the London Film Festival a couple of years ago), also played with deceptive appearances, if in less labyrinthine fashion. The protagonist of the earlier film is a clean-cut young man who infiltrates a sleepy burg's public cable station and sets the townsfolk at each other's throats. This disruption isn't his aim, though it amuses him; his secret agenda is yet more lethal. In the same way, Kint's monologue conceals layers beneath layers, its ostensible purpose a verbal smokescreen for its true one. Or for what, after the final disclosure, we take to be its true one – since it may well be that Soze doesn't exist after all. Or that multiple Sozes exist, offering a mythic persona to be adopted by any underworld boss wanting to terrorise his rivals. 'The greatest trick the Devil ever pulled,' says Kint, 'was convincing the world he didn't exist.' An even greater one, he could have added, was convincing it that he did.

The theological allusion is apt. There's a near-religious intensity to much of the film: Gabriel Byrne's fallen angel of a bent cop, the sacrificial myth of Soze's Hungarian origins and, at the heart of the film, the duel between Kujan and Kint, played out in a tiny, windowless office like a confessional where the Customs agent hounds his captive with all the fervour of a High Inquisitor. All the action scenes, tautly staged though they are, feed back into this claustrophobic space. Palminteri and Spacey play expertly off each other, the one circling and harrying, eyes narrowed and lip jutting, the other slumped in maudlin self-abasement or taking off on another meandering verbal riff. But with the exception of Suzy Amis, stuck with an underwritten token-female role, there's not a weak link in the cast, all responding with relish to Singer's tight direction and McQuarrie's sinewy writing. Dark, tortuous and richly atmospheric, *The Usual Suspects* is the most satisfyingly close-textured thriller for years; even once you know the twist in the tail, there's enough going on here on every level to make it equally rewarding viewing a second time around.

Philip Kemp

BOUND
USA 1996
Directors: Andy Wachowski, Larry Wachowski

Chicago, the present. Just sprung from jail after serving five years for theft, Corky is hired to renovate a flat in a luxurious block. In the lift, she meets Ceasar, a local gangster, and Violet, his moll, who occupy the flat next door. Violet stops by to complain about the noise from Corky's power drill. She then asks Corky over to find an earring dropped down the drain, and attempts to seduce her. The two begin to make love, but are interrupted by Ceasar who, unaware of what has been going on, questions Corky about her shady past. Later, the women consummate their passion.

When Corky sees a man enter Violet's flat, she becomes jealous. Violet explains that it's just business. Later, Corky spies the same man being escorted to the flat by some thugs. She overhears the man, Shelly, being tortured: he has skimmed some $2 million off the 'business'. Violet asks Corky to help her start a new life. Ceasar shows up at Violet's flat with a bag of blood-soaked money: Shelly squealed, but was then killed by the semi-psychotic Johnnie Marconi, son of gangland boss Gino Marzzone and nephew of kingpin Mickey Malnato.

Ceasar washes the money and packs it in a briefcase, which Gino and Johnnie arrange to pick up the next night. Learning that Ceasar and Johnnie hate each other, Corky hatches a plan. The following evening, while Ceasar's in the shower, she lets Corky into the flat; Corky takes the money from the case, replacing it with newspapers. Returning with the Scotch, Violet claims to have seen Johnnie downstairs. Ceasar discovers that the money is gone. When Johnnie and Gino arrive, Ceasar pulls a gun on Johnnie and demands the money. In the ensuing fracas, Johnnie and Gino are killed.

Determined to grab the loot – hidden in a paint drum in Corky's room – Ceasar searches Johnnie's flat. He then informs Mickey that Gino and Johnnie have disappeared. Violet calls Corky to fill her in on events, but she is caught by Ceasar. Corky runs to the rescue, but Ceasar captures and threatens to torture her until she reveals where the money is. Just then, Mickey stops by to pick up the briefcase. Violet rings Ceasar from the bathroom, and Ceasar pretends that it's Gino phoning to tell him that he and Johnnie are in hospital after a car accident. Satisfied, Mickey leaves without the money. While Ceasar inspects the paint drum, Corky escapes. Violet calls Mickey, claiming that Ceasar forced her to help him abscond with the money. Violet shoots Ceasar, and she and Corky make a clean getaway with the cash.

*   *   *

Judging from all the fancy, twirling camerawork in the new thriller *Bound*, the young writer-directors Larry and Andy Wachowski seem hellbent on making a dazzling debut. Ever since another team of brothers, Joel and Ethan Coen, jazzed up a fairly standard film noir plot with jokey pyrotechnics (in *Blood Simple*), a lot of neophyte film-makers have been eager to cut their teeth on such pulpy stuff. Classic 1940s noir, with its murkily lit sets and skewed perspectives, was always among the most self-conscious of Hollywood genres. Contemporary noir takes expressionism to a new extremity. In one typical bit of bombast, the Wachowskis have us peer through an enormous tumbler of Scotch, whose curves and dimples divide the screen prismatically – like the optic field of Al (David) Hedison in *The Fly*. In another scene, the two infatuated heroines press hands against opposite sides of a wall, and the camera glides smoothly over the barrier to reveal that they are touching precisely the same spot.

There are also myriad portentous close-ups of coffee cups and even toilet bowls (since about half the movie seems to take place in the loo). Through it all, the Wachowskis never leave off tracking and panning, as if to externalise the web of betrayal and deceit the spidery protagonists weave around themselves. Old noir was more economical in getting across its smouldering, over-ripe atmosphere. Such campy excess as the Wachowskis favour tends to cool things down rather. But that appears to be the whole point of an ersatz thriller such as *Bound*. You aren't expected to worry too much about who is bumped off or why; you're meant to get your buzz from the chic self-referentiality. Authentic 1940s noir was scarcely innocent of artifice: its habitual twists and double-crosses often fell just short of densely patterned farce. Neo-noir can't resist upping the ante and tumbling over the edge – which may explain why the amoral greed of the characters in John Dahl's *The Last Seduction* or Danny Boyle's *Shallow Grave* comes across more often as funny rather than scary.

Like these films (but unlike, say, Stephen Frears's *The Grifters*), *Bound* is pleased with itself and anxious to induce a similar smugness in the audience. The plot – concerning three people who chase after a grocery bag of money in a silvery Art Deco apartment – is a mere piece of tinsel from which to hang the stylistic baubles. The one bold stroke of revisionism is to make the central figures two carnally driven lesbians and this gimmick reinvigorates quite a few of the clichés. The Wachowskis (whose first major script credit was for the Sylvester Stallone–Antonio Banderas action flick *Assassins*) aren't ones to approach gender politics cap in hand. Despite the duties activist Susie Bright performed in the job of 'technical consultant', neither of the women characters here is plausible as a dyke. But then, neither is conceivable as a human being.

In keeping with the plan of wall-to-wall pastiche, both women resemble stream-lined artefacts from the movie past. The *femme fatale* character Violet (Jennifer Tilly) is a compilation of breathy, fleshy, little-girl mannerisms in the style of Marilyn Monroe. Brooding, slouching, tough-but-vulnerable Corky is, on the other hand, a witty transliteration of James Dean (even if Gina Gershon's brisk, low voice makes her sound more like Jane Fonda). These two bear about as much relation to 'life' as Mrs Danvers does in *Rebecca* – the Wachowskis, though far more sympathetic than Hitchcock, are basically in the same business of exploiting lesbianism for kicks.

Still, it's highly amusing to watch this retro pair slinking around and inspecting each other's cleavage. The undeniable fact about the shallow old movie fakery to which the Wachowskis aspire is that it does invest its stereotypes with heaps of glamour. Violet and Corky (even the names sound phoney) are certainly an iconic breed apart from the prosaic run of modern screen lesbians – and it's arguable whether this sort of preposterous swank isn't ultimately more affirmative than drab, limited realism. The erotic scenes are cartoons of heaving passion, which the brothers linger over with unabashed heterosexual glee. Their porno fantasy treatment is, however, at once so transparent and so hilariously outré that it may be time to admit that voyeurism isn't always such a terrible thing.

Besides, these hot babes have been given brains which – in the movie's rejigging of the noir formula – they are no longer punished for. Indeed, they get away with murder, which in no way compromises their winning qualities. Nowadays, film noir follows Nietzschean ethical standards in judging its crooks above the law. Whoever is strongest, craftiest and bravest receives the audience's vote – a position easily maintained when the tone is so heavily aestheticised. The couple here can also plead from their hearts, which makes *Bound* perhaps the only current mercenary thriller with a hint of old-fashioned sentiment. Their victim, the oily, blustering Ceasar (played by Joe Pantoliano), is your archetypal weak-kneed chump, but the rationale for his killing is novel: since he is a man, and by definition uncomprehending of the women's needs, he deserves to die. The Wachowskis manage to get by with this delirious pseudo-feminist swagger, maybe because they are such accomplished swaggerers themselves.

Peter Matthews

NORMAL LIFE
USA 1995
Director: John McNaughton

Chicago, the present. A bearded, armed man and a blonde woman who are trying to hotwire a car are jumped by an FBI team. The captured man listens on the police car radio as his accomplice is pursued.

Two years earlier, Chris Anderson, a young off-duty cop meets Pam Seaver, a young blonde, in a bar. After an altercation with another couple, Pam cuts her hand. Chris bandages it and they dance. They meet regularly and Pam introduces Chris to her habit of stargazing. Watching the night sky one evening, Chris jokily calls her 'crazy', Pam reacts angrily and storms off. When they are reconciled, she tells him that her mother died in a car accident. They marry, but Pam's drug abuse and overspending provokes huge rows. After one violent disagreement, Chris takes off on his motorbike while Pam drinks heavily and scars herself with a knife. To placate her, Chris buys her a pet dog. When his father dies, Pam turns up at the funeral in rollerblading gear. Chris loses his police job and becomes a security operative. Pam goes into drug therapy.

Deeply in debt, Chris sets up a series of violence-free bank robberies. After several raids, he buys a brand new house. Television coverage of the raids refers to 'The Bearded Bandit'. Pam spots Chris in disguise preparing another raid and insists on joining him. During the raid, she fires a round of bullets into a roof. Chris wants to stop the robberies and run a used bookstore instead. But Pam wants to continue and walks out on Chris when he refuses. Chris relents and they do another job. Chris is captured by the FBI. Pam is pursued by the police and shoots herself. While being tried for the robberies, Chris grabs a warder's gun, shoots two cops and tries to escape, but is shot in the back. Lying injured, he screams out Pam's name and shoots himself.

*   *   *

Normal Life opens promisingly with a botched bank robbery that has cop-turned-thief Chris Anderson listening in helplessly to the police radio wavelength as Pam, his wife and partner-in-crime, is being chased by Chicago cops. It's the film's pivotal moment: the prompt for a flashback to two years earlier when the couple first meet, and the point that is returned to near the end of the film – the culmination of a relationship that resorts to crime in order to avoid dissolution. The most telling moments in John McNaughton's films are often mediated in this way. The consequences of a character's actions are fed back to them at one remove – through video in *Henry: Portrait of a Serial Killer*, photography in *Mad Dog and Glory*, and the radio in *Normal Life*. This is McNaughton's primary motif, a recurring trope of alienation. In *Henry*, the serial killers Henry and Otis embody the outer limits of a white-trash sensibility. The cop in *Mad Dog* maintains a hard man role that he isn't really suited for. *Normal Life* brings it all back home, as it were. Suburban domesticity, the 'normal life' of the title, is what Pam and Chris Anderson try to secure for themselves, only to discover it to be a consumerist mirage in an edge-city wilderness.

Based on the true story of a young middle-class couple's descent into criminality, *Normal Life* nevertheless follows a classic film noir narrative curve; Pam is an unreconstructed *femme fatale* dragging her man behind her in a deadly tailspin. But noir's classic cocktail of fatalism and sexual compulsion is deliberately watered down here. Luke Perry plays Chris as a dutiful husband whose devotion to his unstable wife provokes his turning to crime. He's more of a regular guy gone wrong than a moth-to-a-flame bewitched male. The film turns gradually into the anatomy of a relationship. Pam is a kind of biker-chick version of Emma Bovary, a hotwired bundle of hysterical symptoms. She's also a dope-smoking, Stephen Hawking aficionado: 'Black holes are so intense,' she coos. Ashley Judd plays this death-wish blonde with great intensity. Those who recall her incendiary cameo in *Smoke* as Auggie Wren's errant daughter might expect a fleshed-out version of the same in *Normal Life*. But her character is given little in the way of background: we hear that her mother died in a car accident and that she can't reach orgasm (until Chris starts robbing banks). What we see may be true to the facts of the original case, but the portrayal of Pam unbalances the film's central relationship. Chris's reasons for staying with her are never explored. His rock-like stoicism becomes less and less plausible the more unhinged Pam becomes.

McNaughton gives the film a clinical, almost documentary feel, situating his characters in a desert of car parks and suburban lawns. The couple's demise is structured like a deterministic loop that closes like a pair of handcuffs. Despite this lack of melodrama, Chris's suicide pushes the love story into tragedy. It's a low-key film though, not dissimilar in style to other examinations of domestic discord turning into suburban criminality such as Tony Garnett's *Handgun* and Stacy Cochran's *My New Gun*. McNaughton seems to have found a way to weld his detached examinations of alienated losers to a pared-down, modern-day B-movie style that, while not as brutally dour as that of, say, James B. Harris (*Fast-Walking*, *Cop*, *Boiling Point*), indicates that *Henry* was not the cul-de-sac it was beginning to look like and that McNaughton may yet deliver something just as singular in the future.

Chris Darke

THE THRILLER INSIDE ME

Larry Gross

This World, Then the Fireworks is a short story that the legendary American crimewriter Jim Thompson wrote in the 1950s, but was unable to get published in his lifetime. It tells the story of a grifter named Marty Lakewood, who as well as taking part in the usual minor criminal con games has two striking aspects to his life: he is incestuously involved with his sister Carol, and he has a tendency to murder people, quite abruptly. Though not for profit particularly, nor to advance some other practical agenda. He murders as an avenging angel with a twisted sense of doing what's right.

I read about half of this story and knew immediately that I wanted to try to turn it into a screenplay. The quality that attracted me was this: almost unbearably extreme behaviour, on the part of numerous characters, seemed to arise from a coherent (and therefore credible) set of themes. When a piece of material combines the logical and the illogical in this way, it starts to feel intrinsically cinematic. I write partly to indulge myself – to see almost unimaginable or unthinkable things made real and plausible in screen; things that 'can't happen' somehow happening; behaviour that makes your jaw drop. This story had an abundance of that sort of stuff in it.

For all the violence in cinema, little that we see on-screen is genuinely shocking. Killing people in gory ways, for instance, doesn't shock very often. What does, in my opinion, is the vivid, accurate rendering of extreme emotional states of being, states we have all glimpsed in life, but which are rarely represented. This is why it's so scary when Isabella Rossellini holds a knife in proximity to Kyle MacLachlan's underwear-clothed genitals near the beginning of *Blue Velvet*. The expressed ferocity of her fear, suspicion and rage has enormous impact, despite the fact that the action itself is unexceptional, physically. A great deal of Thompson's story had the same emotional power as this scene.

Because hysteria and madness are part of almost the entire surface of the text, there is very little of what you might call a realistically believable element to the story. An insane narrator, surrounded by grotesques distorted by his point of view, makes for an immediate plunge into unrealism. This was the main challenge for the screenwriter. The critical ambiguity of our movie lies in its relation to thriller machinery. This comes from a split or ambiguity inside Thompson's text. Thompson does three things in his stories that disrupt normal storytelling. First, he focuses on interior psychic states more than external story-oriented thriller writers do. Second, he injects a comic, absurd element that immediately ironises the reader's experience of thriller situations. And third, he exhibits an extreme indifference – whether out of haste, exhaustion or intention – to story logic.

Are Thompson and our movie 'ironic', then, or 'postmodern', in the supposed mode of Tarantino? Are they commentary on genre? In my opinion, no.

There are intentionally ironic authors, but there are more unintentionally ironic ones. I believe Thompson had no intellectual programme to mock the genre tradition he worked in. He ruptured it intuitively, with naive sincerity. I'd make an analogy with the distinction between the primitive or intuitive modernism of Joseph Conrad's novels, say, and the deliberate, self-conscious modernity of Joyce. With Joyce, isn't there a self-conscious, complete separation from realistic convention? But Conrad gropes towards new forms and structures over the bones of the nineteenth-century adventure-novel norms that he never fully repudiates.

Because Thompson's breaches of genre decorum are not systematic, he can at times seem incoherent. That was the danger facing our film. Cinema has a dangerous proclivity for the literal: once you claim to be presenting a story in any kind of real world, then a number of elements of rationality, plausibility and 'realism' have to be taken into account. Part of my job was to make the world of the movie appear a little more real than the world of the story. But if one went too far in that direction, rounding off the mad edges of the Thompson universe to make his world more recognisable, one would just end up with a rather unexceptional and not very terrific crime story. To some degree, this is the flaw of Thompson adaptations such as *The Grifters* or *After Dark, My Sweet*: in both, the decision to move out of Thompson's gothic-degenerate 1950s into the 1990s is intended to make the movies more 'real', and easier to identify with. But it's a choice that is incompatible with the fairytale-like creepiness of the stories.

As compelling 'what-happens-next?' crime drama, there were terrific holes in *This World, Then the Fireworks*. But those holes were more than compensated for by the emotional intensity. In fact, the very disinterest in regular, effective plotting made the piece more compelling. I patched up the holes a bit, but not too much.

I knew that director Michael Oblowitz, who brought me the story to work on, was comfortable with, even in love with Thompson's subversive contempt for conventional moral piety, joined with a certain pessimism about breaking away from conventions. Michael's film-making hero is Fassbinder, who like Thompson utilised commercial narrative forms and then exploded them with his access to unimaginable emotional truth. But Michael is also a great fan of Ridley Scott, who always makes the ugliest realities quite beautiful. The elegance and visual unity that Michael imposed on this material is what makes the screenplay work, to whatever extent it does. Beauty becomes part of the unreality of Marty Lakewood's imagination. The film is shot with a deliberate excess of elegance: the beauty is beyond functional, and this is the sign of an obsessive universe. In addition to this perverse use of visual beauty, the film's unique quality, taken straight from the story, is how verbally over the top it is. For this to work, the actors (especially Billy Zane, who narrates and who has the most outrageous speeches) had to be at the top of their game. Mostly they are. For this, Michael and I are grateful.

I like art that is aggressive and pessimistic, art that wants to try to assert things about the world, while acknowledging the difficulty of assertion. These are qualities and ambitions of *This World, Then the Fireworks* that I am proud of.

THE MOUTH AND THE METHOD

Erik Bauer

The release of *Jackie Brown* represents a watershed for Quentin Tarantino. In the pop-culture terms he himself is so familiar and free with, his third film as director bears the same weight of expectation as any big music act's third CD. There are many jealous of his success who would have been only too willing to savage the film had it been a creative and commercial disappointment. It's not, but the high price of failure may explain how cautious *Jackie Brown* is. Unlike *Reservoir Dogs* (1992) and *Pulp Fiction* (1994), it's an adaptation rather than an original screenplay, it takes great pains to establish character and experiments with long takes of near-Bergmanesque patience, and it shuffles messy violence off-screen. Yet it is Tarantino's film, if only through its instantly identifiable use of language.

Jackie Brown is based on Elmore Leonard's novel *Rum Punch*. Jackie (Pam Grier), a black air hostess in her forties, is caught by cops and customs investigators smuggling a large cash sum into LA from Mexico. They know she is working for Ordell (Samuel L. Jackson), a slick local gun trader, and she agrees to help them set him up, though she knows he is capable of murder. Playing one side off against the other with the help of bail bondsman Max (Robert Forster), she draws Ordell's live-in beach-bum lover Melanie (Bridget Fonda) and his taciturn prison buddy Louis (Robert De Niro) into her elaborate scheme to save her own skin.

Despite the change of tempo in *Jackie Brown*, Tarantino retains his fevered delight in the world he creates. If you take away the scenes of violent confrontation (which admittedly, in his earlier films, is to remove a lot), you are mostly left with characters who are having a good time most of the time – particularly Samuel L. Jackson. Tarantino's people enjoy hanging out and tend not to be burdened by neuroses. All their negative feelings are directed outwards, and reserved for random bursts of anger or disgust. They are practical people, whose needs are clear and who are not to be thwarted. In terms of pure cinema, they are about action not angst, which makes them immensely appealing, as much as the pop-culture references they tend to drop. And Tarantino backs it up with an extraordinary talent for fantasy casting. No other director is gauche fan enough to cast Bridget Fonda as a washed-up beach bum, Robert De Niro as someone really stupid or Michael Keaton as an over-keen cop. It's outrageous wish-fulfilment, free from the po-faced aura that surrounds the casting of the most ludicrous of major Hollywood projects, and only someone with Tarantino's kudos could get away with it.

Some of the new elements are less successful. The choice of soundtrack songs is as good as you'd expect, cementing the blaxploitation connection made by casting Pam Grier in the lead role. But the emotion of the songs, such as the Delfonics 'Didn't I (Blow Your Mind This Time)', is often used as a lazy prod towards what the inscrutable Jackie might be feeling at any moment. In the end, the qualities of *Jackie Brown* that will attract most praise and criticism reside in the dialogue: it has all the rhythm, fizz and humour you'd expect, but many will be offended by its unapologetic use of words such as 'nigger', as our interview with Tarantino confirms.

* * *

Erik Bauer: With *Jackie Brown*, it seems you've gone to great lengths to make the dialogue more naturalistic. It contrasts with the stylised dialogue you're known for.

Quentin Tarantino: I've done two movies before this, so wait until I've done six to start pigeon-holing me. *Reservoir Dogs*, *Pulp Fiction* and my scripts for *True Romance* [Tony Scott, 1993] and *Natural Born Killers* [Oliver Stone, 1994] take place in my own universe, but that doesn't make them fantastical. This movie doesn't take place in my universe – this is Elmore Leonard's universe and it was interesting making a movie outside the little universe I created. Because of that, I wanted it to be ultra-realistic. I used a different cinematographer to get a different look – it still looks great, but it's just a little more down-to-earth, a little less like a movie movie, more like a 1970s *Straight Time*. I like building sets. In *Jackie Brown*, I didn't do that. Every single scene in the movie was shot on location.

Erik Bauer: How have Elmore Leonard's books influenced your writing style?

Quentin Tarantino: When I first started reading his novels I got really caught up in his characters and the way they talked. As I started reading more of them it gave me permission to go my way with characters talking *around* things as opposed to talking *about* them. He showed me that characters can go off at tangents and those tangents are just as valid as anything else. Like the way real people talk. I think his biggest influence on all my things was on *True Romance*. Actually, in *True Romance* I was trying to do my version of an Elmore Leonard novel in script form. I didn't rip it off, there's nothing blatant about it, it's just a feeling – a style I was inspired by.

Erik Bauer: *Jackie Brown* doesn't rely as much on plot reversals as your other films, and what twists you do have are often brought about through dialogue.

Quentin Tarantino: I think it works well. It's always unfolding: it's not a movie about Jackie figuring out in the first ten minutes how to get half a million dollars and doing it – no! It's like little by little by little it starts coming to her, as life and situations change and she's being torn in this direction and that. It slowly evolves, and then from that point on, it's straight ahead until she does it. It's very novelistic, in that the first ninety minutes are just about characterisation. Then, it's all execution: the last half-hour is just them doing it, the money switches and all that.

Erik Bauer: There's more exposition in the dialogue of *Jackie Brown* than in your previous scripts.

Quentin Tarantino: That's for damn sure, yeah.

Erik Bauer: Was that a result of the adaptation process?

Quentin Tarantino: Yeah, that's all that happened in the book. That's part of Max's whole relationship with Jackie: talking about their problems, with him acting as a counsel, trying to help her out. In the second half it's her thinking out loud, she's kind of talking to herself. That's the first time I was dealing in exposition in a big way.

Erik Bauer: What goals did you set for yourself for the screenplay?

Quentin Tarantino: I like the idea of following a female lead character. I think I have an extremely unfair rap from people who say, 'Ah, but can he write women?' The only reason they're saying that is because I did *Reservoir Dogs* first. I really love the idea of following a black woman in her forties. It's funny, but I do feel that Jackie Brown is mine. She's the same character as in the book, but making her black affects her because her life experiences are different and her dialogue is different.

Erik Bauer: Did you do any research for her character?

Quentin Tarantino: No. I actually have known a few women who reminded me of Jackie and that's who I used. I just wanted to find her in myself. I joke about it, but I'm very much a Method writer. I really become all the characters when I'm writing them, and I become one or two when I'm not writing. The entire year I was Ordell. He's the one I identified with the most in the piece. I walked around like him. I talked like him. I spent a whole year basically being Ordell. I couldn't shut him off and I didn't want to. And in a weird way Ordell is the rhythm of the movie.

Erik Bauer: What do you mean by that?

Quentin Tarantino: The way he talks, the way he dresses – everything about him is how this movie should play. He's the old school of soul music, he's the personification of that and I completely identify with it. If I wasn't an artist, I would probably be exactly like Ordell.

Erik Bauer: But it's not his movie.

Quentin Tarantino: It's Jackie's movie, but what's so neat about Jackie's character is that she isn't revealing at all. The story requires her to have a poker face. It requires that you don't know what's going on in her head. One of the things I held on to in the adaptation was that every time she got with Ordell, she would tell him everything she knew about the cops. That would surprise me, no matter how many times she did it. It's like, 'I cannot believe she's fucking him so bad!' I was like, 'God, I hope she isn't fucking Max. I think she's playing straight with us, but I don't know 100 per cent.' Max is the audience – you see the movie through Max's eyes. He's the conscience and the heart of the piece and he's definitely the major human link to the film. Max is the audience, but Ordell is the rhythm, the soul of the movie.

Erik Bauer: Ordell is fascinating because he really seemed to change from the book. He becomes a lot smarter in your script.

Quentin Tarantino: I had a lot of prior knowledge of Ordell, Louis and Melanie because I read *The Switch.* That was the first Leonard book I'd ever read, so even before *Rum Punch* was published I knew these characters because I was doing a little adaptation of *The Switch* in my mind when I was fifteen. And there's a lot of me in Ordell.

Erik Bauer: What elements define the Tarantino universe?

Quentin Tarantino: I try not to get analytical during the writing process. I try just to keep the flow from my brain to my hand and go with the moment and go with my guts. To me, truth is the big thing. Constantly you're writing something and you get to a place where your characters could go this way or that and I just can't lie. The characters have to be true to themselves. And that's something I don't see in a lot of Hollywood movies. I see characters lying all the time. They can't do this because it would affect the movie this way, or this demographic might not like it. To me a character can't do anything good or bad, they can only do something that's true or not. When you're writing, you know every script will have four to six basic scenes that you're going to do. But it's all the scenes in the middle that you've got to write through – that's where your characters really come from. That's how you find them, that's where they live. I think that's how novelists write.

Erik Bauer: Definitely more than most screenwriters, where it's all structure, structure, structure.

Quentin Tarantino: I just don't do that – you know by the first act this has to happen, and so on. I hold no interest in that. It's your voice that's important and I see absolutely no reason why a screenplay can't contain that voice. Now it makes it a hell of a lot easier when you're the writer and the director. But that's not even necessary now, because things are a little more open. There are a lot of bad screenplays, so if you write a good one people are going to respond to it. But if you're just starting your career, it might take a long time to get your work to people who'll appreciate it. It'll just get shot down by all the readers. But if you keep persevering, eventually you'll get past that reader and on to the people who are bored to death reading screenplays. These are the people who really appreciate something new. That was the big thing I had against me starting off in my career – I was writing shit differently, and differently meant I was doing it wrong for that whole reader mentality. Before David Mamet was David Mamet, people probably thought he said 'fuck' too much, too. But once they get to know you, once you get that Good Housekeeper seal of approval, it's a whole different story.

Erik Bauer: Do you use repetitions of a phrase or word in dialogue to enhance its power?

Quentin Tarantino: I do that a lot. I like it. I think that in my dialogue there's a music or poetry, and the repetition of certain words helps give it a beat. It just happens and I just go with it, looking for the rhythm of the scene.

Erik Bauer: Some people have criticised your use of the word 'nigger' in *Jackie Brown* and you respond that no one word should have such power in our culture. I'm not sure I buy that. Aren't you using it to electrify your dialogue?

Quentin Tarantino: There is no word that should stay in word jail. It's all language. And if I was doing what you're saying, I'd be lying. I'd be throwing in a word to get an effect. Well, you do that all the time, you throw in a word to get a laugh, and you throw in a word to get an effect, too, but it's never a situation where that's not what the character would say. You used the example of 'nigger'. In *Pulp Fiction*, 'nigger' is said a bunch of different times by a bunch of different people and it's meant differently each time. It's all about the context in which it's used. When Richard Pryor and Eddie Murphy do their stand-up acts and say 'nigger', you're never offended because they're niggers. You know the context it's coming from. The way Samuel Jackson says 'nigger' as Jules in *Pulp Fiction* is not the way Eric Stoltz as Lance says it, is not the way Ving Rhames as Marcellus says it.

Erik Bauer: How is Ordell's use of the word different from that of the characters in *Pulp Fiction?*

Quentin Tarantino: Ordell probably doesn't use it any differently from Jules. And when Jules and Marcellus use it in *Pulp Fiction* they're coming from the same place, but having it mean different things. Marcellus is very much like, 'You my nigger now', and it was Ving Rhames who came up with that. But Ordell's coming from the same place too, he's a black guy who throws the word around a lot, it's part of the way he talks. If you're writing a black dialect, there are certain words you need to make it musical, and 'nigger' is one of them. If you're writing about that kind of guy, 'motherfucker' is another. Sam Jackson uses 'nigger' all the time in his speech, that's just who he is and where he comes from. So that's the way Ordell talks. Also, I'm a white guy who's not afraid of that word. I just don't feel the whole white guilt and pussyfooting around race issues. I'm completely above all that. I've never worried about what anyone might think of me because I've always believed that the true of heart recognise the true of heart.

Erik Bauer: Do you put a lot of thought into the way you juxtapose humour and violence?

Quentin Tarantino: No more thought than I put into anything else. I love it, I think it's like a Reese's Cup, two great tastes that taste great together. I'm not bending over backwards to try and do it, it just happens. And then when it happens, it's like, 'Whoa, that's great. I got something.'

Erik Bauer: The final scene between Melanie and Louis was taken almost verbatim from the book. But you could have written that scene.

Quentin Tarantino: Yeah, I felt that. And it was so cool – when I actually talked to Elmore Leonard about something like that, or like the scene where Ordell kills Louis, I found he writes like I write. He didn't know Ordell was going to do it. He knew one of them was going to kill the other, but until it actually happened he didn't know how it was going to happen or who it was going to be.

Erik Bauer: Leonard had a lot of time to set up Louis's character that you didn't have. In the book, the violence that comes out of him in that last scene seems like an extension of his character, but in your script it comes as a shock.

Quentin Tarantino: Right, sort of the way violence plays out in your life, all of a sudden. Very rarely does violence build up in real life the way it does in movies. It explodes in your face. I think it gives the movie a dose of reality, especially in the scene we're talking about.

Erik Bauer: But isn't it important for all action to be set up, so people understand why it's taking place?

Quentin Tarantino: It is set up, but Louis is only partially on the page – all right? I remember talking to De Niro about the role and saying, 'Look, this is not like most of the characters that I write.' The reason actors like to do my stuff is because they usually have a lot of cool things to say and they feel cool saying them. I told him, 'You know, Louis is a different character than the ones I ordinarily write. He doesn't say a lot. This is a character that truly needs to be gotten across with body language.' I'm talking to one of the greatest character actors in the world. That's why I wanted him, all right?

Erik Bauer: Did you know who you wanted for all the characters?

Quentin Tarantino: I normally don't. I'll have some people in mind, but this was one where I pretty much had everybody. The one guy that was open was Louis. I thought about De Niro, but I wasn't sure I'd get him.

Erik Bauer: Do you think the audience has an attachment to Melanie when she dies?

Quentin Tarantino: No. I think the audience has a complete love–hate relationship with Melanie. Audiences applaud when Louis shoots her. It's impossible that someone could be asking for it, but she's asking for it. She's a fucking smartass, treacherous and all these things. But we also like her at the same time; she's a totally fun character.

Erik Bauer: You've voiced concern that your own voice might some day become old hat. Was that one of the reasons you decided to go with an adaptation?

Quentin Tarantino: That wasn't the reason, but it does very conveniently serve that purpose. It's a nice way of holding on to my dialogue, of holding on to my gift. I don't want people to take me for granted. The things I have to offer I don't want wasted. When you watch something David Mamet's written you know you've listened to David Mamet dialogue. I want to try and avoid that. I want people to see my new movie, not my next movie. I want each movie to have a life complete unto itself, yet still when you look at it from a certain perspective you can see it all fits. I don't want to do a Woody Allen or a John Sayles thing where one film blurs into the next. Those guys are doing exactly what they want to do, and I'm not putting them down. I just want to do something else.

Erik Bauer: You've said a number of times that you don't want to be known as 'the gun guy'. But *Jackie Brown* and your future projects seem to be all crime stories.

Quentin Tarantino: Well, the next one I do, I think as a director, will be a Western.

Erik Bauer: A Western in the mode of *The Good, the Bad and the Ugly* or *Unforgiven*?

Quentin Tarantino: Actually, it's different. It's a prison Western. It takes place in a prison in Yuma, Yuma Territorial Prison. So it's like a Western *Papillon.*

IN PRAISE OF GOOFING OFF

Jonathan Romney

The success of *Fargo* put to rest a long-held myth about the Coen brothers: that their films were strictly esoteric or enigmatic. This belief seems to be based partly on the way their earlier films are rich in strands that can't easily be assimilated into a conventional narrative pattern – the stray hats in *Miller's Crossing*, the blatantly formal play of circles in *The Hudsucker Proxy* – and partly on the frustrating impression that there is always less to the Coens' work than meets the eye. Every film up until then seemed flawed by the sense that the brothers were being wilfully cavalier, refusing to play their genre games by the rules or, conceivably, just not trying hard enough. Their new film gives some credence to that interpretation: it could almost be subtitled 'In Praise of Goofing Off'.

The Big Lebowski serves as a reminder that the Coens are nothing more enigmatic than this: the most purely ludic of contemporary American film-makers. Played entirely for laughs – at the expense of the audience and of the detective genre – the film warns us from the start not to expect any of its narrative threads to lead anywhere. With a title echoing *The Big Sleep*, we're in for a Raymond Chandler–style entertainment, a labyrinthine route followed solely for the diversions encountered along the way. The story enables us to enjoy a whole catalogue of narrative dead ends, cruel gags and bravura character routines.

The Coens get the jump on us from the opening sequence: the drawling voiceover by the Stranger, a Will Rogers-like philosopher cowboy, makes us expect a Western; but the tumbleweed we see rolls straight into early 1990s LA, an urban wild frontier even more untamed than in Chandler's day, and consequently demanding a rougher and readier Marlowe. We're told Jeff Bridges's superannuated slacker is 'the man for his time and place', and is consequently several degrees of weathered somnolence beyond even Elliott Gould in Robert Altman's 1973 *The Long Goodbye*.

The Dude is on a doomed, albeit humble, quest from the start – to be paid back for his rug, ruined by debt collectors. But he's also out to answer the questions posed by his millionaire namesake: 'What makes a man, Mr Lebowski?' It's a pointed question in a universe which classifies the Dude as effectively a non-person – out of step with a culture of cool, malicious surface, in which he's effectively castrated by the loss of his car.

The Big Lebowski echoes such 1970s neo-Chandlerian thrillers as *Cutter's Way* and Arthur Penn's *Night Moves*, which also recycles *The Big Sleep*'s wayward-nymphet opening premise. Like Penn's detective hero, the Dude will learn that the deeper you work your way into a labyrinth, the less likely you are to get anywhere. But the Coens actually defuse the paranoid implications of the plot complexities, making sinister machinations look like nothing more than obstacles devised to waste the Dude's leisure time. Sent in search of the other Lebowski's missing porn-star wife, the Dude will work his way into a world not so much of evil as of bizarre, misguided pretension. En route, he encounters Lebowski's daughter Maude (Julianne Moore), an artist who does her work suspended in mid-air, and the sinister German nihilist Uli (Peter Stormare), whose prime weapon is a live marmot and whose most menacing threat is to 'sqvishh' the Dude's 'Johnnsonn'.

The Coens seem also to have extended their crime reading to novels by and about 1970s survivors. The hip jokiness suggests Kinky Friedman (*The Love Song of J. Edgar Hoover, God Bless John Wayne*), or the cultivated weariness of the novels of James Crumley (*Mexican Tree Duck*), in which action is measured not in plot points, but in the amount of time spent recovering from benders. The convoluted plot seems designed purely to accommodate its various cameos and acid-inflected nightmare routines, such as a flashy but leaden Busby Berkeley spoof with Julianne Moore as avenging Valkyrie. The range of acting turns is rich, if wayward, with such Coen regulars as Steve Buscemi and John Turturro pointedly reappearing as if to remind us whose film we're watching. Best of all, in a memorably unctuous cameo, is Philip Seymour Hoffman from *Boogie Nights*, the best character-actor find in years. Less plausible are the ludicrous 'moderns': Moore's clipped-voiced practitioner of 'vaginal art' (perhaps jibing at her own loopy Dora Maar in *Surviving Picasso*), a hyper-arch

David Thewlis, and Peter Stormare's hissing heavy. But these characters help to flesh out the Coens' vigorously unglamorous portrait of LA. The Dude shuttles between the dreary nether regions – a bowling milieu all the drabber for such touches of tawdry flash as Turturro's purple-lurex lane shark – and the privileged enclaves where everything is phony, where even the dark secrets that once surrounded Chandler's Sternwood mansion no longer frighten.

Within this world, the Dude – a 1970s activist with the Seattle Seven and signatory of the 'Port Huron Statement' – functions as a resilient lapsed idealist, the old counterculture dreams now regarded as period jokes. He is laudable not for his moral integrity as such, but because deep-ingrained inertia makes him impervious to corruption. He's an aesthetic dissident: honourably out of step with LA *zeitgeist*, he listens to Captain Beefheart and, in a neat reversal of stereotype, recoils when a black cab driver plays the Eagles.

The casting of Jeff Bridges slyly capitalises on his image as Hollywood's last good guy, an actor who can convincingly and affably embody nonconformist righteousness. He makes a wonderfully calibrated double act with John Goodman's irascible Vietnam veteran converted to Judaism ('I don't roll on Shabbas') – a perfect character pairing for what looks like prime sitcom material. That might be finally what this is – a Seinfeld-style 'film about nothing', or about nothing more than the in-jokes that make the Coens giggle (the Dude, by all accounts, is based on a real-life acquaintance of theirs, one Jeff 'the Dude' Dowd, who really was a member of the activist group the Seattle Seven). But then, to make a film this thick with non sequiturs, this defiantly slight, looks like a heroic act in contemporary US cinema. *The Big Lebowski* is at once utterly inconsequential and a blow for a cinematic slacker aesthetic. Its moral payoff is that, like Marlowe, the Dude finally stays the same – he doesn't need to be redeemed, brought into line with the world he inhabits. Likewise, the Coens, flouting the genre rules and gleefully pursuing their own amusement, reserve the right to stay their ineffable, not remotely enigmatic selves.

BLIND DATE

Peter Matthews

It's commonly asserted that pulp fiction is more readily transmissible to the screen than literature. Almost by definition, a major work imposes its own way of seeing, and the adapter – forced to truncate and simplify – usually ends up with a prestige-laden stiff. The second-rate or downright trashy, by contrast, liberates the adapter to improvise freely on its themes and structure, without pangs of conscience that anything too sacred has been violated. But the case of crime novelist Elmore Leonard reminds us that the reverse can also be true: there are writers whose sensibility is so exquisitely minor that finding a screen equivalent is nearly impossible. Leonard ought to be a natural for the movies – his books, after all, consist of page after page of laconic, off-the-wall dialogue alternating with functional descriptions of narrative action. No attempt is made to plumb characters' deeper motives, and even a qualifying adjective seems too much of a compromise. 'If it sounds like writing,' says Leonard, 'I rewrite it.'

It's as if Leonard's thrillers are already movies, with the brevity of language and exteriority a screenwriter is supposed to aim for. But almost without exception the films based on his works (*The Ambassador*, 1984; *Glitz*, 1991; and the recent *Touch*) have been duds – including the three (*Stick*, 1985; *52 Pick-up*, 1986; and *Cat Chaser*, 1989) he scripted himself. It may be that the streamlined ease of Leonard's tone is deceptive – a wealth of concentrated effort has gone into those weightless, zero-degree sentences. There's a true formal rigour in Leonard's approach: he whittles away at words until nothing remains but absolute deadpan – the expression of an attitude as much as a writing style. Leonard's heroes don't let on much, and neither does he. His books aspire to little more than a consummate cool: of style, conception and character. That probably accounts for their enormous cult reputation. Where a major author opens up our perceptions of the world, Leonard narrows it to the articulation of a precise, hip wavelength. For all their lowlife settings and apparent shagginess, Leonard's novels are as neatly self-contained and morally trivial as drawing-room comedies.

Uncorking Soderbergh's id

Perfect shallowness demands its own brand of discipline, and that's where the majority of Leonard's screen translators fail. It's not enough to reproduce the plot twists and zingy one-liners – for something of the spirit of the books to come through requires an exactly calibrated nonchalance in the whole treatment. The breezy, buoyant 1995 film version of *Get Shorty* almost caught it, but faltered ultimately under Barry Sonnenfeld's broad, impersonal direction. Now the screenwriter for that movie, Scott Frank, has teamed up with art-house specialist Steven Soderbergh for *Out of Sight*, based on Leonard's 1996 book and starring George Clooney and Jennifer Lopez.

Out of Sight is just a trifle (though at $49 million, an expensive one), but it strikes me as one of the best formula pictures in years. In case that sounds like a back-handed compliment, it should be remembered that not a few of Hollywood's most memorable entertainments – films that still please audiences after decades – are, strictly speaking, production-line sausages. It's not that *Out of Sight* feels remotely retro: indeed, the loose-limbed contemporary vernacular Soderbergh and Frank employ is one of the movie's singular felicities. But there's an underlying compactness and elegance that puts one in mind of classic Hollywood at its most exemplary. Studio craftsmen of former days – professionals merely doing their jobs – could take conventional genre subjects and turn them adroitly into vital popular art. It's this quality of self-effacing tact that keeps *Bringing up Baby* or *Casablanca* fresh when more pretentious efforts have sunk without a trace. And *Out of Sight* is among the few current movies to suggest that honest commercial know-how isn't entirely dead.

Steven Soderbergh is just about the last person you would think of inviting to direct an Elmore Leonard thriller. His debut feature *sex, lies and videotape* (1989) is commonly said to have put Miramax on the map and American indie films into the shopping mall. With an aggressive marketing campaign and that come-hither title, it could hardly miss – but the multiplex audiences who turned out hoping for something kinky may have been startled to find themselves confronting the work of a chilly formalist. His subsequent flops – *Kafka* (1991) and *King of the Hill* (1993) – were almost fanatically perfectionist in their look, as if the director had felt compelled to chew over the crystalline imagery frame by frame. By the time he made *The Underneath* (1995), a glacial meditation on film noir themes, one had the sense that Soderbergh was as stymied by art-consciousness as his hero was by torpor. Shock treatment was indicated, and it was apparently delivered in the self-financed *Schizopolis* (1996) – so far unseen in Britain, but described by *LA Weekly* reporter Paul Malcolm as a 'screwball, stylistic freak-out … with [a] pointed disdain for narrative coherence and [an] emphasis on sheer momentum'. Given the title and Soderbergh's previous bottled-up style, it's tempting to read *Schizopolis* as the occasion on which the director finally uncorked his id. In *Out of Sight*, he channels this manic high into a technique at once playful and scrupulously controlled.

The movie would appear to be a special case of synchronicity – of the countless things that could be expected to go wrong, going right. I'm not sure Soderbergh has the toughness to make a full career in the mainstream, but serving as a director-for-hire on a project of no importance, he has done better, richer and racier work than he managed as an auteur. Perhaps Soderbergh needed the external discipline of a big-star vehicle to unclench his tight creative personality; in return he invests a purely commercial enterprise with a portion of his fastidiousness. It's not unlike the proverbial bargain struck between Fred and Ginger – Soderbergh gives the movie class, it gives him sex appeal. The synthesis is a flip elegance that isn't miles away from Leonard's notion of cool.

It's well known that Leonard's crime fiction has exerted considerable second-hand influence on contemporary American cinema via the work of his number one fan, Quentin Tarantino. Still, I'm glad it was the meticulous Soderbergh and not the blowhard Tarantino who filmed *Out of Sight*. Judging from the cautious and painfully overextended *Jackie Brown* (based on Leonard's novel *Rum Punch*), when Tarantino approaches his idol too directly he chokes up in bashful reverence. Tarantino's indebtedness to Leonard is more patent in his screenplays for *Reservoir Dogs* and *Pulp Fiction*, and the benchmarks of his cinema-busy but seemingly random plotting, sudden leaps from comedy to carnage, 'humanised' criminals who discuss the merits of consumer items, and non-stop references to movies – are certainly all there in Leonard. But where the author aims at an almost minimalist leanness of effect, the director is a hyperkinetic sensualist who wants to knock the audience flat.

The light touch Soderbergh brings to *Out of Sight* is far more appropriate to Leonard's book than Tarantino's inflated nihilist chic. That's partly because the story is a crime caper through which a delicate, reticent love affair has been threaded. Fugitive bank robber Jack Foley (George Clooney) and Deputy Federal Marshal Karen Sisco (Jennifer Lopez) aren't flamboyant lovers-on-the-lam like the couple in the Tarantino-scripted *True Romance*. They don't burn up the track with erotic friction; instead, their courtship is oddly oblique, tentative and experimental. Karen, we learn, has a history of romantic waywardness, choosing married men or guys who turn out to be felons. Ambitious to rise in a male-dominated profession, she nonetheless feels an obscure yen for more glamour and adventure than can be safely warranted by the law. (Being a Leonard heroine, she never says so – but you intuit it from Lopez's leggy, provocative demeanour and such carefully planted details as her Chanel suit and the silvery-pink shade of lipstick she wears on the job.) Jack, too, longs for something other. A career criminal with nowhere to go but down, facing a thirty-year prison sentence if caught, he harbours the pipe dream of a regular life where people meet for cocktails, talk about movies, get acquainted. The reciprocity of their desires makes them a perfect fit, like the symmetrical couples (played by Cary Grant and Katharine Hepburn or William Powell and Myrna Loy) in 1930s screwball comedies. Movie love in those days could cause difference to crumble instantly, but Jack and Karen recognise there's no future in their developing rapport: he must continue to dodge the law, and she to hunt him down. The sly conceit of the movie is that these official adversaries choose – now and then in isolated pockets of the chase – to bunk off from their public roles and find out what could have been.

Inimical lovers

They indulge their caprice in a handful of the most subtly seductive scenes ever filmed. The first suggests a witty extension (or perhaps contraction) of the 'meet-cute' once mandatory in Hollywood romantic comedy. Escaping from a medium-security Florida prison, Jack is obliged to abduct innocent bystander Karen, whom he bundles into the trunk of a getaway car driven by his accomplice Buddy (Ving Rhames). Then he climbs in himself and, illuminated by the lurid red tail lights, their bodies pressed snugly back to back, the pair soon fall into an easygoing patter about their respective careers and Faye Dunaway movies they have enjoyed. Soderbergh frames this (literal) blind date the only way he can – in huge close-up – yet his darting camerawork offsets the static situation, charging it with emotional expectancy. That trunk stands a decent chance of being as fondly remembered as the motel room across which Clark Gable and Claudette Colbert string the Walls of Jericho in *It Happened One Night* – and it performs a similar function as a sealed-off free zone where inimical lovers can test their true feelings.

That's the beginning for Jack and Karen, but it's also nearly the end. Since their relationship is untenable, it becomes a utopian space within the narrative – the gateway to a parallel universe where a happier story might be told. In Henry Hathaway's 1935 surrealist classic *Peter Ibbetson*, the forcibly estranged sweethearts (played by Gary Cooper and Ann Harding) spend a lifetime visiting each other in dreams. It's almost the same with Jack and Karen. Through some of the most understated techniques of stylisation I've every seen, Soderbergh lends their love duets a hypnotic quality that abstracts them from the rest of the movie. The effect is most pronounced in the sequence where they have cocktails. Sitting alone in a hotel bar high above Detroit, Karen is chatted up by three advertising types, each of whom she repels. Then suddenly Jack appears, as if materialised by thought.

Authorial poker-face

Soderbergh composes their ensuing *tête-à-tête* in lustrous two-shots that fill the frame, connoting a self-sufficient world. At the same time, he faintly flattens the image to the dimensions of a comic strip – insinuating perhaps that this world isn't quite real. It's here that the theme of the movie is most explicitly stated. Talking of making eye contact with someone on the street, Jack muses: 'And the next moment, the person's gone... and it's too late to do anything about it, but you remember it because it was right there and you let it go, and you think, "What if I had stopped and said something?" It might happen only a few times in your life.' To which Karen quietly replies, 'Or once.'

What links Jack and Karen to those flaky 1930s movie couples is their willingness to behave irresponsibly, to leave their hide-bound identities and take a chance. What makes them 1990s figures is the limited nature of their romantic project. Neither is willing to give up the solid world they live in for something as chimerical as love. And yet *Out of Sight* becomes possibly even more romantic because that love crystallises in memory as a lost potential, a regret. As Jack and Karen continue to talk, Soderbergh flashes forward to their single act of consummation (and has the taste not to picture it too graphically). Now we understand why the freeze-frames, which in earlier parts of the film seemed an annoying tic, are necessary to its conception – Jack and Karen are storing up images for the long, cold future. The reserved, slightly ceremonial framing contributes to the mood of subdued gravity: we feel the characters are utterly conscious of each moment as it slips away and already view it with sharp pangs of nostalgia.

Aside from the usual condensations and a changed ending, Frank's script stays extremely faithful to Leonard's book. So why does the movie come across as far more vivid and touching? Perhaps the answer lies partly in the 'reality effect' of cinema. Reading the novel, you admire the craftsman-like way Leonard brings everything to a hard point; but he never gives you the impression of a fully imagined world as a major writer can. That's the downside of his authorial poker-face – the locales lack substance, the people feel disembodied. Yet characters who are ciphers on the page become immediately particularised when actors play them on-screen. This can feel like a loss in film versions of literary masterpieces, but in the case of *Out of Sight* the vast gain in concrete physical detail is a compensation. Of course, it isn't merely by virtue of being photographed that Clooney and Lopez elicit our intense emotional involvement – it's because they act together with such unforced charm. And it isn't just that the movie was shot on location in Miami and Detroit that provides a convincing backdrop – it's that Soderbergh, the cinematographer and the production designer succeed in establishing a strong sense of place.

Most commercial directors these days fall back on grandiose aerial views to portray a city. But Soderbergh stays consistently at street level, which keeps the movie looking self-contained and almost suburban. He has said he was after a rough, imperfect feeling, and you can see what he means: outside the formally orchestrated interludes between Jack and Karen, he judders the camera in muted imitation of *cinéma vérité*. In some of his previous films, Soderbergh would practically quarantine the characters in the tight frame; here it's as if this pan-and-zoom is trying to catch up with them as they go their independent ways.

'Out of Sight 2'

The style is certainly suited to the ramshackle subplot in which Jack, Buddy and a sprinkling of sociopaths conspire to rob millionaire Richard Ripley (Albert Brooks). It's a storyline seemingly composed of ragtags from such 1970s films as *The French Connection* and Sam Peckinpah's *The Getaway*, and indeed there's a flavour of early to mid-1970s American cinema in the movie's veneer of airiness and spontaneity. But the underlying control is very apparent – for instance in the expressionist use of saturated colour, evolving from pink and green pastels in Miami to blues, browns and blacks in Detroit, that plots the darkening course of the love affair. There's perhaps only one spot where Soderbergh's debonair technique goes splat. The crudely staged scene between Jack and criminal confederate Snoopy (Don Cheadle) on the stairs of the Ripley mansion is plainly there to satisfy the meatheads in the audience. And ambiguous though it is, I also object to the new ending in which Karen, tongue faintly in cheek, supplies the *deus ex machina* whereby she and Jack can keep the ball rolling. Frank excises Karen's final words to Jack in the novel – her bleakly realistic: 'I'm afraid, though, thirty years from now I'll feel different about it. I'm sorry, Jack.' The return of Jack and Karen for *Out of Sight 2* feels like a dim possibility – but the melancholy beauty of their romance rests precisely on it being an evanescent flash in their lives, which they will never forget.

THE FLASHBACK KID

Sheila Johnston

When *sex, lies and videotape* won the Palme d'or in Cannes ten years ago, before making more than $100 million worldwide (on a budget of $1.2 million), Steven Soderbergh, then twenty-six, became overnight the poster child of independent American cinema. The blockbuster event movies pioneered by George Lucas and Steven Spielberg in the mid-1970s had dominated international markets for over a decade; Soderbergh's brilliant debut pointed to a different way forward. But then his next movies bombed: the angst-ridden *Kafka* (1991); *King of the Hill* (1993), the story of a small boy struggling to survive the Depression; the glacial film noir *The Underneath* (1995). Interviewed about the last, Soderbergh launched into a long, morose attack: 'I've lost interest in the cinematic baggage you have to use to make a film palatable for a mass audience.'

Unsurprisingly, his career went quiet. He took on a string of behind-the-scenes producing and script-writing assignments including *Pleasantville* and the ill-fated US remake of *Night Watch*. Plans for *Quiz Show* foundered when Robert Redford hijacked the project. Soderbergh the director appeared to be all washed up: a one-hit wonder.

In fact, he had gone to ground to make *Schizopolis*, a no-budget, Dadaesque comedy in which Soderbergh himself plays the tragi-comic hero struggling with his sense of alienation and his failing marriage (his wife was played by the director's own soon-to-be ex-spouse, Betsy Brantley). The film's reception at its Cannes premiere in 1996 was rather more muted than the ovation that had greeted *sex, lies*, with a torrent of bored and bewildered audience members diving for the exit. With his next film, *Gray's Anatomy* (1996), a small-scale piece made with the monologuist Spalding Gray, Soderbergh seemed to have disappeared for good beneath the radar.

But then in 1998 he bounced back triumphantly with an unpromising-sounding assignment as director-for-hire on an adaptation of Elmore Leonard's novel *Out of Sight*, about a failed bank robber and a deputy federal marshal who can't decide whether to arrest the charming felon or fall in love with him. Sexy, elegant and profoundly romantic (a new departure for a director whose work has often been regarded as somewhat cerebral), it was hailed by critics as his best film since *sex, lies*. His return to favour continues with *The Limey*, which played out of competition at Cannes this year. The story of an English ex-convict (Terence Stamp) who travels to Los Angeles to investigate his daughter's death following her involvement with a hedonistic record producer (Peter Fonda), it is on one level a straight revenge thriller with strong echoes of *Get Carter*, while its spaced-out feel and bravura kaleidoscopic editing make it play like a homage to the formal experimentation of 1960s and 1970s cinema.

Soderbergh has been described by one US interviewer, a little patronisingly if not altogether inaccurately, as a 'goofy, balding, loveable geek'. But underneath that persona, thinly concealed, are a steely intelligence and formidable self-awareness. And though he has worked within an astonishing range of registers – from the avant-garde *Schizopolis*, through the quintessential US indie sensibility of *sex, lies* and the arty, black-and-white, middle-European universe of *Kafka*, to such demi-Hollywood genre pieces as *Out of Sight* and *The Limey* – he insists adamantly on the continuity of his work.

* * *

Sheila Johnston: You use a very complex chronological structure in *The Limey* – was that written into the script or created at the editing stage?

Steven Soderbergh: I shot it that way. My whole line while we were making it was, 'If we do our job right this is *Get Carter* as made by Alain Resnais,' which I know spells big box office! I was trying to get a sense of how your mind sifts through things and I felt I could get away with a certain amount of abstraction because the backbone of the movie is so straight. Even so, my first version was so layered and deconstructed even people who had worked on the movie didn't understand it. So I had to start working back to find a balance, which I did through screenings for friends: writers, actors, producers, directors, a new group of guinea pigs each time. At one point Artisan [the production company] wanted a public preview. But I said, 'For a movie like this it's worthless: it's going to score terribly and I'll get nothing I haven't already got by inviting intelligent, creative people to give me ideas.' A week before we were going to do it, they called and said, 'You're right, it's a waste of money. Just finish it the way you're going to finish it and we'll figure out the rest.'

Sheila Johnston: The film's steeped in the mood of the 1960s, though you're a little young to have had much direct experience of that counterculture.

Steven Soderbergh: I've been working for some time on a book of interviews with Richard Lester called *Getting Away with It* and I asked him a lot about that period. Mostly we talked about the gradual shift from optimism to disillusion. I was whining about something and then I added, 'Still, has there ever been a generation that hasn't said, "It's never been this bad"?' He said, 'Yeah, in the 1960s.' But as soon as it became apparent that the youth movement was an ongoing economic force, it began to be co-opted into mainstream culture, and that – combined with other things like harder drugs becoming available – was when things started to shift. When Lester made two trips to San Francisco to research and shoot *Petulia* in 1966 and 1967 he said he could feel a very strong, dark undercurrent on the second visit that wasn't there on the first. That's the feeling that permeates *The Limey*. There's one guy whose dreams of himself were lost in prison and another whose dreams were probably never even his own: he just took everybody else's and made money out of them.

Sheila Johnston: How important was it to cast two icons of 1960s cinema?

Steven Soderbergh: Both Terence Stamp and Peter Fonda have baggage that's not only specific to the 1960s, but has to do with a refusal to compromise: they've stayed pretty true to themselves all these years. But I wasn't trying to turn in a pastiche – though clearly when we had Peter Fonda driving in a fast vehicle up the coast, I thought, 'We've gotta get Steppenwolf.' Terence seemed like a Who kind of guy – in fact his brother, Chris Stamp, was one of the people who discovered them.

Sheila Johnston: One of the film's most remarkable features is your use of scenes from Ken Loach's 1967 movie *Poor Cow*, in which Stamp played another thief, to show his character in flashback.

Steven Soderbergh: In cinema you can follow actors over a long period – you can really see the accumulation of someone's life experience. So the idea of using Ken's film was intriguing, and as far as I know no one had done that before. There was a lengthy process to get the rights because *Poor Cow* was based on a book by Nell Dunn, and Carol White, who was in the scenes we wanted to use, was dead. It went on for months and didn't get completely resolved until we were editing. Then I met with Ken and said, 'Look, I've got this cleared up legally, but morally I can't do it if you think it's offensive.' But when I explained what I was doing, he said it was fine.

Sheila Johnston: When you took receipt of your Palme d'or for *sex, lies and videotape*, you said: 'It's all downhill from here.' Do you now feel that has been true of your career?

Steven Soderbergh: I was being facetious, but what I meant was that it seemed unlikely I would ever again be the recipient of such unified acclaim. A lot of people never are and to get it for my first movie seemed almost comical. The Palme d'or helped me hugely – it made a name for me in Europe, where people sometimes like my movies more than they do in the States – but if *sex, lies* had made only half a million dollars nobody would be talking about it today. It was a modest piece with modest aspirations that happened to be what people wanted to see in a way I obviously haven't been able to duplicate. It was pure chance: I have a strong feeling that had it been made a year later it wouldn't have hit in the same way.

Sheila Johnston: Unlike many younger American independent film-makers, you didn't use the success of your first film as a springboard to a commercial Hollywood career. Are you happy now with the choices you made?

Steven Soderbergh: Let's put it this way, I don't regret any of them. There have been good ones and bad ones, but I look back and think, 'That's an eclectic group of movies that, for better or worse, belong to me.' I turned down a lot of studio stuff – or rather traditional studio stuff, because two of my films were made by Universal – until *Out of Sight*, which seemed the perfect blend of what I do and the resources a studio can provide.

Sheila Johnston: What is the difference between coming in on a pre-existing project and creating a film from scratch?

Steven Soderbergh: With a screenplay that didn't come from you, you get on that train and it takes a while to start driving it. But you work your way through each car until you get to the front, and once you're close to shooting there's really no difference. By then you usually have a healthy disrespect for – or sense of detachment from – the material, even if you've written it yourself. When we rehearsed *Out of Sight* I started cutting lines because, though Elmore Leonard writes great dialogue, it seemed in scenes like the last one there wasn't a lot to be said. That's one of the differences between a book and a movie. I met someone recently who was in *Days of Heaven* and she said there was lots of dialogue in the script, but when they got on the set Terrence Malick would go, 'Don't say anything.' When you look at the film you realise that he ended up having to write all that voiceover in post-production because nobody said anything, so nobody knew what was going on! You think, 'Oh, that's such a great example of stripping everything away,' and then you find out why he did it. Sometimes it's better not to know too much.

INDEPENDENTS DAZE

Kim Newman

It is no longer possible to define easily what is meant by 'American independent cinema'. Spike Lee's *Do the Right Thing* (1989) seems like a textbook example of what we mean when we use the term – a personal project, inexpensive but inventive, engaged with topical issues, cast without 'names', hard to squeeze even into a genre as broad as 'social realism' – but it is, like the bulk of Lee's work, a studio project, financed, distributed (and supported) by Universal. James Cameron's *Terminator 2: Judgment Day* (1991), equally typical of the type of summer blockbuster associated with the majors – a sequel to a proven hit, packed with star power and big effects, and clearly a genre movie (sci-fi/action) – is actually an independent, backed by short-lived player Carolco.

Moreover, both films are the work of director–writers who have worked cannily to preserve a creative and commercial identity in an increasingly corporate industry, with Cameron's film just as much as Lee's stamped with the personality and distinctive interests of a creator whose films demand to be taken as part of developing bodies of work as much as they do as one-off works. From the perspective of auteur criticism, such films are thought of as artistic progressions, each new work drawing on what has gone before, often revising or revisiting earlier themes to present an update – Lee's *Summer of Sam*, 1999, for instance, refers constantly to *Do the Right Thing*; from the perspective of genre analysis, they are labelled as sequels, spin-offs or rip-offs.

Once upon a time, independent American cinema was – aside from the works of industry fringe figures such as John Cassavetes or estranged-from-Hollywood 'underground' artists such as Jack Smith and Andy Warhol – all about genre. Even Cassavetes' films often play as riffs on familiar film forms such as the backstage drama (*Opening Night*, 1977) or the gangster film (*The Killing of a Chinese Bookie*, 1976; *Gloria*, 1980), and most of the 1960s underground film-makers were so in love with Hollywood that they would have relished the chance that their works might be bracketed with a Maria Montez fantasy or a Shirley Temple musical. Otherwise, the only way commercial independent film-makers could get any screen space at all in America was to make the sort of film bookers understood, which – from the 1950s through to the 1970s – meant the type of genre movie that could play on triple-features in drive-ins: horror films, violent thrillers, pop musicals, sexploitation.

Thanks to Roger Corman, who made the vital leap from writer–director to producer–distributor, it became possible for young film-makers to circumvent the established career structure of old Hollywood and make their first features outside the studios, which were themselves no longer the 'dream factories' of the 1920s, 1930s and 1940s, and becoming corporate distribution outlets. Thanks to Corman and his grasp of the hot genres of the moment, we have a horror film by Francis Ford Coppola (*Dementia 13*, 1963), Westerns by Monte Hellman (*The Shooting*, *Ride in the Whirlwind*, both 1966), a gothic horror/serial killer picture from Peter Bogdanovich (*Targets*, 1968), car chase/gangster movies from Martin Scorsese (*Boxcar Bertha*, 1972) and Jonathan Demme (*Crazy Mama*, 1975), a fishy monster picture from Joe Dante (*Piranha*, 1978) and a clutch of other early credits for now-mainstream creatives from Sylvester Stallone and Jack Nicholson to Menahem Golan and Robert Towne, not to mention a grounding in special effects for James Cameron. Corman even had one connection with the 'underground' – Curtis Harrington's *Night Tide* (1960) – and would develop the career of a rare Andy Warhol 'superstar' to make it in legitimate movies – Mary Woronov (*The Chelsea Girls*, Warhol, 1968; *Death Race 2000*, Paul Bartel, 1975).

However, the attitude to genre in these various Corman-shepherded pictures is subtly different from that of his older competitors in the exploitation business. When a major studio B unit or an outfit such as American International Pictures (which backed Corman as a director in the 1950s and 1960s) assigned a horror movie or a gangster film, the intention was to fill a slot, sometimes coming up with a film to fit a pre-sold title or poster art (*Beast with a Million Eyes*, David Kramarsky, 1956) and almost inevitably failing to deliver on the promise. Corman's protégés – also known as 'film students who would work cheap' – were given far more latitude: just so long as they delivered something that could be classed as a genre picture and kept it fast and entertaining enough not to alienate hardened drive-in audiences, they could do almost anything they wanted. A film such as *Targets* – made because Bogdanovich found a way of using up a few days Boris Karloff owed Corman on an old contract – touches base with genre, but is actually unlike any other American psycho movie up to that date, emphasising not the gothicism of the Bates Motel with its corpse in the fruit cellar and swamp-of-the-subconscious out back, but the normality of an all-American home whose Tab Hunter lookalike son addresses his father as 'sir' and shows the proper interest in marriage and hunting, but still ends up for no apparent reason on a water tower sniping at passers-by.

The point in the 1970s was for a young director to get a couple of Corman credits out of the way and then go on to make films which didn't have to fit the strait-jacket of genre (typical 'break-out' pictures are Scorsese's *Mean Streets*, 1973, and Demme's *Melvin and Howard*, 1980), but conform more to our expectation of what an 'independent' film (on the model of Cassavetes or Robert Altman) might be. Then, the young film-maker would land a career with major studio backing, hoping for a reputation-building commercial and critical hit such as Coppola's *The Godfather* (1971), and leave the drive-ins behind. It is notable that Coppola, for instance, has devoted the bulk of his post-Corman career to making gangster films, war pictures, juvenile delinquent quickies and monster movies. At some point in the 1970s – when *Jaws* (Steven Spielberg, 1975), a pared-down monster movie, replaced *The Godfather* and *The Exorcist* (William Friedkin, 1973), jumped-up envelope-breaking gangster and horror films, respectively, as a box-office champion – genre became respectable commercially. But, equally – when it became possible for Westerns (*Dances with Wolves*, Kevin Costner, 1990; *Unforgiven*, Clint Eastwood, 1992), a horror film (*The Silence of the Lambs*, Demme, 1991) and a disaster movie (*Titanic*, Cameron, 1997) to take home Best Picture Oscars – genre also became critically respectable.

With changes in strategies of production and distribution in the low-budget sector, prompted especially by the downfall of the drive-in and grindhouse theatrical circuits and the rise of ancillary markets such as home video and cable TV, the career model for American film-makers that emerged under Corman – in which independence was a rebellious but proving stage like adolescence before the adult responsibilities of major studio film-making set in – ceased to be viable. Roger Corman still makes movies by the dozen, but no one since Cameron has graduated to the big leagues and a recent Corman picture is more likely to be directed by a frank hack such as Jim Wynorski (*The Wasp Woman*, 1996) than an ambitious kid who will figure in the Oscar nominations in 2010. Now, the goal of everyone who wants a career as a director is to get a self-financed apprentice picture accepted at the Sundance Festival and then fish for a deal with Miramax or one of the other independent outfits which have become attached to majors, just as niche market music labels form part of vast conglomerates. The result of this is that if modern first features have a genre model, it is a genre defined by previous independent auteur films – note the recycling of *Mean Streets* in works as varied as Quentin Tarantino's *Reservoir Dogs* (1992), Nick Lopez's *Laws of Gravity* (1991) and Alan Taylor's *Palookaville* (1996), or the plethora of ethnic ghetto violence movies modelled on the breakthroughs of Spike Lee and John Singleton, such as the Hughes brothers' *Menace II Society* (1993) and Boaz Yakin's *Fresh* (1994).

The young directors of the past thirty years are without exception cine-literate enough – even on the video-store clerk level of a Tarantino or Kevin Smith – to know all about genre, but there has been a shift from those who loved and admired the likes of Cassavetes, John Ford, Sam Fuller (a key figure for the independent sector) and

Robert Altman to those who revere not so much the films of Tarantino, Steven Soderbergh, Martin Scorsese, Spike Lee, Bryan Singer or John Singleton as their career trajectories. Now, the heroes of these desperate wannabes are liable to be Eduardo Sanchez and Daniel Myrick, whose *The Blair Witch Project* (1999) has been more often dissected as an economic phenomenon or a radical rethink of the role of the director than it has for its genuine engagement with the broad spectrum of the horror genre in film and literature and even its specific precedents in the 1970s wave of mock documentary monster movies or Ruggero Deodato's *Cannibal Holocaust* (1980). *Blair Witch* (picked up by indie distributor Artisan, which had handled Darren Arnofsky's *Pi*, 1998), stands also as a break with the increasingly slick, soulless horror style of Dimension/Miramax, whose *Scream* films work hard at smoothing off all the rough edges in the genre and reducing the variable but distinctive Wes Craven to the sort of hired hand whose idea of a personal project casts Meryl Streep as a music teacher working with underprivileged kids.

In an era when dozens of *Reservoir Dogs* spin-off quirky crime comedies tussle for their spots at Sundance, it becomes easier to appreciate the true independence of creative spirit exemplified in very different ways by genuine mavericks such as David Cronenberg, David Lynch and Abel Ferrara. These directors started out well off the chart, with essentially underground works (Ferrara even made a hardcore porno in *9 Lives of a Wet Pussy*, 1976, while Cronenberg and Lynch came to cinema through other arts and turned out first features well outside anyone's mainstream), then passed through a phase of involvement with a brand of horror/crime/melodrama cinema made possible by off-Hollywood creators such as George A. Romero and Wes Craven before coming into their own as film-makers whose works are *sui generis*. Romero and Craven constantly ask themselves what a horror movie is and see if the form will bend in the ways they want it to – and John Carpenter tried to make films exactly like the pictures he imagined Howard Hawks or William Castle were making when he first saw them as a twelve-year-old. But Cronenberg, Lynch and Ferrara made pictures as if they were only told halfway through shooting that they would be sold as horror movies, though they had not until that moment considered them to be anything but personal projects dressed up with licks borrowed from pictures they liked, but didn't love: hence the detours into Bergmanesque pain of *Shivers* (1976) and *The Brood* (1979), the mutation of soap opera and classic melodrama in *Eraserhead* (1977) and *Blue Velvet* (1985), and the mix of Scorsese–Paul Morrissey New York and Polanski interior chill shot through *The Driller Killer* (1979) and *Ms. 45* (1981).

This pursuit of the personal through popular forms may lead these film-makers to blind alleys. Though I mostly admire the films, I can't help but find *Naked Lunch* (1991) and *Crash* (1996) disappointing because Cronenberg allows his own personality to be eclipsed by those of William Burroughs and J. G. Ballard who, for all their merits, mean a lot less to me than he does. And it now seems clear that, with the best will in the world, *Dune* (1984) was a vast folly, due as much to underlying problems with Frank Herbert as to the runaway production methods of the De Laurentiis company. It also means that, as with the now sadly inactive Larry Cohen, you have to take the embarrassments along with the great to arrive at the totality. Their most 'achieved' films – *The Fly* (1986) and *Dead Ringers* (1989), *The Elephant Man* (1980) and *The Straight*

Story (1999), *King of New York* (1990) and *The Addiction* (1993) – are their most generic, inhabiting entirely their generic forms while retaining their makers' personalities, but these pictures only exist because the blanks are filled in by untidy, often-misunderstood, against-the-odds – but great – pictures such as *Videodrome* (1984) and *eXistenZ* (1999), *Twin Peaks: Fire Walk with Me* (1992) and *Lost Highway* (1997), *Bad Lieutenant* (1992) and *The Blackout* (1997) – not to mention misfires and sports such as *Fast Company* (1979), *Wild at Heart* (1991) and *Dangerous Game* (1993).

What sets Cronenberg, Lynch and Ferrara apart is that they are open to influences from well outside the cinema, which often means that they get lumped together as exponents of an extreme sensibility. Accused of being obsessed with sex and violence, Cronenberg once mildly turned the question on the interviewer with: 'Yes, but sex and violence are very interesting, don't you think?' It is possible that their survival as artists depends on the mismatch of their genuinely-held interests and an audience demand for lurid product that has scarcely diminished since the Corman days. When Lynch offers something as 'tame' as *The Straight Story* as opposed to an exercise in self-pastiche such as *Wild at Heart*, there is a faint disappointment on the parts of those who habitually condemn or demonise the director as much as of those of his 'fans', who pride themselves on being able to take weirdness beyond the sensibility of the average filmgoer.

Though no longer apt to turn out a stream of women-in-prison or toothy monster movies (now the province of big studio effects and direct-to-video fodder), the independent sector often feels a need to compete with the big boys by cutting off ears or gunning down half the population of Mexico. The odd thing is that Tarantino, Robert Rodriguez and Kevin Williamson, to pick three of the more notable names at random and stereotype their not-uninteresting oeuvres, seem not to be that interested in sex and violence, but suspect they need to include those elements either as part of a strategy of reference – the torture scene of *Pulp Fiction* (1994) springs not from real-life tortures, in the way that Craven's *Last House on the Left* (1971) does, but from torture scenes in numberless earlier movies – or out of a desire to get noticed, which is as much to do with landing a distribution deal as with being the centre of attention. Ever since *Targets*, indie and apprentice film-makers have been accused of making movies about movies as opposed to movies about life. Craven's *Scream* (1996) or Rodriguez's *The Faculty* (1998) are movies about what life means in the movies, but *Targets* is a movie about what movies mean in life, a very different and considerably more important project. Kevin Williamson–scripted 1990s movies such as *The Faculty* use irony and awareness to bracket their shameless and footnoted appropriation of basic horror and science-fiction plots, whereas *Targets* climaxes with a confrontation between a cinematically conceived bogeyman (an ageing Boris Karloff) and a sniper whose blank monstrousness cannot be constrained or understood within the crumbling walls of the horror genre.

Index